P9-DXH-508

DATE DUE

NO 13 01			
DE 19 01			
MY 27 '03			

DEMCO 38-296

CORPORATE BUSINESS AND CAPITALIST CLASSES

CORPORATE BUSINESS
AND CAPITALIST CLASSES

John Scott

OXFORD UNIVERSITY PRESS

1997

DP

Mexico City Nairobi Paris Singapore
Taipei Tokyo Toronto
and associated companies in
Berlin Ibadan

Oxford is a trade mark of Oxford University Press

Published in the United States
by Oxford University Press Inc., New York

British Library Cataloguing in Publication Data
Data available

Library of Congress Cataloging in Publication Data
Data available
ISBN 0–19–828076–9
ISBN 0–19–828075–0 (Pbk)

Typeset by Hope Services (Abingdon) Ltd.
Printed in Great Britain
on acid-free paper by
Biddles Ltd.,
Guildford & King's Lynn

Acknowledgements

Corporations, Classes and Capitalism was first published in 1979, and a second edition was necessary in 1985. For that second edition, I completely rewrote the text and updated much of the material. When I prepared what was to be the third edition, it was again necessary to completely rework the text as well as to update the empirical material. In consequence, this book is so different from its initial form that only a new title could mark its distinctiveness. Although I hate to lose the beautifully alliterative title—despite the fact that others could never remember the words of the title in the correct order—it was decided to recognize this as an essentially new book and to give it the title *Corporate Business and Capitalist Classes*.

I welcome this opportunity to again recognize the ways in which this book builds on the work of those with whom I was associated in the Research Group on Intercorporate Structure and the researchers associated with the MACNET group: Meindert Fennema, Catherine Griff, Beth Mintz, Michael Schwartz, Frans Stokman, and Rolf Ziegler. The translation of the first edition into Japanese brought contacts with many Japanese scholars whose comments and suggestions have been invaluable to me. Continuing contacts with those I met on my lecture tour have been essential to the development of my argument, and much of this help is indicated in the Bibliography. Of particular help have been Akira Kaneko, Hiroshi Okumura, Masaki Nakata, and Yoshiaki Ueda. I am grateful to Mizuha Nakamura and Akihisa Uetake for undertaking the translation that made these contacts possible. I am also grateful to Hisashi Hamabuchi, who read through much of the manuscript of this book and provided me with many helpful comments. Others who have read and commented on various parts of the manuscript and its argument include David Lee, and Julio Portales.

The manuscript was largely completed while I was living a peripatetic academic existence (thankfully now at an end), travelling between my home in Leicester and the Department of Sociology at Essex. It could not have been completed without the intellectual support offered by the Department, which helped to counter the depression of living with the collapse in the housing market. My colleagues at Essex have contributed to the book in ways that few of them will recognize from its contents. By creating a lively and exciting intellectual environment for the development of sociological ideas, the Department has helped to sharpen and clarify many of my ideas.

John Scott

Colchester
April 1996

Contents

List of Tables

1

BIG BUSINESS AND CORPORATE POWER

F EW people appreciate the extent to which large multinational business enterprises are able to shape our lives. The products and services that we use in the course of our routine daily activities—the food that we eat, the newspapers that we read, the cars that we drive, the houses that we live in, and so on—are all today the products of mass-market business enterprises. These commodities can be produced for us only if other enterprises produce the boilers, printing presses, machine tools, and bricks that are required in their production. The majority of people in paid employment are paid by these same businesses to work in the factories, shops, and offices that produce these goods, and the production and consumption of goods requires the use of cash, credit cards, and bank accounts that are operated by large banking enterprises. News reports on the movement of the *Financial Times* share index, the exchange rates, and the international currency markets in which these enterprises are involved do not refer to matters that are peripheral to 'real' events, but to processes that help to ensure or prevent the availability of goods, services, and jobs. All of us, whether as 'consumers' or 'workers', are inextricably tied into a global web of financial connections that stretch from our corner shop to the Tokyo money market.

How is the power and significance of big business to be understood and explained? The brand names and products that lie behind anonymous corporate identities can be discovered fairly easily from the numerous reference books that are available in most libraries, but the identities of the people that actually run their affairs and determine their policies are rather more difficult to discover. The entrepreneur of the nineteenth century, as both the owner and the controller of a business, was easily identifiable as a business leader, but this immediate and direct link between ownership and control has now been broken. With the wider use of the 'company' or 'corporation' from the last part of the nineteenth century on, it became possible for the 'owners'—those who hold the 'shares' in a company and so provide the capital—to become divorced from any effective control over the actual operations of the business.[1] In order to expand their activities, companies must draw on large pools of disposable wealth, and as the number of shareholders becomes larger and more diverse, so direct owner-control becomes progressively more attenuated.

The aim of this book is to explore the implications of these changes for the exercise of power within the business systems of the advanced industrial economies. This involves a consideration not only of the narrow issues of power within particular business enterprises, but also of the power of business enterprises in general to influence economic development and state policies. Such considerations raise, in turn, broader issues about the nature of the class relations that are associated with the exercise of corporate power.

Questions of Corporate Governance

The term 'corporate governance' has come into use during the last ten years to designate a new area of academic specialism, though many of its central themes have been subjects of debate in sociology and economics for many years. Motivated by an attempt to understand changes in the legal and financial organization of business and in patterns of political intervention in business, lawyers and accountants in schools of business and management have taken the lead in the development of this new specialism. In setting out their new discipline, writers on corporate governance have rediscovered some of the classic works of the first half of the twentieth century, in which these matters were first systematically explored; and they have sought to build on them, to construct realistic analyses of business enterprise and to draw prescriptive conclusions for legislation and

---

[1] In Britain the legal form is described as the 'joint stock company', while American law terms it the 'corporation'. Although there are numerous technical differences, these legal forms may be referred to simply as companies or corporations.

regulation. Their concern, then, is to start out from legal and official frameworks of norms, regulation, and supervision, and to explore the social context in which these operate to shape the governance of business.

Central to corporate governance are the legal norms that establish the constitutional framework of business enterprise. The company law that applies in an economy, together with aspects of its laws of property and contract, define the legal relations that must exist between the shareholders and the directors of a company. The shareholders are those who invest their wealth in a company by purchasing a 'share' of its total capital. In return for providing a portion of the capital that the enterprise requires for its business operations, shareholders are given rights of attendance at company meetings and rights to vote in the election of its directors. The directors, for their part, are the legally recognized officials who can enter into contracts on behalf of the company, and who are responsible for ensuring that it meets its legal obligations. Questions of corporate governance arise in relation to the property rights and *de facto* powers of shareholders and those who lend money to a company, including such issues as their ability to constrain the behaviour of the directors (Tricker 1984).

Each national system of company law is different, and so these constitutional arrangements vary from one economy to another. In countries that have adopted the general framework of English law—most particularly the United States, Australia, Canada, New Zealand, and Britain itself—there is a uniform pattern of property, contract, and company law, and a similar form of corporate undertaking. This legal framework defines a joint stock company or corporation as a body with a permanent legal existence and whose capital is jointly provided by its 'members' (Scott 1986: ch. 2). These members are shareholders, each contributing a share of the capital and having the right to receive a 'dividend' income from their shares and the right to participate in company affairs. The members may be individuals or they may be other companies, and the shares of a company may be more or less dispersed, depending on the size of the company and the extent to which its shares are traded as a commodity on a stock exchange.

A company is legally the owner of its business assets, and the shareholding members have only the rights that are attached to their ownership of share capital. It is this legal 'separation' of share ownership from ownership of the business assets that creates a problem of control: if shareholders do not own the assets of the company, then who is able to decide how they are to be used? The day-to-day running of the business is undertaken by 'directors', and the law prescribes a particular system of corporate administration: the directors sit as members of a single board whose rights and obligations are indivisible and inalienable. Directors are appointed by the shareholders at an annual general meeting and, through their board meetings—generally held once a month, but sometimes more often—they are responsible to the shareholders (Bacon and Brown 1977; Bank of England 1979). Board members may be 'executive' or 'non-executive' directors. Although this distinction is not specified in company law, executive and non-executive directors have different contracts of employment and, therefore, different responsibilities. The executive directors are the full-time 'officers' or 'insiders' of a corporation and bear the main day-to-day responsibilities. The non-executive directors are the part-time, or 'outside', directors whose involvement may be less regular and less frequent. The chief executive or managing director (the 'president' in the United States) is appointed by the board of directors, and the board itself is headed by a chairman. There is not, in general, any legal requirement that the two posts of chairman and chief executive be separated, though they are often, in practice, held by different people.

The business enterprise in the Anglo-American world, then, is organized in relation to this specific legal framework. As a company, or a linked group of companies, an enterprise must meet the requirements of company, property, and commercial law in undertaking its business. Enterprises are, however, complex *social* organizations, and not mere *legal* entities, and the legal framework is only an approximate guide to how they actually operate. The relations among the various categories of employee—'managers', 'workers', 'clerks', and so on—are regulated by their contracts of employment to the company and by other relevant laws (such as health and safety legislation or laws relating to collective bargaining and taxation), but their actions cannot simply be deduced from their legally defined roles. The relations between managers, directors, and shareholders, for example, are both complex and variable (Child 1969a: 14). It is these broader social relations with which specialists in corporate governance have increasingly had to concern themselves.

The legal framework of the Anglo-American world and its system of business organization comprises only one of numerous systems of corporate governance that exist. The legal codes of Germany,

Austria, Switzerland, and the Netherlands prescribe what can be described as a 'German' system of governance for joint stock companies (*Aktiengesellschaft* or *Naamloze Vennootschap*). This is a two-board system in which an executive board (the *Vorstand* or *Raad van Bestuur*) is responsible for overseeing the managerial hierarchy, while a supervisory board of non-executives (the *Aufsichtsrat* or *Raad van Commissarissen*) meets three or four times a year and is responsible for monitoring the activities of the executive board through its formal meetings and through informal meetings and subcommittees (Grossfeld and Ebke 1978; Ziegler 1993: 300–1; Charkham 1994: ch. 2).[2] The supervisory board is elected by the shareholders[3] and it, in turn, appoints the members of the executive board. The executive board has collective responsibility in law, though the tendency has been to appoint a chairperson with the powers of a chief executive officer. In this two-board system, the board of executive directors is legally recognized as a distinct element in corporate governance, while executive directors in the Anglo-American system have the same rights and obligations as the non-executive directors. Actual practice in the Anglo-American economies over the last twenty years, however, has gradually led to the establishment of informal committees of executives and to the formation of audit committees, remuneration committees, and recruitment committees that have increasingly formalized the distinction between the roles of executive and non-executive directors.

In Germany itself, the two-board system is further complicated by the system of worker-shareholder 'co-determination' that exists in the largest companies. This dates back to the early 1920s, when Works Councils were given the right to appoint two of their members to sit on the supervisory board. Although this right was abolished by the Nazi government in 1934, a degree of co-determination was re-introduced by the post-war occupying authorities, and this was codified in a law of 1976. Under the 1976 co-determination laws, the shareholders of a company elect only half the members of its supervisory board, while the workforce and the unions elect the other half. Shareholders do, however, retain distinct and superior

---

[2] Not all corporations in these countries are organized as public joint stock corporations, but the various limited liability companies and corporate partnerships approximate to this pattern. Swiss law in fact recognizes both the 'German' two-board system and the 'Latin' system described below.

[3] The Dutch *Raad van Commissarissen* perpetuates itself through co-optation, but the appointment of directors is subject to agreement or veto by the shareholders.

legal rights, most notably veto powers over certain constitutional and structural matters and the right to appoint the chairman.

In France, Belgium, Italy, and Spain, the governance of joint stock companies (*Société Anonyme*, *Società per Azioni*, or *Sociedad Anonima*) involves what may be called a 'Latin' variant of the two-board system. Although a German-style two-board system was introduced as an option in France in 1966, most companies continue to use the Latin variant.[4] An administrative board (*Conseil d'administration* or *Consiglio d'amministrazione*) combines both supervisory and executive responsibilities, and operates in much the same way as the single board of the Anglo-American system. A separate auditing board (*Commissaires aux comptes* or *Collegio sindicale*) is also appointed by the shareholders and has responsibility for monitoring the financial probity of the enterprise, but it has no managerial responsibility. The auditing board operates very much as an internalized form of the external auditing function in the Anglo-American system, under which independent firms of auditors work under contract to large numbers of enterprises.

Japanese corporate law is different again. It was initially constructed along European lines, drawing particularly on English and German law and practice, but many American features were added during the post-war occupation (Yazawa 1963). The original Meiji commercial code established joint stock companies (*kabushiki kaisha*) with an English-style single board, although financial monitors were introduced as a system of corporate regulation in the 1960s and this was formalized in 1994 as a requirement that all large companies establish monitoring boards. These boards have no executive powers and do not act as German-style supervisory boards, but have a role similar to the auditing boards of the Latin system. On the main boards themselves, there are few non-executive directors or true 'outside' directors, and many of the key executive decisions are delegated to separate management committees (*jomukai*) in which the presidents play a key role.

Central to the discussion of corporate governance and corporate power have been investigations into the actual powers of directors and shareholders, as opposed to their legal rights and obligations. Comparative studies of directors have usually treated members of the single board of the Anglo-American system, the two boards of the German system, and the administrative board of the Latin sys-

---

[4] In the German-style two-board system set up in France, a supervisory *Conseil de surveillance* is distinguished from an *executive directoire*.

tem as 'directors' for purposes of comparative research (Bacon and Brown 1977). This allows researchers to investigate the activities of the various categories of directors (for example, executive and non-executive) and the relations among them. Recruitment to company boards occurs for a variety of reasons that will be reviewed later in this book, and it is quite frequently the case that people hold directorships in two or more companies and so may accumulate multiple directorships. Where these multiple directorships are within a single enterprise—directorships in, for example, both the parent company and its subsidiaries[5]—they have little wider significance; but where they occur between legally independent enterprises, 'interlocking directorships' (or, more simply, 'interlocks') are established. Individual companies become tied into a more or less extensive network of interlocking directorships, and the significance of these has been much discussed (Di Donnata et al. 1988).

At the very least, interlocking directorships constitute channels of communication between enterprises: a person who sits on two or more boards—a 'multiple director'—has access to the inside information of each company and has an opportunity to 'transmit' this information from one board to another (Scott 1985; Scott and Griff 1984). At their strongest, however, interlocking directorships may be relations of power. If information flows predominantly one way, or if there is a capital or commercial relation between the companies, then the interlocking directorship may become a means through which one enterprise is able to dominate the affairs of another. Particular significance has been attached to the 'primary interlocks' that are created when an executive director of one enterprise holds non-executive directorships in others. It can often seem natural to assign a direction to these relations and to see them as relations of control (Sweezy 1939). A bank executive, for example, may represent the bank on the boards of its client and associated enterprises, and so effect a directed relation of 'bank control'. Many proponents of a model of 'finance capital', for example, have interpreted bank interlocks in this way (Fitch and Oppenheimer 1970a; 1970b; 1970c), but the situation may not be so simple. It may well be the case that a bank insists that one of its executives be placed on the board of an enterprise that it seeks to dominate; but it is equally possible that an enterprise might co-opt a bank executive onto its board in order to enhance its own power. All that can be concluded at a general level

[5] A parent company is one that owns all the shares, or a majority of them, in another, subsidiary company.

is that primary interlocks are more likely to be stable, institutionalized relations (Palmer 1983a; Ornstein 1982), and that they may therefore indicate deeper social relations. Where a person holds non-executive directorships in two companies—and these are by far the most common type of interlocking directorship—the relationship is less likely to be a direct and overt channel of power. Such interlocks are more likely to be associated simply with the communication of information, the informal monitoring of behaviour, and the exercise of influence. Both types of interlock play a part in corporate affairs, primary interlocks being embedded in more extensive networks of communication among enterprises.

The question of the powers of directors highlights the related question of the powers of shareholders and lenders. While directors may be legally distinct from shareholders, there may actually be very close relationships between them. Shareholders are those who own one or more of the shares issued by a company, and they are accorded particular rights in company law. Individual shareholders have the right to stand for election to the board of directors as well as to vote in these elections, and they have a range of other constitutional and financial rights, but they may also have powers that go beyond their formal legal rights. Voting power, for example, depends on the number of shares that are owned, and so large shareholders have greater power than small shareholders. It is important for companies to maintain good relations with their large shareholders—on whom they may wish to call if they intend to issue more shares—and these shareholders may seek to exercise a continuing influence over the policies that are followed by directors. It is for this reason that studies of corporate power must uncover the identities not only of directors but also of shareholders. It is not always an easy matter to identify the shareholders of a company, despite the fact that the legal systems of many countries require that companies maintain a share register that shows the names and addresses of its shareholders, together with the number of shares that they hold. In countries such as Britain, summary information is presented in published accounts (Wearing 1984; Wearing and Seaton 1985), but more comprehensive information is available in the share registers. Share registers are often available for public inspection, and so it might seem to be an easy task to discover who owns a company's shares; but the registers are not as transparent as they might seem. The 'registered shareholdings'—termed 'shareholdings of record' in the United States—are often listed under anonymous bank accounts or custodian 'nominees' that mask the identities of the real beneficial owners. The task of identification is even more difficult in countries where the law requires no registers and shares are merely issued to the 'bearer'. In these circumstances, the legal rights of ownership may be exercised without any need for owners to identify themselves.

The fact that shareholders have this potential for anonymity has been seen to pose critical questions of corporate governance. Much recent discussion of this issue has taken place in relation to the question of 'insider dealing' in shares by directors, and the conflicts of interests that may exist between directors and shareholders and among the various categories of shareholder. It has been suggested, for example, that directors and others may be able to use the anonymity of the share registers to mask their share dealings and, therefore, to secure personal advantages rather than to act in relation to their legal responsibility to the shareholders collectively. The scope for such actions is greater where shares have become widely dispersed, rather than being concentrated in the hands of one or two founding families. These days, however, many of the largest shareholders are banks, insurance companies, pension funds, and other corporations, and this has raised the question of the relationship between directors and shareholders in a particularly acute form. Discussions of corporate governance have increasingly come to be concerned with the legitimate role of large shareholders in the shaping of corporate policy. It is at this point that the new debates over corporate governance merge with older debates over management control and finance capital. Issues such as the degree of separation that exists between shareholders and directors, and of the extent to which interlocking directorships and capital relations lead to the formation of 'groups' of enterprises that are able to pursue a common policy, have come to the forefront of attention (Prentice and Holland 1993; McCahery et al. 1993. See also Cadbury 1992; Maw et al. 1994).

Studies of corporate governance have barely begun to take account of the detailed studies of these matters that have already been undertaken by sociologists and economists concerned with the issues of corporate power. Paradoxically, these studies originated in the earlier works of those who sought to establish an understanding of the realities of power in corporate business at a time when the majority of legal and financial theorists approached these matters in a highly abstract way. Berle and Means (1932), for example, sought to combine legal and economic methods to study the actual distribution of power in business, while Florence (1953) called for the establishment of a 'realistic' approach to business organization that would show how legal and other processes interact to shape the actual patterns of business practice. The precursors for these intellectual efforts were the Marxist and managerialist writers whose views shaped theories of capitalist society and of industrial society. In the Marxist tradition such concerns have centred around the idea of 'finance capital', while managerialist writers have explored the nature of 'management control'. In this chapter I will examine these rival conceptualizations of business power, and I will show that their key ideas are, in fact, complementary to one another. Each has an important part to play in a comprehensive conceptualization of corporate governance and corporate control.

Contending Theories of Business Power

The complexities that arise in assessing the power and significance of big business enterprises have generated a number of rival theoretical interpretations. The main contending views have their roots in two overarching themes in social thought, each of which has provided the basis for a well-developed theory of the development of industrial capitalism. These are the themes of 'industrialism' and 'capitalism' (Giddens 1973: 141–2). The theme of industrialism highlights the transformation of human labour through the use of inanimate sources of energy in productive activity and the resulting physical proximity of workers and machines in systems of factory production. Its focus, then, is on systems of industrial technology. The theme of capitalism, on the other hand, highlights the organization of production through a search for the realization of profit on privately owned capital, and the broader system of market exchange for which commodities are produced. Its focus is on financial organization. Industrial capitalism is a system of economic life that combines these two processes, but the two most influential theories of industrial capitalism have each stressed one theme to the virtual exclusion of the other. These contending theories are the theory of industrial society and the theory of capitalist society.

Mainstream sociology has its origins in the work of Saint-Simon and Comte, both of whom saw 'modern' societies as developing into specifically 'industrial' ones, run by the expert managers who shape industrial technology (Giddens 1976; 1971: 245 ff.; 1973: ch. 8;

Kumar 1978; Scott 1995).[6] Modern societies were, in this fundamental respect, distinguished from all preceding 'traditional' societies. This conception of modernity and of the task of sociology to produce a compelling theory of industrial society lay at the heart of mainstream sociology, and it had a major impact on neighbouring disciplines. In sociology, economics, and political science, and in the new disciplines of management and business studies, the theme of industrialism has been paramount.

The clearest statements of this point of view, in so far as it relates to the business enterprise, are to be found in a number of influential works produced in the 1950s and 1960s by Aron, Bell, Galbraith, and Kerr, and it has been a central element in the sociological theories of Parsons and the economic theories of Rostow. According to these writers, industrial technology reflects the growth and application of scientific knowledge. Modern society embodies the rational, scientific organisation of production:

Modern societies are defined first and foremost by their organisation of labour; that is, by their relationship to the external world, their use of machinery, the application of scientific methods, and the social and economic consequences of the rationalisation of production. (Aron 1967: 15; see also Lenski 1966: 298–9)

The theory of industrial society holds that the basic features of culture and society are to be explained as consequences of the unfolding of tendencies that are inherent in the organization of industrial technology.[7] The structures of industrial society follow from the development of technology, from the 'logic' of industrialism (Kerr *et al.* 1960: 42–3; Aron 1968: 53).[8] All industrial societies, regardless of their starting-points, will converge towards a common structural pattern because of their common dependence on the forces of indus-

---

[6] Giddens (1976: 727) claims that this theory is the substantive correlate of structural functionalism and of a positivist philosophy of science. See also Fay (1975: 55 ff.).

[7] See the important criticisms of this larger deterministic theory in Goldthorpe (1964; 1972; 1974).

[8] This argument has spawned a mass of work in the sociology of development, according to which 'underdeveloped' societies develop on the basis of the transfer of technology from the already-'developed' societies. See Hoselitz (1960), Hoselitz and Moore (1966), McClelland (1961), and Rostow (1960). These approaches are criticized in Hoogvelt (1976) and Spybey (1992). In political sociology the approach has been associated with the 'pluralist' and 'managerialist' perspectives on the state that are found in Lipset (1960), Aron (1960), Bell (1973), and other sources. These are criticized in Alford and Friedland (1985), Parry (1969), and Keller (1963).

trialism.

Galbraith has, perhaps, been the most forceful advocate of the view that the central dynamic of industrial society—its rational technology—is to be found in the large business enterprise. He has argued that the core of the economy consists of about 500 'technically dynamic, massively capitalised and highly organised corporations' (Galbraith 1967: 9; Pavitt and Worboys 1977: ch. 4). The increasing scale of production within the large enterprise requires such great amounts of capital that enterprises must sell larger and larger numbers of shares in order to finance their expansion. Eventually, the number of shareholders increases to the point where no individual or group of individuals is able to use their share ownership as a basis for control over the enterprise's activities. As Galbraith (1967: 80) has characteristically claimed: 'Corporate size, the passage of time and the dispersion of stock ownership do not disenfranchise the stockholder. Rather, he can vote but his vote is valueless.'

At the same time, as Bendix (1956: 226) has argued, the number of managers grows: 'As the enterprise increases in size, it becomes necessary for the owner-manager to delegate to subordinates responsibility for many functions, which he (sic) has performed personally in the past. Subsequently, it becomes necessary to delegate further managerial functions.' The owners of company shares lose their power of control, and the resulting power vacuum creates the conditions under which professional, salaried managers are able to usurp effective control. Capitalist forms of control have given way to 'management control'. Dahrendorf has built similar arguments into his attempts to reconstruct Marx's sociology, arguing that class relations do not depend on legal ownership but are 'relations of factual control and subordination in the enterprises of industrial production'. As such, he holds, classes are identified by their 'exercise of, or exclusion from, authority' (Dahrendorf 1959: 21,136; Bendix 1956: 13). He concludes that:

Control over the means of production is but a special case of authority, and the connection of control with legal property an incidental phenomenon of the industrialising societies of Europe and the United States (Dahrendorf 1959: 136–7)

The theory of industrial society provides a coherent and, in many respects, convincing account of the business enterprise. Versions of it have been widely used as the basis for attempts to construct a new perspective in microeconomics, and it has taken the lead in theoretical and empirical work. In the course of this book many criticisms of the 'managerialism' of the theory of industrial society will be made, but it will also be argued that any adequate understanding of big business must recognize its real, though limited, achievements.

The theory of capitalist society has its origins in the work of Marx, and has provided a radically different image of big business to that found in the theory of industrial society. Marx (1865) discussed the joint stock company in *Capital*, though the unfinished character of his remarks required later Marxists to expand on his fragmentary remarks. Hilferding (1910) and Bukharin (1918) were the leading theorists in the development of this theory, though it became familiar to later researchers mainly through the programmatic formulations offered by Lenin (1917a) and a number of Marxist textbooks.[9] This body of theory has inspired numerous Russian, American, and British researchers in their investigations into contemporary capitalist businesses.

Lenin drew on Hilferding's and Bukharin's analyses of 'organized capitalism' as the outcome of the growth of industrial concentration and combination from the apex of competitive capitalism in the 1860s to the 'monopoly' forms of the 1890s.[10] The introduction of the joint stock company was an essential element in this monopolization of capital, as it allowed enterprises to grow through internal capital accumulation and through merger and amalgamation with other enterprises. Individual enterprises achieved greater economic power in the markets in which they operated, and separate enterprises became more closely linked together through cartels, trusts, interweaving shareholdings, and interlocking directorships (Lenin 1917a: 39, 45 ff.). In this situation, banks acquire a critical importance as shareholders, mobilizers of capital, organizers of cartels, and providers of directors. Finance capital, then, results in bank control and bank influence.

Organized capitalism constituted a 'new social order, a transi-

[9] The most popular textbooks include Bukharin and Preobrazhensky (1920), Kuusinen et al. (1959), Eaton (1963), and Ryndina and Chernikov (1974).

[10] Lenin's formulation of the theory of imperialism and the state (1917a and b) drew heavily on the work of Bukharin, though the latter's theory was not published in full until a year after Lenin's pamphlets. Lenin and other Bolshevik writers preferred the term 'monopoly capitalism' to 'organized capitalism', seeing the latter term as being too closely identified with the reformist social democracy of the Second International. This terminological difference now seems of minor importance.

tional one from complete free competition to complete socialization' (Lenin 1917*a*: 23). It is a consequence of the separation of the increasingly socialized productive assets from the still-privatized appropriation of surplus value that became possible in the joint stock company: 'Production becomes social, but appropriation remains private' (ibid.: 56, 119). The period between 1890 and 1917 represented, for Lenin, the 'highest stage' of capitalist development, and it signalled that private production was beginning to give way to socialized production. The idea that capitalism had entered a 'transitional' phase has been more difficult to sustain as the length of this supposed transitional phase has increased. Orthodox Marxism continued to stress the transient character of organized capitalism, but more novel variants of Marxism have sought to arrive at alternative interpretations of the apparent stability of what has variously been described as 'contemporary capitalism', 'modern capitalism', or 'late capitalism'.

Most striking is the position taken by Habermas (1973). In his critical extension of Marxism, he has argued that the expansion of industrial technology has produced a number of changes in the structure of capitalism, and that fundamental alterations to Marxist theory must be made if these changes are to be properly theorized. To be true to its spirit, he holds, it is necessary to depart from the letter of Marxism (Habermas 1976). In the stage of 'late capitalism', Habermas argued, the economic-crisis tendencies that are generated in the market have come to be regulated by the state, but the price that is paid for this is the translation of these tendencies into the structure and operations of the state itself. In order to finance the expenditure that is required for effective intervention in the economy states have to borrow or raise taxation, and so experience fiscal problems that cannot easily be resolved. They also experience internal structural dislocations among their various departments, agencies, and branches, making it impossible to successfully resolve their fiscal problems or to regulate economies. These dislocations of policy constitute a 'rationality crisis' for capitalist states, which results from 'a snare of relations into which the advanced-capitalist state fumbles and in which its contradictory activities must become more and more muddled' (Habermas 1973: 63. See also Offe 1972).[11] Like the theory of industrial society, the theory of capitalist society con-

---

[11] Habermas related this 'rationality crisis' to broader sociocultural problems of legitimation that cannot be discussed here. See Habermas (1976: part 4), Offe

tains many important and useful ideas. Nevertheless, the contrary positions proposed from within Marxism show that the theory is not without its internal difficulties. Any alternative explanation of the role of the business enterprise must build on its powerful, though flawed, arguments.

Corporations in the Contemporary World

The two theories that I have discussed in this chapter have generated the most influential contemporary views of business enterprise. Each theory offers a clear and coherent account of the development of industrial capitalism, and each has a considerable degree of plausibility. While much of the empirical research that has been carried out into business ownership and organization has been shaped by the arguments of the two theories, the most sophisticated researchers have begun to move beyond the limits of these theories. Ever since Zeitlin's (1974) codification of a critical anti-managerialist position, empirical research and theoretical innovation have begun to advance together (see also Mizruchi 1987). The arguments presented in this book draw upon this theoretical work and the accumulating mass of empirical evidence, and I aim to set out an alternative account of the development of the business enterprise that has the scope of its two predecessor theories as well as maintaining the capacity to generate further empirical advance in the understanding of corporate governance and corporate power.

My argument, in summary, is that industrial capitalist societies have undergone a transition from *personal* to *impersonal* forms of ownership and control. The joint stock company, the stock-exchange system, and the introduction of new forms of investment have allowed enterprises to expand beyond the resources of individual entrepreneurs and families. The organization of production, distribution, and consumption is increasingly shaped by the ownership of shares and the allocation of loans, and this is now structured largely through an impersonal system of finance capital. Those shareholders that are able to mobilize votes in sufficient numbers, through the ownership of large percentage blocks of shares or through the acquisition of voting control over the shares owned by

(1970), and the more general account in Habermas (1981*a* and 1981*b*). Habermas's general approach to sociology is discussed in Scott (1978) and Scott (1995: ch. 10).

others, have the power to intervene in corporate affairs and to ensure that their views are influential. Although individuals and families have often been able to maintain or achieve this power, it is increasingly the case that the principal owners of company shares are other companies and financial intermediaries. Banks, insurance companies, pension funds, and investment companies have become the most important agents in the capital markets and the dominant forces in share ownership. These share-owning enterprises are, in their turn, subject to the same form of ownership; and, as a result, extensive networks of intercorporate capital relations have been formed in all of the advanced capitalist economies.

Both the theory of industrial society and the theory of capitalist society have assumed a unitary model of capitalist development, holding that all industrial, capitalist societies will follow a similar pattern of development. While they have different images of this common pattern, the assumption that there *is* a common pattern is shared. It is my contention that the assumption of a unitary pattern of capitalist development must be rejected, and that attention must be paid to variant forms of capitalism. The move to impersonal possession is, indeed, a common feature of all industrial, capitalist economies, though it develops unevenly and its concrete forms reflect varying national patterns of capitalist development. Personal forms of possession by individuals and families, for example, persist more strongly in some economies than in others, and the role of banks is highly variable. In some economies banks are the leading members of cohesive groups of industrial and financial interests, while in others a more generalized dominance in capital markets is exercised by banks and other financial intermediaries. These variations mean that the rise of impersonal possession cannot be equated simply with the rise of bank control.

I will argue that a number of distinctive patterns of capitalist development, related to systems of corporate law, can be identified. In Britain and the United States—the heartlands of the theoretical debates that I have considered—a characteristic 'Anglo-American' pattern can be found. In these societies, *entrepreneurial* forms of personal possession, as found in relatively small-scale family concerns, have given way to *institutional* mechanisms of capital mobilization, as the scale of economic activity has increased. Financial institutions have become the principal shareholders, and the intercorporate network is central to what I call 'control through a constellation of interests'. This, and not 'management control', is the predominant form of corporate control in these societies. In Germany and Austria, on the other hand, a 'German' pattern of capitalist development centres around the mobilization of capital through a banking mechanism that makes long-term capital available to client enterprises. The intercorporate network is vertically organized into corporate filiations around the big banks, each of which is linked to a number of dependent enterprises. A third pattern of capitalist development is the 'Japanese' pattern, in which there is a clustering of enterprises into tightly integrated sets within which capital is circulated from one enterprise to another in order to sustain the long-term investment strategy of the group as a whole. These corporate sets initially took a vertical form, in which company groups were subject to family control; but they subsequently developed into more decentralized forms of impersonal possession. The intercorporate network in Japan ties together banks, trading companies, insurance companies, and industrial companies into tight and cohesive enterprise groups. In France and Italy, by contrast, the move from personal to impersonal possession shows a 'Latin' pattern that involves the use of corporate webs in which the shareholdings of families, banks, and investment companies intersect in mutually supporting ways, to form patterns of control that allow the continuation of family influence within a more depersonalized system of investment funding.

These four patterns—the Anglo-American, the German, the Japanese, and the Latin—are the most important patterns of capitalist development to be found in the core of the capitalist world-economy, but they are not the only forms of capitalism that can be discovered. Outside the capitalist core, a number of other patterns have emerged as economies have industrialized. Of particular importance is the 'Chinese' pattern found in the newly industrializing economies of East Asia. In these economies, a system of corporate co-operation based on the solidarities of kinship and communal commitments allows the formation of large, but rather short-lived, groups of enterprises. This form of possession has been the basis of their rapid state-sponsored economic growth in the period since the Second World War. In the emerging economies of Central and Eastern Europe, on the other hand, the collapse of Communism has been followed by the emergence of a variety of structures that reflect differing historical experiences, and it is unclear which will persist and whether capitalist relations of production will be consolidated. In all the post-Communist economies, however, a system of haggling, bargaining, and barter is central to capital mobilization, and the erstwhile *nomenklatura*—ex-Communist officials—have established formal and informal mechanisms of corporate collusion to protect their own positions in the emerging systems of impersonal capitalist possession.

These variant patterns of impersonal possession are associated with a number of other features of business enterprise. Large enterprises have experienced a bureaucratization of management that involves a growth of managerial hierarchies and a structural alteration in the form of administration. In place of the personal systems of supervision found in entrepreneurial and family firms, large enterprises rely on impersonal mechanisms, such as the budgetary constraints imposed on corporate divisions, the bureaucratic constraints imposed on career executives, and the technical constraints imposed on factory and office work. The form taken by this process of bureaucratization and impersonal monitoring has varied over time, and it shows considerable variation among the differing patterns of capitalist development. 'Holding companies', 'functional organization', 'multidivisional organization', and varying patterns of 'flexibility' can be found. It will be argued that the move from personal to impersonal forms of possession and administration is a central aspect of the move from 'liberal capitalism' to 'organized capitalism', and that the growth of 'flexibility' in corporate administration reflects a further shift towards what has been called 'disorganized' capitalism. This process of 'disorganization' is most apparent at the level of the administrative and productive processes, but its effects are also becoming apparent at the level of corporate ownership and control: financial systems have become increasingly deregulated, and this has had major implications for patterns of control.

This move towards more 'disorganized' forms of capitalism is inextricably linked to the growing globalization of the world-economy. In contemporary capitalist markets a small number of large, oligopolistic enterprises control the bulk of all corporate assets and activity, though these enterprises are surrounded by a dependent fringe of small and medium-sized firms—often subcontractors—that operate in markets in which some of the features of atomistic competition are still to be found. These large enterprises have a great autonomy within their markets and possess considerable market power. In the post-war period, these enterprises have become more multinational in their ownership and operation. Overseas investment has been centred in large multinational enterprises, and the multinational enterprises based in the advanced economies of the capitalist core have increasingly turned their attention to investment and sales in other advanced economies. This has led to an increase in the number of capital relations, commercial relations, and interlocking directorships that connect enterprises of varying nationalities. This interconnection has resulted in a progressive 'disarticulation' of national economies that has reinforced their internal 'deregulating' processes. Instead of being linked into a cohesive national economy, the various elements in the advanced economies are tied into an extensive, but decentralized, global network of intercorporate relations. National economies have become disarticulated and are ceasing to be, in any meaningful sense, units of economic activity.

By virtue of their global disarticulation, these economies are less and less subject to effective control and planning by nation states. In all of the advanced capitalist societies, states have taken an increasingly interventionist role, rather than seeking simply to facilitate private production; they have expanded their budgets to finance new areas of expenditure, and have undertaken economic planning and the restructuring of economic activity. The modes and intensities of state intervention have varied from one society to another, and reflect not only the structures of their economies, but also the policies and practices of their capitalist classes. The economic powers of nation states have, however, been increasingly undermined by the globalization of the world-economy, and many of the principal economic variables are now beyond their control, resulting in characteristic 'rationality' crises. Following a drive towards interventionist and regulatory practices in many societies during the 1960s and 1970s, recent decades have seen the adoption of policies that have promoted the very processes of 'disorganization' and 'disarticulation' that have weakened nation states. Systems of financial and economic regulation have been dismantled, and there has been a systematic 'privatization' of state economic assets, aimed at establishing a more 'liberal' and competitive regime of capital accumulation.

Class structure, in turn, reflects the economic and political transformations that these societies have undergone. Propertied capitalist classes can still be identified: the impersonal structure of possession has not resulted in the loss of power by wealthy, propertied persons. Yet these capitalist classes are no longer merely collections of individually powerful families. Wealthy families have spread their shareholdings across a large number of companies, rather than holding controlling blocks in particular companies, and they form a pool from which the top corporate managers are recruited. A propertied capitalist class has interests throughout the corporate system, and is able to ensure its continuity over time through its monopolization of the educational system as well as its monopolization of wealth. It stands at the top of the stratification system, enjoying superior life chances to those in the subordinate service class that fill the rungs of the corporate hierarchies. As processes of ownership have become more globalized, so capitalist classes have become less 'national' in character. Reflecting the disarticulation of national economies, capitalist classes have themselves become increasingly disarticulated.

This alternative interpretation of industrial capitalism will be presented in more detail in the remainder of this book. It will be argued that the theories of industrial society and of capitalist society, although they have generated much relevant empirical data and theoretical insights, must now be buried and that further advance requires their transcendence. Chapter 2 discusses the finance capital and managerialist perspectives in greater detail, while Chapter 3 builds on these to set out the model of corporate governance and control used in Chapters 4, 5, and 6 to explain the various patterns of capitalist development that can be found in the advanced societies. Patterns of corporate rule, administration, and 'flexibility' are discussed in Chapter 7, the national and international economies and the role of the state are discussed in Chapter 8, and in Chapter 9 the development of corporate capital is related to transformations in class structure.

2

MANAGERIALIST AND MARXIST PERSPECTIVES

....

POWER in the contemporary business enterprise rests upon the legal form of the joint stock company or corporation. It was through this legal form that enterprises were able to increase in size, to merge with or to acquire other enterprises, and to establish extensive internal hierarchies of authority. At the heart of the dispute between the theory of industrial society and the theory of capitalist society is a disagreement over the social consequences that are assumed to follow from this legal form. In the theory of industrial society, the corporate form allows a separation of ownership from control to emerge; and this in turn results in an enhancement of the power of the managers of the enterprises. For the theory of capitalist society, on the other hand, the corporate form is the basis of a fusion of banking and industrial capital that results in the rise to power of finance capitalists.

The issues that are addressed in these theories are those of corporate governance, of the control and regulation of the business enterprises that have been made possible by the extension of the corporate legal form. A critical assessment of their conflicting views, however, is limited by unnecessary differences of terminology between the two theories, and by their tendency to focus on different conceptual issues. If a proper critical assessment is to be undertaken, a clear and coherent conceptual framework must be established, as this is the only basis on which their rival views can be appraised. In order to assess whether large enterprises are controlled by their managers, for example, it is essential that there be an agreed concept of 'management control'. Without such conceptual agreement, researchers will continue to talk past one another and there will be neither theoretical dialogue nor empirical advance.

My task in this and the following chapter is to begin to construct such a conceptual framework. I will examine the ways in which the central concepts of 'finance capital' and 'management control' have been formulated in the two theoretical approaches, and I will then set out a model of corporate control that seeks to draw on both approaches and to enlarge their respective concerns.

Financiers and Finance Capital

The most influential conceptualization of finance capital is to be found in the works of the 'Austro-Marxists' Renner and Hilferding, who built their analyses from Marx's fragmentary remarks on joint stock capital and the corporate form. Marx had claimed that the social relations of production were relations of effective possession that had to be distinguished from the legal property rights on which they were based. Relations of production, he said, in a characteristically cryptic statement, 'develop unevenly as legal relations', and so possession must always be considered as part of a 'more concrete substratum'. Legal relations and social relations do not coincide in a one-to-one way, and so 'The influence of laws in stabilizing relations of distribution, and hence their effect on production, requires to be determined in each specific instance' (Marx 1857: 98, 102, 109). Study of law in the abstract is a poor guide to actual relations of possession, since legal rights and relations must be seen in relation to the concrete historical contexts that give them their structural significance. It was this insight that Marx tried to apply to the relationship between the legal form of the joint stock company and actual patterns of capitalist business enterprise. In the modern enterprise, he argued, 'capital as property' is separated from 'capital as a function', but this 'divorce' develops gradually as part of the expansion of the credit system: 'Stock companies in general—developed with the credit system—have an increasing tendency to separate this work of management as a function from the ownership of capital, be it self-owned or borrowed' (Marx 1865–7: 380). The function of capital in the process of production—subordination of the labour process to the expansion of capital—is 'institutionalized' in the business enterprise itself, and so is separated from the individual property owners who supply the capital. Those engaged in the 'work of management and supervision' through which the function of capital is met are employees of the corporation, and may not be its legal owners (Marx 1865–7: 372, 376, 378–9, 428; see also Marx 1864–6).

The model of finance capital was developed in response to the late and rapid industrial development of Germany and Austria, which brought out forcefully the issues that were involved in the emergence of the joint stock company and the growth of monopoly. In these countries, capitalism developed in a highly 'organized' form that involved a high degree of concentration in banking and in industry. Renner (1904) and Hilferding (1910) developed closely related analyses of joint stock capital that went well beyond Marx's rather terse statements. Renner held that the legal institution of property comprises a set of legal imperatives that regulate the 'detention' of, or access to, social objects. The legal relation of 'ownership', then, comprises 'a person's all-embracing legal power over a tangible object' (ibid.: 81). A particularly important area of property law concerns access to the social objects that are involved in the production of goods and services (Renner 1904: 53, 73–4). As Marx had suggested, the actual social relations that constitute a society rarely correspond exactly to its codified legal forms. To reduce social relations to their legal expressions involves 'fetishism', as social relations are transformed into things. Legal ownership is not the same as social ownership. While in legal theory 'ownership is reduced to a mere legal title' and is thereby fetishized (ibid.: 147), legal forms must in reality be seen as simply one of the conditions of actual social relations. It is the 'social function' of the legal forms that is crucial: a legal relation of ownership can have varying social meanings depending upon the larger social context of which it is a part. The social relation of ownership—the actually effective power of 'possession'—may diverge from the legal relation of ownership, even though the latter is one of its essential conditions. Renner argues that the relations of effective possession are structured in ways that establish relations of social *power*:

Without any change in the norm, below the threshold of collective consciousness, a *de facto* right is added to the personal absolute domination over a corporeal thing. This right is not based upon a special legal provision. It is a power of control, the power to issue commands and to enforce them. (Ibid.: 107, 117)

Legal institutions give rise to social relations, but they are then themselves subject to transformation as these social relations develop. There will always be a greater or lesser lack of correspondence between legal property relations and the social relations of possession.

In the individually owned capitalist enterprise, the capital that is available for production is directly provided by its owners. The scale of production is therefore limited by the personal wealth of the capitalist owner. The entrepreneurial capitalist is the legal owner of the business and has actual possession of its capital. In these circumstances, there is a long-term and active participation by 'working capitalists who must combine ownership with the entrepreneurial function' (Hilferding 1910: 121). The productive, functioning capitalist earns 'profit' on this invested capital, and this is the basis of the income that he or she receives. As the enterprise grows in size it requires more capital than can be provided by one individual or family, and the legal forms of ownership become fetters on its further growth. The joint stock company provided a solution to these problems and opened up new possibilities of social development by allowing enterprises to raise large amounts of capital. Individual capitalists subscribe only a part of the capital that is required by a particular enterprise. As their capital is provided jointly with others, the individual capitalists cease to be 'industrial capitalists'. Instead they are creditors, owners of money capital who have no necessary connection with the uses to which the credit is put. Investors in joint stock companies may include, for example, landowners, retired persons, and various other categories of individuals who have money to spare. They are mere shareholders. The shareholder, as a 'money capitalist', earns 'interest' from profitable investments (Renner 1904: 142–3), but no longer has effective possession of the means of production. Legal ownership of company stock or shares gives a person the right to benefit from corporate activities,[1] but legal ownership of the corporate assets themselves is vested in the joint stock company as a corporate body.

These tendencies in joint stock capital created a problem of control: if the company is legal owner of the means of production, then who has the actual power to determine the uses to which these means are put (ibid.: 198, 268, 275)? Renner's answer was that this power—the 'social power of command' (ibid.: 283)—is vested in the organizational activities of salaried managers, who combine it with

---

[1] Renner terms this 'economic ownership', but this term has not been used in the present discussion because it has recently been employed by other writers in a very different sense. Renner's own position is discussed in Kinsey (1983).

the exercise of their technical expertise in the process of production. This social power, the 'capitalist function', is separated from the shareholding capitalists, who nevertheless retain the right to appropriate surplus value in the form of interest. In Hilferding's work this conclusion was allied with an analysis of the growing importance of banks and other financial intermediaries in the ownership of money capital. He held that there had been a fusion of banking and industry into 'finance capital', a process that removed most of the shareholding capitalists even further from actual production.

According to Lenin, industrial enterprises were becoming vast monopolies of productive capital, but, at the same time, the banks 'grow from modest middlemen into powerful monopolies having at their command almost the whole of the money capital of all the capitalists and small businessmen' (Lenin 1917a: 28). Monopoly in banking gave the banks economic power over manufacturing enterprises and, as a result, banking and industry was gradually fused into this new form of capital, 'finance capital'.[2] In this system, banking and industry are allied with one another through shareholdings, credit relations, and interlocking directorships. The major banks own shares in industry; industrial combines own shares in banks; and there is an exchange of directors between the boards of the banks and the leading industrials. The credit system is enlarged with the emergence of new and expanded roles for savings banks, insurance companies, investment trusts, pension funds, and other novel forms of savings and investment. This is the basis of finance capital, a form of capital that is not restricted to any one particular sphere of economic activity and that comes under the control of the banks. Industrial enterprises become increasingly dependent on bank loans and other forms of finance capital for expansion, and this consolidates the dominance of finance capital over productive capital (Rochester 1936: 13).

In place of the numerous competing enterprises of liberal capitalism, the system of finance capital is organized into a much smaller number of distinct and competing 'financial groups' or 'empires of high finance'. These are clusters of connected enterprises within which co-ordination and control by dominant over subordinate enterprises is established. At the heart of each financial group is a closely allied group of monopolies that pursue a common policy and

[2] In addition to Hilferding (1910), the concept of finance capital appeared in the works of Kautsky (1902) and Luxemburg (1913). Hilferding's work draws on the work of the liberal writer Hobson (1906). For a general review see Kiernan (1974).

that can exercise control over a large number of operating companies in various branches of the economy. Interlocking directorships, cross-shareholdings, and other types of connection create 'associations of capital which at most have a common direction and at the least a common interest in avoiding conflicts of interest' (Aaronovitch 1961: 79, emphasis removed; 1955: 12, 54 ff.; Rochester 1936: 104). Perlo claimed that by the 1950s the 'ties which interlock the monopolies have become tighter and more complex. The control of corporations is more and more centralised in knots of financial power' (1957: 15).

According to Perlo, the leaders of the separate financial groups were families and coalitions of families, and the separate groups were themselves connected into a nationwide 'spider web' of business interests:

Strong ties of ownership cemented with interlocking directorates link financial institutions of different kinds in an inner circle of co-ordinated power. Similar strands extend from the inner circle to the great corporations of industry, transport and utilities, through which billions of profits extracted from the population of this and other countries are funnelled to the central oligarchy. (Perlo 1957: 61–2; see also Bukharin 1918: 72; Rochester 1936: 104–6; Menshikov 1969: 216)

This 'inner circle' of finance capitalists consists of rentier capitalists who are dependent on the incomes that they earn from the shares that they own and who are, therefore, parasitic upon those who actually manage productive capital (Lenin 1917a: 56; Bukharin and Preobrazhensky 1920: 141–8; Rochester 1936: 85). Recruited from wealthy families and sitting on the boards of the big banks and other joint stock companies, they form a financial oligarchy, a clique of 'a few hundred or at most a few thousand men (sic) of wealth' who comprise the dominant social class (Perlo 1957: 13; Aaronovitch 1961: 70). The dominant social class in organized capitalism, then, is a class of rentier, finance capitalists rather than of entrepreneurial capitalists.

Where the theory of industrial society sees a separation of ownership from control as allowing the rise of a new dominant class of managers, the theory of capitalist society draws different conclusions from the differentiation of finance capital from productive capital. The argument is that the day-to-day running of production is delegated to subordinate managers, engineers, and clerks, but that finance capitalists retain the power to determine the general policies that are implemented by their subordinate managers. Finance capitalists have the power to hire and fire managers, and they appropriate the proceeds of production (Menshikov 1969: 80–1, 132–4, 318–20). They continue, therefore, to play a central role in the reproduction of capitalist relations of production: they are involved in the buying and selling of shares, the manipulation of blocks of shares, the provision or withholding of loans, and the many other financial machinations that emerged in the stage of organized capitalism.

These finance capitalists, Hilferding claimed, constitute the leading edge of the capitalist class, and they are able to ensure that the powers of salaried managers are exercised on their behalf (Hilferding 1910: 119–20; Renner 1904: 114 ff.). Capitalist development, then, is shaped by the interplay of finance capitalists and the subordinate managers that Renner (1953) was later to term the 'service class'. Both writers agreed that the rise of the joint stock company pointed to the eventual demise of the capitalist class. Because capitalists were no longer the direct holders of the social power of command, they had become technically redundant to the actual process of production. The residual control that was exercised by the finance capitalists no longer had any basis in the technical development of the forces of production.

One particular strand of Marxist theory, however, has drawn conclusions that bring it close to managerialist theory. Baran and Sweezy (1966), in attempting to rebuild Marxist micro-economics, argued that much day-to-day power has, in fact, passed to salaried managers. They rejected the idea that industrial enterprises were now dominated by bankers. Large enterprises, they held, are units of 'monopoly capital', not of 'finance capital'. A monopoly enterprise has considerable power in its markets, but it is still constrained by the countervailing power of other monopoly enterprises. This effectively reduces the discretion of those who fill the top levels of the corporate hierarchy. Whether the shareholders have withdrawn from production or not is irrelevant, as business leaders must follow the logic of the market. The market mechanisms of monopoly capital ensure that the policy followed by an enterprise is dictated solely by an economic logic, and not by the particular preferences of bankers, shareholders, or executives. Large enterprises pursue growth or revenue within their markets, and this involves no fundamental departure from the conditions of capitalist production. The continuing constraint of market profitability ensures the continuity of capitalist relations. The managerial enterprise expresses these conditions in a particularly clear and systematic way, devoid of any of the 'irrational'

characteristics of family enterprise. This form of 'Marxist managerialism', then, converges with conventional managerialism and sees
the rational action of the large enterprise as the visible hand of
monopoly capital.

Organized capitalism is also seen as showing a growth in state
intervention and of interlocking between finance capital and the
state (Rochester 1936: 287 ff.; Aaronovitch 1955: 66, 73 ff.). This partnership of capital and the state helps to promote domestic profitability and the socialization of unprofitable activities, and it
facilitates the international expansion of national monopolies.
Bukharin went so far as to claim that there was a tendency for each
national economy to become 'a single combined enterprise with an
organization connection between all the branches of production'
and the state (Bukharin 1915: 70), but few subsequent writers have
followed him in this. Whether formed into a single combine or a
small number of competing financial groups, the relationship
between capital and the state becomes central to the whole social
structure. The state takes on more and more economic functions,
including such macro-economic activities as the maintenance of
profitability, the creation of demand, the redistribution of national
income, and a whole range of other activities from direct state enterprise to international military and political entanglements. The
orthodox Marxist writers of the 1920s and 1930s saw this as leading
to a change in the internal structure of the state, and they saw the fascist states of Italy, Germany, and Japan as indicative of the form of
state that would eventually develop in the other advanced capitalist
societies (Varga 1928: 12: Radek 1934: 9 ff.). More generally, the
claim is simply that dictatorship and other forms of centralized,
authoritarian government are more appropriate than democracy for
systems of organized capitalism. 'State monopoly capitalism' continually evolves in this authoritarian direction, with the state
machine acting in the interests of the most powerful capitalist
groups and serving the interests of the financial oligarchy
(Aaronovitch 1955: 75):

Finance capital is not one interest among many which may lobby an impar-
tial government and whose legitimate rights such a government should
seek to satisfy. It is built into and controls the entire government and
administration of this country for its own profit and against the wider interests of the nation. (Aaronovitch 1961: 162)[3]

---

[3] See also Gollan (1956), Harvey and Hood (1958), Frankel (1970), Rochester
(1936: ch. 8), and Perlo (1957: ch. 15). Similar arguments can be found in Lenin

At a global level, state monopoly capitalism is seen as involving imperialism and militarism. Faced with declining opportunities for profitable investment in their national economies, financial groups begin to export capital through investment in other parts of the world. Through the establishment of colonies they secure the production of the minerals, raw materials, and agricultural products that are required by capitalist enterprises in the imperial centres. An international division of labour develops in which the industrial development of the colonies is subordinated to the needs of the imperialist powers (Lenin 1917a: 77).

Managers and the Managerial Revolution

The late and rapid industrialization of the United States stimulated considerable discussion about the joint stock company and the power of the investment bankers who formed these companies into large, monopolistic enterprises. One of the earliest discussions of managers in the new, large enterprises was that of Veblen (1924), who claimed that corporate organization involved the 'alienation of control' by owners. Shareholders become absentee owners, and the investment bankers who participate in strategic control also tend to adopt an 'absentee' orientation in so far as they are concerned with financial matters rather than with the people and physical goods involved in the work of production. While shareholders and financiers have a 'pecuniary' orientation, engineers and skilled workers adopt an 'industrial' orientation which is held in check by their subordination to proprietary and banking interests (Veblen 1919; see also Banks 1959). For Veblen, the creative powers of industrial craftsmanship could be released by liberating them from financial bondage.

The most influential contribution to these debates was a study by Berle and Means (1932), who echoed the claim of Veblen that ownership was being separated from control in large enterprises. Berle and Means argued that the corporation involved a dissolution of 'the traditional logic of property', according to which the supplier of capital was able to determine how that capital was to be used. The individual owner of industrial property had full rights to both use and to

(1917b), though the argument there is more complex. For critical discussions see Jessop (1990).

benefit from this property, but in the era of the corporation this had changed. The modern corporation involved 'the surrender and regrouping of the incidence of ownership, which formerly bracketed full power of manual disposition with complete right to enjoy the use, the fruits, and the proceeds of physical assets' (Berle and Means 1932: 8). Stocks and shares provide their owners with a financial interest in an enterprise, but they are not necessarily associated with any significant control over its assets. The dissolution of the traditional property rights means that those who supply the capital of a joint stock company may not be the same people as those who determine the uses to which the capital is put (ibid.: 433 ff.; Berle 1955: 17). In these circumstances, it is possible to distinguish 'nominal ownership' from 'effective ownership'. Nominal ownership is the legal right to receive an income in return for risking one's wealth by investing in a company, while effective ownership is the actual ability to control the corporate assets.[4] Thus, Berle and Means are in agreement with Renner that it is necessary to go beyond mere legal forms to the 'economic and social background of law' (Berle and Means 1932: 339). While the corporation emerged as a purely *legal* institution, it rapidly became the basis of business enterprise as a 'social institution' to which the law had to be continually adapted. Corporate enterprise, then, is not a mere creature of the law, it is 'not fictitious, but factual' (Berle 1955: 9).

In a corporate enterprise, the shareholders are not the actual owners of the assets. The assets are legally owned by the corporation itself and are, therefore, effectively controlled by whoever is able to determine corporate policy. In the same way as Renner and Hilferding, Berle and Means saw the problem of 'control', rather than legal ownership, as being at the heart of the modern corporation. Central to their argument was the claim that shareholders were gradually being forced to withdraw from any significant involvement in actual control. When there are very few shareholders in a company they may, if they wish, continue to co-operate in the management of the corporation; but as they increase in number, this becomes more difficult. The composition of the board of directors and, thereby, the company policy is decided by the majority vote of the shareholders; and so the dispersal of shareholdings to ever larger numbers of people makes it progressively more difficult to mobilize a majority of the shares. When shares are dispersed among a great

---

[4] Berle and Means somewhat confusingly term these two aspects 'passive' and 'active', but these terms are rather unhelpful.

number of individual investors, each of whom has only a very small holding, no one has sufficient shares to give them a decisive voice in the company's affairs. The mass of shareholders can no longer be regarded as 'capitalists' in the strict sense, as they have merely a beneficial, and very small, interest in the affairs of the companies of which they are the nominal owners. When owner control is weakened, non-owners may have greater opportunities to participate in control, and Berle and Means saw the internal executives as the main contenders for this control. 'Management control' exists where those who are able to dominate the composition of the board of directors are almost totally divorced from the legal ownership of the corporation (Berle and Means 1932: 80–4). This change in control is seen as a precondition for important changes in corporate behaviour:

The separation of ownership and control produces a condition where the interests of owner and of ultimate manager may, and often do diverge, and where many of the checks which formerly operated to limit the use of power disappear. (Berle and Means 1932: 6, 121–2)

The power of control becomes divorced from legal ownership, and it is no longer appropriate to regard the enterprise as a capitalist one at all. It is, instead, a managerial enterprise, subject to management control, and it is effectively free from the constraints of capitalist property ownership. The managers are able to run the enterprise with a more general public interest in mind. The 'democratization' of shareholdings means that if the business system is still to be described as capitalist, then it must be described as 'People's Capitalism' (Berle 1960).

A particularly systematic statement of this view has been given by Bell, who sees the rise of the managers—the 'managerial revolution'—as the end result of a long process of social transformation. A series of economic crises at the beginning of the twentieth century, he argues, enhanced the power of the investment bankers who played a leading role in reconstructing failing enterprises. This system of banking power was, however, short-lived. Because of the expansion of the financial system, capital became more easily available and soon became less critical for production than the technical knowledge and expertise that was required to operate large-scale systems of production. As a result, the professional managers who had been recruited by the bankers became the indispensable 'corporate organizers' of the whole system (Bell 1957: 40–1).

With these social changes, the inheritance of capital or position through the family became increasingly less important for economic power, and technical skill became more important. Industrial societies experienced a 'break-up' of the old ruling class: the mere possession of wealth could no longer guarantee access to economic power (Bell 1958: 50 ff.; Lenski 1966: 343). Parsons and Smelser (1957: 289), for example, claimed that 'the kinship–property combination typical of classical capitalism' had given way to the 'bureaucratization' of production, and in this situation, they hold, the theories of Weber are more relevant than those of Marx. For these reasons, then, managers become a new class that is capable of consolidating the further development of industrialism, and which gradually replaces the capitalist propertied class of entrepreneurs. The managerial class is not tight and closed, but 'broad and diffuse . . . with several loosely integrated components', based not on property ownership but on 'occupational status and occupational earnings' (Parsons 1954a: 431; Lenski 1966: 352).[5]

Writers associated with this 'managerialist' point of view differ in the conclusions that they draw from the rise of the managers. The predominant conclusion is what Nichols (1969), in his critical review, has termed 'non-sectional managerialism'. This sees the separation of ownership from control as allowing managers to depart from the profit orientation that had characterized the capitalist entrepreneur. Managers are no longer constrained by the financial demands of shareholders, and they are motivated by a broader outlook that eschews sectional financial interests and embodies a sense of social 'responsibility'. The manager holds a fiduciary or 'trust' role on behalf of the community as a whole, and corporate policy becomes 'benevolent' or even 'soulful' (Kaysen 1957; Mayo 1949; Drucker 1951). This is the basis of Berle's (1960) 'People's Capitalism', a phase of industrialism in which large enterprises are able to 'judge society's needs in a more conscious fashion and . . . to do so on the basis of some explicit conception of the "public interest" ' (Bell 1974: 284).[6]

Other writers, however, have drawn the conclusions that Nichols has summarized as 'sectional managerialism'. This view has been particularly strong among economists, involving the claim that the

---

[5] This viewpoint underlies much of the so-called 'functionalist' theory of stratification. See Davis and Moore (1945) and Parsons (1954a). Much of the debate is reprinted in Scott (1996b).

[6] Variants of this non-sectional managerialism can also be found in Dahrendorf (1959) and Crosland (1962; 1956).

separation of ownership from control allows managers to give free rein to their own sectional interests. As a result, corporate policy reflects a drive to maximize growth, revenue, and managerial salaries (Galbraith 1967). The traditional theory of the firm, an integral part of the neo-classical theory of relative prices, assumed that market mechanisms guided the behaviour of profit-maximizing enterprises and ensured an appropriate level of output. Sectional managerialists, however, see the separation of ownership from control as weakening the commitment of the new managerial controllers to the goal of profit-maximization. Large enterprises, therefore, have a greater autonomy in their markets, and their managers are able to co-ordinate the flow of resources in relative freedom from competitive market forces: 'the visible hand of management replaced what Adam Smith referred to as the invisible hand of market forces' (Chandler 1977: 1).

Sectional managerialists hold that this view of the enterprise as a 'visible hand' has to be incorporated into alternative theories of pricing behaviour. A common starting-point has been Simon's rational choice model of 'satisfactory' rather than 'optimal' behaviour (Simon 1945: ch. 4; March and Simon 1963: ch. 6). According to this model, enterprises do not 'maximize' their income, they 'satisfice'. They do not have the kind of information that would allow them to make a rational calculation of the chances of maximizing their income and so they aim at achieving a satisfactory level of profit, given the constraints under which they operate. Thus, Williamson (1964) and Marris (1964) have argued that salaried managers are oriented towards 'satisficing' the rewards associated with their occupational position: they pursue large salaries, fringe benefits, work autonomy, and prestige. All of these rewards are seen as associated with the size of an enterprise, and so managers are held to be motivated towards the growth of their department and their enterprise, subject only to earning a sufficient surplus to keep the shareholders happy. Large and rapidly growing enterprises provide the rewards that managers pursue.[7] While non-sectionalist managerialists claim that the managerial class is the carrier of a new social ethic of responsibility, sectionalist managerialists argue that it pursues its own self-interest.

These two viewpoints—the managerialist and the Marxist—have much in common in their recognition of the fundamental changes to

---

[7] See also Baumol (1959) and the contributions in Mason (1959).

the structure of business that follow from the introduction and growth of the corporate form. There is a common recognition of the need to move away from a purely legalistic framework of analysis in order to recognize the changing nature of 'ownership' and the implications of the rise of 'management'. The substantive conclusions that are drawn in the two traditions differ, however, and they present radically variant images of capitalist development. My aim in the rest of this book is to draw on the common elements in the two approaches in order to construct a model of corporate control that is better able to grasp the various forms of capitalist enterprise that have developed in the contemporary world. That task begins in the next chapter, where the conceptual insights of Marxists and managerialists are combined with the conceptual innovations of those who have engaged, theoretically and empirically, with these two traditions.

3

STRUCTURES OF CORPORATE CONTROL

ITH the emergence of the legal form of the joint stock company, the corporation itself is the owner of its assets. It is this that makes the question of who is able to control the corporation and to determine its behaviour all-important. 'Control', in the strict sense, designates a structural relation in which particular individual or collective actors have the *de facto* capacity to mobilize the powers that are legally vested in the corporation. As such, it constitutes a power potential. Control should be distinguished from 'rule', by which is meant actual involvement in decision-making or participation in business leadership (Scott 1990*a*: 352–3). The rulers of an enterprise are those who wield the actual powers that are inherent in the ownership of corporate assets, and the exercise of rule is always constrained by the structure of control. In many situations, the distinction between control and rule need not be emphasized: rule can be considered as an aspect of control in its broadest sense, and the word 'control' can be used to encompass both processes. It must always be borne in mind, however, that control and rule *are* distinct from one another and that important empirical questions may be asked about the relationship between them.

Berle and Means's (1932: 69) conception of control in a corporation is focused on the ability to determine the composition of its board of directors, though it has been stressed that this reflects 'the power of determining the broad policies guiding the corporation' (Goldsmith and Parmelee 1940: 99).[1] Control consists, then, in the

---

[1] Perhaps the earliest formulation of the position that control over the 'managerial function' was to be defined in terms of control over recruitment to top

power to determine the fundamental elements in corporate behaviour, and centres on the power to determine the composition of the ruling body of corporate leaders. Thus, non-board members, such as bankers or family shareholders, may nevertheless have powers of control because they are able to place their nominees on the board and so ensure a compliant ruling directorate.

It is useful to see control and rule as occurring at two levels within the enterprise: the 'strategic' level of structural decision-making, and the 'operational' level of day-to-day management.[2] Those with strategic power are those who determine the strategic, structural decisions within an enterprise (De Vroey 1973: 82–3; Eisenberg 1969: 11–13). Strategic control shapes the decisions that are taken by corporate rulers in relation to 'the determination of the basic long-term goals and objectives of the enterprise, and the adoption of courses of action and the allocation of resources necessary for carrying out these goals' (Chandler 1962: 13; Ansoff 1965). Strategic decisions set or alter the structure of the basic parameters within which an enterprise acts. They concern such matters as the source and level of investment funds, the allocation of these funds to alternative uses, calculation of the rates of profit that are to be earned in different branches of the enterprise, the recruitment of the top executives, and the resolution of such constitutional issues as mergers, take-overs, and liquidation. Operational power, on the other hand, involves the detailed implementation of corporate strategy and thus concerns the immediate day-to-day administration of corporate operations at plant and divisional level.

Operational managers exercise their rule within a general framework that is set by those who determine the corporate strategy, and in most cases the controllers of a large enterprise will not seek to participate in the actual making of operational decisions. Strategic power sets the financial constraints within which the tasks of operational management are undertaken. At its highest levels, operational management involves budgetary decisions about the achievement of

management was in Weber (1914). See also Larner (1970: 2), Villarejo (1961a: 49), Domhoff (1967: 50), Barratt Brown (1968a: 53–4), Francis (1980a), and Zeitlin (1974: 1091–2).

[2] The distinction between strategic and operational control has appeared, often implicitly, in many sources, although Pahl and Winkler (1974: 15) were the first to make the distinction an explicit point of reference in their work. For related views see Parsons (1956: 30–1), Peterson (1965: 2), Juran and Louden (1966), Lundberg (1969: 169), Jancovici (1972: 80), Burch (1972: 18), Poulantzas (1974: 119), Westergaard and Resler (1975: 163), Soref (1976: 362), and Cutler et al. (1977: 308–9).

strategic objectives, and management tasks at these levels involve the calculation of material and labour matters in monetary terms. At the lower levels, operational management involves calculation in terms of physical quantities and the direct supervision of labour together with the technical conditions under which it takes place. Economic theories of the firm have tended to emphasize operational issues concerned with materials management: the acquisition and maintenance of raw materials, product research and development, and marketing and market research. Sociological discussions of operational management, on the other hand, have focused on managerial power over the labour process: most particularly, over work relations, employment relations, and industrial relations (Gospel 1983a: 12 ff.).

Corporate control, then, involves the regulation of an extensive system of tasks, ranging from long-term structural matters to the everyday monitoring and disciplining of labour—from top-level financial direction to shop-floor supervision. It is strategic control, however, that is crucial with respect to the mobilization and accumulation of capital; and that lies at the centre of the theoretical concerns of both Marxists and managerialists.

Shareholders, Financiers, and Managers

The classic entrepreneurial firm was organized around *direct personal possession*. In this situation, an individual or family owns a factory or workshop and is the personal employer of labour to work in it. Control and rule are unified in the person of the entrepreneur, and the profits generated in the enterprise form the personal income of the entrepreneur. The joint stock company separates the right to determine the use of assets from the right to benefit from them, but this is a *legal* separation and not an absolute divorce. For this reason, the basic power relations of a corporation are always matters of *control* rather than of ownership *per se*. In the words of Berle and Means, 'control is more often factual than legal, depending upon strategic positions secured through a measure of ownership, a share in management or an external circumstance important to the conduct of the enterprise' (1932: 79). The nominal legal owners of the corporation 'become no more than creditors' (Westergaard and Resler 1975: 154) who can be regarded 'as legitimate claimants to some fixed share of the profits' (Bell 1974: 295). This means that individual investors of all sorts become rentiers and become aware that this is what they are. Their property consists less and less of their ownership of some part of the corporation's physical plant and stock of materials and products than of their right to a revenue from the ability of the corporation to manoeuvre profitably. (MacPherson 1973: 154; see also Tawney 1920 and Levy 1950)

The property rights of individuals are transformed into mere financial claims upon the company, together with the right to transfer these entitlements to others simply by selling the shares (Jones 1982: 86–92; Hadden 1977; see also Hollowell 1982; Causer 1982; Becker 1977). Shareholders do, however, have certain constitutional rights as 'members' of the company, most particularly the right to attend the annual general meeting and to vote on the selection of the directors who will be responsible for running the company and for seeing that the legal interests of the shareholders are protected.

Shareholders, therefore, are legal beneficiaries of the use of corporate capital, but their participation in its control is much attenuated. It is possible, nevertheless, for a group from among the body of the shareholders to exercise this control. As Poulantzas emphasized, not all shareholders are equal:

not every share or interest taken by a shareholder in a firm's capital corresponds to an equivalent or proportionate share in economic ownership and real control. This ownership is wielded as a whole by a few large shareholders, not necessarily a majority, who by various means . . . concentrate in their hands the powers that derive from it. (Poulantzas 1974: 119)

In other words, 'the relationship between ownership and control can be viewed as one consisting of several *degrees of separation* determined by the extent of the effective involvement of the owners in decision-making' (De Vroey 1976: 12). The large shareholders may 'retain real ownership through a partial legal ownership' of the whole corporation (Carchedi 1975: 49).

When a unified group of personal shareholders continue to exercise the effective powers of control in full, entrepreneurial control takes the form of *indirect personal possession*. In this situation, an individual or family owns the shares in a company, and it is the company itself that owns the unit of production and that enters into contracts of employment with workers. The profits that are generated by a company become the income of the entrepreneurial group only when they are paid out in the form of a dividend on the shares. It is possible, however, that shareholders may not be able to sustain their dominance, and salaried managers or external finance capitalists may be able to take advantage of the new circumstances. These three groups—shareholders, executive managers,[3] and financiers—become the protagonists in a struggle for corporate power, and it is precisely this struggle that lies at the heart of the debates that I considered in the previous chapter.[4] Recent work has interpreted the relationship between shareholders and directors as a quasi-contractual relation between 'principals' and 'agents' in which there are express and implicit assumptions about the nature of the continuing relation between the shareholders and the directors and executives. The shareholder is seen as having a contract with the directors of the company and they must, therefore, establish mechanisms to monitor their behaviour and to ensure that their interests are protected. The stock market is the mechanism through which shareholders must achieve this (Jensen and Meckly 1976; Fama 1980; Fama and Jensen 1983; see also Bradley 1993; Ross 1978; Fligstein and Froeland 1995).

The capacity that shareholders have to participate in the running of an enterprise is limited by the countervailing power of the other contenders for control. Managers have their primary power-base in command situations in the organizational hierarchy of the enterprise and in the expertise and credentials that allow them to occupy these positions. According to advocates of the theory of industrial society, this power-base enables them to subvert the residual powers of shareholders and to rule the corporation for themselves. Whatever the merits of this claim—which I will explore in the following chapters—it is important to recognize that technical expertise, and the ability of full-time executives to use their positions to regulate the information available to shareholders and other 'outsiders', does provide a power-base for management. Managers may be able to manipulate the passive shareholders and their representatives, and so pre-empt the decisions taken by the board of directors (Pahl and Winkler 1974). It is financiers who have been cast in the role of the main rivals to shareholders by those who have been influenced by the theory of capitalist society. Those who determine

---

[3] 'Manager' is often used in a very broad sense to include all the directors of an enterprise. This was, in fact, the way that Berle and Means tended to use the word. In my discussion I have generally limited the term to salaried executive managers, who may or may not be members of the board of directors.

[4] Some of the themes in this debate have been reviewed in Zeitlin (1974), Kotz (1978), Useem (1980), and Glasberg and Schwartz (1983). Zeitlin's article has been reprinted in Zeitlin (1989b).

the availability of credit for investment are able to specify the conditions under which enterprises can have access to this credit, and so are able to determine the chances that they have to take up investment opportunities and to implement an investment strategy. Financiers, it is argued, have the power to impose their will on enterprises, and so to subordinate managers and to displace individual shareholders (Soref 1980; Zeitlin 1980).

Shareholders, financiers, and executive managers are, of course, analytical categories, and they do not necessarily refer to separate and distinct individuals. The financiers who provide loan capital, for example, may also be large shareholders, and major shareholders may be members of the executive hierarchy. This overlap becomes even more marked when the shareholders and the providers of capital are themselves 'corporate' entities rather than individual persons. In these circumstances the true financiers, for example, are banks and other lending institutions, and their interests have to be represented by their own directors or managers. It is important to know, therefore, in what capacity people sit on company boards. Managers of financial institutions, for example, may act very differently in their role as representatives of the institutions on other boards than they do in their role as managers in their base institution. In the former case they are likely to be acting in the role of 'financier'—a representative of the corporate provider of capital—while in the latter case they may be acting in the role of 'manager'. Similarly, the manager of an insurance company that invests heavily in the capital of an enterprise, and who sits on that enterprise's board, is likely to be acting in the role of 'shareholder'—representative of the corporate or institutional shareholder—rather than that of the 'manager' that he or she is in the base institution.

An influential strand of theory has concluded, from the increasing importance of 'corporate' as against individual shareholders, that the question of which individuals are able to control an enterprise is now all but meaningless (Cutler *et al.* 1977; Kitahara 1980; 1985). It is claimed that as property and company law recognize the company as an agent capable of 'possession' and of entering into contracts, so the 'enterprise' becomes an economic agent that unites possession with the function of capital within a unit of production (Cutler *et al.* 1977: 249, 275).[5] The enterprise, as a collective agent, is a locus of

---

[5] The concept of 'possession' used by Cutler *et al.* (1977) corresponds closely to what Poulantzas termed 'economic ownership', and they depart usefully from Poulantzas's own concept of 'possession'. See also Bettelheim (1970).

decision and action in its own right. Its actions cannot be reduced to the actions and motives of its individual managers, directors, and shareholders. Rather, its actions are the outcome of the specific institutionalized practices and mechanisms of 'calculation' and 'supervision' through which decisions are made and implemented. The autonomy of the enterprise as a social organization is manifested through a rational calculation that is 'effected by an organizational apparatus involving both individuals and machines (e.g. computers, tabulators, and sorters, etc.) so that the products of calculation can in no way be reduced to the work of any human individual' (Cutler *et al*. 1977: 277; see also Kitahara 1980: 31–2). Managers, as those who direct the operations of the enterprise, act merely as 'delegates' or 'supports' of the enterprise (Cutler *et al*. 1977: 304). They do not themselves possess the means of production but are mere functionaries who are recruited through specialized labour markets to carry out the requirements of the capitalist enterprise itself (Hirst 1979: 131–2; Tomlinson 1982; Kinsey 1983). These writers also hold that, just as managers cannot be considered to be 'capitalists', neither can shareholders or financiers. Insurance policies, bank deposits, and individually owned shares are not capital, and so individual shareholders and beneficiaries are not capitalists (Hirst 1979: 135). The money of individuals only functions as capital when it is brought together into a unit of possession that is directed as a single agency of production. Shares, for example, are financial claims that only become capital if they are owned by financial intermediaries that use them as centralized credit funds in their own corporate activities.

The conclusion that individuals are not 'capitalists' because the enterprise is the personification of capital is not, however, compelling. The significance of the corporate form is that it creates the conditions under which various groups may struggle for the social power of command. The growth of corporate and institutional shareholdings is the basis of a transition from indirect personal possession to *impersonal possession*, though this does not mean that individuals are no longer essential elements in corporate control. Collective agents, for all their undisputed autonomy, manifest their actions through the actions of individuals, and these individuals are not mere ciphers or puppets of structural 'requirements'. The question of *who* is most active in shaping the 'calculations' of an enterprise is an important matter; corporate behaviour is not totally determined by market constraints. The 'dominant coalition' that comprises the active leadership group in an enterprise is able to exercise a certain amount of choice within these constraints (Child 1972). Its members may be unaware of the constraints, or they may even choose to ignore them. Corporate behaviour is the result of actions that may be undertaken with partial or incorrect information about the circumstances in which enterprises are located. As a result, enterprises can, and do, act against the 'requirements' of the market, even though this may result in their financial failure. It is important, therefore, to investigate the interests of the various contenders for control, the information that is available to them, the conditions under which each may enter into the dominant coalition, and the consequences for corporate behaviour that follow from the particular composition of the coalition. In a situation of impersonal possession, control is structured through corporate and institutional shareholdings, but corporate rule is exercised by the individual agents who represent the shareholders and financiers or who may be employed as executives. The corporate strategy that is formulated by the corporate rulers is the outcome of their struggle to determine corporate behaviour. The questions of control and rule are therefore fundamental to an understanding of corporate behaviour.

Corporate Control and Intercorporate Relations

Through the joint stock company, strategic control became the means through which the legal forms of property relations are institutionally mediated (Giddens 1973: 121; Clement 1975a: 13). It is therefore important to look at the various modes of institutional mediation through which legal ownership is translated into strategic control. This has often been approached in a formal and ahistorical way, though the classic discussions involve an implicit historical interpretation of capitalist development. Berle and Means recognized that possession and control rest not on legal forms *per se*, but on the social context of legal relations, and they saw a transition occurring from those situations where strategic control rests upon the legal right to vote a majority of the shares, to those in which there are dispersed shareholdings and management control. Between these two extremes were various intermediate cases where groups of shareholders have less than a majority of the shares but are able to supplement their shareholdings with other means of control. Their typology of modes of control, then, ranged from forms of majority control, through minority control, to management control.

Where control is based on almost complete ownership or on the holding of a majority of the shares by a single individual or group, the degree of dissociation between nominal ownership and effective possession is not very great; Berle and Means describe this as either 'majority ownership' or 'majority control'. The legal rights inherent in the ownership of a majority of the shares are sufficient to give the majority shareholders the full powers of control. As the controlling group reduces its percentage holding below the majority level, this majority control gives way to 'minority control', in which a small group with less than 50 per cent of the shares has 'working control' owing to the absence of any other holdings large enough to oppose them. The lowest level of shareholding at which minority control becomes possible is dependent on the way in which the remaining shares are distributed. Where a minority shareholder is confronted by other minority shareholders who can mobilize a countervailing block of shares, their minority control is precarious or non-existent; but if all the remaining shares are widely dispersed among a large number of small shareholders, the minority shareholder is less likely to face any serious opposition.

The level of shareholding that is required for minority control is, then, dependent on the dispersal of the remaining shares, and this level will vary over time with trends in the general pattern of share distribution. In 1910 Hilferding had suggested that minority control required between a quarter and a third of the shares (1910: 118–19), but Berle and Means had felt that the appropriate level in the 1920s was 20 per cent. More recent writers have suggested that the wider dispersal of share ownership that has occurred since then makes minority control possible with 10 per cent, 5 per cent, or even less (Larner 1970; Burch 1972; Scott and Hughes 1976). Zeitlin (1974) held that the critical figure will vary according to the unique circumstances of particular enterprises. It is nevertheless possible to turn to models of voting and rational choice to reduce the arbitrariness that is involved in determining the cut-off threshold for minority control. Florence (1951), for example, showed that a resolute group with a 6 per cent holding and faced with a mass of indifferent small shareholders can exercise minority control with a 96 per cent probability of success (see also Scott 1986: 55–6). A broad picture of the extent of minority control in an economy can be obtained by using Florence's methods to arrive at a cut-off threshold. On this basis, it has been concluded that a 10 per cent threshold is appropriate for the Anglo-American economies in the post-war period (Scott 1986: 58 ff.).

Zeitlin and his coworkers have argued that minority control is the most widespread form of control in contemporary American capitalism, this fact allowing minority shareholders to spread their interests across the system:

Minority control is one of the most important consequences of the development of the corporation as the decisive unit of productive property: the great majority of shareowners are stripped of control by a small segment of the capitalist class made up of the principal shareowners of the large corporations, who are thus able to extend their control of capital (and of the political economy) far beyond the limits of their ownership. (Zeitlin *et al.* 1975: 92)

Whether these writers are correct in their assessment of the extent of minority control will be examined in later chapters, but the general import of their statement is clear. This is that minority control makes possible 'the simultaneous development of diffused ownership and of concentrated control' (Cole 1948: 124). But minority control is inherently precarious, as there is always the possibility that other shareholders may increase the size of their holdings to the point at which they can challenge the established controllers. The position of a minority controller can be buttressed by such things as their easier access to the voting machinery, which is administered by the current members of the board of directors. This power enables a board to solicit the votes of shareholders who are not able to attend the general meeting, and this voting by 'proxy' can be a powerful tool in the hands of the controlling group.[6] On the other hand, an assertive rival group may be able to force a 'proxy fight' by attempting to solicit the votes of the normally uninvolved shareholders.

Unless a controlling group wishes to relinquish its control, it can be assumed that they will try to keep sufficient shares to maintain their controlling block. To a significant extent, then, the degree of dispersal in share ownership is a consequence of calculations that are made by the current controllers about how many shares they can afford to sell before their control is threatened. In a growing enterprise, those who are in control will be willing to issue additional

---

[6] The word 'proxy' refers to the form on which the shareholder who does not wish to attend a company meeting is invited to delegate a board member (or some other person) to vote on his or her behalf, normally in favour of the management's own proposals.

shares to raise capital so long as they feel that their chances of retaining control are high. New issues, mergers, acquisitions, and other capital restructurings, create a complex and shifting pattern in the distribution of shareholdings, and in the course of this restructuring some groups may be weakened and new alliances may be strengthened. If the controllers calculate that they are likely to lose control, then they will be forced to withdraw their expansion plans or to try and maintain a controlling block of shares by forming alliances with other groups of shareholders. Controlling groups must base their calculations on their knowledge of the distribution of the shares in the company, the identity of the various shareholders, and their probable voting behaviour (Pitelis 1987: 16 ff.). In large enterprises with many thousands of shareholders, who often hold their shares in anonymous bank accounts or in 'nominee' companies, it is difficult to monitor the pattern accurately, and the possibility of miscalculation is great.

Where minority controllers miscalculate the necessary size for a minority holding, or deliberately reduce their holding below the critical level, they can no longer exercise minority control. It is in this situation that Berle and Means saw 'management control' emerging. This mode of strategic control rests on the advantages of incumbency that directors enjoy in a situation of dispersed share ownership. No shareholder has sufficient shares for minority control, and so the members of the board—who may have only minimal shareholdings in the company—have the opportunity of becoming a self-perpetuating ruling group insulated from any external influence. The directors face a mass of small and passive shareholders, whose preferences they may safely ignore. In these circumstances, a 'challenge to management comes only from the occasional shareholder or group of holders who together possess a relatively substantial minority position that can serve as a base to offset the advantages inherent in management's position' (Baum and Stiles 1965: 12–13). The management will, in this situation, use their access to the proxy voting machinery to buttress their rule. If a proxy fight occurs, if a group of shareholders is able to form an alliance, or if a large holder increases the size of its holding, then the incumbent management may lose their power.[7]

---

[7] One of the best-studied proxy fights between a management group and a minority shareholder is Rockefeller's battle for the control of Standard Oil of Indiana in 1929. This is discussed in Baum and Stiles (1965: 13), Baran and Sweezy (1966: 32 ff.), Fitch and Oppenheimer (1970a: 88), and Blumberg (1975: 93).

Management control has often been seen as heralding fundamental changes in corporate strategy. Shareholders have an interest in the value of their shares and in the dividend that they can earn, while non-owning managers have no such interest. Managers, it is held, are less committed to the need to make a high return on the value of a company's shares and so they are able to take a longer-term, less sectional approach towards investment. Larner, for example, has claimed that 'the management, in the absence of gross incompetence or serious misfortune, has open to it a wide range of discretionary behaviour in which it can, without fear of punitive action by stockholders, pursue policies which serve its own interests at the expense of the [legal] owners' (1970: 3). The interests of the small shareholders, in a situation of management control, 'serve as a constraint rather than as the dominant motivating factor' (ibid.: 4). This argument, in fact, conflates two distinct claims: first, that the management acquires an autonomy from the *particular* interests of its own shareholders, and second, that it acquires an independence from *any* shareholder interest. To show that managers can achieve a partial autonomy from the large mass of passive shareholders in the enterprise that they manage is not necessarily to establish that they are completely free from any shareholding interest or that 'the managers' are a distinct social group from 'the owners'. Managers are not infrequently shareholders themselves, and will be motivated, in part, by their shareholder interests. Managers may also be subject to influence from other 'outside' interests, such as financiers. Gordon has argued that external financial interests may influence managers and therefore participate in 'control', even if this influence does not involve direct intervention in the decision-making process.

A powerful interest group, because it is powerful, possesses a certain degree of influence in the affairs of a corporation; that is, its desires, opinions, advice, remonstrances, or cajolings tend to be heeded by management. However, this sort of pressure is not decision-making if . . . management itself . . . makes the final decision. (Gordon 1945: 151)

Managers are involved in actual decision-making, in corporate 'rule'. Financiers and shareholders, on the other hand, whether they are represented on the board or not, may have the capacity for 'non-decision-making'. Outside interests call the tune and set the agenda by virtue of their constraining financial power. They effect a 'mobilization of bias' that ensures that some options are precluded before matters even reach the stage of decision-making.[8] This argument points to the limits of the concept of management control: where managerial autonomy is reduced in this way, it no longer seems sensible to speak of management control at all.

This point becomes particularly pertinent if the assumption of the increasing dispersal of shares is questioned. The Berle and Means classification is based on the assumption that as share-ownership becomes more and more dispersed, so control passes from majority to minority and finally to management control. Management control, they held, occurs when the outstanding shares are so widely dispersed that no individual or united group of associates holds sufficient shares to counterbalance the power of the incumbent management. This process of dispersal, however, is not inexorable. The growth of shareownership by insurance companies, unit trusts, and pension funds that has occurred with the rise of impersonal possession has involved a renewed concentration of shareholdings. These financial institutions extend the principles behind the joint stock company and the stock exchange: the growth of a market for securities allows investors to attain 'independence of the fate of the particular enterprise in which he has invested his money' (Sweezy 1942: 258), and the growth of 'indirect investment' is the completion of this process so far as the individual investor is concerned (Cole 1948: 25; Parsons 1958: 112; Hirst 1979: 135; Hilferding 1910). In a situation of indirect investment, individuals put their money in savings institutions or invest in financial intermediaries rather than investing directly in industrial enterprises, and the financial 'institutions' gradually become the most important holders of company shares as well as the major financiers of enterprises through bank loans and other forms of credit (Berle 1960; Child 1969a: 46). The growth of institutional and other forms of intercorporate shareholding reverses any trend towards dispersal, so increasing the power that shareholders can exert over managers. In a context of growing intercorporate shareholdings, then, the concept of management control becomes less useful. This reconcentration may not involve the resurgence of majority or minority control. A single institution rarely holds a majority or minority block, and institutions in general tend to regard themselves as 'outsiders' rather than 'insiders'. That is to say, institutions are less directly involved in corporate rule than are the

---

[8] On non-decision-making and the mobilization of bias see Bachrach and Baratz (1962a and b) and the general discussion in Lukes (1974).

majority and minority shareholders who regard themselves as having a legitimate right to an inside role in business affairs.

In the Anglo-American economies the growth of intercorporate shareholdings has been the basis of what may be termed 'control through a constellation of interests', which many commentators have failed to distinguish from the classic concept of management control that was formulated by Berle and Means to describe control in large American enterprises.[9] The origin of this concept lies in Weber's contrast between domination by virtue of authority and that by virtue of a constellation of interests. He argued that this latter situation is typical of monopolistic domination in the market, which is 'based upon influence derived exclusively from the possession of goods or marketable skills guaranteed in some way and acting upon the conduct of those dominated, who remain, however, formally free and are motivated simply by the pursuit of their own interests' (1914: 943). A large bank, for example, may have a dominating influence in the market and so may be able to influence the behaviour of its potential debtors for the sake of its own financial interests. The mutual accommodation of interests between the bank and its customers places the bank in a dominant position. If, however, the bank is able to place some of its directors on the customer's board and these directors are given specific rights of command as a condition for the grant of credit, then the form of domination is transformed into a relation of 'authority' rather than a mere constellation of interests (ibid.: 943–4).

Weber's concept of a constellation of interests accords closely with one important outcome of the growth of intercorporate shareholdings. It describes the situation where the largest shareholders have sufficient shares to exercise a real and effective constraint over the corporate rulers, but are unable to exercise minority control. The exercise of minority control requires that the leading shareholders comprise a small and compact grouping, willing and able to intervene in a united way in pursuit of its interests. Where the principal shareholders are not close associates of one another, they do not have the unity necessary for minority control (Gordon 1945: 36, 44). The largest shareholders may collectively hold a block of shares that would be large enough to give minority, or even majority, control to a united group, yet they lack the basis for collective organiza-

---

[9] Morin (1974a: 22) gives a useful discussion of some aspects of this matter, but he writes of 'technocratic' control. See also Barratt Brown (1968: 43–4) on the role of 'co-ordinating controllers'.

tion that would enable them to act as such a cohesive controlling group. No coalition is able to achieve a stable position of minority control, and any temporary coalition based around a subset of the principal holders is likely to be countered by a coalition based around a different subset. The co-operation of these competing institutions is limited to their very broad and shared interests in the activities of the companies in which they invest (Hill 1995: 262). In situations where the leading shareholders have effective possession of the enterprise but they do not constitute a united coalition of associates, the mode of strategic control must differ from both the minority and the management forms.

While the large institutional shareholders may be able to co-operate whenever necessary, their normal business operations divide them competitively. Insurance companies, for example, compete with one another for insurance business, and they compete with banks and other fund managers for pension business. The word 'constellation' is appropriate in these circumstances, because there is no group cohesion among the controlling shareholders. The principal shareholders have effective possession, yet this constellation of ownership interests has no real unity and little possibility for concerted action. Each institution pursues its own interests, and the interests that they have in common are limited to their common shareholding involvements with particular companies. The board of directors, however, is unable to disregard the interests of those who hold substantial amounts of the capital, as they depend on them for future capital needs and they must have support if they are to be re-elected or to have their policies endorsed. It is in this way that controlling constellations exercise a continuing constraint over executive managers:

While avoiding formal and even informal alliance, *de facto* the institutions often acted in concert. With access to the same information and sharing similar concerns, they took parallel actions whose aggregate impact was virtually the same as if formally coordinated. (Useem 1993: 42)

The board of directors reflects and is responsive to the 'congeries of intercorporate relationships', the balance of power, and the 'intricate interweaving of interests' among its major shareholders (Zeitlin *et al.* 1975: 102, 106; see also Blumberg 1975: 93; De Alessi 1973: 844), though not necessarily in an immediate and direct manner. The board cannot achieve the autonomy from particular shareholder interests that is characteristic of management control. But, at the same time, the board is not the mere instrument of a cohesive controlling group.[10]

I have so far talked loosely of the 'leading shareholders', and it is important to discuss what might be the size of a typical controlling constellation. As with the cut-off threshold for minority control, no operational definition can encompass all the variations in particular circumstances. Some guidance can, however, be given. It can be assumed that a controlling constellation must have a total shareholding that is at least equivalent in size to that of a controlling minority holding. But this does not resolve the question of the number of large holders who can participate in this controlling constellation. A group that is too large would be unable to co-operate at even the minimal level that is required for any kind of control, while a very small group is best seen as having or sharing in minority control. Using probability theories of statistics and rational decision-making, Florence (1947) had argued that a group of twenty is about the maximum number of shareholders that could participate in control. The controlling group may be smaller than this, but it is unlikely to be much bigger. Florence concluded that a procedure that investigates the number of shares, held by the twenty largest shareholders in a company, is likely to lead to the correct identification of the locus of its control.[11] Control through a constellation of interests, therefore, can be operationally defined as the situation where the top twenty shareholders collectively hold a minority (or perhaps a majority) block of shares and no subset of these twenty shareholders constitutes a unified group of minority controllers.

The basis for management control is a distribution of shareholdings that allows no individual or group of owners to become a serious threat to the internal management. Shareholding must be so distributed that no shareholder has anything other than a minute

[10] Fennema, commenting on the first edition of this book, suggested that 'strong components' in a network of interlocking directorships are equivalent to constellations of interests. I do not agree. This argument rests on a fallacious definition of a 'constellation' as 'a financial group in which no definite locus of control can be distinguished' (Fennema 1982: 144). As should be clear, my argument is that constellations of interests are not to be seen as financial groups of this kind.

[11] Florence was writing about minority control and its forms at a time when institutional ownership had not progressed very far. His conclusions on voting behaviour, however, remain relevant to the discussion of control through a constellation of interests. My discussion concentrates on mechanisms for maintaining control rather than the mechanisms which outsiders may use to attain control. On the latter see Chevalier (1970: 42) and Blumberg (1975: 92, 145).

fraction of the share capital. Control through a constellation of interests, on the other hand, occurs where a substantial block of shares can be concentrated in the hands of a small but diffuse group of shareholders and the remaining shares are widely dispersed. Unless shares are completely dispersed, the original concept of management control cannot be applied. In view of the growth of intercorporate shareholdings and the concentration of shares in the hands of a small number of corporate shareholders, Herman (1981) has modified the original Berle and Means concept, and talks of 'constrained management control'. This is undoubtedly a more realistic designation, but retention of the phrase 'management control' implies the kind of dispersal envisaged by Berle and Means. To avoid unnecessary confusion, I prefer the term 'control through a constellation of interests'.[12]

Control through a constellation of interests is just one of the forms taken by corporate control when intercorporate shareholdings are formed into structures of impersonal possession. As will be seen, it is characteristic of the Anglo-American economies, where a specific structure of banking and credit has encouraged the building of large financial intermediaries. This structure of institutional shareholding has meant that corporate constellations differ markedly from the tight financial interest-groups depicted in Marxist theory. In many economies, however, intercorporate relations have been formed into groups that do correspond more closely to these. In later chapters I will consider these in more detail, but some indications can be given here. One such variant occurs where intercorporate relations are formed into *corporate sets* through the reciprocal shareholdings of aligned enterprises. These arise where conditions encourage the establishment of stable, long-term control relations in the context of a weak entrepreneurial system. In other circumstances, looser *corporate webs* have been formed around investment-holding companies in which wealthy families continue to play an important part. Corporate webs can arise wherever conditions encourage or require the formation of investment companies that combine a diversified portfolio of investments with a willingness to participate in the control of enterprises on a long-term basis. The other major pattern of intercorporate relations that I will consider is that of the *corporate filiations*. Here, enterprises are grouped together into overlapping vertical filiations, but the groups have no enduring

---

[12] This view is supported by Mizruchi (1983b: 432).

identity or overlap with one another. At the heart of this system are substantial bank participations that have been encouraged by state policies as mechanisms of industrial growth.

Corporate constellations, corporate sets, corporate webs, and corporate filiations are or have been found in all the major economies of the capitalist core, though their importance and their persistence varies from one to another. It is the balance between them that defines the characteristics of the major forms of capitalist development and their particular structures of impersonal possession. What I have called the Japanese system is one where corporate sets have been central to the whole history of capitalist development and have shaped the emergence of Japan's 'alliance capitalism' (Gerlach 1992). In the Latin system, on the other hand, corporate webs have predominated. Although they have played an important part in the Anglo-American economies, it is in the Latin economies that they have acquired a central and enduring role, partly through the encouragement given to them by states. The German system, finally, is characterized by the predominance of corporate filiations that have resulted from a distinctive and highly concentrated banking system.

Mechanisms of Control

Having discussed various modes of strategic control, it is necessary to examine in more detail the mechanisms through which strategic control can be exercised.[13] A basic distinction can be made between 'active' (or direct) and 'passive' (or indirect) mechanisms of control. Direct mechanisms of control are those where shareholders or financiers are actually represented on a company's board, and control is translated directly into rule. The ultimate basis of this power is the ability of the controlling shareholders to use their voting strength to alter the composition of the board, and thereby to hire and fire the top managers.

If some or all of the board members are direct appointees of the major shareholders, then their advice and opinions may be regarded as *de facto* authoritative instructions: managers may feel that they must obey their 'advice' (Weber 1914: 944; Gordon 1945: 151). This is

[13] For a consideration of the mechanisms through which outsiders can try to attain control see Chevalier (1970: 42) and Blumberg (1975: 92, 145).

especially characteristic of situations where shareholders are regarded as 'insiders': situations of majority or minority control, and those where control is structured through corporate webs, sets, and filiations. Majority or minority control involve looser relations of intervention than is the case with parent–subsidiary relations, though they tend to seek direct involvement. Where intercorporate shareholdings tie enterprises into cohesive groupings of various kinds, the leading shareholders in an enterprise are likely to co-operate with one another and relations of control will be more stable and institutionalized, allowing a regular and continuous involvement in corporate affairs. In situations of control through constellations of interests, where control rests upon institutional shareholdings, the authoritative involvement of controllers is less likely. These controllers regard themselves, and are regarded by enterprises, as 'outsiders' and are more likely to delay active intervention until it is no longer avoidable. Intervention is likely to occur if an enterprise runs into serious financial or legal difficulties; but the more routine are the decisions, the less likely the controllers to need to intervene. Institutional shareholders will tend to exert 'a milder sort of continuing pressure . . . plus reserve power to act when the occasion requires' (Peterson 1965: 20; Gordon 1945: 57, 187; Monsen et al. 1968: 437).

In normal or routine circumstances other, indirect mechanisms of control are available to large shareholders, especially the institutional outsiders. Gordon has argued that indirect control

usually implies approval rather than initiation of decisions, and may imply merely an indirect influence rather than direct approval or veto. The purpose of control is normally to further or protect particular interests of the controlling group, and this may be done without participating in the formation of many, perhaps most, policies. (Gordon 1945: 173)

At its most general level, this indirect form of control is manifest in the power to sell shares or to withdraw credit. All shareholders have an interest in the income and capital gains that their investments can yield, and any corporate strategy must meet these interests (De Alessi 1973: 843; Peterson 1965: 18). The large shareholders will, of course, exercise a much greater constraint over managers than do the small shareholders, since any dissatisfaction that they feel could lead to substantial share sales. This is a particularly important power in a takeover situation. As Manne (1965) pointed out, the struggle for shares in a takeover bid—and the desire of managers to avoid their enterprise becoming the target of an unwelcome bid—are important constraints that compel managers to pay serious attention to the interests of those shareholders whose holdings are most likely to be critical in the case of a bid. In the Anglo-American economies, these shareholders are the financial institutions.

The sale of large blocks of shares has a considerable effect on share prices, and a rapid and sustained decline in the share price will create considerable difficulties for an enterprise that is hoping to expand. As this is something that managers will seek to avoid, large shareholders may constrain management decisions without direct intervention. Their influence on corporate strategy 'does not require active participation. . . . The power . . . to sell a large block of capital can be enough—if clashes of policy between major shareholders and company directorate should occur' (Westergaard and Resler 1975: 160; Gordon 1945: 57).

Intermediate between these indirect constraints and the more active forms of direct intervention are a number of mechanisms through which major shareholders are able to ensure that the management is particularly responsive to their interests. The large shareholders tend to be better informed about business matters and to have greater access to the enterprise's management. Those making company policy will, then, be particularly influenced by the pressure and advice that the principal shareholders are able to offer. While small shareholders cannot afford the time or money necessary to keep closely in touch with the affairs of the companies in which they invest, large shareholders have a financial incentive to monitor the behaviour of directors and managers and will expect to be consulted about and involved in major structural decisions (Milgrom and Roberts 1992: 497; Eisenberg 1969: 45–6; Hill 1995: 258–9). Enterprises have increasingly had to establish departments to maintain shareholder relations with the big financial institutions and the stock-market analysts who advise them (Useem 1993).

Corporate and institutional shareholders in particular will be well-informed and well-placed to make their views known to management. As institutional holdings have grown in size, Eisenberg argues, 'the predisposition to vote in management's favour seems to be breaking down' (ibid.: 52). Financial intermediaries have the kind of administrative and supervisory apparatus that allows them to collect, analyse, and act upon business information, and so they can ensure that management is more responsive to them than it is to the small shareholders (Baum and Stiles 1965: 165, Blumberg 1975: 94; Beed 1966: 13).

The rarity of direct intervention 'indicates that such intervention is not often necessary because, in the generality of cases, . . . share-holders are satisfied that their interests are reasonably well-served' (Nichols 1969: 104). It is when major strategic issues arise that the controllers will strive to influence the board and to see that their wishes are carried through (Zald 1969: 107). A move to exercise direct control over the managers need not, however, involve overt conflict or a dramatic and public struggle: there may instead be a gradual but firm imposition of the interests of the controlling group over the company's management. Where actual intervention does occur, it is likely that the composition of the board will become more and more representative of the controlling interests and of the balance of power among them (Clement 1975a: 23).

It is important to emphasize that similar mechanisms of control are available to non-shareholders with a substantial financial interest in the company, such as the banks and the holders of the company's loan stock. Strategic control concerns the use of capital, and all those that influence the flow of capital to an enterprise may be able to participate in its control. Banking interests, for example, may be able to exercise considerable influence over the minority- and management-controlled companies in which they have a significant stake (Chevalier 1970: 45–6; Morin 1974a: 35). Very often, of course, those who are creditors of a company are also owners of its share capital, either as direct beneficiaries or as trustees. This is particularly the case in the corporate sets, webs, and filiations, and for enterprises that are controlled through constellations of interests. As Zeitlin has rightly concluded, the pattern of control in a corporation can be discovered only if it is examined in relation to 'the concrete situation within the corporation and the constellation of intercorporate relations in which it is involved' (1974: 1091, 1107–8: see also Marris 1964: 15; Mace 1971; Zeitlin et al. 1975: 110 ff.).

The view of corporate control and corporate rule that I have outlined in this chapter has been drawn from a wide range of sources in order to show the great deal of consensus that exists about the concepts necessary to study control in the large business enterprise. The major lines of theoretical contention in contemporary debates on corporate governance centre on the differing interpretations that have been given to the available empirical material. The rest of this book is an attempt to marshal this evidence, and to use my model of corporate control to illustrate the theoretical interpretation that was outlined in Chapter 1.

4

CORPORATE CONSTELLATIONS IN THE ANGLO-AMERICAN SYSTEM

THE managerialist contention that there has been a separation of ownership from control in the capitalist business enterprise has been hotly debated in the United States. Berle and Means (1932) were motivated to undertake their classic study by the reflections of their contemporaries on the development of American capitalism during the first thirty years of the twentieth century. If the theory has any application, it should, surely, apply to corporate life in America. Managerialist theory posits the demise of family capitalism and the disappearance of the classic entrepreneur. The joint stock company, it is argued, dissolves the framework of personal property-holding and allows the emergence of a structural differentiation between a mass of small, powerless shareholders and a small body of powerful executive managers. My aim in this chapter is to review the evidence in support of this claim, drawing on the research of those who have examined its main tenets.

I have suggested that the American economy can usefully be seen as a member of a larger group of 'Anglo-American' economies that exhibit similar patterns of corporate development and capital mobilization, rooted in their specific cultural, economic, and political characteristics. An assessment of managerialism, then, cannot be limited to the American case alone. In countries such as the United States, Britain, Australia, Canada, New Zealand, and South Africa, that follow English legal practices, a uniform pattern of property, contract, and company law has emerged. This legal pattern prescribes a common form of corporate enterprise with one and only one board, its rights and obligations being indivisible and inalien-able. All directors, executives and non-executives, are appointed by the controlling shareholders and, through their monthly meetings, are responsible to the annual shareholders' meeting (Bacon and Brown 1977; Bank of England 1979). It is necessary to consider whether this common legal framework is indeed associated with a common structure of ownership and control and, in particular, whether managerialism offers an adequate account of the develop-ment of these economies.

I will argue that the managerialist view, in its classic formulation, cannot be sustained as an account of any of the Anglo-American economies. While it correctly depicts the decline—though not the disappearance—of family ownership and control, it fails to grasp the significance of the growth of financial shareholdings. The form of ownership and control that results from this growth, I will argue, is better seen as control through a constellation of interests.

Corporate Power and Control in the United States

While the question of corporate power has a long history in the United States, the terms of the debate on ownership and control have been dominated by the ideas and methods of Berle and Means (1932). Writing in the wake of the great financial crash that ruined many investors, they claimed that the long-term dispersal of share-holdings in large enterprises had destroyed owner control and cre-ated the conditions for management control. The sheer scale of the American economy, and the rapid growth of giant enterprises oper-ating on a national scale that were central features of organized cap-italism in the United States, necessitated the mobilization of capital from outside the immediate circle of the entrepreneurs who had founded the enterprises. The joint stock company and the stock-exchange system were the vehicles for meeting this need, and at the turn of the century this system of capital mobilization was domi-nated by the New York banks. These banks restructured the capital and the systems of production of enterprises in order to float them on the stock exchange, and many owning families were forced to reduce their holdings in their enterprises. Berle and Means saw this as a first step in the dissolution of family capital. Families were now less likely to have complete ownership of their enterprises, and they had to rely more and more on majority ownership. Between 1914 and 1928 a further move, from majority to minority control, began to occur as large enterprises expanded the scale of their operations from the national to the international. This trend became even more marked during the 1930s, and there was a massive growth in the number of enterprises without dominant ownership interests (Berle and Means 1932: 84–9; Berle 1960: ch. 2).

Table 1 shows that when Berle and Means began their investigations, in 1929, the number of shareholders in the largest corporations was already very great, and this number had increased substantially by 1974. There was, in consequence, a very clear increase in the dispersal of shareholdings over the 45-year period. Almost half the corporations that could be classified in 1929 had 20,000 or more shareholders; by 1974 this was the case for over 90 per cent of the top corporations. The number of corporations with more than 100,000 shareholders increased over this period from 10 to 70.

This rise in the number of shareholders in large enterprises was a continuous trend over the whole period, resulting in a continuous fall in the average size of personal shareholdings. A Senate committee of investigation reported that in 1937 most shareholders in the

Table 1. Shareholders in the top 200 US non-financial enterprises (1929 and 1974)

	Number of enterprises	
Number of holders	1929	1974
Less than 5,000	41	1
5,000–20,000	53	8
20,000–50,000	39	52
50,000–100,000	22	69
100,000–200,000	7	43
200,000–500,000	3	27
Unclassified	35	–
Totals	200	200

Source: Adapted from Berle and Means (1932: 49) and Herman (1981: Table 3.6).
Note: The unclassified companies of 1929 were mainly owned through legal devices such as voting trusts. Size bands are shown as in the original sources.

top 200 corporations owned fewer than 100 shares each, and that only 0.25 per cent of shareholders held more than 5,000 shares each (Goldsmith and Parmelee 1940: 27, 36; Anderson *et al.* 1941). By 1951, Villarejo reported, the typical large corporation was characterized by a wide dispersal in its shareholdings: the majority of its shareholders owned just over thirty shares each (1961*a*: 49). It is clear that one major plank of the Berle and Means thesis is confirmed by this evidence. There was a tendency for corporate capital to be spread among a very large number of shareholders, most of whom own very small amounts of shares.

Berle and Means concluded that share dispersal would lead to the disappearance of the traditional capitalist forms of private and majority ownership, which would survive mainly in smaller enterprises whose capital requirements were not so great. Control in large enterprises depended more and more on minority holdings. In the 1920s and 1930s, minority and other substantial shareholders were able to dominate the boardrooms of the largest enterprises and were becoming the main shapers of corporate strategy. Most big enterprises were still influenced by their largest shareholders, and within this structure of indirect personal possession 'the separation of ownership and control has not yet become complete'. The mass of small shareholders have no significant influence over company policies, and 'those actually in control are usually stockholders though in many cases owning but a very small proportion of the total stock' (Berle and Means 1932: 343). This was a trend that Berle and Means saw continuing. As share-ownership became more dispersed, they argued, the proportion of shares represented on the board of directors would fall even further, and the separation of ownership from control would move towards completion. As complete separation was approached, so the power chances of career executives would increase and they would become the major force in enterprises. Those enterprises in which there were no longer any dominant ownership interests would become subject to 'management control'. These expectations would seem to be confirmed by the data presented in Table 2, which puts the Berle and Means data alongside those from other studies. Just under one quarter of large enterprises in 1900–1 were without a dominant owning interest. This proportion had risen to just over 40 per cent by 1929 and to over 85 per cent by 1975.[1] On the basis of research undertaken in 1963, Larner had

[1] Eight of the 173 companies listed in Table 2 as having no dominant interest were separated out by Herman as having minority controllers that held 5 to 9 per

claimed that 'it would appear that Berle and Means in 1929 were observing a "managerial revolution" in process. Now, thirty years later, that revolution seems close to complete' (Larner 1966: 786–7). Larner had recognized, nevertheless, that owner control remained an important characteristic of smaller enterprises, a fact that was confirmed in research undertaken on the 500 largest enterprises of 1965 (see Table 3). Enterprises believed to be subject to management control were heavily concentrated among the top 125, while owner control remained more important outside the top 200.

Table 2. Ultimate strategic control in the top US non-financial enterprises (1900–1975)

	Number of companies			
Mode of control	Top 40 of 1900–1	Top 200 of 1929	Top 200 of 1963	Top 200 of 1975
Private control	–	10	–	1
Majority control	5	9	6	3
Minority control	13	65	18	21
No dominant interest	9.5	81	167	173
Financial control	12.5	23.5	–	1
Legal device	–	9.5	9	–
In receivership	–	2	–	1
Totals	40	200	200	200

Source: Adapted from Berle and Means (1932: 106), Herman (1981: Tables 3.2, 3.4, 3.5, and 7.1), and Larner (1970: 12–13, Table 1).
Note: The figures for 1929 incorporate Herman's corrections and adjustments to the original Berle and Means data. The cut-off level for minority control in 1963 and 1975 was 10 per cent; in the earlier periods it was 20 per cent. 'Private control' refers to the situation where the majority block is 80 per cent or more. Those companies subject to joint control were split between the categories according to the control position of their joint controllers.

It might appear, then, that the kind of personal, owner control found in nineteenth-century liberal capitalism had gradually given way to management control, especially in very large enterprises. As a result, it might be anticipated that internal, career executives would have become the dominant members of the corporate directorate. This conclusion would, however, be hasty, as a number of

cent of their shares. This qualification to his conclusion is discussed later in this chapter.

Table 3. Strategic control in the top 500 US industrial enterprises (1965)

Mode of control	Rank by sales				Totals
	1–125	126–250	251–375	376–500	
Owner-controlled	24	45	48	44	161
Management-controlled	101	75	73	78	327
Unknown	0	5	4	3	12
Totals	125	125	125	125	500

Source: Adapted from Palmer (1972: 57, Table 1).
Note: The cut-off point for owner control is 10 per cent.

serious reservations must be noted. The various studies that I have considered all have serious technical and methodological shortcomings, and a re-examination of their data shows that the continuing importance of both family control and financial influence has been underestimated.

The technical and methodological difficulties inherent in this kind of research appear so great that De Vroey has gone so far as to claim that 'procedural choices are almost shaping the very nature of the conclusion' (1976: 29). One particular problem concerns the cut-off level that is used for the identification of minority control: Berle and Means used a 20 per cent threshold, while Larner and later writers have taken 10 per cent or even less as being an appropriate figure. The extent of minority control that is found in a particular study depends, of course, on the cut-off threshold adopted, and a more restrictive threshold will make the extent of minority control appear particularly low. As I showed in Chapter 3, any cut-off threshold is arbitrary, but the use of a particular cut-off threshold can be justified if there is supporting evidence on the overall distribution of shareholdings. On these grounds Herman (1981: 24–5) came to the sensible conclusion that, in the post-war period, holdings of 5 per cent or less are unrealistic bases for control in even the largest enterprises, and that owners of 5 to 10 per cent may exercise, at best, a very limited form of minority control. For the post-war period, then, a 10-per-cent threshold seems appropriate. For the period prior to the War, when shareholdings were less dispersed, there are good reasons for accepting Berle and Means's more restrictive cut-off point of 20 per cent. On this basis, then, the broad trends shown in Table 2 are an accurate reflection of developments in ownership and control over the period considered.

A more significant technical problem concerns the treatment that is accorded to intercorporate shareholdings. Berle and Means used the category of control through a 'legal device' to designate those situations where majority or minority holdings are organized into a voting trust or into a structure of intercorporate holdings. The organization of company shares by financial enterprises in this way was widespread in the 1920s as a result of an expansion in the number of investment trusts and investment-holding companies, most of which were affiliated to the big banks (Carosso 1970: ch. 14). In these situations, the majority or minority controller is another company, which may itself be controlled by yet another company, and so on. The response of Berle and Means was to distinguish between 'immediate' and 'ultimate' control. While the immediate control of such an enterprise may be control through a legal device, its ultimate control, they held, was the same as that of its parent company. An enterprise subject to 'immediate' minority control by an enterprise that was itself management-controlled was to be regarded as subject to 'ultimate' management control. This distinction between immediate and ultimate control does, of course, bring out some important features of corporate control, but it tends to overstate the significance of 'management control' and can lead to unwarranted conclusions about the autonomy of the internal management of enterprises controlled through legal devices. For this reason Herman (1981) separated out these enterprises for particular attention, and he reclassified enterprises from the 'legal device' category to either 'minority' or 'financial' control (see also Zeitlin et al. 1975: 97).

The implications of these different measurement decisions are brought out in Table 4, which shows the findings of the Senate Committee of 1937. Basing its estimates on 'immediate control', the Committee found that the number of majority-controlled enterprises in 1937 was considerably greater than the number in 1929 (see Table 2). Berle and Means had not included majority-controlled subsidiaries in their 'top 200', but the Senate Committee included all these subsidiaries and so considerably inflated the figure for majority control.[2] Neither approach can be regarded as absolutely prefer-

[2] Herman has shown that excluding these subsidiaries from the figures in Table 4 leaves fifteen majority-controlled and fifty-two minority-controlled, a result that is much more consistent with the trend shown in Table 2 (Herman 1981: 72).

Table 4. Immediate strategic control in the 200 largest US non-financial enterprises (1937)

Mode of control	Number of corporations	% of corporations
Majority ownership	42	21.0
Predominant minority	37	18.5
Substantial minority	47	23.5
Small minority	13	6.5
No dominant shareholders	61	30.5
Totals	200	100.0

Source: Calculated from Goldsmith and Parmelee (1940: Appendix XI, 1486).
Note: Control is measured by the proportion of voting stock held and by representation in the company's management. The dividing line between 'predominant' and 'substantial' minority is set at 30 per cent and that between 'substantial' and 'small' is set at 10 per cent.

able to the other; the approach that is chosen must depend upon the particular questions that are to be investigated. It is obvious, however, that researchers who include subsidiaries and classify them according to their immediate control should make this explicit in the presentation of their results.

The final technical problem in this kind of research is the absence of complete or comprehensive information on corporate ownership. Much research has relied, for the most part, on estimation and guesswork based on inside information and newspaper sources. In many cases the quality of the data was simply unknown. Much difficulty arises from the use of 'nominee' accounts by shareholders. While the ownership of each share must be registered in the company's share register, shares are often listed under anonymous accounts or 'street names' that conceal the identity of the beneficial owner. Even where access to the register is achieved, it may not be possible to identify the leading shareholders because of the prevalence of such nominee holdings. Berle and Means, however, did not even have access to this kind of information. Half of the corporations that they classified as management-controlled were simply 'presumed' to fall into this category on the basis of little or no information at all (Zeitlin 1974: 1081; De Vroey 1976: 16 ff.). For this reason, the figures for 1929 in Table 2 incorporate corrections made by Herman, using information that was unavailable to Berle and Means.

There is, nevertheless, some evidence that, even after correcting for these technical problems, the absolute level of family control

may have been underestimated. In a re-analysis of the 1929 data produced by Berle and Means, Burch has estimated that the true figure
for family control in the top 200 lay between 37 and 45 per cent.
Burch made this claim on the grounds that enterprises might still be
controlled by particular families even if these families had only a
very small block of shares (1972: 114–15). I have already shown that
the threshold level for minority control must not be drawn too low,
but Burch's point is particularly significant if extended families and
groups of families are considered. The leading members of a family
may, for example, have a relatively small holding, but wider kin may
have further holdings that can normally be relied upon to buttress
the core family block. Recognizing this point, the Senate Committee
had argued that particular families held control of 40 of the top 200
enterprises in 1937, and that groups of families controlled a further
35. Including those subsidiaries that were ultimately controlled by
families, the Committee's researchers concluded that family control
accounted for about two-fifths of the top enterprises. Thirteen principal family groups were identified—including those of the Ford, Du
Pont, Mellon, and Rockefeller families—and Burch's re-analysis of
the 1937 data supported their conclusions about the extent of family
control and the prominence of family groups (Anderson *et al.* 1941:
1723).

Despite his claim that the Committee had overstated their case,
Gordon has produced evidence on family holdings that supports this

Table 5. Family control in the ninety-three largest US manufacturers (1939)

| Size of shareholding block (%) | Number of enterprises in which block held by | | | | |
	Single family	Two or more families	Family and enterprise	No family	Totals
More than 50	4	3	0	0	7
30–49	9	5	1	1	17
10–29	10	11	4	1	26
Less than 10	5	4	0	0	9
No dominant interest	–	–	–	34	34
Totals	28	23	5	37	93

Source: Gordon (1945: 40–1), calculated from *Temporary National Economic Committee* data.
Note: The category for 'no family' includes three cases where another enterprise held the controlling block.

general picture. Table 5 shows that family groups held majority or minority control in 42 of the 93 largest manufacturers of 1937–9 and held smaller blocks in a further 9, though Gordon rightly pointed out that it must not be assumed that the largest shareholding families in an enterprise always comprised a 'compact and unified group' (1945: 42). Research carried out during the 1950s suggested that family control remained important in the post-war period. Villarejo, for example, estimated that almost two-thirds of the 232 enterprises that he studied in 1951 had a controlling block of shares held by their directors or by other dominant interests (1961a: Appendices I and II), while Kolko found that 72 of the top 100 of 1937 had the same dominant shareholders in 1957. In 22 of these enterprises the same families were dominant, though the size of their shareholdings had generally fallen (1962: 62). Even Larner's study found that 14 per cent of the top 200 in 1963 were family-controlled, a conclusion that was confirmed by Sheehan (1967) on the basis of journalistic information. Re-analysing Larner's data, Burch claimed that the true figure for family control in 1965 was 40 per cent, and that a further 18 per cent were 'possibly' family-controlled. Burch recognized, however, that family control was less widespread in the vary large enterprises that made up the top 50 (1972: 68). Family shareholdings were invariably associated with family representation on the board of directors, and Burch suggested that this had lasted for much of the post-war period (ibid.: 96, 101). A study of the top 250 American enterprises of 1980 found that 32 were controlled by families or individuals, virtually all of these being minority-controlled (see Table 12, p. 74). A further three enterprises were jointly controlled by families and corporate interests. The only family to control more than one enterprise was the Mellon family, controlling Mellon National Bank, Alcoa, and Gulf Oil.

What conclusions can be drawn about family control in the United States? There can be little doubt that many cases of family control through majority or large minority blocks can be found in each period that has been studied, but it is doubtful whether family holdings of less than 5 per cent can be taken as signifying family 'control', especially if these holdings are dispersed among a large extended family. Holdings of between 5 and 10 per cent may provide the potential for control, but this control would be rather limited. Such situations may be regarded as cases of limited minority control or of family influence rather than secure minority control. Chandler's judgement is, for the most part, correct:

What Burch's data does show is that wealthy Americans invest in the securities of large corporations, that some families of the entrepreneurs who helped to found a company still retained as much as five per cent of the stock in those companies, and that members of those families often have jobs in that enterprise. Burch helps to document the fact that wealthy families, particularly those of the founders of modern business enterprises, are the beneficiaries of managerial capitalism, but gives little evidence that these families make basic decisions concerning the operations of modern capitalistic enterprises and of the economy in which they operate. (Chandler 1977: 584)

It remains the case, nevertheless, that the presence of family shareholdings and the representation of these families on company boards significantly qualifies the conventional view of the undisputed rise to power of the internal executives. Family *influence* may continue to be an important factor, even in those enterprises that are not subject to family control.

The picture that I have drawn so far is of a trend towards dispersal in shareholdings and a consequent reduction in—though not a disappearance of—family control and influence. The conclusion drawn by Berle and Means, Larner, and many others is that those enterprises in which family control has indisputably disappeared may be regarded as 'management-controlled'. I wish to question this conclusion, which ignores the significance of the growth in shareholdings by financial institutions in precisely these enterprises. Table 2 provides some background information for this claim in its tabulation of the importance of financial control. The high level of 'financial control' in the first half of the twentieth century reflects the role that was played by the big banks in the amalgamation and 'rationalization' of industrial and commercial enterprises. These banks built up substantial minority shareholdings in the companies that they brought to the stock exchange or whose expansion they promoted. As the enterprises have grown, these bank holdings have declined, but there has been a corresponding growth in shareholdings by financial intermediaries since the 1930s (see Table 6). While shareholdings by investment banks have declined, insurance companies and pension funds have gradually acquired larger numbers of company shares.

Table 6 shows that the proportion of shares that were owned by financial enterprises rose from 6.7 per cent in 1900 to 34.7 per cent in 1978. By 1981 this figure had risen to 38 per cent, and by 1990 institutions owned 53.3 per cent of company shares (Charkham 1994).

Table 6. Beneficial ownership of US company shares (1900–1978)

Type of holder	% of corporate stock held by each category			
	1900	1939	1974	1978
Bank-managed trusts	4.3	12.9	11.1	8.9
Pension funds	–	0.2	9.9	13.6
Investment companies	–	1.2	5.4	3.5
Life insurance companies	0.5	0.6	3.5	3.4
Other financials	1.9	2.1	3.3	5.3
Totals	6.7	17.0	33.3	34.7

Source: Kotz (1978: Table 1) and Herman (1981: Table 4.4).

Villarejo (1961a: 49) produced complementary evidence on personal shareholdings, showing that in 1951 the mass of small personal shareholders in large enterprises typically accounted for less than 10 per cent of their shares. As the *number* of shareholders has increased, the *proportion* of shares held by individuals has declined and that held by institutions has increased. The gradual, but partial, replacement of personal shareholders by 'institutional' shareholders occurred most rapidly during the post-war period. The pension fund became the most important type of financial shareholder, and by the 1970s pension funds had become the largest single source of new investment capital. Because many of these pension funds were under bank management, the banks had increased their significance, and hence their power, in the overall mobilization of capital (Drucker 1976: 1; Rifkin and Barber 1978: 10, 234; see also Goldsmith 1958; Cox 1963: 52; Baum and Stiles 1965: 31 ff., 54–5).

A pension fund is a trust fund, financed by employer and employee contributions; the fund invests in shares, bonds, property, and other income-producing assets in order to generate a stable income from which to pay the pensions of its retired members (Schuller 1986). Pension funds, like bank deposits and insurance policies, are controlled by people other than the ultimate beneficiaries: those who are currently in employment contribute a part of their salary to ensure a future pension benefit for themselves, but they play little part in determining the uses to which the investment funds are put. Radical writers have claimed that the question of control is raised in an especially acute form in the pension fund, because employees do not make individual decisions to hand over money to professional managers as is the case with shareholders in joint stock companies. Pension contributions are generally decided as part of a package of conditions of employment, and decisions on the management of the fund are taken or supervised by the employer. Thus, pension-fund capital is a form of socialized capital that has been institutionalized under private control.

Pension-fund and insurance-company investment, then, does not represent a 'democratization' of capital, but a renewal of bank power and an increase in the power of financial institutions generally. Although private individuals may be the ultimate beneficiaries of pension and insurance investment, 'the great bulk of financial institution stockholdings are of a character that cannot by any stretch of the imagination be regarded as representing ownership by masses of the population' (Perlo 1958: 30). Pensioners and the insured are neither owners nor controllers of the capital from which they benefit. Institutional shareholding reflects a move towards much greater concentration in corporate capital, a fact that led a Congressional Committee to report in 1968 that

the trend of the last 30 or 40 years toward a separation of ownership from control because of the fragmentation of stock ownership has been radically changed towards a concentration of voting power in the hands of a relatively few financial institutions, while the fragmentation in the distribution of cash payments has been continued. (Patman Report 1968: 13)

I argued in Chapter 3 that the growth of financial shareholdings might give rise to control through a constellation of interests rather than to management control in those enterprises without dominant shareholding interests. If this is indeed the case, then this should be apparent from data on the numbers of shares that are held by the twenty largest shareholders in major companies. Table 7 presents figures for 1937 and 1976 that give considerable support to this view. In almost half of the large enterprises of 1937 the twenty largest shareholders held 30 per cent or more of their shares. This degree of concentration, however, generally reflected the existence of one or two very large holdings and a mass of smaller holdings. Thirty-two of the 57 enterprises with more than 50 per cent of their shares in the hands of the top twenty holders were, in fact, majority-controlled by a single shareholder (Goldsmith and Parmelee 1940: 89–91).

The aggregate data for 1937, then, discloses little evidence for the existence of constellations of financial interests. The pattern of

Table 7. Holdings by the twenty largest shareholders in the largest US non-financial enterprises (1937 and 1976)

% of shares held by top 20 holders	1938: 208 share issues		1976: 122 corporations	
	Number	%	Number	%
More than 50	57	28	7	6
40–49	36	17	4	3
30–39			9	7
20–29	69	33	31	25
10–19			47	39
5–10			11	9
1–5	46	22	12	10
< 1			11	
Totals	208	100	122	100

Source: Goldsmith and Parmelee (1940: 81) and Herman (1981: 102).
Note: The 1937 figures are based on 208 share issues for the 200 largest corporations.

shareholding in many large enterprises where shareholdings were relatively dispersed can, however, be seen from a particular case study. The Union Pacific railway company had been classified as management-controlled in 1929, when its twenty largest shareholders owned 10.4 per cent of its share capital (Berle and Means 1932: 99). By 1937 their collective holding had increased to 14.47 per cent, and Table 8 shows that the top twenty holders included four family groups. These were the Harriman, Harkness, Vanderbilt, and Goelet families. Most of the large shareholders at this time were bank and trust companies that held shares on behalf of individuals and had only limited voting rights in these shares. In this situation, family shareholders and internal managers would both appear to have a basis for control, and financial constraints would be relatively loose.

Perlo has argued that the growth in financial shareholdings resulted in an increase in the proportion of shares held by the twenty largest shareholders in large enterprises between 1937 and 1954, and Eisenberg showed that the holdings of the ten largest holders had become even larger by 1961 (Perlo 1958: 29–30; Eisenberg 1969: 43–4). This was also glimpsed in Chevalier's work, which demonstrated that the top fifty enterprises of 1965 showed the highest

Table 8. Top twenty shareholders in Union Pacific (1937 and 1980)

1937		1980	
Shareholder	%	Shareholder	%
1 Harriman interests	2.99	Prudential Insurance	2.14
2 NV. Administratie-kantoor	2.66	Harriman family	2.09
3 Central Hanover Bank & Trust	1.18	Equitable Life Assurance	1.76
4 City Bank Farmers Trust	1.12	Mellon National Bank	1.50
5 Harkness interests	0.92	Citicorp	1.48
6 Kuhn Loeb	0.78	Rothschild family	1.45
7 Chase National Bank	0.75	J P Morgan & Co.	1.33
8 United States Trust	0.60	University of California	1.20
9 Chemical Bank & Trust	0.49	Bankamerica	1.15
10 { J W Davis & Co.	0.45	Manufacturers Hanover	1.13
{ Vanderbilt family	0.45	Rowe Price & Associates	0.86
12 Goelet family	0.43	Chemical New York	0.85
13 Dominick and Dominick	0.38	New York State Pension Fund	0.78
14 Bankers Trust	0.35	New Jersey Division of Investments	0.74
		Kirby family	0.74
{ Home Insurance	0.34		
15 { Massachusetts Investment	0.34	Hospital Trust	0.68
{ Trust			
17	–	Bank of New York	0.67
18	–	Kemper family	0.60
19	–	Du Pont family	0.59
20	–	Donaldson Lukfin & Jenrette	0.59
Totals of top 20	14.47		22.43

Source: 1938 list from Goldsmith and Parmelee (1940), 1980 list from CDE (1981).
Note: The original 1938 list was based on registered shareholders and included a number of obviously connected holdings. After combining these holdings only sixteen large shareholders remained.

dispersal in shareholdings. At other levels of the top 200 he discovered the importance of limited minority holdings of 5 per cent and 'predominant interests' of just under 5 per cent (see Table 9 and Table 10). In twenty-eight of the enterprises that might conventionally be classified as 'management-controlled', banks exercised a significant influence through shareholding and board representation. Altogether the six largest banks had limited minority participations or significant influence in forty enterprises (Chevalier 1970: 115,166).

Table 9. Strategic control in the top 200 US non-financial enterprises (1965)

Mode of control	Rank by size				Totals
	1–50	51–100	101–150	151–200	
Majority ownership	1	3	3	4	11
Minority ownership	14	24	25	30	93
Predominant influence	5	6	4	1	16
Management control	30	17	18	15	80
Totals	50	50	50	50	200

Source: Chevalier (1970: 67).
Note: Minority control involves more than 5 per cent of shares as well as representation on the board. 'Predominant influence' is the situation where there is strong influence on the board, even if there is no evidence of a 5-per-cent holding.

Table 10. Identity of controllers in the top 200 US non-financial enterprises (1965)

Mode of control	Type of controller					Totals
	Families	Banks	Other financials	Board	Other	
Majority ownership	7	0	0	0	4	11
Minority control	58	14	5	16	0	93
Predominant influence	4	12	0	0	0	16
Management control	–	–	–	–	80	80
Totals	69	26	5	16	84	200

Source: Chevalier (1970: 67).

    Claims such as these led to the setting up of a Congressional Committee on bank shareholdings, the evidence from which led Blumberg to conclude that financial enterprises held at least 10 per cent of the shares in each of the top ten US enterprises of 1969. All except one of these ten companies had been classified by Larner (1970) as 'management-controlled'. In eight of these enterprises, the top ten shareholders held between 30 and 40 per cent of the share capital (Blumberg 1975: 98–9). The five largest shareholders in the top 500 industrials of 1980 owned, on average, 28.8 per cent of the capital (Schleifer and Vishny 1986). Kotz (1978) has interpreted such evidence as indicative of a growth in bank minority control, and Table 11 shows Kotz's estimate that financials had minority control in thirteen large enterprises and 'partial control', with between 5 and 10 per cent, in a further ninety-three. This appears to be impressive evidence for financial control—minority control by financial enterprises—in almost a third of the top 200 enterprises, a finding that stands in stark contrast to Herman's discovery of just one case (see Table 2).

Table 11. Financial control in the top 200 US non-financial enterprises (1969)

Type of control	Number of corporations	% of corporations
Full financial control	13	6.5
Full owner control	3	15.5
Partial financial control	46	23.0
Partial owner control	2	1.0
Partial financial and owner	10	5.0
No centre of control	93	46.5
Other	5	2.5
Totals	200	100.0

Source: Kotz (1978: Table 3 on 97).
Note: 'Full' control refers to control on the basis of 10 per cent or more of the shares, while 'partial' control is based on 5–10 per cent.

These discrepant conclusions suggest that Kotz and others have produced evidence not for 'financial control' or bank minority control, but for control through a constellation of interests. This is the form of impersonal possession generated by the strengthening of institutional share ownership. The major financial intermediaries have become central agents in the mobilization of capital and are, in consequence, central to strategic control. It is not generally the case, however, that single financial enterprises have acquired the 10 per cent holdings that I have suggested are necessary for minority control. Instead, minority blocks have been acquired by large and diverse constellations of interests. Table 7 shows, for example, that by 1976 there had been a doubling in the proportion of large enterprises in which the top twenty shareholders owned between 10 and 30 per cent. Table 12 shows the pattern of control in the largest

American financial and non-financial enterprises of 1980. At least 154 of the top 250 were controlled through constellations of interests. In none of these did the twenty largest shareholders have less than 10 per cent, and in no case did they have more than 50 per cent. In none of the enterprises for which information was available was the degree of dispersal great enough for them to be regarded as management-controlled.

The outcome of this trend can again be illustrated from the case of Union Pacific, whose shareholder list is given in Table 8. Union Pacific's twenty largest shareholders in 1980 owned 22.43 per cent of its share capital, and most of the numerous bank holdings were held on behalf of pension funds. What is particularly remarkable is the appearance of five family groups on the 1980 list, one of which had been the largest holder in 1937. There appears, therefore, to be considerable support for Burch's claim that family influence has persisted even when shareholdings have been dispersed. In many cases families remained as important participants in controlling constellations and they retained a degree of influence over corporate affairs: almost two-thirds of the controlling constellations, included family participants. Indeed, the Ford family and Ford Foundation participated in seventeen controlling constellations, though this was exceptional. Other families to participate in two or more constellations were the Rockefellers, Du Ponts, Templetons, and Phipps (Scott 1986: 144).

How do institutional shareholders act in a situation of control through a constellation of interests? It is often held that institutions have no need to intervene in corporate affairs. An institution that is dissatisfied with the way that a company is run can simply sell its shares and invest elsewhere. This may not always be possible, however, as institutional shareholders are such large shareholders that it is often difficult for them to find purchasers for their shares. The capital market is dominated by institutions, and if one institution is dissatisfied with a company's performance, then others are likely to be dissatisfied too. Even where a potential purchaser can be found, the actual sale of a large holding may not be possible without a massive drop in the share price, which would be financially damaging to the shareholder. Institutions, then, tend to become 'locked in' to the enterprises in which they invest (Baum and Stiles 1965: 11; Davies 1993: 83–4). For this reason, argue Fitch and Oppenheimer (1970b: 62–3), they are impelled to adopt a strategy of intervention. Only by making their views known can they safeguard their investments.

Table 12. Identity of controllers in the top 252 US enterprises (1980)

	Type of controller					
		Corporate				
Mode of control	Personal	US	Foreign	Mixed	Other	Totals
Exclusive majority	2	1	4	0	0	7
Shared majority	0	0	0	1	0	1
Exclusive minority	26	21	0	0	0	47
Limited minority	3	0	0	0	0	3
Shared minority	1	0	0	2	0	3
Mutual	–	–	–	–	11	11
Constellation of interests	–	–	–	154	–	154
Not known	–	–	–	–	–	26
Totals	32	22	4	157	37	252

Source: Scott (1986: Table 6.1 on 137).

Table 13. Strategic control in the 200 largest US commercial banks (1962)

Mode of control	Number of banks	% of banks	% of assets
Private ownership	1	0.5	0.1
Majority control	4	2.0	0.6
Minority control:			
20–50%	22	11.0	6.2
10–20%	17	8.5	3.1
No dominant interest	149	74.5	87.5
Not known	7	3.5	2.5
Totals	200	100.0	100.0

Source: Adapted from Vernon (1970: Table 1).
Note: The analysis refers to those banks that are members of the Federal Reserve System, i.e. all the major commercial banks.

Thus, the growth of bank and other institutional shareholding has led to a progressive move away from a passive or neutral stance and towards one of more active involvement in corporate control. As Chevalier said of banks some years ago:

In spite of the banks' apparent reluctance to intervene in the administration of corporations, it appears likely that they will be progressively impelled to give up their neutrality, in so far as the volume of stock they hold obliges them to shed the simple role of institutional investor. (Chevalier 1969: 168)

At a minimal level this might involve seeking representation on the boards of enterprises in which they invest, or at least ensuring that these boards include a suitably 'independent' outside influence (Allen 1976: 889–90; Blumberg 1975: 168). An institutional share-holder may, for example, be happy to see a politician, a prominent public figure, or even a director of a rival enterprise sitting on a board if they feel that they can be relied upon to counterbalance the inter-nal management and safeguard shareholder interests. A stronger, more direct strategy for substantial investors might involve surveil-lance, the continual monitoring of an enterprise's affairs through regular visits to examine the accounts and consult with manage-ment. Baum and Stiles, for example, have shown that the large insti-tutional shareholders have privileged access to business information on plans and markets, and have the expertise and means to make the best use of this through a constant scrutiny of all the companies in which they invest (Baum and Stiles 1965: 346; Useem 1993):

institutional investors are in a position to obtain corporate information not available to other shareholders. This position springs from the power of large holdings and from the ability as a day-to-day matter to send compe-tent men (*sic*) into the field to question management, not to mention the fact that institutions are themselves big business and, thus, their executives are the natural associates of industrial executives. (Baum and Stiles 1965: 65, 162–3; Chevalier 1970: 202)

In extreme cases institutions may vote against the management or attempt to alter the composition of the board. Cases of direct inter-vention have, until recently, been rare (Herman 1973: 20–1; O'Connor 1971: 139, 143). They have mainly been in response to crises, and when the crisis is on its way to resolution institutions have returned to the 'normal' processes of surveillance (Glasberg 1981; see also Gogel and Koenig 1981).

In most normal situations, the controlling interests prefer to remain as 'outsiders' and to allow the internal management to run an enterprise with minimal shareholder intervention. As Chandler (1990: 740 n. 53) has shown, insiders have detailed information about the complexities facing enterprises in their day-to-day activities, and they have an understanding of 'the realities of alternative courses of action as well as the ability to carry out decisions and to review and revise them'. Outsiders, on the other hand, have a power potential that is used when an enterprise gets into difficulties or there is a takeover bid. The outsiders 'have helped create, maintain, or destroy existing capabilities, but they cannot maintain a healthy, competitive enterprise without the support of a management hierarchy with product-specific administrative and financial skills' (ibid.).

It became apparent during the 1970s not only that surveillance and pressure were crucial aspects of strategic decision-making but also that intervention by institutional shareholders was increasing in both Britain and the United States. In the United States this was due to pressure from government, the unions, and the newly-formed Council of Institutional Investors to take more seriously their fiduciary role in relation to their beneficiaries. Indeed, pension funds are required by law to vote their shares and to disclose how they have voted. The surveillance and pressure has often been informal and behind-the-scenes, as institutions have sought to avoid any publicity that might make an enterprise's financial problems any worse.

During the 1980s institutions have been far less reluctant to intervene in public and often confrontational ways if this has seemed necessary to safeguard their interests (Useem 1993). They are, for example, more likely to vote their shares themselves than to assign their proxies to executives. This has particularly been the case for public funds, as opposed to funds for private-sector employees. Public sector funds such as TIAA-CREF in the United States (the world's largest pension fund) have no need to sustain an internal management or to maintain relations of reciprocity with other pension funds. As a result, there are fewer obstacles to them taking a more active role in corporate governance. In addition to issues of corporate strategy, the very practices of corporate governance themselves have become foci of institutional attention. Pension funds and their managers have sought seats on company boards and on the institutional audit committees that oversee executives, and they have been increasingly willing to vote their shares in contentious elections, especially in relation to such issues as executive remuneration and conditions of service. There have been highly public institutional interventions in the affairs of GM, IBM, and American Express, and in 1995 TIAA-CREF mobilized other institutions to depose the Chairman of W. R. Grace and to reduce its board size and the average age of its directors. Members of the controlling constellations in large enterprises, then, have been moving from passive and indirect mechanisms of control to more active and direct ones.

I have concentrated so far on the ownership of non-financial enterprises, and I have shown that they are increasingly controlled by constellations of financial interests. If financial intermediaries control the large non-financials, then who owns and controls the financials? Vernon's study of strategic control in the big commercial banks in the 1960s (see Table 13) found that most of these banks were without a dominant shareholder. The larger the bank, the more likely was this to be the case (Vernon 1970: 654). The main source of information on bank ownership is the series of reports produced by the Patman Committee, which found, in Chevalier's words, that 'the most important shareholders of the banks are the banks themselves' (1970: 115). In 1966, almost all of the top 210 banks held some of their own shares, over a half held more than 5 per cent, and over a quarter held more than 10 per cent. Additionally, there were significant cross-holdings of bank shares: in each of the top six New York banks, between 12 and 20 per cent of the shares were held by these same six banks (Patman Report 1966: 817, Table VI; CDE 1980b: 13). The Patman Committee also discovered that subsidiary banks held shares in their own parent, and in the parent companies of other banks as well (Patman Report 1967: 918 ff.). There are also high levels of bank-share ownership by other financial institutions. Almost a half of the top 275 banks of 1966 had 5 per cent or more of their shares held by other financials. J. P. Morgan, which with Morgan Guaranty held substantial shareholdings in many of the largest American enterprises, had 27.6 per cent of its capital held by its twenty largest shareholders (CDE 1980a).[3] This bank, like many others, is included in the tabulation shown in Table 12, confirming the conclusion that the ownership patterns of financial and non-financial enterprises are similar. As Chevalier argues, 'the American banks are linked amongst themselves by an extremely dense network of financial participations' (1970: 117). Many banks, then, are controlled through constellations of interests and are themselves members of the constellations that control other enterprises.

[3] The exceptions to this rule are the mutual insurance companies which are, strictly speaking, controlled by their policy-holders. The only study of control in mutuals (Gessell and Howe 1941) concluded that financial interests controlled the companies through proxy voting and complex electoral arrangements. See also Perlo (1957: 82) and O'Hara (1981).

The American evidence suggests that large enterprises have undergone a transition from the personal possession by particular families that characterized liberal capitalism to a situation of impersonal possession through an interweaving of ownership interests that characterizes contemporary 'disorganized' capitalism. This transition did not involve a simple unilinear movement. The initial move towards greater dispersal of share ownership that occurred with the rise of organized capitalism introduced indirect forms of personal possession and, during the 1930s, a large number of management-controlled enterprises. By the 1950s, management control was, indeed, a characteristic of many large enterprises (Useem 1984: 175–9), though family ownership and influence persisted in many areas of the economy. Since the 1950s, however, managerial enterprises and surviving family enterprises have declined in number as enterprises in which intercorporate 'institutional' shareholdings are the dominant form of ownership have grown in number. Even Herman, an advocate of the most sophisticated version of the managerial position, has recognized that enterprises without dominant ownership interests are subject to considerable influence from their institutional shareholders. He shows that many of these enterprises had significant share stakes held by financial intermediaries, and that many of these shareholding interests were represented on the boards (Herman 1981: 58–9). He described this situation as one of 'constrained managerial control' (ibid.: 15), though the evidence that I have presented suggests that it can far more appropriately be termed 'control through a constellation of interests'. Internal executive managers have the power to make decisions, but this power is constrained by the power that banks and other financials have to limit the choices that are open to them. Internal executives cannot ignore the interests of the financial constellations that comprise their principal shareholders. This 'negative' constraint (Herman 1981: 19) by financial intermediaries provides the potential for active intervention in decision-making by representatives of the financial institutions, should this become necessary. Control through a constellation of interests has become the dominant form of strategic control in the largest American enterprises.

Controlling Constellations in Britain

There has been far less discussion of and research into the question of ownership and control in Britain than there has in the United States. British capitalist business remained 'entrepreneurial' in character for most of the nineteenth century, and few changes in the structure of liberal capitalism were apparent to observers before the First World War. Only the liberal economist Hobson, and the Fabian socialists, seemed to sense any signs of change resulting from the rise of the joint stock company. Hobson recognized that a spate of company flotations after the 1870s had allowed company shares to be sold on the stock exchange at a profit without undermining the position of the original owners, who could hold onto a large enough block of shares for continued control. He concluded that 'diffused ownership with concentrated control is the distinctive feature of the company' and that 'the monetary support of the public is wanted but not their direction' (Hobson 1906: 240). The implications of Hobson's work had been developed in a strikingly similar direction by the Fabians, who held that the bulk of the shareholders in joint stock companies were purely passive, and that the few large shareholders adopted a 'rentier' orientation (Clarke 1889; Macrosty 1901). By the inter-war years, the Fabians felt, capitalism had become more 'organized' and a leading role in business was being played by the 'financiers and bankers who monopolize the art of collecting millions of spare money' (Shaw 1928: 181). Managers were employed as the subordinate 'brain workers': the 'intellectual proletariat' who served the capitalist rentiers (Webb and Webb 1923: 56–8).

Apart from some scattered investigations by financial journalists, only one researcher gave any serious attention to the issue during the whole of the period from the 1930s to the 1950s (Florence 1947; 1953; 1961). The matter entered the arena of public debate during the 1950s with the initiation of a wider debate on socialist policy for economic change and the future of the left. Managerialist theory posited the demise of the capitalist class just as 'embourgeoisement' theories posited the transformation of the working class; and those who sought to 'modernize' Labour-Party policies saw the managerialist view of the business enterprise as a major plank in their critique of inherited doctrines (Crosland 1956 and 1962; but see also Hall *et al.* 1957). The outcome of these political debates for research on ownership and control was fairly limited. While the debate over the embourgeoisement of the working class generated a massive and continuing programme of research (Goldthorpe *et al.* 1968*a*, 1968*b*, 1969), the debate over managerialism had no similar impact. Indeed, the basic tenets of managerialist theory seemed to become part of the taken-for-granted assumptions of economists and sociologists alike. An important survey of aggregate trends in share-ownership was undertaken (Stone *et al.* 1966), but no real theoretical discussions took place until Nichols (1969) and Child (1969*a*) published their reviews of the American debates and outlined their relevance to the British situation. Even then, debate was very subdued until the mid-1970s, when a number of empirical studies by economists and sociologists began to appear.

This lack of research is rather paradoxical, given that useful data is more easily available in Britain than in the United States. British company share-registers are available for study in a public archive, and these registers show the name, address, and size of holding for all shareholders. Despite the widespread use of 'nominee' accounts, a clear picture of share-ownership can generally be obtained. Filed along with the share registers are other company documents, including those that list the names and affiliations of all of the directors.

Like the United States, Britain has experienced a long-term decline in the number of large family-owned enterprises. The formation of a 'big business' sector, however, was somewhat slower in Britain, and the smaller size of the British national economy meant that the founding entrepreneurs and their heirs came under far less pressure to dilute their controlling shareholdings until relatively late in the present century. Many of the largest enterprises at the turn of the century were the long-established railway, dock, and canal companies in which more dispersed forms of ownership already existed; but a large number of them, especially those in manufacturing industry, were family-owned, and this number increased for the first part of the century. Hannah (1980: 53) has shown that the proportion of the top 200 enterprises with family representatives on their boards increased from 55 per cent in 1919 to 70 per cent in 1930. This high figure for 1930 can be accounted for by the changing composition of the top 200 following the amalgamation of the numerous non-family railway companies into four large enterprises in the 1920s, and the consequent entry into the top 200 of many family-owned manufacturers. The number of family firms fell between the 1930s and the Second World War, standing at 60 per cent of the top 200 in 1948, but the figure seems unlikely to have fallen to any great extent between the War and the middle of the 1960s. About a third of the top 120 enterprises were family-owned in both 1954 and 1966 (see Table 14). The increase in the number of large enterprises shown as dominated by their internal managers in 1954 and 1966 is a result of an expansion in the number of foreign subsidiaries operating in Britain, which Barratt Brown (1968a) treated as controlled by their local management. While this may be appropriate for many purposes, it overstates the importance of local managers in the ultimate control of these subsidiary enterprises.

A more detailed view of this trend can be found in the pathbreaking work of Florence, the first person in Britain to have investigated the question of the supposed decline in owner control in a direct and

Table 14. Board representation in the top 120 British enterprises (1954 and 1966)

Dominant interest on board	1954	1966
Family or tycoon	36	38
External interests	53	47
Internal management	31	35
Totals	120	120

Source: Adapted from Barratt Brown (1968a: 45, Table 7).

Table 15. Strategic control in large English non-financial enterprises (1936 and 1951)

	Number of companies	
Mode of control	1936	1951
Majority control	9	6
Minority control	13	11
Other owner control, 20% cut-off	47	36
Other owner control, 10–19%	15	28
No dominant interest	10	17
Totals	94	98

Source: Calculated from Florence (1961: 112–15, Tables Va and Vb).
Note: 'Other owner control' refers to the holdings of the twenty largest registered shareholders.

systematic way. In a series of investigations of share-ownership Florence discovered not only that wholly owned subsidiaries comprised a much larger proportion of large enterprises in England than in the United States, but also that shareholdings generally were less dispersed in England (Florence 1953: 189). Table 15 shows nevertheless that, after excluding wholly owned subsidiaries, there was a trend towards greater share dispersal between 1936 and 1951: the average percentage of shares held by the principal shareholders in large enterprises fell from 30 to 19 per cent over this period. In 1936, twenty-one of the large enterprises were majority or minority-controlled by personal shareholders, and a further sixteen of the 'other owner' enterprises were, in fact, controlled by families or family groups. By 1951, just seventeen enterprises had personal majority or minority controllers, and only nine of the 'other owner' enterprises were subject to personal control, a decline of almost one-third. Florence's data suggest an overall decline in personal-owner control, together with a shift from majority to minority control among those enterprises remaining under personal control.

Florence's data also suggest that the decline in family ownership

Table 16. Identity of controllers in the top 250 British enterprises (1976)

Mode of control	Type of controller						
	Personal	British Corporate	Foreign Corporate	State	Mixed	Other	Totals
Public corporations	–	–	–	13	–	–	13
Wholly-owned	7	1	28	2	0	0	38
Exclusive majority	14	1	9	1	0	0	25
Shared majority	0	12		1	2	0	15
Exclusive minority	19	12	5	0	0	0	36
Shared minority	0	2	0	1	8	0	11
Limited minority	3	1	0	0	0	0	4
Mutual	–	–	–	–	–	8	8
Constellation of interests	–	–	–	–	100	0	100
Totals	43	71		18	110	8	250

Source: Scott (1986: Table 4.1 on 53).
Note: Table 4.2 on p. 64 of Scott (1986) classifies these same companies with a more refined measure of minority control, but concludes that the classification given here is a valid picture of the broad features of corporate control.

Table 17. Mode of control in the top 250 British enterprises (1976 and 1988)

	Number of companies	
Mode of control	1976	1988
Public corporations	13	11
Wholly-owned	38	54
Other majority	40	15
Minority control	51	45
Non-proprietary	9	12
Constellation of interests	100	113
Totals	250	250

Source: Scott (1990a: Table 1 on 362).

was associated with a shift from personal shareholding to institutional shareholding and a consequent increase in the number of enterprises that were controlled through constellations of interests. Although there was an increase in the number of enterprises without a dominant ownership interest, there was also an increase in the number where the top twenty shareholders held between 10 and 20 per cent of the capital. This move towards control through a constellation of interests was strongly confirmed in a study for 1975, which found that 39 per cent of the top 250 British non-financials had no holder with as much as 5 per cent of the capital, and a further 10 per cent of enterprises in which no holder held more than 10 per cent. Almost half the large enterprises were, however, found still to be majority- or minority-controlled by a cohesive group (Nyman and Silberston 1978: Table 1; Francis 1980a). The data presented in Table 16 confirm this picture. About a third of the top 250 of 1976 were wholly owned or majority controlled, and a further 20 per cent were minority controlled (Scott 1986). Over a half of the top 250, then, were subject to control by a dominant shareholding interest or a group of closely allied interests. Among the companies with a dominant controlling interest, the largest single category comprised the 46 family-controlled enterprises, this personal ownership being equally divided between the majority and minority forms. Foreign ownership, overwhelmingly North American, accounted for 43 of the top 250, and this predominantly took the form of wholly-owned subsidiaries. The still-significant state sector was apparent in the thirteen public corporations and the five other enterprises in which the state had control or influence.[4] Forty per cent of all the enterprises were controlled through a constellation of interests.

Evidence from Scotland shows this same pattern. The Scottish economy is a regional enclave within the British economy, and has higher levels of both family and foreign ownership than is the case in Britain as a whole or in the United States. The top sixty-two Scottish non-financials of 1973 included twenty-four cases of family or individual control, fifteen cases of 'foreign' control,[5] and seven cases of control through a constellation of interests (Scott and Hughes 1980b: Table 4c, p. 244). The spread of control through a constellation of interests has been inhibited partly by the continued vitality of family enterprise and partly by the expansion of English and American ownership into Scotland in the post-war period.

Underlying the move towards control through a constellation of interests in Britain, as in the United States, was the growth of 'institutional' shareholdings. There has, of course, been a massive increase in the total number of shareholders in large enterprises, but this has run in parallel with a concentration of the bulk of company shares in institutional hands. In 1942 most shareholders in the thirty large companies analyzed by Parkinson were individuals holding shares valued at less than £100, and companies such as the London, Midland, and Scottish Railway had over 200,000 registered shareholders (1951: 51, 122, 125, 128–9). Although institutions began to hold company shares much earlier, the big growth in institutional ownership occurred during the inter-war period, and particularly rapidly from the 1950s. Investment trusts had been set up in the late nineteenth century to invest in company shares; they had rapidly became major investors, and were followed by the new unit trusts from the 1930s. Life-insurance companies shifted their growing funds in a major way from government securities to ordinary shares during the inter-war years, and by 1956 insurance companies collectively held 6 per cent of Dunlop and ICI, 15 per cent of GEC, and 34 per cent of the Steel Company of Wales (Scott 1986: 89). Pension funds grew rapidly from the 1960s and soon became a significant element in the capital market. Imperial Tobacco illustrates this trend well. In 1942 it had 94,690 shareholders, but by 1985 this had

---

[4] 'Public corporation' is, in Britain, a legal category for corporations established by the state with no share capital and under the direct control of a ministry.

[5] In this context 'foreign' includes English enterprises.

increased to 134,484.[6] 92 per cent of these shareholders were individuals or families, the great bulk of them holding fewer than 1,000 shares. Indeed, the 65,070 shareholders with 1,000 or fewer shares held just 4 per cent of the company's shares in total. Banks, insurance companies, pension funds, and other institutions were a mere 8 per cent of the shareholders in number, but their holdings represented 74 per cent of the total share capital. This progressive marginalization of personal shareholders—despite their large numbers—is a feature of all large British companies and has led to a steady decline in the total number of personal shareholders in large enterprises during the 1970s and 1980s. A relatively small number of institutional shareholders have become the principal owners of company shares, and it is the institutions that now dominate the capital markets.

These trends are apparent from Table 18, which shows the growth in financial shareholdings and the relative decline in personal shareholdings throughout the corporate sector during the post-war period. The proportion of shares held by individuals and families, as measured by their market value, declined consistently from 65.8 per cent in 1957 to 17.7 per cent in 1993. While the total number of shares owned by individuals has increased, their percentage holding has fallen. Conversely, holdings by financial institutions increased from 21.3 to 61.2 per cent over the same period. Indeed, the voting power of financial institutions is even greater than these figures imply, as shares held in personal equity plans—controlled by fund managers—were included by the CSO under the category for 'individual' shareholdings, as were other shares beneficially owned by individuals but actually managed by financial institutions. The main area of growth has been shareholdings by insurance and pension funds, largely as a consequence of the extension of occupational and private pension schemes during the 1970s and 1980s (Diamond Report 1975*b*: 11–12; Erritt and Alexander 1977; Wilson Report 1977; Briston and Dobbins 1978; Lash and Urry 1994). Despite a fall-back in the percentage of shares owned by insurance companies in the 1980s, pension fund holdings have continued to rise and have reached a level almost double that of 1975. Funds such as Hermes (the Royal Mail and British Telecom fund)[7] have now become the

---

[6] By the 1980s the company had been renamed Imperial Group. These and the following figures are calculated from the company's Annual Report.

[7] When the Post Office was split up and the telephone service privatized as British Telecom, the pension fund remained a joint fund separate from the privatized enterprise.

Table 18. Beneficial share-ownership in British enterprises (1957–1981)

| | % of market value held | | | | | | |
Category of owner	1957	1963	1969	1975	1981	1989	1993
Persons	65.8	54.0	47.4	37.5	28.2	21.3	17.7
Banks	0.9	1.3	1.7	0.7	0.3	0.9	0.6
Insurance companies	8.8	10.0	12.2	15.9	20.5	18.4	17.3
Pension funds	3.4	6.4	9.0	16.8	26.7	30.4	34.2
Other financials	8.2	12.6	13.0	14.6	10.4	9.1	9.7
Public sector	3.9	1.5	2.6	3.6	3.0	2.0	1.3
Overseas	4.4	7.0	6.6	5.6	3.6	12.4	16.3
Other	4.6	7.2	7.5	5.3	7.3	5.6	3.1
Totals	100	100	100	100	100	100	100

Source: From Stock Exchange (1983), Table 2.16; CSO (1991: Table C; 1994).
Note: Data relate to stratified samples of quoted companies. See Stone *et al.* (1966), Moyle (1971), and Department of Industry (1979). Figures for 1957 involve an estimate for 'other financial', which may account for the apparent rise between 1957 and 1963.

leading investors in the capital market. Over this same period, American pensions funds have diversified their holdings into Europe and have become important holders of British company shares.

The consequences of these trends at enterprise level are illustrated in Table 19. Florence had concluded that his studies of 1936 and 1951 had produced no evidence of a managerial 'revolution', but he did feel that there were definite indications of a managerial 'evolution' (1961: 187). The facts that led him to this conclusion were a decline in the percentage holdings by the board of directors and by the twenty largest shareholders. It can be seen from Table 19 that the total shareholding by directors did indeed decline continuously from 1936 to 1976 in the four largest enterprises studied by Florence. By 1976, the directors held less than two in a thousand shares in each of these enterprises. It can also be seen that in three of the enterprises the holdings of the twenty largest shareholders fell between 1936 and 1951; in the fourth case it increased from a very low level. In 1951, the holding of the top twenty shareholders exceeded 10 per cent only in the case of Imperial Group. Even Nichols (1969: 77) concluded that these figures showed Dunlop to be 'the epitomy (*sic*) of the "management-controlled" company'. But a comparison of the figures for 1951 and 1976 shows that these judgements were premature. During the post-war period of growth in institutional holdings, the proportion of shares held by the top twenty shareholders increased to the point at which they held more than 10 per cent in all four of the large enterprises. In a detailed investigation of ICI in 1957, Hall *et al.* (1957) showed the progress of this growth: 9 per cent of the shares of this enterprise were held by the 11 largest shareholders, and many of these shareholders were represented on the board. The fragmentation of small and medium-sized holdings among a large number of individuals gave effective control to the leading shareholders.

Table 19. Development of control in Britain (1936–1976)

	% held by board			% held by top 20		
Enterprise	1936	1951	1976	1936	1951	1976
Courtaulds	3.3	1.2	0.011	21.0	7.1	18.49
ICI	0.2	0.1	0.006	10.1	9.3	13.60
Imperial Group	10.4	4.2	0.038	19.0	15.8	17.39
Dunlop	0.09	0.03	0.015	5.1	9.6	20.14

Source: Florence (1961), Appendix, and data collected by author; see also Nichols (1969: 76, Table 6.3).
Note: In a similar comparison by Nichols, British American Tobacco and Unilever were included. These have been excluded because both were special cases of high-vote concentration.

It has sometimes been questioned whether institutional shareholders really do have the potential for control. To test this idea, Cubbin and Leech (1983) constructed a model of voting behaviour analogous to that discussed in Chapter 3. They applied this to data collected by Collett and Yarrow (1976), who discovered that in none of their selection of eighty-five large industrials of 1970–1 did the twenty largest registered shareholders hold less than 10 per cent of the shares. Cubbin and Leech showed that these twenty shareholders always held a block larger than that necessary to ensure control.[8]

[8] Cubbin and Leech attempted to show that minority control could be exercised by one of the twenty largest holders in some of these enterprises. They claimed this as a possibility in twenty-five of the seventy-one without a dominant interest. In fact, these are best seen as, at most, cases of limited minority control, as they conclude that a holding of less than 10 per cent by an institution is a less secure base of control than a similar holding by an internal family executive (1983: 366). Their analysis, therefore, confirms the picture of control through a constellation of interests. For a similar discussion of the American situation see Leech (1987*a*; 1987*b*).

This growth in institutional holdings has enhanced the power of those banks that manage the institutional funds. Minns (1980; 1982) has shown that the bulk of the shares owned by pension funds are actually managed by banks or by insurance companies and big stockbrokers. Although banks had direct ownership of only 0.7 per cent of shares in 1975, they had voting control over 17.6 per cent. The same is true of other large fund-managers: Prudential Assurance now manages pension funds worth twice the value of its own insurance business. The computerization of share trading has made small investors more likely to place their shares in nominee companies run by their stockbrokers or bankers in order to gain administrative savings, and this often means that individuals lose the right, *de jure* or *de facto*, to vote their own shares. In this way, the voting power of the institutions can vastly exceed that implied by the level of their direct beneficial share ownership. Through these and similar means, banks and insurance companies dominate the mobilization of capital and now have voting rights in about one-third of all corporate capital. By virtue of their holdings, they become 'locked-in' to the affairs of the enterprises in which they invest, and they must consider the possibility of intervention whenever their interests are threatened (Wilson Report 1977: 26). There has, in fact, been an increasing tendency over the 1980s for insurance companies and pension-funds to exercise the voting rights in the shares that they own. While only one-third of shares are actually voted, large institutions have a greater tendency to vote than do small shareholders, and so their voting-power is greater than is suggested by figures on ownership (Mallin 1995). This is what happens when enterprises are controlled through constellations of interests. The directors of financial institutions who sit on company boards as 'external interests' (see Table 14) are the 'co-ordinating controllers' (Barratt Brown 1968a) that represent the major corporate shareholders and creditors.

It has been found that 100 of the top 250 enterprises in 1976 were controlled through constellations of interests (see Table 16). In each of these enterprises, the twenty largest shareholders owned between 10 and 50 per cent of the capital,[9] and shareholdings outside the 'top twenty shareholders tailed off rapidly to negligible levels. An analysis

---

[9] Florence's analysis was based on the largest registered shareholders, termed 'shareholders of record' in the United States. The data presented in Table 15 are based on an identification of the beneficiaries, or vote-holders, and this involved grouping shares that were subject to a common management. An analysis limited to registered shareholdings underestimates the concentration of votes.

of these 100 enterprises showed that 192 shareholders participated in their controlling constellations (Scott 1986: 101 ff.). Sixty of these participants were themselves members of the top 250, and they accounted for just over two-thirds of all the shareholding participations. Prudential Assurance, Britain's largest institutional shareholder, was a member of 88 of the 100 controlling constellations, and in 43 cases it was the single largest shareholder. Virtually all the participants in the controlling constellations were financial intermediaries, the great majority of them being British enterprises. There was, however, a significant involvement in controlling constellations by the Kuwait Investment Office, by American banks such as Morgan Guaranty, Bankers Trust, and Citicorp, and by the French shareholding trust SICOVAM. In a number of cases, however, families were participants in controlling constellations, showing that family influence could continue even when family control had disappeared. This kind of family influence was apparent in one-third of those enterprises controlled through constellations of interests, the sizes of the influential family holdings typically being less than 2 per cent.

Holdings by the top twenty shareholders in those enterprises that were controlled through a constellation of interests in 1976 are shown in Table 20. In most cases the top twenty held between 20 and 30 per cent of the capital, and in no case did their block fall below 10 per cent. Table 21 illustrates this using data from two of Britain's largest enterprises. In neither case did the largest single holder have sufficient votes to exercise minority control on its own, and there were no cohesive sub-groups within the top twenty that could together form a controlling minority block. The extent of the overlap among the controlling constellations of Britain's largest enterprises is strikingly illustrated by the fact that the two enterprises had nine of their top twenty shareholders in common.

The restructuring of the British economy since the late 1970s has led to some changes in patterns of ownership and control, as can be seen in Table 17. This restructuring had particularly marked effects within the financial sector, where the principal financial markets were deregulated. Associated with the deregulation of the financial markets, discussed more fully in Chapter 5, was an encouragement of foreign inward investment and the privatization of state assets, trends which further weakened family control. The number of majority-owned enterprises in the top 250 declined considerably between 1976 and 1988. Where families owned the whole share

Table 20. Holdings by the twenty largest shareholders in large British enterprises (1976)

% of shares held by top 20 holders	Number of companies
More than 50	0
40–49	4
30–39	13
20–29	61
10–19	22
Less than 10	0
Totals	100

Source: See Scott (1986: 95, Table 5.2).
Note: Data based on the 100 enterprises in Table 16 that were controlled through a constellation of interests.

capital of their company they were often able to survive, but where they had less than complete ownership they fared less well. Only seven of the majority-controlled non-financial enterprises of 1988 were controlled by families or entrepreneurs—half the number that there had been twelve years previously. Some families had, as a rational calculation or through misfortune, failed to buy sufficient new shares to retain the size of their percentage holdings as their companies increased in size, and their enterprises passed from majority control to minority control. Others proved unable to provide the finance that was needed to meet increased foreign competition, and they simply declined, dropping out of the top 250.

Family majority control in the financial sector—almost exclusively found among the merchant banks—declined significantly over the period from 1976 to 1988. Merchant banks had grown markedly in size during the 1970s and 1980s, and many controlling family holdings had declined to minority levels or to mere elements in controlling constellations. Wholly owned merchant banks fared relatively better until the 1990s.

The policy of privatizing state assets had been intended to encourage wider share-ownership, but the programme has actually resulted in an increase in the proportion of shares that are held by financial institutions. Privatization occurred on a fairly limited scale until the sale of British Telecom shares in 1984 and of TSB and British Gas in 1986. Although these and other privatization issues led to an initial

Table 21. Top twenty shareholders in ICI and Prudential Assurance (1976)

Imperial Chemical Industries		Prudential Assurance	
Shareholder	%	Shareholder	%
1 Prudential Assurance	3.36	Britannic Assurance	3.09
2 Imperial Chemical Industries	1.84	EMI	2.19
3 Commercial Union	0.78	Legal and General Assurance	1.71
4 Mercury Securities	0.71	Electricity Council	1.58
5 Royal Insurance	0.69	Prudential Assurance	1.36
6 Legal and General Assurance	0.63	Mercury Securities	1.18
7 Kuwait Investment Office	0.59	Midland Bank	1.17
8 Oil Transport and Trading	0.54	Hill Samuel	0.94
9 Electricity Council	0.47	Standard Life Assurance	0.91
10 Britannic Assurance	0.47	Barclays Bank	0.79
11 National Westminster Bank	0.40	Oil Transport and Trading	0.76
12 Baring Brothers	0.37	Baring Brothers	0.48
13 Norwich Union	0.37	British Airways	0.47
14 Robert Fleming	0.37	British Gas	0.47
15 Hill Samuel	0.36	Lucas Industries	0.46
16 Standard Life Assurance	0.34	Eagle Star Insurance	0.44
17 Hambros	0.34	Scottish Provident Institution	0.44
18 Equity and Law Life Assurance	0.31	Philip Hill Trusts	0.43
19 Barclays Bank	0.31	Morgan Grenfell	0.42
20 Co-operative group	0.31	National Coal Board	0.42
Totals of top 20	13.60		19.72

Source: Listings for 100 enterprises controlled through constellations of interests, contained in J. Scott, 'The Controlling Constellations', booklet available through British Lending Library and the national copyright libraries.

Note: 'Oil Transport and Trading' in the above lists is the pseudonym of a large British oil company. All holdings in the names of non-financial enterprises were, in fact, holdings by their pension funds.

increase in personal share-ownership, most individual shareholders sold quickly and the total number of individual shareholders fell back again. There has nevertheless been an increase in the percentage of the population that owns shares, combined with a continuing decline in the percentage of shares that they hold. In conjunction with declining family ownership and with policies aimed at deregulating the financial sector, this has resulted in a substantial increase in the number of companies that were controlled through constellations of interests. The number of such enterprises among the top 250 increased from 100 to 113 over the twelve-year period between 1976 and 1988.

A particularly striking feature of the British economy in 1988 was the substantial growth in foreign ownership that it experienced. The number of foreign-owned subsidiaries among the top 200 non-financials increased from 28 in 1976 to 39 in 1988, a growth that occurred very much at the expense of family control and influence. This internationalization of control in the manufacturing sector was not exclusively a process of 'Americanization', as the number of subsidiaries of companies based in other European countries also increased substantially. The shift in control patterns reflected a Europe-wide restructuring of capital in anticipation of the 1992 changes in European Community customs barriers and the move towards a single market.

In Britain, then, a transition from personal to impersonal possession has taken place. As in the United States, the personal, family-based forms of ownership characteristic of liberal capitalism gave way to indirect forms of personal possession in the stage of organized capitalism and then, with the growth of institutional shareholdings, to the impersonal possession characteristic of disorganized capitalism. The overall trend from personal to impersonal possession is manifest in the increasing replacement of entrepreneurial capital by institutional capital and control through a constellation of interests.

Corporate Control: Anglo-American Variations

The pattern of capitalist development found in Britain and the United States has been described as an Anglo-American pattern. While there are substantial differences between the two economies, their similarities are great enough for them to be considered as variations on a common pattern. Management control became a significant feature of the American economy in the 1930s and persisted as the dominant characteristic of the very largest enterprises until the 1950s. Although the dispersal of shareholdings remains greater in the United States than it is in Britain (compare Table 7 with Table 20), the growth of 'institutional' holdings, which began earlier and progressed more rapidly in Britain (compare Table 6 and Table 18), has meant that 'management control' has increasingly been replaced by control through constellations of interests in both countries. This form of control now seems to characterize all large British and American enterprises without dominant ownership interests. It is worth emphasizing once more that a constellation of interests must not be seen as a cohesive group that is sharply separated from other controlling groups. From the standpoint of any particular enterprise it may be possible to identify a controlling constellation; but most financial institutions will be members of a great many such controlling constellations, and so enterprises become elements in a complex network of interweaving shareholdings. The boundaries of the corporate constellations within such a network are loose and amorphous, and they overlap in complex ways. The members of the constellations alter their relative positions as they buy and sell shares in the stock market and, over time, the composition of the various constellations changes.

Although control through a constellation of interests is characteristic of most large enterprises in the United States and Britain, family control persists and is especially important among the smallest of the large enterprises. Foreign ownership is an important form of business in Britain. By contrast, Herman's study found only one foreign-controlled enterprise in the American top 200 of 1976. This varying significance of foreign ownership reflects the relative size of the two economies in an increasingly globalized world-economy. American enterprises are large enough to expand overseas on a scale that is impossible for their British counterparts.

Britain has, however, been an important global force. British colonial and, later, industrial expansion brought a number of areas of the world into peripheral locations within the expanding capitalist world-system. Canada, Australia, and New Zealand grew as countries of massive inward migration, whose indigenous populations were swamped, much as had happened with European migration to North America. Southern and East Africa and parts of South America, on the other hand, developed as minority-settler economies with substantial inward investment in mining and ranching. The forms of business that developed in most of these areas were shaped by the established forms of British and American enterprise, and local legislation established supportive legal frameworks that reflected British and American company law. In these areas, then, an Anglo-American pattern of capitalist development has firm roots.

British enterprise has been important in the economic development of the former colonial economies of Australia, Canada, and

New Zealand, and these economies now show high levels of both British and American ownership. Evidence from all three economies supports the claim that there has been a transition from personal to impersonal possession that has involved the supplementing of family ownership by control through a constellation of interests.

Academic and political debates over these issues in Canada have centred on Canada's position as a 'satellite' economy within the capitalist core. The Canadian economy developed as a dependent satellite on more powerful economic enterprises, and it has always shown a high level of foreign ownership. First British and later American enterprises have dominated Canadian trade and industry, and have influenced the activities of indigenous enterprises. A study of the 'top 100' Canadian enterprises[10] over the period from 1946 to 1976 shows that their Canadian-owned proportion declined from 68 per cent in 1946 to 56 per cent in 1966, and rose again to 61 per cent in 1976 (Carroll 1982: 97–8). According to Carroll, these figures show fluctuation rather than any long-term trend, and the basic feature of the post-war period has been the constantly high level of foreign ownership.

It is in this context that studies of ownership and control must be interpreted. Table 22 shows data collected by Porter in the first such study undertaken in Canada. The sixty-four large enterprises that he studied accounted for most of Canadian industrial output: in almost

Table 22. Strategic control in Australian and Canadian enterprises (1955 and 1960)

	Number of enterprises	
Mode of control	Australia (1955)	Canada (1960)
Private ownership	2	11
Other majority	6	16
Minority control	33	23
No dominant interest	32	3
Not known	0	11
Totals	73	64

Source: Wheelwright (1957) and Porter (1965: 589, Table 12).

[10] In fact the number of companies selected in each year varied between 103 and 116. For a related study of an earlier period see Piedalue (1976).

Table 23. Strategic control in large Canadian enterprises (1975)

Mode of control	Type of controller					Totals
	Personal	Corp.	Foreign	Mixed	None	
Majority control (80%)	10	0	61	0	–	71
Majority control (50–79%)	14	1	51	3	–	69
Minority control	24	0	18	1	–	43
Limited minority control	2	–	–	–	–	2
No dominant interest	–	–	–	–	20	20
Totals	50	1	130	4	20	205

Source: Calculated from Niosi (1978: 11–16, Table 11) and Niosi (1981).
Note: The cut-off point for minority control is 10 per cent, and limited minority control is based on holdings by directors of 5–9 per cent. The figures above are calculated from the raw data given by Niosi, and there seem to be certain discrepancies with the various summaries calculated by Niosi himself. The corporate holdings in the 'corporate' and 'mixed' categories are mainly by investment and holding companies. It is impossible to assess how many of these were, in fact, family holdings.

a half of these there was some form of majority control, only slightly fewer were subject to minority control, and relatively few of those on which there was information were without a dominant shareholder. Table 23 provides a more detailed breakdown for 205 large enterprises in 1975,[11] and the small proportion of enterprises without a dominant interest is confirmed by these more recent data (see Dhingra 1983; Antoniou and Rowley 1986). It is also clear that those enterprises where families or other personal shareholders had majority control must be distinguished from those where foreign interests were the majority shareholders. Dominant in the 'indigenous' family-controlled enterprises were the Molson, Eaton, Weston, Bronfman, Desmarais, Webster, and Irving families, while British and American enterprises were the principal foreign owners.

There has been much argument over whether those enterprises in which there were no dominant interests could be regarded as management-controlled. Niosi has observed that financial institutions have accumulated large shareholdings in these enterprises and that, for this reason, 'management control' may not be the most

[11] For a classification of control in forty-eight large French Canadian enterprises see Niosi (1981), table 3.1.

appropriate designation (1978: 83, 100, 168). Shareholdings in these enterprises are not dispersed among the mass of small shareholders, but are concentrated in constellations of interests. The eleven largest registered shareholders in Abitibi Paper, for example, held 34 per cent of its shares—making it a clear case of control through a constellation of interests (ibid.: 82).[12]

There is some evidence to suggest that the pattern of ownership and control in Canada has changed during the 1980s. In a situation of heightened international competition, great pressure has been placed on Canadian enterprises, and those most susceptible to takeover have been those controlled through constellations of interests. Many of these enterprises have been acquired by investment-holding companies run by new and dynamic entrepreneurial capitalists. These entrepreneurs have used their investment companies to build huge chains of corporate connections, tying numerous enterprises into massive corporate webs through intersecting minority holdings.

The situation in Australia is consistent with the idea that there are distinctively Anglo-American forms of ownership and control. In a study of the large Australian enterprises of 1955 that were not subject to foreign ownership (see Table 22), Wheelwright (1957) found the overwhelming majority to be either minority-controlled or to be without a dominant shareholding interest. A larger and more systematic investigation of the 299 largest manufacturers of 1963 found that foreign enterprises had majority control in 127 and minority control in fifteen.[13] Other enterprises had foreign minority controllers, though some of these involved joint control with Australian partners. It is clear that a major role in the Australian economy was played by foreign corporate interests, with or without the support of Australian enterprises (Wheelwright and Miskelly 1967).[14] Indigenous Australian enterprises tended to be controlled by personal owners with majority or minority holdings. In almost a quarter of the top 299 enterprises of 1963, families or individuals held 10

[12] See the evidence on this in Niosi (1981).

[13] A 20 per cent cut-off threshold was used in this study.

[14] These figures are based on recalculations from the original sources, because Wheelwright and Miskelly based their definition of 'owner control' on the total of all personal shareholdings, regardless of their size and regardless of what connections may or may not exist among these shareholders. The figures reported in this paragraph are based on calculations comparable with those used in the other studies discussion in this book.

per cent or more of the capital—and, as in the earlier study, most were cases of minority control.

Forty-six Australian enterprises in 1963 were without dominant ownership interests. While Wheelwright and Miskelly designated them as 'management' or 'unclassified' enterprises, they observed that the high degree of institutional share ownership indicated the need for 'a new category of control by financial institutions' (ibid.: 8; see also Wheelwright 1974: 131; Connell 1976). In fact, a closer examination of the original data confirms that these enterprises were controlled through constellations of interests. The holdings of their top twenty shareholders varied from 12.4 per cent in Broken Hill Proprietary to 47.1 per cent in Tom Piper. In most cases, the top twenty held between 20 and 40 per cent. What distinguishes these somewhat from the constellations found in Britain and America, however, is the large number of family and non-financial participants that they have.

Table 24. Strategic control in large Australian enterprises (1975)

Mode of control	Directors	Type of controller			None	Totals
		Australian corpns.	Foreign corpns.	Joint corporate		
Majority control	11	6	28	3	–	48
Minority (15%)	–	22	11	1	–	⎫
Minority (10%)	65	–	–	–	–	⎬ 99
No dominant interest	–	–	–	–	79	79
Totals	76	28	39	4	79	226

Source: Calculated from Lawriwsky (1984: Table 1.1 and Figure 5.3).

Though not directly comparable, data produced by Lawriwsky (see Table 24) confirms the conclusion that a high proportion of Australian enterprises are subject to family minority control. Lawriwsky did claim, however, that institutional holdings in enterprises without dominant interests are actually higher than in Britain (Lawriwsky 1984: 38). Almost three-quarters of enterprises with dispersed ownership had financial institutions with aggregate holdings of 20 per cent or more among their top twenty shareholders. In many of these enterprises, the largest shareholder was an institution with 5 per cent or more—generally Australian Mutual Provident, the largest Australian insurer (ibid.: 108–9; Crough 1980). Of the seventy-nine enterprises without a dominant shareholder, twenty-one had strong family participants in their controlling constellations: such families held between 4 per cent and 9 per cent of the capital and were represented on the board.[15] Family control by the leading dynasties remained important, though it was being progressively supplemented by 'institutional' and foreign ownership (Encel 1970: 330–9, 376 ff.).

Fogelberg's (1980) study of share ownership in New Zealand looked only at the 43 largest enterprises of 1962 and 1974, but it confirms the general picture found for the Anglo-American economies. Between these two years the number of shareholders increased markedly, but there was also a concentration of shareholdings and of voting-power in the hands of the largest shareholders. Table 25 shows the overall distribution of shareholdings in these enterprises, bringing out clearly the declining significance of personal shareholdings and an increase in insurance-company investment.

In terms of ownership and control these shifts in shareholding resulted in a decline in the number of enterprises that were

Table 25. Registered shareholdings in the top 43 New Zealand enterprises (1962 and 1974)

	Percentage of shares held	
	1962	1974
Persons	39	24
Insurance companies	12	27
Investment companies	6	6
Trustee companies	7	9
Nominees	3	4
Other companies	26	2
Government	6	2
Totals	99	100

Source: Fogelberg (1980: Table 2 on 57).
Note: Totals do not add to 100 because of rounding.

[15] There were also family shareholders, with smaller holdings or no board representation, in the membership of the controlling constellations.

Table 26. Ownership and control in the top 43 New Zealand enterprises (1962 and 1974)

	Type of controller							
	Family		Corporate		Mixed		Total	
	1962	1974	1962	1974	1962	1974	1962	1974
Majority	4	2	3	2	1	1	8	5
Exclusive minority	7	2	2	5	0	0	4	7
Shared minority	4	4	0	0	0	3	4	7
Limited minority	2	0	0	0	0	0	2	0
Constellation of interests	–	–	–	–	20	24	20	24
Totals	17	8	5	7	21	28	43	43

Source: Recalculated from original data in Fogelberg (1980).

majority- or minority-controlled by families, and a corresponding increase in the number whose shares were largely held by financial institutions (see Table 26). It seems reasonable to interpret the latter, from the evidence available, as being controlled through constellations of interests rather than as management-controlled. In no case did the largest shareholder have more than 5 per cent, but in the nine analysed in detail by Fogelberg (1978), the twenty largest shareholders consistently held between 15 and 40 per cent of the shares. Most of the large holders were insurance companies, the number of these in each controlling constellation ranging from six to ten.[16] By 1981, Chandler (1982: 7) shows, more family enterprises had either disappeared through takeover or had undergone a transition to control through a constellation of interests. Indeed, three-quarters of the surviving large enterprises of 1974 were controlled through constellations of interests by 1981. Drawing on evidence from a much larger selection of 204 large enterprises, Chandler found one-third to be

---

[16] The enterprises with dispersed capital in 1962 seemed closer in type to those found in Britain and the United States during the 1920s and 1930s, when the principal participants were families.

controlled by families, one-third controlled by other corporations, and one-third controlled through constellations of interests.[17]

South Africa has been studied in some detail and shows an interesting variation on the Anglo-American pattern. The country was an area of more limited British and American settlement, and it developed in its early years through extensive inward investment in mining and ranching. The practices of investment-holding company finance proved remarkably successful in allowing the expansion of gold and diamond mining and the later expansion of mining enterprises into other industries. Investment-holding companies, unlike investment trusts, took large share participations in enterprises that they sought to control or, at least, to participate in their control in an active and deliberate way. Investment-holding companies and syndicates of these companies frequently held substantial minority holdings, and often buttressed control by families or financial interests. The early strength of the investment-holding companies meant that there was a weaker drive towards impersonal possession and a corresponding long-lasting survival of entrepreneurial forms of capital. These investment-holding companies were predominantly British-based, and Afrikaner opposition to British colonial power led to the formation of a number of state agencies charged with supporting Afrikaner business enterprises and aiding their rivalry of established British-controlled enterprises. As a result, extensive webs of corporate interests and of state participation became important features of the South African economy. Data produced by Savage (1978 and 1985) shows the consequences of this for patterns of ownership and control (see Table 27).

Six of the top 100 enterprises in 1977 were majority-controlled by state agencies, and in five more control was shared by the state and private interests. When these same 100 enterprises are analysed in terms of 'ultimate control', however, the continuing significance of webs of cross-cutting investments becomes apparent. Many of the majority-controlled and minority-controlled enterprises were links in chains of control that tied them to one another and to investment-holding companies. This was the case, Savage suggests, for at least 27 of the top 100 of 1977. The three biggest corporate webs were the Oppenheimer group, the Sanlam group, and the SA Mutual group. Intercorporate holdings, then, showed a different pattern from that found in Britain and the United States in the same period.

---

[17] Like Fogelberg, Chandler describes the latter as 'management-controlled'.

Table 27. Immediate control in the top 100
South African enterprises (1977 and 1984)

Mode of control	1977	1985
Exclusive majority	52	61
Shared minority	10	8
Exclusive minority	27	22
Shared minority	8	9
No dominant interest	3	0
Totals	100	100

Source: Calculated from the original data lists in
Savage (1977 and 1985).
Note: These figures differ from Savage's own tabula-
tions as I have classified enterprises on the same basis
as in Table 15.

Corresponding to this, the number of enterprises that were controlled through constellations of interests was very small: just three
enterprises in 1977, and none in 1984.[18]

Corporate webs have been found in some other Anglo-American
economies. In Britain, for example, they were an important feature
of the transport and electrical sectors in the inter-war years (Scott
1993), and I have shown their growing importance in Canada. Only
in South Africa, however, have they been at all pervasive or enduring,
reflecting the role of the state and of the colonial mining houses.
Savage suggests that this has prevented the kind of fragmentation of
shareholdings that has occurred in the other Anglo-American
economies. He suggested in his initial paper that the growth of insurance-company investment might be expected to increase the number of enterprises that were controlled through constellations of
interests; but the evidence for 1984 does not support this view.
Insurance-company investment has taken place, to a considerable
extent, *within* the corporate webs; and while the webs have loosened
somewhat, they have not fragmented into constellations of interests.

There was much change in the South African economy between
1977 and 1984: the number of state-controlled enterprises declined

[18] Savage defines those without dominant interests as 'management-controlled',
though he shows that they arise from the growth of institutional holdings. He classifies one 1984 enterprise as management-controlled, though his own listing shows
it to be minority-controlled at the 10-per-cent threshold.

because of privatization, the number of foreign-controlled enterprises also declined, and the number of enterprises connected into corporate webs fell from twenty-seven to nineteen. The biggest change, however, was an increase in the number that were majority-controlled by other large South African enterprises. The early 1980s, it would appear, were a phase of economic concentration and corporate restructuring in which foreign, state, and web control was being replaced by the expanding interests of the large indigenous industrial enterprises. Savage may yet be correct in anticipating that, in due course, these enterprises will exhibit the same kind of dispersed patterns of control that are found in the other Anglo-American economies.

The United States and Britain, I have argued, exemplify an Anglo-American pattern, in which the development from personal to impersonal possession has been characterized by the emergence of large enterprises controlled through constellations of interests. It would appear that Australia, Canada, New Zealand, and South Africa followed the Anglo-American pattern of development towards impersonal possession as a result of the growth of institutional holdings. This common trend was weakened by the fact that there was a high level of external ownership in all the economies except the United States, and in South Africa it was further weakened by the powerful corporate webs. The major foreign owners in these economies were, of course, Britain and the United States, with the latter being an important foreign shareholder in Britain itself. Foreign subsidiaries in the other Anglo-American economies are elements in British and, particularly, in American multinational enterprises that are themselves increasingly subject to ultimate control through a constellation of interests. In Canada, however, there is evidence that control through a constellation of interests has been supplemented by the kind of entrepreneur-led corporate webs that have long played an important role in South Africa.

5

STRUCTURES OF FINANCE CAPITAL

THE arguments of the managerialist theory of the business enterprise were my point of departure in the previous chapter, and I
showed that it is a theory which fails to provide an accurate account
of the relationship between ownership and control in the Anglo-
American economies. Managerialism fails, in particular, to appreciate the significance of the growth of financial shareholdings that
have resulted in what I have called 'control through a constellation
of interests'. In this chapter, I consider a range of issues that surround the Marxist concept of finance capital and its view of contemporary economic relations in the Anglo-American economies.
'Finance capital'—the organizational fusion of 'banking capital' and
'industrial capital'—was seen by Hilferding (1910) as centring on the
formation of alliances and coalitions among enterprises in different
economic sectors and the building of extensive networks of intercorporate linkages. A small inner circle of financiers, he held,
ensures a degree of co-ordination and intercorporate unity through
the directorships that they hold in the institutions that determine the
availability of capital.

Similar views about an 'inner circle' had appeared in liberal com-
mentary on the 'Money Trust' in the United States and in radical cri-
tiques of the 'City' in Britain. The common theme in these
arguments was the claim that banks and other enterprises involved
in the granting of credit have interests that are, in important respects,
opposed to those of manufacturing enterprises. The two types of
enterprise are seen as forced into antagonistic relations, in which
banks are able to assert their dominance by coercing manufacturers

to act under conditions that serve financial rather than productive interests.

A number of confusions run through these debates. Although Hilferding clearly stated that 'finance capital' was to be seen as a fusion of banking and industrial capital, his emphasis on the organizational centrality of banks has led many subsequent commentators to interpret him as proposing a theory of bank control. While there is some textual support for this interpretation, it is clear that Hilferding was positing a more general account, and that the model of bank control was simply one variant of this. This confusion is linked to a persistent confusion of 'finance capital' with the 'financial sector'. The financial sector comprises all those enterprises that operate in the monetary sphere, and it is distinguished from the 'non-financial' sector of commercial, service, and manufacturing enterprises. 'Finance', on the other hand, refers to the monetary resources of an enterprise and involves the idea of a specific relationship between the monetary (financial) sphere and the activities of enterprises. It is not correct, then, to see Hilferding as positing a contrast or separation between 'financial capital' and 'industrial capital', between 'banks' and 'industry'. For Hilferding, manufacturers that adopted joint stock organization were compelled to enter into the monetary sphere themselves. Through their involvement in the stock exchange, and their need to deal in stocks and currency, they become 'financial' as well as 'industrial' enterprises (see also Sweezy 1971: 31; De Vroey 1975a: 8–9). At the same time banks, insurance companies, and other enterprises involved primarily in monetary processes come into closer contact with manufacturers and traders. Large enterprises, whatever their primary area of economic activity, are increasingly likely to be involved in both 'financial' and 'non-financial' activities, and they are likely to enter into various forms of organizational alignment and co-operation. It is this fusion of the financial and the industrial that Hilferding described as the system of 'finance capital'.

This does not, of course, resolve the empirical question of whether the model of finance capital—or the derived model of bank control—is at all accurate as a description of contemporary capitalism. To answer this question it is necessary to investigate the organization of the 'financial' sectors of the Anglo-American economies and to explore their relations to other sectors. This involves considering whether the institutional shareholdings that have brought about a closer alignment of financial and 'non-financial' enterprises has also given the institutions an enhanced role in strategic control. Do banks and other 'financials' become involved in corporate decision-making and impose their interests on other enterprises?

The Money Trust and Bank Control in the United States

For most of the nineteenth century, the American economy comprised a large number of small manufacturing and retail enterprises operating in local and regional markets. These enterprises depended on local and personal capital, and they had recourse to banks only for day-to-day payment and lending facilities. Indeed, the banking system itself was highly localized in its operations and in its ownership and control. It was the development of the railway system in the middle of the century that began the transformation of the American financial system, the great capital needs of railway finance requiring the bigger New York banks to play a more active role. Through promoting and floating railways these banks developed new skills of corporate finance, which they continued to employ in the expansion of the railway system. As a result, wealthy and powerful New York bankers were well-placed to play a leading role in the rapid industrialization of the American economy in the 1890s. These investment bankers applied the same techniques of business finance to the new industrials as they had to the railways, and they brought into being new, giant enterprises in which were merged their smaller predecessors. These enterprises were able to operate on a national scale and they began to enter international markets.

The ability of the investment bankers to mobilize the savings of large numbers of individuals and to make them available to industry was the basis of their power to intervene in the formation, merger, and expansion of enterprises and to engineer the formation of 'trusts' and 'cartels' in important markets. Though the banks played a critical role in the emergence of highly concentrated markets, a system of 'bank control' was not established. It was not, in general, possible for a single bank to raise all the capital that was required by a large enterprise, and banks had to form themselves into loose underwriting syndicates for the issue and sale of shares. Each bank would participate in a number of syndicates and so would be involved in financing a number of different enterprises. The biggest of the banks, however, could act as lead banks in their syndicates, and

were in a position to offer 'advice' to the directors of the new enterprises and even to place their representatives on their boards
(Carosso 1970: ch. 3; Sweezy 1940; 1941).

This developing system of bank power was the source of much
concern in liberal public opinion. For many commentators, the
emerging 'Money Trust' or 'financial oligarchy' was seen as likely to
use its immense power to undermine the competitive nature of the
market economy (Veblen 1904; Pratt 1905). The financial writer John
Moody countered such criticisms with an apologia for contemporary
business practices, arguing that the trusts created by Morgan,
Rockefeller, Vanderbilt, and Harriman had, in fact, been responsible
for America's economic success (Moody 1904; see also Bunting 1986:
5–14). Populist distrust of the power of the 'Money Kings', the
'Masters of Capital', and the 'Captains of Industry' nevertheless grew,
and by 1910 this had crystallized into a broad political debate about
the powers and responsibilities of the 'Money Trust'. A
Congressional committee of investigation—the Pujo Committee—
was set up in 1912 (Bunting 1976: 7–8; Andrews 1982; Roe 1994), and
its report made the first published reference to the phenomenon of
the 'interlocking directorate' in the United States (Pujo Report 1913).

An interlocking directorship, it will be recalled, occurs whenever
one person is a member of two or more boards, and the 'interlocking directorate' is the whole web of corporate connections that is
built up from these interlocking directorships.[1] Interlocks tie enterprises together and thereby increase the overall level of concentration in an economy, and it is this concentrating effect of interlocks
that has led their critics to see them as being anti-competitive. Louis
Brandeis, a lawyer and anti-trust campaigner, popularized the Pujo
Committee's findings in a much-quoted claim that 'The practice of
interlocking directorates is the root of many evils. It offends laws
human and divine' (1914: 35). Large enterprises, he argued, were
connected through a chain of interlocks that created a 'vicious circle
of control' in which 'each controlled corporation is entwined with
many others' (Brandeis 1914: 38). Brandeis was critical of the
bankers' use of 'other people's money' to enhance the economic
power of large enterprises and to pursue anti-competitive policies.

---

[1] Strictly speaking, a 'directorate' is a board of directors and, by extension, the
whole body of directors in an economy. In many American studies, however, the
word has been used interchangeably with 'directorship', which refers to the occupancy of the role of director. In this book I have tried to use 'directorate' and 'directorship' in their proper and distinct senses.

These and similar attacks were instrumental in securing legislation and regulation aimed at maintaining competition. Insurance companies had been limited, since 1906, from owning any company shares, and the Pujo Committee report led to increased restrictions on banking and, later, on the ability of mutual funds to accumulate controlling blocks of shares. Following the First World War public opinion seemed less critical of banking power, and, in restating his defence of the Money Trust, Moody argued that the war had effectively ended the unpopularity of big business (Moody 1919). Only in the 1930s, in the wake of the Great Crash, did critical views of business once more become prominent in government circles. Brandeis's book on the Pujo investigations was reissued in 1933, at the same time that Berle and Means (1932) were extending the scope of the debate to a concern with the inner workings of the large corporation. Brandeis and Means were, in fact, closely associated with one another in official work. Means's work for the *National Resources Committee* built important links between official and academic work by drawing on specially commissioned research reports by Paul Sweezy (1939) on the economic significance of financial groups (Means *et al.* 1939). At about the same time, the *Temporary National Economic Committee* (Goldsmith and Parmelee 1940) had been set up at the instigation of 'New Deal' liberals who shared Brandeis's concern about the responsibility of big business for the economic problems of the 1930s. The debate over ownership and control reviewed in Chapter 3 was the outcome of this long series of political debates.

From Brandeis's strictures on the 'vicious circle' of control, to the research undertaken by Means and by Sweezy, interlocking directorships have been seen as key indicators of economic power. Interlocks were built up in the latter half of the nineteenth century among banking, insurance, and railway enterprises as the New York bankers sought to monopolize corporate finance and emerging railway systems sought to monitor their rivals and their suppliers. From these strategic alliances there resulted an extensive community of financial interests, a network of intercorporate connections (Bunting 1983). By the 1880s, enterprises in coal mining and telegraphs were tightly linked together into this community of interest, and in the following decade the expanding manufacturers had become part of it (Roy 1983*a* and *b*; Kotz 1978).[2] Wall Street banks and stockbrokers had become central to the financing of big business, becoming

---

[2] This is discussed further in Scott and Griff (1984: ch. 5).

multiple directors on a large scale, and by the beginning of the twentieth century, as shown in Table 28, they had become the dominant players in the intercorporate network (Roy 1983b; Mizruchi 1982; 1983a).

Table 28. The distribution of directorships in the top 167 US enterprises (1899–1974)

No. of directorships per person	1899	1905	1912	1919	1935	1964	1969	1974
1	1530	1632	1786	1915	2040	2437	2527	2402
2–5	244	292	297	333	306	371	403	371
6 or more	16	20	27	14	3	4	2	0
Totals	1790	1944	2110	2262	2349	2812	2932	2773

Source: Bunting (1976: part 1, Table 3; part 2, Table 3). See also Dooley (1969: 315), Bunting and Barbour (1971: 324) and Herman (1981: 199).

The total number of directors in the top 167 enterprises increased continuously from 1899 to 1969, as shown in Table 28. Those with two or more directorships, however, achieved their greatest significance between 1905 and 1919, when they comprised between 15 and 16 per cent of the overall directorate. A substantial number of these multiple directors held six or more directorships: twenty-seven directors held this number of directorships in 1912, but by 1935 the figure had fallen to three.

The argument that a 'Money Trust' existed in the period between the 1890s and the First World War seems, therefore, to be confirmed. Wall Street bankers had become the central agents in an extensive intercorporate network, many holding six or more directorships. The Pujo Committee reported that six banks and their dependent trust companies made up the heart of the corporate system: the private banks of Morgan, Kuhn Loeb, Lee Higginson, and Kidder Peabody, and two commercial banks (First National Bank and National City Bank).[3] Morgan and the two commercial banks, in which Morgan had shareholdings, were described as the 'inner

---

[3] Commercial banks are those involved in 'retail' deposit banking through national 'high-street' branch systems. In Britain they are normally described as 'clearing banks'.

group' to which the others were affiliated, and all six banks were surrounded by their numerous associates and clients (Pujo Report 1913: ii, 1102–3). For many contemporary commentators, Morgan interests were seen as having overwhelming power in the system of big business.

By 1914 commercial banks were already challenging private bankers as the principal source of investment banking capital, and this opening-up of the capital market was reflected in a loosening of the interlock network. Investment banking remained a powerful force in the American economy throughout the 1920s, however, and the big banks played an active part in the formation of the many general investment and utility-holding companies[4] that took stakes in industrial and commercial enterprises. It was through the minority shareholdings built up by these investment and holding companies that the 'legal device' of pyramiding became such a prominent feature of the corporate scene as to appear to Berle and Means as a distinct form of control. The activities of the investment funds were also at the heart of the stock market boom that culminated in the 'Great Crash' of 1929 (Carosso 1970; Galbraith 1954). While the crash finally broke the power of the investment bankers, it merely confirmed a decline that had deeper causes. The big industrial enterprises had grown and established themselves in their markets, and their ability to secure internal resources for expansion lessened their dependence on the investment bankers. The growth of 'institutional' investment, primarily by insurance companies, also weakened the power of the investment bankers by encouraging the private placement of corporate shares with financial intermediaries (Gordon 1945: 214–16; Sweezy 1941: 190–3; 1942: 267). Although insurance companies were prevented from taking direct ownership of company shares until the early 1950s, their influence in the capital markets grew. In 1951 they were allowed to invest a maximum of 2 per cent in their own name, but this was increased gradually to 5 per cent, and insurance investment was completely deregulated in 1984 (Roe 1994: ch. 6).

These trends seem to confirm one strand in the theory of finance capital—that there has been a growing fusion of the financial and industrial sectors—but the theory also holds that intercorporate networks are structured into distinct 'financial empires'. These empires are seen as groups of enterprises that are subject to a degree of

---

[4] The 'utility' sector refers to electricity, water, and gas companies.

central co-ordination and that enter into competitive relations with other groups (Pastré 1979).[5] While there is some evidence of such groups in the United States, there appears to be a very high level of overlap among them. Mizruchi (1982), for example, found evidence that a number of powerful, bank-centred financial groups existed in the period from the 1890s to 1919. These groups had numerous commercial relations with one another as members of overlapping syndicates and they were tied together through the network of inter-locking directorships. The directors of the Morgan bank, for example, had such extensive connections in this network that they were central to its cohesion and acted as the *de facto* leaders of the corporate world.

Sweezy's study for the *National Resources Committee* discovered eight 'interest groups' in the top 200 enterprises of 1935. Most of these groups were family-based, the most prominent being the Morgan, Rockefeller, and Mellon groups, and each group was tied together through majority and minority holdings, bank credit, and interlocks (Sweezy 1939: 168; Poland 1939; Means *et al.* 1939).[6] Sweezy also found a considerable overlap of membership among them. A re-examination by Mizruchi (1982) of this 1935 data showed clearly that there were not eight distinct and competing 'empires' but a linked network of more loosely structured groups. The groups were not as strong and cohesive as those of the earlier part of the century, and the power of the Morgan bank to hold the system together had declined from its high point prior to the First World War. Regionalism had also become a marked feature of the intercorporate network, due partly to the sheer territorial scale of the United States and partly to legal restrictions on banks operating in more than one state. As a result, the groups often had a regional base.[7]

[5] These groups are distinct from the purely legal conception of a group of companies, in which restrictive legal criteria are used for defining group membership. In the legal sense, a 'group' of companies is an integrated enterprise whose constituent companies are linked through tight ownership relations as parents, subsidiaries, and associates. The kind of group depicted in the model of finance capital is a looser cluster of otherwise autonomous enterprises. These issues are explored in Blumberg (1993), Hadden (1993), and Teubner (1993).

[6] See also Anderson *et al.* (1941: 25) and Goldsmith and Parmelee (1940: 129–30). The evidence produced by Sweezy was similar to the more speculative suggestions of Rochester (1936: chs. 2–5).

[7] A general review of various attempts to identify interest groups and a comparison of their allocation of enterprises to groups can be found in Fennema (1982: 26–9). Herman (1981: 217 ff.) discusses the concept of interest group, and Allen (1978*a*) discusses various methods for identifying groups.

By the 1960s, the power of the investment banks had declined considerably. The proportion of multiple directors with four or five directorships declined after 1935 and the solid core of multiple directors has been those with two or three top directorships. Directors have, however, tended to accumulate additional directorships outside the very top ranks of the corporate system, giving a hierarchical character to interlocking directorships (Bunting and Barbour 1971; Dooley 1969).[8] The interest groups identified by Villarejo were loose communities of interest rather than financial empires (1961b: 60). This loosening of the groups is apparent in Dooley's suggestion that the top 250 enterprises of 1965 were formed into fifteen groups, each being smaller and less cohesive than the groups of the earlier period. The eight groups that had been identified by Sweezy thirty years earlier could still be identified, but they were mere shadows of their former existence. Especially striking was the regional character of group formation (Sweezy 1969: 320–1).[9] A study by Allen (1978a), using data for 1970, showed a similar picture: the groups identified in 1970 were smaller and less cohesive than those of 1935, they were regional in character, and they were likely to be based on interlocks alone rather than on capital and commercial relations together with interlocks. Similarly, Sonquist et al. (1976) discovered thirty-two regional groups ranging in size from three to fifteen. They did, however, find that banks held a central position in over half of the groups.

The American intercorporate network, then, has become less dense and cohesive since the First World War, change becoming especially rapid after the inter-war years. At the height of the Money Trust interlocking directorships had been particularly intense, with enterprises often being linked through two or three common directors. In the post-war period, each link had become less intense and enterprises were linked to one another mainly through single common directors. On this basis a smaller proportion of multiple directors with fewer directorships could spread their influence over a larger number of enterprises. The 'endless chain' of interlocks that

---

[8] The two sources cited disagree as to whether the proportion of multiple directors declined very slightly or remained constant over the period 1935–65. This disagreement is partly due to the use of different data selection criteria. Table 29, which extends the trend to 1974, shows clearly that the period since 1935 can be characterized by a long-term constancy in the proportion of multiple directors, particular years showing only minor fluctuations around this constant figure.

[9] The fact that the groups were loose and overlapping was also recognized by most Marxist commentators: see Menshikov (1969: 216–21, 229) and Chevalier (1970: 123 ff.).

had been identified by Brandeis had grown to incorporate more and more enterprises into an extensive national network (Dooley 1969: 315, table 2; Allen 1974: 404; Bunting and Barbour 1971: 330–4; Bunting 1986: 119).[10] The groups that could be identified within it were loose, overlapping regional clusters, not sharply divided financial empires. New York and the Wall Street financials continued to play the dominant part in this network, the system being structured into 'a giant national wheel of interlocking directorates with the New York hub dominating the many spokes that spread out from and back to it' (Warner and Unwalla 1967: 146).

Table 29. The distribution of interlocks in the top 250 US enterprises (1975)

No. of interlocks per enterprise	Number of enterprises		
	200 non-financials	50 financials	top 250
0	15	1	16
1–4	54	7	61
5–9	62	13	75
10–14	44	12	56
15 or more	25	17	42
Totals	200	50	250

Source: Calculated from Herman (1981: 201, Table 6.5).

The extent of this intercorporate network is clear from Table 29, which shows the number of interlocks that were carried by each of the top 250 enterprises in 1975. All but sixteen enterprises were interlocked within the top 250 and, while many had more than fifteen interlocks each, most had fewer than ten. Financials were considerably more likely to be interlocked—and to be interlocked at a high level—than were the non-financials, and large numbers of interlocks ran between the two sectors. Research on a similar data set for 1976 showed the network of interlocking directorships to have a density of 0.034 (Bearden and Mintz 1984).[11]

[10] See also Baran and Sweezy (1966: 31), Fennema and Schijf (1978: 11–12), Smith (1970: 48–9), Smith and Desfosses (1972: 66), Patman Report (1967: 965), and Antitrust Committee (1965).

[11] The density of a network of interlocking directorships is the ratio of the

The most thorough and influential account of this network has been produced by the MACNET group of researchers.[12] Reflecting on the growing number of connections between financial and industrial enterprises, the discovery of loose regional groups, and the fact that banks invariably appear at the centre of such groups, these researchers constructed a powerful and persuasive model of the American intercorporate network. They hold that there is an overall national network of interlocks that is extensive but loosely connected, and that this contains denser regional groups that are built from intercorporate shareholdings, indebtedness, and 'primary' (executive officer) interlocks (Bearden et al. 1975: 50; Mariolis 1975: 433–5). The regional groups are loose, bank-centred clusters of small and medium-sized enterprises that are tied into an extensive national network through the leading banks (Mintz and Schwartz 1981a and b; 1983; Bearden and Mintz 1985).[13] This view is confirmed by a separate study of interweaving shareholdings among the 91 leading participants in the controlling constellations of the largest American enterprises of 1980. This network of shareholdings showed there to be a division between the New York institutions that adopted nationwide investment strategies, and those institutions with

number of actually existing interlocks to the maximum possible number of interlocks that can exist in the network. It is, therefore, a measure of the completeness of the connections. The measure of density used here varies between 0 and 1, a density of 0.034 indicating that 3.4 per cent of all possible interlocks actually occur. Density values should be compared only for networks of roughly similar size and character, as the value varies with the size of the network. These technical issues are discussed in Scott (1992: ch. 4) and Scott and Griff (1984: ch. 1).

[12] The MACNET group developed from early work by Michael Schwartz and his students and colleagues at Stony Brook, though members of the group are now to be found in many universities and colleges. The group is unified by its original orientation towards a massive data set, described in Mariolis (1975), and common procedures of analysis. Its most active leaders include Schwartz, Mintz, and Mizruchi, and the group has close links with the work of Bunting. The group is an offshoot of the productive network of 'structural analysts' trained by Harrison White at Harvard, the larger network including Levine and Berkowitz in the field of interlocks. The origins of the group at Harvard are described in Mullins (1973), and its shared methodology is set out in Berkowitz (1982) and in Wellman and Berkowitz (1988).

[13] Palmer (1983a and b) raises serious doubts about the strong variants of the interest-group theory proposed by writers such as Kotz (1978) and Knowles (1973). Levine (1978) criticizes Mariolis (1975) and attempts to reassert a strong case for bank control. See also the reply in Mariolis (1978). The overall research strategy of the MACNET group has been criticized in Andrews (1982). On regional structuring see Galaskiewicz and Wasserman (1981) and Ratcliff (1980).

regional bases. While there was no evidence for sharply defined regional groups in the network of shareholdings, the research does support the contention that regionalism is an important characteristic of intercorporate relations in the United States (Scott 1986: 150). The MACNET researchers highlight the interdependence of national and regional foci, arguing that

the integration of New York, Boston, Philadelphia and California centers of business into a national and even international network of corporations has occurred simultaneously with the maintenance and further development of interest groups which continue to organize and coordinate intercorporate cooperation and control. (Bearden *et al.* 1975: 50)

A striking feature to emerge from all of the research reviewed is the existence of bank centrality in the American intercorporate network. The twenty enterprises with the largest number of interlocks in 1969 included eight banks and three insurance companies. Three banks (Morgan Guaranty, First National City Bank, and Chase Manhattan) had more interlocks than any other enterprises. It is noteworthy that the successor banks to Morgan and the two commercial banks that had been highlighted by the Pujo investigators as the 'inner group' at the turn of the century were among the three most interlocked banks in the 1970s, while Chase Manhattan is widely regarded as a surviving member of the Rockefeller interests. Although large industrials showed year-to-year variations in the level of their interlocking, four-fifths of the heavily interlocked banks in 1962 held a similar position in the network of 1969. The MACNET researchers concluded that 'banks are the foundation of intercorporate networks. While other firms may rise into momentary prominence and a few remain there for some years, the major commercial banks persist from year to year' (ibid.: 59).

The MACNET model of the contemporary intercorporate network depicts the main New York commercial banks as the peaks of the national network, each being the hub of numerous connections to major insurance companies and large industrials (such as AT&T and United States Steel). Regional banks in Chicago, Pennsylvania, Boston, California, and a few other areas are linked to the national hubs through insurance companies and through big regional industrials, and, at the same time, these regional banks are hubs for connections to the smaller financial and non-financial enterprises of their own region. Inter-bank conflict at the national level, and conflicts between New York and the regions, are contained within a wider network of intercorporate unity.

The City and Corporate Power in Britain

The early industrial development of Britain was largely undertaken by small entrepreneurial firms in the North and the Midlands (Berg 1994). These firms financed their investments from family capital, and were able to raise additional capital from the small 'country banks' in their regions. As a rule, the founding family provided capital for investment and the local banks supplied short-term working capital (Kennedy 1987; Mathias 1969; Payne 1967, 1974; Hobsbawm 1968; Kindleberger 1984: 92–4). Country banks were locally owned and had only one or two offices, though some were formed into moderately sized regional chains. Their links with the London banks were, in general, limited to commercial banking transactions and correspondent business.

The City of London financials themselves had a long history and had a long association with agrarian and mercantile capitalism, though they concentrated on government loans and foreign investment rather than long-term industrial finance. Merchants, merchant banks, and discount houses were central to the financing of international trade, and the clearing banks and private banks acted as the providers of funds to the active dealers in the money market. There was, as a result, a sharp separation of City financiers from provincial manufacturers (Scott 1982b; Rubinstein 1976). As the banking system grew in the later part of the nineteenth century the majority of the country banks were incorporated into national chains headed by the large City banks. As a result, they were forced to adapt to City practices and all but withdrew from industrial finance. While some regional joint stock banks remained separate from the City and played a limited role in financing manufacturers in their region, the most noticeable feature of the British economy at the turn of the century was the stark separation that existed between City capital and provincial capital (Scott and Griff 1984: ch. 6; Ingham 1984; 1982).

The City banks were not, however, completely isolated from other enterprises. Through capital relations and interlocks they were connected with enterprises involved in all aspects of credit and commerce, and most especially with those in insurance, railways, and shipping. While shipping and insurance had been long-standing areas of City involvement, the flotation of canal companies and, later, of railway companies that depended on stock-exchange finance brought the City enterprises into the new and lucrative business of capital mobilization. The role played by the British banks in capital mobilization differed, however, from that of their American counterparts.

In the United States railway finance had been led by bankers, and the development of the railways produced a banking system that was able to respond proactively to the turn-of-the-century industrial mergers and to incorporate the new giant enterprises into their existing network of connections. In Britain, on the other hand, railway finance had much more of a regional base, and few of the private City banks took a leading role in company promotion and finance. Some smaller banks did become actively involved with manufacturing industry in the American way, but their role was limited by the scale of their funds (Hannah 1980: 55). The period before the First World War in Britain did not, therefore, see the emergence of a Money Trust of the kind found in the United States. The British economy was, however, dominated by City of London enterprises concerned with banking, insurance, commerce, and transport.

Commentators before the First World War showed little interest in discussing the implications of this separation of 'City' and industry. Almost unique among his contemporaries was Hobson, who drew explicitly on the American debates and suggested that the industrial amalgamations of the turn of the century in Britain had been created by a 'financial class' of promoters, bankers, and brokers who operated as intermediaries between the investors and those who actually ran the enterprises (1906: 242). Hobson recognized, however, that the big banks were not the leading agents in this process, and that financiers had not generally become involved in the management of industrial enterprises.[14]

The pattern of interlocking directorships at the time that Hobson was writing can be seen in Table 30, which shows that 197 of the top 250 enterprises of 1904 were interlocked with one another. This high level of interlocking is due to the extremely large number of railway companies that appeared in the top 250 at the time, as railways were

---

[14] Hobson (1906: 265 ff.) presented an analysis of interlocks between City financiers and South African mining enterprises, the first analysis of interlocks to be carried out in Britain. The financing of gold and diamond mines in Imperial territories was not, however, incompatible with the City's traditional role. The 1906 edition of Hobson's book, which included this analysis, was seen by him as the definitive statement of his position. The 1926 edition is identical, except for the addition of a supplementary chapter.

Table 30. The distribution of directorships in the top 250 British enterprises (1904–1988)

No. of directorships per person	1904	1938	1976	1988
1	1901	1844	2400	not known
2	234	218	195	199
3–5	68	102	85	89
6 or more	1	9	2	2
Totals	2204	2173	2682	–
Inclusiveness	197	201	189	203
Density	0.013	0.019	0.017	0.017

Source: Scott and Griff (1984: Table 2.7).
Note: 'Inclusiveness' is simply the number of companies with interlocks. 'Density' is the ratio of the actual to the possible number of interlocks. The enterprises analysed are those discussed in Table 16 and a similar data-set for 1988.

especially well-connected to the City of London or to regional enterprises. The proportion of directors who held two or more directorships was somewhat lower than it was in the United States (see Table 32), and the proportion with six or more was considerably lower: just one British director held this many directorships in the top 250. Table 31 shows that only a quarter of interlocked enterprises at this time had six or more connections within the top 250. The ten enterprises with the largest number of interlocks comprised two banks, two insurers, four railways, and just two industrials (a mine and a steel producer). The enterprise with the largest number of interlocks, an insurance company, had just eighteen. In the United States, by contrast, sixteen of the top 167 enterprises of 1905 had more than fifty interlocks each (Bunting 1976). It is clear, therefore, that the level of interlocking in Britain before the First World War was considerably lower than it was in the United States, that the banks were far less prominent in the intercorporate network, and that the network included fewer industrial enterprises (Scott and Griff 1984).

This changed during the inter-war years. While the American intercorporate network was becoming less dense and less dominated by the banks, the British network was moving in the opposite direction. The two economies were converging on a common

Table 31. The distribution of interlocks in the top 250 British enterprises (1904–1988)

No. of interlocks per person	1904	1938	1976	1988
0	53	49	61	47
1–5	148	116	112	129
6–10	39	63	54	54
11 or more	10	22	23	20
Totals	250	250	250	250

Source: Scott and Griff (1984: Table 6.3).
Note: As Table 32.

pattern. The City was faced by declining opportunities for profitable foreign investment and so was forced to look more closely at domestic outlets for its funds. These funds were, at the same time, being swollen by the growth of life insurance. Of particular importance in bringing about a realignment of the City with the provinces was its response to the economic problems of the 1920s and 1930s. The recession pushed many large enterprises to the point of bankruptcy, and the clearing banks were forced to become involved in their affairs. Although they were the providers only of short-term overdrafts, they had to become much more actively involved in the long-term future of enterprises in difficulties. In normal circumstances, a bank might have been able to withstand the bankruptcy of one of its customers, but the sheer scale of industrial collapse meant that each bank was faced with the possible bankruptcy of many of its largest customers (Pollard 1962; Hannah 1976c: chs. 3 and 5; Payne 1978; W. Thomas 1978; Clarke 1967). The banks had to become involved in reconstructing the affairs of their ailing customers, and they became the reluctant holders of industrial shares and loan stock. The Bank of England co-ordinated industrial rescue and reconstruction by finance agencies to support the banks. In order to spread their risks, the banks drew the growing insurance companies into industrial finance, and the boards of industrial enterprises began to include representatives of the financial intermediaries. This is apparent from Tables 30 and 31, which show an increase between 1904 and 1938 in the average number of directorships held by each director, an increase in the density of the network from 0.013 to 0.019, and a substantial increase in the proportion of enterprises with six or more interlocks. Of the 98 large enterprises studied by Florence in 1936, 56 were interlocked with one another (Florence 1961: 88). Interlocking, then, was becoming the norm for the largest enterprises, and the inter-war period saw the consolidation of 'finance capital' in Britain. By the Second World War the intercorporate network had become truly national in scope and, though organized around the City financials, it incorporated both financial and non-financial enterprises.

Since the 1930s, and especially since the late 1950s, the City has become less exclusively involved in commercial activities. Although the clearing banks withdrew from long-term involvement in industrial enterprises as soon as their economic recovery permitted, their involvement remained much closer than it had been during the first part of the century. The growth of institutional shareholdings and the property and takeover booms of the post-war period brought all sectors of the economy into a closer alignment with the financial intermediaries, and the post-war expansion in economic activity further consolidated the coalescence of banking and industry. At the same time, the City enterprises were themselves undergoing a transformation. Merchant banks became more active in industrial investment and fund management, and the clearing banks (no longer controlled by City merchants) became involved in these same areas, as well as entering into such activities as consumer credit, domestic mortgages, and industrial leasing. The clearing banks and some of the big merchant banks and insurance companies became massive diversified financial conglomerates (Channon 1977).

In the wake of an official report on the role of City bankers in a leakage of secret information (Radcliffe Report 1959; Lupton and Wilson 1959), the operation of the City came under critical scrutiny and the existence of financial interest groups began to be discussed. Marxist writers on both the orthodox and 'new left' wings saw the dominance of the 'City' over 'industry' as an endemic feature of British capitalism, arguing that the City dominated the flow of capital and diverted it abroad at the expense of domestic industry. Britain's long-term economic decline, it was argued, was due to the starving of manufacturing industry by City institutions that pursued their sectional interests and also had a preponderant influence over state policy (Anderson 1964; Nairn 1972 and 1977; see also Longstreth 1979).

Aaronovitch (1961: 78 ff.) and Barratt Brown (1968a: 58–60) suggested that ten or more financial empires had been formed around the major banks and insurers. Central positions in these groups were claimed for the big five clearing banks (Barclays, Lloyds, Midland, National Provincial, and Westminster) and for merchant banks such as Rothschild, Lazard, and Morgan Grenfell (part-owned by the American Morgan bank). It was held that these banks were able to ensure a degree of co-ordination and lack of competition among the members of the groups. The research was not, however, as systematic as that undertaken in the United States, and the desired conclusions seem to have shaped the results. More systematic research has not confirmed the existence of such sharply divided groups. Research for 1971 showed that all the major financials of the City were closely tied together and had close links to the large industrials. Although the banks had more interlocks than other enterprises, conforming to the picture of bank centrality found in the United States, they did not maintain exclusive connections with particular interest groups. Rather, they formed parts of a unified and diffuse intercorporate network (Whitley 1973 and 1974; Stanworth and Giddens 1975).

By the 1970s the British intercorporate network had come to resemble that of the United States very closely: 189 of the top 250 British enterprises of 1976 and 203 of those of 1988 were interlocked, the bulk of them being connected through a chain of interlocks into a single network component. The enterprises most likely to inter-

Table 32. Multiple directorships in the top 250 British and US enterprises (1976)

Number of directorships per person	% of directorships held	
	Britain	United States
2	69	64
3	21	24
4	6	8
5	3	3
6–10	1	1
11 or more	0	0
Totals	100 (N=282)	100 (N=564)

Source: Stokman and Wasseur (1985: Table 2.2 and Fig. 2.1).
Note: Tables 31 and 32 relate to the same group of British directors. The US data are based on 3,108 directors in total.

lock were those controlled through constellations of interests, the state enterprises, and enterprises with shared control. Family-owned enterprises generally showed a low propensity to interlock. About one third of the foreign subsidiaries were interlocked, though wholly owned American subsidiaries were less likely to interlock than were those of other nationalities (Scott 1986: 78–80). Table 32 shows that the number of multiple directors in the United States at this time was considerably larger, but that the distribution of their directorships was very similar.

In both Britain and the United States there is strong evidence for the existence of bank centrality. The ten British enterprises with the largest number of interlocks included the Bank of England, all four big clearing banks, a specialist industrial credit bank, and a merchant bank.[15] Banks were especially important in the network of primary interlocks, though there was little evidence of any regionalism in this network. Despite the absence of regional groupings, there were some striking parallels between the British situation and the findings of the MACNET researchers. The British banks stood at the centre of loose and overlapping groups of enterprises created through primary interlocks, although these were less sharply divided from one another than were those found in the United States. The heart of the British economy consisted of an intercorporate network in which 'City' enterprises were closely integrated with 'non-financial' enterprises (Moran 1984). There was no real separation of 'City' and 'industry': the intercorporate network formed and connected units of finance capital.

The relative weakness of regionalism in Britain reflects the smaller scale of its economy, and it was only in Scotland that any significant degree of regionalism persisted. A study of large Scottish enterprises found that they showed a tendency to ally themselves with the large Scottish banks rather than with the London banks (Scott and Hughes 1980; Scott and Griff 1984: chs. 2, 4). The Scottish enterprises tended to be closely interlocked into a Scottish intercorporate network with close relations to England, and the banks and insurance companies were central in this network (Scott and Hughes 1976; 1980a). Banks and industry were allied in a system of finance capital in which Scottish interests played an important role in linking Scottish to foreign enterprises (Scott and Griff 1984: ch. 2).

---

[15] The others were an oil company, an insurance company, and a metal producer.

The major difference between Britain and the United States lies in the number of uninterlocked enterprises. Over 90 per cent of the American top 250 of 1976 were interlocked, compared with only 75 per cent in Britain. As a result, the British network of interlocks had a density of 0.017, compared with the 0.034 found in the United States. There are two main reasons for this difference. First, as I have shown, the British network included many foreign subsidiaries that tended not to interlock with other British companies, while the American network included few such subsidiaries. In Britain, 37 of the 61 non-interlocked enterprises of 1976 were foreign subsidiaries. Second, family ownership was stronger in Britain than in the United States, and family enterprises in both countries were less likely to interlock with other enterprises. Thirty-nine of the top 250 enterprises in Britain had families or individuals with majority or minority control, and a further thirty-six had family participants in their controlling constellations. The stronger the family influence, the less likely was the enterprise to interlock within the top 250 (Scott and Griff 1984: Table 4.3; A. B. Thomas 1978).

The growth of institutional investment has strengthened the short-term orientation that the City has always adopted towards industry. City institutions look for a rapid return on their investments and they are unable to tie up their assets on a long-term basis. The stock exchange and commercial banking system are central to this short-termism, as they allow investors to convert assets into cash as easily as possible and whenever desired. A typical clearing bank makes over a half of its lending for terms of less than one year, and less than one-fifth of its lending is spread over five years or more (Hutton 1995: 149). Small and medium-sized enterprises, in particular, are dependent on the provision of short-term overdraft lending. This high degree of liquidity is the benchmark for all forms of investment. For this reason, companies have to pay high and regular dividends to their shareholders in order to prevent them from selling their shares, leading to a stress on stable cash-flow and high returns for safe investments. The threat of takeover—always present in a system that is organized around stock-exchange finance—impels enterprises to boost their short-term profitability by all means possible in order to sustain their dividend payments. An enterprise may, for example, sell an under-performing subsidiary or division, rather than try to build up its long-term strength. British enterprises have, then, become risk-averse and unable to tie up their funds over a long term.

Both Britain and the United States, then, show a move away from the liberal-capitalist economy of entrepreneurial capital through a more 'organized' phase of trusts, cartels, and communities of interests to more diffuse intercorporate networks. The diffuse interlock networks of the phase of 'disorganized capitalism' corresponded to the diffuse networks of interweaving shareholdings that resulted from the growth of control through a constellation of interests. Whereas investment funds in the small entrepreneurial firm derived from the individual owner and from his or her family and associates, the large enterprise acquires its investment funds through the credit system as 'finance' in the form of share capital, loan stock, or bank credit. To this extent, the concept of finance capital captures an important dimension of the economic transformations that have occurred in Britain and the United States (Edwards 1938; Hussain 1976). During the 1970s and 1980s, new financial conglomerates and similar American enterprises extended their activities into the heart of the old City by buying stakes in stockbrokers and jobbers, Lloyd's insurance syndicates, and discount houses. This restructuring of the City has begun to alter the British intercorporate network, breaking up the old groups and further disorganizing the pattern of interlocking directorships.

The transition from entrepreneurial capital to finance capital has involved the development of a close relationship between the 'financial' and the 'non-financial' sectors. The integration of the two sectors, and the consequent conversion of all big businesses into units of finance capital, has in each country been accelerated during periods of industrial change when company formation and amalgamation have resulted in higher levels of concentration. In the United States, the Morgan-dominated community of interest that emerged at the turn of the century was gradually transformed into a more extensive and more inclusive national network that, until the 1930s, was organized around the overlapping remnants of the financial groupings built by the investment bankers. By the 1970s regional groupings were the most prominent feature of the network of primary interlocks, though these groups were embedded within a larger and cohesive framework of intercorporate relations in which the New York banks held central positions. In Britain the move from entrepreneurial capital to finance capital was slower and followed a slightly different pattern. The City of London banks allied themselves with provincial manufacturers only slowly, and it took a deep recession before a national network could emerge. It was only during the 1950s and 1960s that the British intercorporate network was forged into an extensive and cohesive network structured around the big clearing banks. These banks have been involved in loose and overlapping groups of enterprises, but they do not have the regional character that exists in the United States.

Intercorporate Relations: Anglo-American Variations

Canada's economy centres on a highly concentrated financial system. Through most of the post-war period, the big four chartered commercial banks[16] (Bank of Montreal, Bank of Nova Scotia, Royal Bank, and Canadian National Bank) and the large insurance companies such as Sun Life and Manufacturer's Life have stood at the heart of this system. Of particular importance in share ownership have been a number of shareholding trust companies, which, though ostensibly independent of the chartered banks, were for a long time tied to them through interlocking directorships and shareholdings. These institutions have followed the British practice of avoiding any significant involvement in long-term industrial finance. Separate from these dominant enterprises were a small number of investment banks that, like their American counterparts, were involved in company promotions and mergers in the first part of the century, but declined in importance from the 1930s.

Discussion of the development of finance capital in Canada has centred on the question of whether corporate directors are oriented primarily towards the Canadian national economy or towards the 'metropolitan' economies of Britain and the United States that have owned and controlled much of Canadian business. Clement (1975a) and Niosi (1981) have argued that the Canadian directorate can be divided into an 'indigenous' group which controls the Canadian-owned enterprises, and a 'comprador' group which acts as the executive managers of foreign-owned subsidiaries. Carroll (1982), however, has argued against this view, claiming that the multiple directors should be seen as a unified group of finance capitalists with interests in both the domestic and the overseas sectors of the economy. He holds that the 'indigenous' enterprises should not be seen as subordinate to or dependent on foreign interests, as they control

[16] These banks were formed as joint stock companies by Royal Charter and pre-dated modern Company Law.

a significant proportion of corporate assets. Canadian-owned enterprises are controlled by an indigenous 'national bourgeoisie' of finance capitalists who operate in both the industrial and the banking sector and are relatively autonomous from foreign interests (Carroll 1986; see also Carroll 1985).

Table 33. Interlocking directorships in Canadian industrial enterprises (1951 and 1972)

No. of directorships per person	1951		1972	
	No. of people	No. of directorships	No. of people	No. of directorships
1	704	704	672	672
2	112	224	155	310
3	43	129	58	174
4	21	84	28	112
5	13	65	20	100
6	7	42	6	36
7	3	21	6	42
8	2	16	1	8
9	1	9	–	–
10	1	10	–	–
Totals	907	1304	946	1454
No. of companies	170		113	

Source: Adapted from Porter (1965: 589, Table 12) and Clement (1975: 166, Table 18).

Indigenous Canadian ownership has been the dominant element in the financial sector and it has been a substantial factor in the industrial sector. The two sectors have been closely interlocked at board level over the whole of the post-war period. Carroll's (1986) data show that the Canadian intercorporate network was much more dense than those of Britain and the United States (see also Ornstein 1989).[17] This view is supported by Porter's earlier finding that 22 per

---

[17] Carroll's own figures for density are calculated for multiple interlocks only, and relate to the top 100 enterprises. Recalculations for all interlocks show a level of 0.100 in 1946 and 0.134 in 1966. These density levels are much higher than those found in Scotland, where a similar number of enterprises were studied (Scott and Hughes 1982). Primary interlocks in Canada are discussed in Ornstein (1982).

cent of directors in 1951 held two or more directorships in the top
170 enterprises. The corresponding figure for the top 113 of 1972
was 30 per cent (see Table 33). The figures for Britain and the United
States never reached such high levels, even at the height of the power
of the Money Trust. The explanation for this high level of interlocking seems to be the large number of foreign subsidiaries operating in
Canada and the tendency for these subsidiaries to recruit Canadian
directors to sit alongside their own executives (Safarian 1966: 64;
Gonick 1970: 51).

Table 34. Density of interlocking directorships in the top 100 Canadian enterprises
(1946–1976)

	1946	1951	1956	1961	1966	1971	1976
Density	0.096	0.115	0.120	0.120	0.128	0.113	0.127

Source: Calculated from Carroll (1986: Table 5.2 on 104).

Carroll's (1986; 1982) investigation of the top 100 enterprises has
shown that there was a rise in network density between 1946 and
1966 (see Table 34). Although there was a slight fall during the 1970s,
the overall level was broadly constant after an initial rise in the
immediate post-war period. There are, however, interesting variations behind this pattern. It was found, for example, that as the interlocking between the long-established indigenous enterprises and
American subsidiaries declined over the period, so the level of interlocking among indigenous enterprises has increased (Carroll 1986:
113–16). Interlocking between indigenous and British companies
also declined during the 1970s, and the interlock network can be said
to have become more 'Canadian' in character over the post-war
period. Carroll concluded that there had indeed been a fusion of
indigenous banking and industry into a structure of 'finance capital',
albeit a form of finance capital in which foreign ownership plays a
considerable part. The Canadian economy is not the dependent
'branch plant' economy that it has sometimes been depicted as, and
foreign-owned enterprises adopt a strategy of co-optation that ties
them into the domestic economy and, in particular, to the banking
sector. Even Clement (1975a: 159) has argued that the banking establishment has gradually moved into a close association with those
industrial sectors that have been developed and made profitable by

foreign capital. There is, then, no evidence for any significant separation of indigenous and 'comprador' groups within the corporate
directorate.

Over the post-war period, the Canadian economy has shown the
development of the same kind of bank-centred groupings that have
been found in the United States and in Britain. In 1946, the core of
the economy was a large cluster of enterprises that was Montreal-
based and centred around the big banks and trusts. By 1976, however, this had expanded to include many more companies, and had
fragmented into five overlapping clusters associated with particular
banks (Carroll 1986: 141–3).

It appears, however, that the Canadian economy has been funda-
mentally transformed in recent years. Legislation in 1967 separated
trust companies from the commercial banks, leading them to begin
moving apart from one another. The trust companies, the main
managers of pension fund capital, have come under the control of
entrepreneurial investment companies that have been able to use
their economic power to expand further into the financial and non-
financial sectors. Heightened international competition in the 1970s
and 1980s, together with the deregulation of the credit system, loosened the hold of the chartered banks over Canadian industry
(Richardson 1988, 1992; Carroll 1989; Carroll and Lewis 1991). The
corporate network of 1986 was no longer organized simply around
a core of established financials, but had fragmented into a number of
separate components. Alongside the Montreal-based financial core
were a number of webs of corporate connections centred on investment-holding companies such as Brascan, a number of which had
acquired large insurance companies and merchant banks to service
their webs of connection (Carroll and Lewis 1991: 496; Carroll 1986:
177 ff.). Those who sit on the boards of the large Canadian enterprises are no longer simply the finance capitalists who express the
fusion of banking and industry and the interests of the established
institutions. The directors of the largest banks, who held nearly a
quarter of all directorships in the top industrial enterprises of 1951
(Porter 1965: 579, 234) have been joined by the new entrepreneurial
capitalists who have built the investment holding companies and
extended their shareholdings. The 'disorganization' of Canadian
capitalism, then, has involved a growth of those corporate webs that,
I will show, have been central to economic development in France
and the other 'Latin' economies.

Australia, like Canada, developed through a close dependence on

Table 35. Multiple directorships in the top 250 Australian enterprises (1959–1991)

No. of directorships per person	% of directorships held			
	1959	1979	1986	1991
2	63	45	48	55
3	21	26	25	18
4	12	18	14	9
5	4	3	8	12
6 or more	0	8	5	6
Totals	100 (N=397)	100 (N=751)	100 (N=836)	100 (N=555)

Source: Calculated from Alexander and Murray (1992: Tables 2 and 3), Stening and Wan (1984). Additional information from M. Alexander.

British capital and ownership, but American ownership has never been as pervasive as in Canada. The long-term trends in Australian finance capital are difficult to assess, as there has, until recently, been very little research on the subject. An early study by Rolfe (1967) showed that 12 per cent of the directors of the top fifty Australian enterprises of 1962 held a quarter of all directorships in these enterprises. A large proportion of those directors who sat on financial boards were drawn from wealthy families, reflecting the high level of family enterprise in Australia (Encel 1970: 396). Stening and his colleagues undertook a major study of interlocking directorships in the top 250 Australian enterprises (Stening and Wan 1984; Carroll *et al.* 1990), and Alexander and Murray (1992) have provided some corrections for these data and have extended its coverage. Table 35 shows that the level of interlocking increased substantially over the period between 1959 and 1986. By 1986, 320 multiple directors held 39 per cent of all directorships in the top 250 and the density of the network of interlocks was 0.025. Levels of interlocking were broadly comparable with American levels, and were a little above those in Britain. Directors with four or more top directorships were rather more significant in Australia than they were in Britain or the United States. The figures for 1991, however, show a fall in the level of interlocking: multiple directors in that year held only 27 per cent of all top directorships, and the network density fell to 0.017. This may reflect, in part, the different selection criteria used for the 1991 data, but

Alexander and Murray suggest that it may also be explained as a response to the restructuring of the banking system that took place during the 1980s. Their interpretation is strengthened by the finding that, among the multiple directors, the 'big linkers' with four or more directorships have become a more significant element in the economy. The overall shape of the interlock network is now highly dependent on the activities of the big linkers, and as Australian boards are small, they have also become a more significant force in the boards on which they sit. In the continuing 'colonial' situation faced by Australian enterprises, the big linkers are the focus of attempts to strengthen indigenous corporate power, their position having become more marked as the globalization of the economy has proceeded (Alexander *et al.* 1994: 26).

Table 36. Interlocking directorships in the top 100 South African enterprises (1977 and 1984)

No. of directorships per person	1977		1984	
	No. of people	No. of dirships.	No. of people	No. of dirships.
1	592	592	631	631
2	87	174	72	144
3	27	81	38	114
4	18	72	11	44
5	2	10	10	50
6	2	12	6	36
7	1	7	4	28
8	1	8	0	0
9			1	9
10			1	10
Totals	730	956	774	1066

Source: Savage (1978: 37, Table 5) and (1985: 28, Table 10).

The similarity of South Africa to the other Anglo-American economies is apparent from patterns of interlocking directorships (see Table 36). The level of interlocking among the top 100 enterprises was fairly stable through the 1970s, but it increased substantially with restructuring in the early 1980s. Between 1977 and 1984 there was a slight increase in the number of multiple directors and a very sharp increase in the number of directorships they held. As more of the large enterprises became subsidiaries of other large enterprises, so the number of interlocks connecting them increased. As a result, the inclusiveness of the interlock network increased from 84 per cent to 93 per cent and the density increased from 0.037 to 0.099, though this might be expected to fall back somewhat as restructuring comes to an end. The South African interlock network also showed the characteristic Anglo-American pattern of bank centrality. The five largest banks of 1984 interlocked with 61 of the top 100 enterprises, and the two largest banks each interlocked with more than one-fifth of these enterprises.

Bank Power and Financial Hegemony

Banks have been found to play a central role in the intercorporate networks of all the Anglo-American economies. There has, however, been much debate over whether their role is one of control or merely of influence. For many Marxists and for others influenced by the theory of capitalist society, banks are seen as centres of control that are able to coerce other enterprises into acting against their own interests. One variant of the model of bank control sees banks exercising their power over the particular clusters of enterprises that form their 'financial empires' or 'interest groups'. I have already suggested that there is little evidence for the existence of such groups of enterprises in the Anglo-American economies (see also Glasberg and Schwartz 1983: 316–17). Another variant of the model holds simply that banks are more powerful than industrials and will exercise their power whenever it suits them. According to this argument, industrials may be controlled by particular banks, but it is equally possible that a particular industrial will be subject to pressure from many different banks. It is the collective power of banks that is important, and they may cooperate and collude in order to pursue their interests. A prominent advocate of this view is Fitch, who has claimed that interlocking directorships between banks and industrials express 'the exercise of raw economic power' and that they are one of the means through which banks can force industrials into 'buying and selling goods on the basis of considerations other than price, quality, and service' (Fitch 1972: 107). This is a particularly strong claim, as it involves the argument that banks are able to coerce the managers of industrial enterprises into taking decisions that run counter to profit calculations that they would make using purely 'market' criteria. On this view, then, the interests of the banks become the predominant force in shaping corporate strategy in the industrial sector.

The bases on which banks may be able to exercise this kind of economic power are capital relations and interlocking directorships.[18] Capital relations arise from the granting or withholding of credit, varying rates of interest, buying and selling large blocks of shares, and exercising the voting rights attached to shares. Banks are able to reinforce capital relations through interlocking directorships, which allow them to monitor the behaviour of the enterprises with which they are involved and to gather knowledge and information about business conditions that can be used or passed on to their clients and to other enterprises with which they are interlocked (Baum and Stiles 1965: 36; Patman Report 1968: 19, 23 ff.; Mintz and Schwartz 1981b). The ultimate source of power for a bank is undoubtedly the network of capital relations in which it is involved, as an interlocking directorship without such an institutional base is only a weak source of bank power. An assessment of the idea of bank control, then, must begin with an analysis of the lending and shareholder relations of banks and other financial institutions.

Loans and shareholdings are the two main forms of 'external' funding available to enterprises, which must otherwise rely on 'internal' funding from their retained earnings. Managerialists have seen internal funding as the principal way in which executives are able to increase their autonomy from shareholders and financiers, and high levels of internal funding have been seen as evidence against the idea of bank control. Thus, one leading managerialist has claimed that 'only a minor proportion of corporate capital today is raised through the sale of equity capital. A more significant portion of capital comes through self-financing' (Bell 1974: 294). From the standpoint of Marxist managerialism, Sweezy (1941) has claimed that the decline of the investment banker in America was a result of an increase in the level of internal funding during the 1930s.

In the most systematic empirical study of this matter, Lintner (1959) found that 'the proportion of funds from external sources in American non-financials stood at 40–42 per cent throughout the

---

[18] Scott (1982a and 1991) sets out the distinction between capital, commercial, and personal relations. In the case of banks their commercial relations with other enterprises mainly involve the granting or withholding of credit, and so are indistinguishable from capital relations.

period 1900–25, fell to 37 per cent in the late 1920s, and varied between 37 and 42 per cent in the period 1930–49' (1959: 181; see also Kuznets 1961). This evidence provides some support for Sweezy's view, though not, perhaps, as much as would be required to fully substantiate his claim. The level of external funding increased over the period from 1949 to 1957 to a level of about 44 per cent, returning to the level at which it had stood at the turn of the century. Lintner argued that these figures show a high degree of stability in the source of funds over the course of the century, the only discernible long-term trend being a very slight rise in the level of external funding.

Berle arrived at a slightly lower estimate than did Lintner for the level of external funding in the United States in the immediate post-war period, though his findings confirm Lintner's broad conclusions (Berle 1960: 25–6). Fitch and Oppenheimer suggested that the level of external funding increased more sharply during the 1960s, their estimates showing that the level varied from 30 per cent in 1964 to 39 per cent in 1966 and 43 per cent in 1968. Fitch has subsequently claimed that this increase was sustained into the 1970s (Fitch and Oppenheimer 1970b: 74; Fitch 1971: 156). Unpublished evidence by Stearns has extended and updated Lintner's data, and has supported his conclusion that there has been no long-term decline in corporate dependence on external funding (cited in Mizruchi 1987: 11).

Comparable long-term figures for Britain are not available, but the proportion of funds from external sources has been shown to have stood at around 30 per cent between 1950 and 1970. Thompson (1977: 254–5), however, has suggested that the figure may have been as low as 23 per cent in 1950. External sources are mainly important for the funding of expansion, and Barratt Brown (1968b) has estimated that the fastest-growing enterprises during the early 1950s obtained half their funds from external sources (see also Williams et al. 1968: 111–12). A stock exchange study during the 1970s confirmed this view, showing higher rates of external funding when growth was at its greatest (Stock Exchange 1977: 14, Table 3).

Figures on internal and external funding are complex to compile and to assess, and any general conclusions must be treated with care (Herman 1973: 26). The evidence does not, however, seem to support the managerialist thesis. Large enterprises are tightly constrained by their need to secure external capital, but they are not simply dependent on bank loans. It is generally possible for enterprises to choose between share issues and bank loans when external funds are required, and if bank loans are taken this is because of specific conditions in the financial markets and not simply because they are submitting to bank power. The crucial issue, then, is that of the autonomy that enterprises have to choose between external and internal sources of finance. The availability of internal funds is dependent on the profitability of an enterprise, and Fitch and Oppenheimer (1970b: 75) suggested that its level of internal funding will vary with its profit rate. Where there are cash-flow problems, enterprises will be forced to use external funds. Observed trends in external funding, therefore, may best be seen as the counter-trend to aggregate corporate profitability: a long-term rise in external funding reflects a long-term decline in profitability. External funding, therefore, will vary with general economic circumstances. If enterprises have to use external funds and they are unable to raise these funds through share issues, they may have to borrow money under terms decided by the banks. Fitch and Oppenheimer concluded that the rise in external funding during the 1960s was a sign of worsened industrial profitability and was associated with a consequent enhancement of banking power. Their final conclusion, however, is fallacious, unless it can be shown that enterprises were unable to make share issues in this period—and there seems little evidence that this was the case (Thompson 1977). The only secure conclusion is that declining profitability will lead to an increase in external funding and that this gives banks a potential for power. Whether this potential can be actualized depends on the specific capital market conditions that prevail at the time. Evidence on external funding cannot, in itself, provide evidence for bank power. Conversely, of course, evidence on internal funding cannot, in itself, provide evidence for managerial power.

The thesis of bank control is also weakened by the unrealistic assumptions that are made about banking strategy. It is assumed that banks are concerned with increasing the indebtedness of industrial enterprises, allowing bank profits to rise at the expense of industrial profits. However, banks are not necessarily interested in increasing the indebtedness of the enterprises with which they deal, as an indebted company is likely to be a poor risk for further lending, and this is a poor prospect for a bank. An enterprise with a good cash-flow will be preferred by a bank and will be seen as a good customer. This means, however, that if such an enterprise decides to fund its investments from external sources it is in a good position to choose the bank to which it will give its business. Cash-flow provides the basis for freedom from bank dependence (Sweezy 1971: 13; Beed 1966: 39). Conversely, of course, low profitability will reduce cash-flow and so increase dependence on banks.

The evidence on internal and external funding, then, gives direct support neither for the managerialist nor for the bank control argument. Because of the great importance of share issues and loan stock as compared with bank loans, any shift to external funding will strengthen the position of the big institutional shareholders rather than the banks. It must be recalled, however, that banks play a major role in the management of institutional funds through their trust and investment departments, and it may well be that institutional shareholdings, and particularly the holdings of pension funds, may buttress bank power. Such bank power would be based ultimately on shareholdings rather than indebtedness.

The growth of pension funds does not, in itself, strengthen the case for bank control. Those who manage pension funds—whether they are banks, insurance companies, or stockbrokers—are legally regarded as custodians or trustees of the funds that they manage. Many pension funds are, in any case, run 'in-house' by an employer,[19] although others have their management delegated to banks, insurance companies, or stockbrokers. Where the funds are managed by banks they may become 'captive funds' (Rifkin and Barber 1978: 95) that can be used by banks in support of their investment and corporate finance dealings, and not simply maintained as trustee holdings. Banks may, for example, use institutional funds to bolster the position of their clients by voting on their side in a takeover struggle or by using them to take up a share issue (Minns 1980; Schuller and Hyman 1984). Drucker has concluded that banks could be encouraged to make more active use of their captive funds in support of long-term investment banking (Drucker 1976: 72–3), though he recognizes that this is not currently the case.

The issue of bank power, then, is one aspect of the wider issue of institutional power, of the power of pension funds, insurance companies, unit trusts, and other financial institutions. It is on this basis that the capital relations in which banks are involved can be assessed. Banks are critically important members of the constellations of interests through which the majority of large business enterprises are now controlled in the Anglo-American economies, and their

[19] Control over these funds remains a problem, as they may be used as adjuncts to the normal business operations of the enterprise, or as a way of manipulating its share price, rather than as a mere trustee investment.

powers are exercised alongside those of other institutional share-holders and through similar mechanisms.

Because of their role in the capital markets, banks and other financial institutions are able to shape the consequences that follow from the activities of other enterprises. This ability lies, as Glasberg (1989; 1987) has shown, in the fact that 'normal' and 'crisis' situations are, to a considerable degree, social constructions. Banks and other financial institutions always have a degree of latitude in deciding how they will define financial situations and, therefore, in deciding on appropriate forms of action and intervention.

Where banks and other institutions define the financial situation of an enterprise as 'normal', they are likely to support it by providing loans and by buying stock through their pension and trust funds. If, however, a situation is defined as a 'problem', they are more likely to deny loans or sell large blocks of shares. It is in this way that 'problems' may become 'crises':

A corporate crisis is not always a mechanical economic reaction of the invisible hand of the market brought on simply by low profitability. Rather, it is a reflexive definitional process, involving shifting levels of discretion and constraint that can seriously damage a firm's long-term business trajectory. (Glasberg 1989: 19)

If the leading banks and big investors act in this way, smaller investors will tend to follow their example and there is likely to be a serious shift in an enterprise's standing in the capital market. A problematic situation in which banks have predicted a crisis becomes a real crisis, and the leading institutions are likely to have to intervene in the shaping of corporate strategy.

The argument for bank control has also pointed to interlocking directorships and bank centrality in interlock networks as indicators of control, and this aspect of the argument must also be assessed. The composition of corporate boards can be seen as 'reflecting the organization's perceived need to deal differentially with various important sectors or organizations in the environment' (Pfeffer 1972: 220; Aaronovitch and Sawyer 1975: 261), and interlocking directorships between financial and non-financial enterprises are a result of a two-way recruitment mechanism. From the standpoint of the industrials, this means ensuring that their boards are adapted to the interests of the constellations of major shareholders, to sources of credit, and to suppliers and competitors (Pennings 1980: ch. 6; Allen 1974). The commercial and capital relations that bring credit, partners for mergers, and opportunities for successful share issues also bring access to the expertise and information that permits a more rational and planned strategy to be constructed (Herman 1973: 25–6). Banks are not only managers of institutional funds and providers of credit, but are continually involved in corporate advice and corporate finance; it is on this basis that bank centrality in inter-corporate networks can be explained.

Banks and the large institutional shareholders are able to provide capital or to ease the availability of capital; they have access to business information about the financial markets and the activities of the enterprises in which they invest, and so their directors and executives are particularly attractive recruits for industrial boards. On the other hand, financials seek to secure board representation that will protect their interests and will also recruit leading industrial executives to their boards in order to enhance board knowledge of business conditions. Directors of industrial and commercial enterprises, for their part, will also seek out financial directorships in order to obtain access to the accumulated expertise and knowledge that they possess. Through these processes, directors of banks—whether their main base is in an industrial or a financial company—acquire a prominent position in the network of interlocking directorships. Bank directors become 'the most important carriers of information and opinion from one sector of the business establishment to another' (Domhoff 1967: 53; Smith 1970: 49).

Over and above their role in the flow of capital, then, banks are the 'nerve centres of the communication network' between enterprises (Mokken and Stokman 1974: 30). They are the foci through which information flows from one part of the network to another. The network of interlocks generates a 'unification of outlook and policy' (Mills 1956: 123) and reinforces the informality of kinship and friendship by creating 'well-oiled communication channels through which business deals of a wide variety can be furthered' (Sonquist et al. 1975: 199; see also Koenig et al. 1979; Koenig and Gogel 1981). This ability to control the flow of information, whether used intentionally or unintentionally, is a way of influencing corporate strategy. Capital and commercial relations are fundamental to the structure of the inter-corporate network, but these may be expressed in and reinforced by interlocks carried by bank and industrial executives (Fennema 1982: 140). The influence that banks can exercise over enterprises with which they interlock is greatest when these interlocks reinforce capital and commercial relations between banker and client.

The co-optation of directors to large enterprises tends to follow commercial and capital relations. Banks tend to recruit their outside directors from among their own clients and associates, while industrials tend to recruit directors from their primary bank (Bearden 1987: 53). As a result, interlocking between banks and industrials does not occur at random but along established lines of customer–client relations. In this way, banks emerge as the centres of loose spheres of enterprises. The fact that large enterprises have credit relations with more than one bank, however, means that these spheres tend to overlap and to form a larger intercorporate network. Where there is regionalism in bank operations, as in the United States, the spheres will tend to have a regional character also. These spheres are not financial interest groups of the kind depicted in Marxist theory, but bank-centred spheres of influence, clusters of enterprises that share a common orientation to a particular bank whose board-room provides a meeting place for the discussion of common concerns. The bank is not a centre of control or of direct power, but it is a central forum in which common business interests can be pursued. Banks, then, are arenas of influence within a structure of intercorporate unity.

The structure of intercorporate capital relations and of primary, executive officer interlocks is overlaid by a structure of weaker interlocking directorships that have no direct institutional base. Retired business leaders, retired civil servants and military officers, politicians, landowners, and even trade unionists are recruited to corporate boards in large numbers, and those who are recruited to more than one board create secondary interlocking directorships. It is this network of relations that researchers in the Anglo-American economies have found to be both diffuse and national in scope. These weaker interlocks consolidate the outlines of the bank-centred spheres of influence and determine the overall shape and cohesion of the network of interlocking directorships. The structure of this network is not the result of direct, control-oriented actions by all-powerful banks. It is, rather, the unintended consequence of a myriad of individual recruitment decisions, but it nevertheless persists over time and shows a degree of stability (Levine and Roy 1977; Warner and Unwalla 1967: 124–5; Scott and Griff 1984: ch. 1).

It is this structure of relations that exhibits bank centrality, and understanding the structure as an unintended consequence of director recruitment under the contemporary conditions of the capital and product markets allows a proper interpretation to be given to the significance of bank centrality. Banks are foci of influence within the spheres that surround them, but they are not involved in regular or recurrent long-term relations of power and control over the members of these spheres. The strong ties created by primary interlocks are overlaid by weaker ties that nevertheless act as important channels of communication between enterprises (Granovetter 1973). Banks are central in this structure of weak ties as well as in the structure of primary interlocks, and this enhances their role as centres of communication (Mokken and Stokman 1976). For this reason, a bank's *influence* may be far greater than its direct *control* (Allen 1976: 889–90).

The Anglo-American economies are systems of finance capital in so far as the availability of monetary advances determines when and where production will take place. Even when enterprises rely on internal funding, they are dependent upon stock-market valuations and on the need to maintain a satisfactory cash-flow. In most large enterprises, internal funding no longer involves a deduction from the income of an entrepreneur. It is, instead, a deduction from the incomes of the institutional shareholders that advance capital. The growth of institutional shareholdings, reflected in the spread of control through a constellation of interests, has produced a system of business finance in which each individual enterprise is embedded in an extensive network of intercorporate shareholdings and interlocking directorships. With the rise of organized capitalism, the large corporate enterprise supplemented the 'invisible hand' of the market with the 'visible hand' of corporate planning, bureaucratic hierarchy, and cohesive intercorporate relations. The growth of institutional shareholding has helped to create a pattern of 'disorganized' or deregulated capitalism that has led to the emergence of the 'invisible handshake' (Okun 1981) that connects enterprises into diffuse intercorporate networks.[20] With some simplification, this development from liberal to organized and to disorganized capitalism can be characterized as involving a shift from 'market' to 'hierarchy' to 'network' in intercorporate relations.[21]

The form of intercorporate structure found in the Anglo-

---

[20] This idea of the 'invisible handshake' has a number of sources. Michael Mann suggested the idea of a new invisible hand in a seminar discussion of my work in 1983, and Useem (1984: 181) set out a similar idea of the 'collective hand'. Okun's idea of the 'invisible handshake' is the best formulation of this idea. See also Herman (1981: 297).

[21] This view will be discussed more fully in Chapter 7.

American economies can best be described as a system of polyarchic financial hegemony (Mintz and Schwartz 1985; 1986).[22] Numerous large financial institutions hold powerful positions within the business world, but they do not exercise direct control over particular dependent enterprises. Their collective control over the availability of capital, however, gives them the power to determine the broad conditions under which other enterprises must decide their corporate strategies. Those enterprises that are involved in the provision of credit through the granting of loans and the purchasing of shares are those in which is institutionalized the collective power to constrain corporate decision-making. This power of constraint is exercised without deliberate or overt intervention:

> Bank and insurance company decisions regarding the most promising locales for capital investment lead to the nurturance of some industries or firms and the decline of others. Since most companies are dependent upon outside funds, they will adapt to conditions placed upon available funding, thus allowing financial suppliers to influence and coordinate the activities of industrial companies without necessarily intruding on their decision-making processes or tampering with executive autonomy. (Glasberg and Schwartz 1983, 318)

An analysis of the participations of the top 250 British enterprises of 1976 and the top 252 American enterprises of 1980 in the capital of the enterprises that were controlled through constellations of interests showed that their shareholdings tied them together into a well-connected network. Interweaving shareholdings, like interlocking directorships, formed a continuous chain of connections in which there were no sharp boundaries of the kind that is hypothesized in the idea of 'financial empires'. There was, however, a clear hierarchical structure to the network: the hegemonic controllers and their close associates were distinguished from the subordinate enterprises that they controlled (Scott 1986: 117–19, 150–1). In each country, a diverse category of banks, insurers, and public and private enterprises with large in-house pension funds stood at the heart of this network of polyarchic hegemony.

Within this structure of polyarchic financial hegemony, banks play a key role by virtue of their part in the management of institutional funds and in corporate advice. They are the dominant agents within

[22] As will be shown in Chapter 6, the system is 'polyarchic', by contrast with the 'oligarchic' bank hegemony found in some other economies.

the hegemonic system. A diverse set of credit institutions controls access to capital, but bank boards are the institutional arenas in which the major credit-givers and credit-recipients come together to determine the constraints under which that credit can be used. Banks have considerable power and influence in the business world, even though they may not deliberately seek out such a role. Bank dominance in the hegemonic system is the basis of bank centrality in the network of interlocking directorships; and the fusion of banking and industry is expressed in the structure of property ownership, the mode of corporate control, and the structure of intercorporate relations.

6

VARIANT PATTERNS OF
CAPITALIST DEVELOPMENT

THE Anglo-American pattern that I have described in Chapters 4 and 5 rests upon a particular framework of property, contract, and commercial law, though the 'social function' of these legal norms is shaped by the specific economic, cultural, and political circumstances shared by the Anglo-American economies. In Chapter 1, however, I showed that there are a number of other legal frameworks of business regulation, and I suggested that these might be associated with differences in banking practice and share-ownership, with variations in patterns of class structure and wealth-holding, and with divergent state strategies. From this complex of factors have emerged the German, Latin, post-Communist, Japanese, and Chinese patterns of capitalist development that I will discuss in this chapter.

In Germany and Austria, a weak entrepreneurial system gave way very early on to a system of oligarchic bank hegemony and corporate filiations. Japan, like Germany, had a weak entrepreneurial sector, but this was transformed through the emergence of a number of powerful families that, under state sponsorship, built massive corporate sets. France and Belgium had a rather stronger entrepreneurial sector than did Germany or Japan, but they developed a system of investment-holding companies that became the bases of extensive corporate webs. Corporate filiations, corporate sets, and corporate webs structured the 'organized' form of capitalism in the German, Japanese, and Latin economies, and each has subsequently developed into a more 'disorganized' form of impersonal possession. Corporate filiations in the German system have become more intermeshed and less hierarchical; corporate sets in the Japanese system have become more 'horizontal' than vertical in structure and have more extensive interconnections with one another; and corporate webs in the Latin system have developed into larger, but looser, 'ensembles' of interlinked webs.

The Communist systems of Russia and eastern Europe were highly 'organized' command economies, but they were not, of course, specifically capitalist systems. With the breakdown of these systems, however, they have moved towards systems of capitalist enterprise that have a dispersed, 'disorganized' character, but which do not yet seem to have acquired a stable and persistent form. The Chinese systems of south-east Asia developed as networked systems of family enterprise that provided a powerful motor for rapid economic growth. As these economies expand, however, they face the problem of evolving a more impersonal mechanism of capital mobilization, and it is unclear as yet how their states will respond to this.

Although capitalist industrialism has involved a generic transition from entrepreneurial capital to finance capital, and from personal to more impersonal forms of possession, the mechanisms involved, the route followed, and the current stage reached have varied from one country to another. This chapter will document these variations.

Corporate Filiations: The German Pattern

Germany remained an almost exclusively agrarian society, with only a very small and weak commercial bourgeoisie, for much of the nineteenth century. Its limited industrial development relied heavily on foreign capital, as neither entrepreneurs nor the banking system could generate sufficient funds to finance industry on any significant scale. The strong Prussian state had encouraged an influx of foreign capital in the hope of creating an opportunity for indigenous mechanisms of capital mobilization to establish themselves (Kitchen 1978). In pursuit of this policy, new banks modelled on the French *Crédit Mobilier* were set up during the 1850s to promote investment in the railways. Unlike their French counterparts, however, these so-called 'universal banks' combined long-term industrial investment with both deposit and merchant banking, garnering savings and surplus assets from a wide range of sources and making these available as capital for investment. These banks were intended by the government to be the means through which the rapid accumulation of industrial capital would take place, and as the pace of railway development slowed down they were encouraged to move into industrial finance. They did this by floating companies, providing long-term credit, taking substantial shareholdings, and managing shares owned by others. They became heavily involved in utility and transport companies as well as in the manufacturing of producer goods and, during the 1870s, they became closely involved in a number of industrial promotions and mergers (Chandler 1990: 416–17; Kocka 1978: 542).

As banking became more concentrated, the big banks of Berlin achieved a dominant position in the expanding economy. These banks formed large national chains of affiliates and associates that dominated the supervisory boards of industrial enterprises and took the leading part in all aspects of business. Their power over industrial enterprises lay in their trustee holdings—the shares that they held on behalf of their customers and for which they held the legal voting-rights. Through these trustee holdings and through their own direct participations, the big banks acquired large stakes in the coal, iron, steel, engineering, and chemicals industries, and they were actively involved in the formation of the cartels that organized and regulated these industries (Henderson 1961: 62 ff.). As industrial enterprises became more profitable, their surplus earnings could be recycled by the banks to finance other enterprises. In this way, a sustained cycle of long-term capital accumulation was generated by the universal banking system (Landes 1969: 205; Gille 1970).

Because of the scale of the funds that were needed as production became concentrated into larger units, syndicates of banks were formed. At the same time, a series of banking mergers around the turn of the century concentrated bank shareholdings even further, giving them large controlling blocks in industrial enterprises and creating a pattern of interweaving participations and corporate filiations (Milward and Saul 1977: 47; Henderson 1961: 62 ff.; Kocka 1980: 90; Tilly 1974; Kocka 1978, 565–70). As industrial enterprises grew in size, however, so did their opportunities for internal funding and, therefore, their chances of greater autonomy from the banks. The relationship between the big banks and the big industrials became more of a two-way affair. Nevertheless, on the verge of the First World War the big five banks owned 10 per cent of all industrial capital (Tilly 1986).

This close relationship between banking and industry gave German industrialization a highly 'organized' form. The leading bankers, together with pioneer entrepreneurial families and government officials, stood at the top of a vertically structured system of corporate filiations. The banks were—both individually and collectively—a hegemonic force in the economy. Businesses operated in an economy that was dominated by banks and by large bank-controlled and bank-allied enterprises, a situation that can be described as one of oligarchic bank hegemony. This was not, it must be emphasized, a system of direct bank control. Power relations existed between the banks collectively and industrial enterprises. The banks tended to have minority holdings in large industrial enterprises, but each enterprise was generally affiliated to more than one bank. Bank boards were forums that brought together bank executives and industrialists into a union of interests that determined the strategy that a bank would pursue in relation to its clients. It was through this oligarchic system that banking strategies determined the conditions under which other enterprises formulated and implemented their own strategies.

The earliest study of this system was undertaken by Jeidels (1905), who investigated the number of directorships in large enterprises that were held by those who sat on the boards of the big Berlin banks. This analysis became the cornerstone of Hilferding's (1910) model of finance capital, though Hilferding assumed that the situation described by Jeidels was common to all capitalist economies because the effects of the credit system on industry would be the same everywhere. As I have shown in Chapters 4 and 5, the development of the Anglo-American economies differed greatly from Hilferding's model. The German system as it existed at the turn of the century represents simply one form of finance capital, not its only form.

The German economy was severely disrupted by the Second World War and the subsequent partition of Germany into east and west sectors. American support for the Federal Republic, however, allowed its economy to recover rapidly, and key manufacturers were able to reorganize themselves for expansion in post-war Europe. The banks, too, were able to recover much of their pre-war power, and the big three banks—the *Deutsche*, *Commerz*, and *Dresdner*—came to dominate the newer regional and co-operative banks.

Institutional funds outside the banking system were of only limited importance in the west German economy. Insurance companies such as *Allianz* have been important investors, but legal restraints on insurance company share-ownership have meant that they have invested more in loan stock and government bonds. Pensions have generally been met from the current incomes of enterprises, rather than from separate funds, and those few pension schemes that have been incorporated as funds since the 1970s have generally had banks appointed as their advisers and managers (Readman *et al.* 1973: ch. 5). Most industrial share capital, then, has been closely held by banks and insurance companies and by a small number of families and private foundations. Share capital is, in any case, less important than is bank lending for industrial funding, giving German enterprises a very different capital structure to that found in the Anglo-American economies. Banks hold their shares as long-term participations and so the stock exchange is insignificant as a secondary market in shares. Those who wish to buy or sell shares and those enterprises that wish to issue shares must do so through the banks. The shares of only sixty or seventy companies are actively traded on the exchange, and hostile takeover bids are virtually unknown. Reliable figures on the distribution of shareholdings are difficult to obtain because of the widespread use of bearer shares, but it has been estimated that insurance companies and pension funds held only 11.28 per cent of shares in 1990. Banks, on the other hand, held up to 10 per cent of all shares, while individuals held just 16 per cent. Table 37 shows figures estimated on a slightly different basis, though the broad pattern is clear.

Bank holdings are reflected in the importance of bank loans in corporate finance, the banks following a strategy of long-term

Table 37. Distribution of share ownership in Germany and France (1988 and 1989)

	Proportion of shares held	
	Germany (1988)	France (1989)
Individuals	19.4	23.9
Banks	8.1	3.5
Insurance cos., pension funds	2.7	2.6
Unit trusts	3.4	2.5
Non-financial enterprises	39.3	50.5
Government	7.1	4.3
Foreign	20.0	12.8

Source: Charkham (1994: 105, Table 3.11).

'relationship banking' rather than one-off 'transaction banking'. This is apparent at all levels of the economy. While large national and multinational enterprises are affiliated with the big three banks, regional and smaller enterprises have close links with regional banks. Over the whole period from 1970 to 1990, bank loans have accounted for 90 per cent of all external finance, and a large German bank will have over a half of its lending tied up for long-term periods of four or more years (Hutton 1995: 149). The banking multiplier mechanism, therefore, has underpinned German economic growth. This multiplier operates through cycles of lending: when banks lend to a customer, money is deposited in the customer's bank account and can be re-lent to another customer, and so on. This multiplier effect allows a small amount of saving to generate a high level of industrial investment (Carrington and Edwards 1979: 192). By contrast, the Anglo-American reliance on the stock market means that much capital is dissipated in the secondary stock market, where institutions buy shares that are already in issue and so represent no addition to the capital stock of enterprises.

Table 38. Strategic control in large German enterprises (1961–1970)

Mode of control	Number of companies		
	1961	1966	1970
Family ownership (25%+)	74	63	47
Other owner (25%+)	147	213	220
No dominant interest	22	18	15
Unknown	68	29	15
Total	311	323	297

Source: Thonet and Poensgen (1979: 26, Table 1).

Table 38 shows the structure of corporate ownership in western Germany during the 1960s and 1970s, showing clearly the continuing importance of family ownership and of ownership by banks, non-financials, and state enterprises. Minority control with a holding of 25 per cent or more was an especially strong form of control in Germany, as a legal requirement for 75 per cent support for certain corporate decisions gave an effective veto to these minority shareholders. Families such as Krupp, Thyssen, Flick, and Quandt survived from the pre-war period as significant corporate controllers, and they were joined by newer entrepreneurs such as Grundig and Springer (Krejci 1976; Dyas and Thanheiser 1976). Families had majority control in four of the top twenty-two non-financials of 1970 and held a minority veto in a further two (Jacquemin and De Jong 1977: 166, based on Vogl 1973). A study of the thirty-one largest manufacturers in the early 1970s showed family control or influence in nine of these (Francko 1976: 5), and individuals, families, and foundations had substantial interests in thirty of the top 100 non-financials of 1978 (E. O. Smith 1983: 206–7). In 1991, enterprises subject to family ownership accounted for 12 per cent of the turnover of the top 100 enterprises. In some enterprises, special voting rights buttressed family holdings: the Siemens family, for example, held just 1 per cent of the shares in Siemens, but these shares carried 10 per cent of the votes.

Table 39. Bank shareholdings in the seventy-four largest German enterprises (1974–1975)

	% directly owned	% as trustee	Total holding
Big three banks	6.1	28.8	34.9
Other banks and investment companies	3.0	24.8	27.8
Totals	9.1	53.6	62.7

Source: E. O. Smith (1983).

Table 39 shows the influence exercised by banks over non-financial enterprises in the 1970s. The big three banks directly owned 6.1 per cent of the capital of the top seventy-four enterprises, but they controlled a further 28.8 per cent through their trust departments. Through direct and indirect ownership, then, their total voting control came to over one-third of the issued capital of the enterprises.[1] A

---

[1] Many German companies issue bearer shares rather than registered shares. That is to say, the shares are not registered in the name of a particular shareholder, as in the Anglo-American system, but are regarded as the property of whoever is the current bearer of the certificate. Individually owned bearer shares are generally deposited with the banks and so enhance the voting power of banks. On legal forms of business enterprise in Germany see E. O. Smith (1983: ch. 7), where it is calculated that two-thirds of the top 100 in 1978 were *Aktiengesellschaften*.

similar proportion of shares were held by investment companies, and banks and investment companies together owned almost two-thirds of the capital of the seventy-four enterprises. These bank holdings were not spread evenly through all enterprises, but were highly concentrated. In 1978 the holdings of the big three banks were found to be concentrated in twenty-six of the top 100 enterprises, and bank holdings ranged from 25 to 50 per cent in twenty-two of these (E. O. Smith 1983: 206–7). In 1986, banks held stakes of 5 per cent or more in twenty of the top 100 enterprises, and in eight enterprises a single bank held more than 20 per cent. The big three banks held 32.5 per cent of Siemens, 54.5 per cent of Bayer, 51.7 per cent of BASF, and they had many other large holdings in giant enterprises. These direct holdings were generally magnified by the voting-power of the funds managed by other banks. Thus, the *Deutsche Bank* held 28.5 per cent of Daimler Benz, but the big three banks collectively controlled 61.7 per cent of its votes (Baums 1993b: 160). The big three banks typically exercise well over half the votes actually cast at the AGMs of large enterprises (Roe 1994: Table 6, 173).

These big banks were, then, important foci of power. Bank holdings were not, however, the basis of exclusive minority control, but of oligarchic forms of shared control and co-operation by various banks. Indeed, much loan capital comes from regional banks that are independent of the big banks, and that act as co-ordinating centres rather than pivots of bank control (Edwards and Fischer 1994). Windolf and Beyer (1994: 10) showed that one in ten of the largest 623 enterprises of 1992 owned substantial blocks of shares in other large enterprises: one in five held shares in two or more enterprises. These enterprises were involved in a network of share participations with an overall density of 0.0016. While this was much lower than the density of the intercorporate network among a similar number of enterprises in Britain, German shareholdings were far more structured around enterprises—financial and non-financial—that were the foci of 'star'-pattern clusters.

Other important owners of shares were the federal and local states—which had majority control in six enterprises and minority participations in a further ten—and foreign enterprises and governments that had minority holdings in thirteen of the top 100 of 1978. Franks and Meyer (1992: 26) showed that in 85 per cent of large quoted companies in Germany in 1986 at least one shareholder had more than 25 per cent of the capital—a firm basis for minority control. The big three banks themselves had no predominating shareholders, though their autonomy was enhanced by virtue of their control over their own shares: *Deutsche Bank* controlled 47 per cent of its own shares, 59 per cent of the shares of the *Dresdner Bank* were controlled by the bank itself, and *Commerzbank* controlled 30 per cent of its own share capital (Charkham 1994: 36).

Table 40. Directorships held by multiple directors in Europe (1976)

No. of directorships per person	% of directorships held in the top 250 enterprises in						
	Austria	Germany	Switzerland	Netherlands	Belgium	France	Italy
2	65	60	67	64	57	60	63
3	17	20	19	17	19	19	17
4	9	9	6	8	9	9	7
5	4	5	2	6	6	6	5
6–10	4	5	5	5	6	6	7
11+	2	1	1	0	2	0	1
Totals	100	100	100	100	100	100	100
No. of multiple directors	271	420	405	357	373	378	322
Inclusiveness (%)	62.7	76.1	82.4	77.6	70.4	80.4	77.6
Density	0.027	0.038	0.032	0.031	0.039	0.034	0.029

Source: Stokman and Wasseur (1984: Table 2.2 and Figure 2.1), and calculated from (1984: 25, Table 2.3).

Table 40 shows the way in which this pattern of ownership was reflected in the network of interlocking directorships. Multiple directors made up 10.7 per cent of the directorate of the top 250 German enterprises of 1976, and they tied over three-quarters of the enterprises into an extensive network of connections. The density of this network, at 0.038, was higher than that found in any of the Anglo-American economies, reflecting the high proportion of multiple directors who held four or more directorships. Bank directors were especially important in this network. Of all interlocks in 1976, 28 per cent were carried by executives, about a half of these by executives in financials—most of them from the big three banks (Ziegler, Bender, and Biehler 1985; Ziegler 1993; Biehler 1986; Schonwitz and Weber 1980; Franks and Meyer 1992). Interlocking directorships are also strongly associated with shareholding relations (Windolf and Beyer 1994: 18). The supervisory board of a typical large enterprise includes four executives from other enterprises and sends four of its directors to the executive boards of other enterprises. Bank directors sat on the supervisory boards of 75 of the top 100 industrials in 1986, accounting for one-fifth of all their shareholder-elected directors. Almost two-thirds of the directorships held by bank directors were held by directors of the big three banks, and the chairs of supervisory boards were invariably held by bank directors.

The reunification of eastern with western Germany in 1990 appears to have had little effect on the overall shape of ownership and control in Germany. State-owned combinations in the east were transferred to a privatization agency that adopted a strategy of breaking them up into their saleable parts. These more viable concerns were generally sold to Western enterprises, and where privatization partners could not be found the concerns went directly into bankruptcy (Blum and Siegmund 1993: 404–5). Virtually all large enterprises are now controlled from the west, the independent enterprises in the east being only small or medium-sized. Although the costs of the restructuring of industry in the east have been considerable for the Federal government, eastern business and industry has had to adapt to western structures and practices. In the new Germany, the top 10 non-financial enterprises of 1991 accounted for 46 per cent of the turnover of the top 100 enterprises (Charkham 1994: 33).

This 'German' system of capital mobilization is not limited to Germany itself. Variants of it are also found in Austria and Switzerland, where German cultural and political influence has been strong, and in Sweden. Until the inter-war years, the 'German' system prevailed through much of Central Europe, including many of the economies that were subsequently drawn into the Soviet bloc. German and French banks provided the capital and leadership in the late nineteenth century for the *Credit Anstalt* and other Austrian banks that operated as universal banks and became greatly involved in industrial finance (Eigner 1994). Indeed, it has been claimed that Austria, not Germany, is the true exemplar of universal banking, and it was the opinion of Hilferding that Austria was the clearest case of bank hegemony (Teichova 1992: 18). This system of oligarchic bank hegemony was transformed during the inter-war period by the failure and subsequent nationalization of the *Credit Anstalt* together with its industrial participations. The Austrian government established a system of state support for the banking mechanism, and the economic role of the state was considerably expanded during the post-war period, when the government nationalized leading financial and non-financial enterprises to prevent their confiscation by the Soviet Union as 'German' property. Despite some subsequent denationalization, the banking system remains firmly under the control of the state, and the oligarchic system has been transformed into a unitary system of state–bank hegemony within a 'corporatist' framework. State and local government ownership accounted for 71 of the top 250 enterprises in 1976. The state banks were the peaks of the intercorporate network (see Table 40) and, though they exercised considerable power over other enterprises, they were themselves subject to regulation by the political authorities (Ziegler, Reissner, and Bender 1985).

In Switzerland, banking was dominated by small private banks until the 1850s, when three German-style universal banks were formed with foreign backing. Their primary concern, however, was not the development of Swiss domestic industry, but the expansion of its overseas markets. Only as they began to acquire a number of the private banks did they achieve any significance in the domestic sector of the Swiss economy. The banks have therefore had a particularly close relationship to Swiss multinationals, tying them into an intercorporate network that is similar to that of Germany. In 1976 (see Table 40), a large number of the top 250 Swiss enterprises were interlocked into a dense network in which the big three banks— *Crédit Suisse*, the Union Bank, and the Swiss Bank—held central positions (Rusterholz 1985; Schreiner 1984).

Although it does not have a German two-board system, the Swedish economy has a number of similarities with the German pattern of capital mobilization. Swedish industrial development followed closely on the establishment in 1856 of the *Stockholm Enskilda Bank* as a universal bank controlled by a single family, the Wallenbergs (Kindleberger 1984: 131–4). By 1903 a tightly integrated business network existed, with sugar, mining, and railway enterprises closely tied to banks and insurance companies. Ottosson (1993: 55) has shown that the density of the network of the top 125 enterprises increased steadily from 0.027 in 1903 to 0.056 in 1924, the main increase taking place prior to 1912. Throughout this period the most central enterprise was a bank, the *Skandinaviska Kreditaktiebolaget*, which was interlocked with 18 of the top 125 enterprises in 1903 and 42 of those in 1924. Over this period banks and other financials increased their centrality, and their interlocks reflected their shareholdings in non-financial enterprises. Indeed, each of the big three banks was associated with a distinct cluster of enterprises. Following the collapse of the massive Kreuger financial group, the economy was restructured as the banks sought to rescue its constituent enterprises (Larsson 1991). As a result, the density of the network had declined slightly by 1939, although bank centrality had increased. The Swedish economy remained highly concentrated.

By the 1960s, fifteen families owned enterprises employing almost a half of those working in private industry, and the Wallenberg family alone was responsible for the employment of 20 per cent of those in the private sector. Through the use of shares with special voting rights, the family controls seventy Swedish enterprises, including Electrolux, Saab-Scania, L. M. Ericsson, Swedish Match, Astra, Alfa-Laval, and SKF, and since 1994 it has also become a major influence in Volvo. Many of these shareholdings are co-ordinated through Investor, the Wallenbergs' investment holding company. The only significant counterweight to the Wallenberg family is the *Svenska Handelsbanken*, which operates through an investment-holding company and has large stakes in Aga and a number of other enterprises. Concentration of shareholdings in Swedish enterprises was so great in the 1960s that the ten largest shareholders had a majority of the shares in all corporations quoted on the Stockholm stock exchange (Commission on Concentration 1968: 37; Gustavsen 1976). While the Social Democrats introduced the 'Meidner Plan' for employee shareholding-funds in 1975, this policy was repudiated in the early 1980s by the Conservative government, and it had little impact on patterns of ownership and control.

Germany, Austria, Switzerland, and Sweden, then, show variations on a common pattern of bank-dominated industrial development. This model did not, however, extend to Scandinavian countries other than Sweden. In Norway, for example, banks have been far less important for industrial development, and the network of interlocking directorships is much less dense than in any of the German economies. Private capital is relatively weak and small-scale in Norway, although it is highly concentrated. A study for 1963 found that the twenty largest shareholders in Norwegian enterprises typically held over 50 per cent of the shares, with a majority block generally being held by fewer than ten shareholders (Higley *et al.* 1976: 132; see also Seierstad 1968: 100–1; Andersen *et al.* 1989). Bank finance played little part in the activities of these enterprises, and the Norwegian network of the period 1975–94 showed little evidence of bank or other financial centrality (Grønmo 1995a: 15; 1995b: 44–5, 53). Similarly the Finnish economy, with a much lower level of industrialization than Sweden, had great similarities to the Norwegian economy (Heiskanen and Johanson 1985). In both countries, the state and the co-operative sectors were important, and industry showed a low level of concentration.

The Netherlands, on the other hand, combines elements of both the German and the Anglo-American pattern. The economy has always had a marked overseas economic orientation, and big business was not characteristic of the manufacturing sector until late in the nineteenth century. About three-quarters of the Dutch labour-force was employed in small enterprises prior to 1900, but by 1909 this figure had fallen to half as industry became more concentrated (De Vries 1978: 10). An analysis of interlocks among the top 142 enterprises of 1886 showed a great similarity between the Netherlands and Britain at that time, though the overall density of interlocks was higher in the Dutch network (see Table 41). At the heart of this interlock network were financial and commercial enterprises, the most central including a large number of banks together with insurers, railways, and shippers. Wibaut's (1913) analysis of interlocks in 1910 tried to show that Jeidel's (1905) model of German interlocks could be extended to the Netherlands, but Schijf (1993; 1984) has shown that there is little evidence that the Dutch banks were following German practices. Wibaut's error had been to start from the banks and trace their interlocks, so building bank centrality into his data. Schijf, by taking a larger selection of enterprises, put bank interlocks in context and showed that there were close interlocks between banks, other financials, and colonial traders, but relatively few interlocks between banks and industry (see Table 41).[2]

Manufacturers such as Philips, Van den Berghs, and Jürgens arose independently of the banking system, and even Royal Dutch Petroleum, which traded throughout the Dutch colonial territories, had few links with the Amsterdam banks. Industrial development in the early twentieth century, however, did stimulate some concentration in the banking sector, leading to the emergence of a 'big five' between 1911 and 1930. Later industrial mergers were associated with a further burst of bank mergers in 1964, reducing the number of big banks to just two—AMRO and ABN—though some rival

---

[2] Schijf (1979) presented some provisional results, which are corrected in Schijf (1993). The earlier paper does, however, include some additional data for 1894 and 1910.

Table 41. Distribution of directorships in the Netherlands (1886–1969)

No. of directorships per person	Number of directors		
	Top 142 of 1886	Top 104 of 1902	Top 147 of 1969
2	115	76	190
3	47	27	103
4	22	10	70
5	9	10	35
6	4	5	26
7		3	10
8 or more		3	21
Totals	197	134	455

Source: 1886 and 1902 from Schijf (1993: Tables 6.1 and 8.3), 1969 from Helmers et al. (1975: Table 5.3).
Note: Schijf selected the top 142 companies of 1886 and traced the survivors of this selection in 1902. The only truly cross-sectional data, therefore, are those for 1886 and 1969.

co-operative banks were set up during the 1970s (De Vries 1978: 25–6). In the post-war period, therefore, the Dutch economy had become focused around a small number of big banks and large industrials such as Unilever, Royal Dutch, Philips, AKZO, and Hoogevens, and the relationship between banks and industry conformed closely to the Anglo-American pattern. Banks acted as intermediaries in the underwriting and private placement of share issues, but they were otherwise involved only in the provision of short-term credit. Equally, 'institutional' shareholders have had a far greater importance in the Netherlands than they have in Germany, France, or Belgium (Readman et al. 1973: ch. 6).

The Dutch pattern of interlocking directorships, however, differed significantly from the Anglo-American economies. A study for 1969 (see Table 41) found a high proportion of multiple directors with large numbers of directorships, reflecting a relatively dense network of interlocks. The commercial banks were involved in more of these interlocks than were any other enterprises (Mokken and Stokman 1974: 12; Helmers et al. 1975). The top 250 enterprises of 1976 formed a network whose density of 0.031 was higher than the figure of 0.022 found by Schijf for the top 142 of 1886. While there was a low level of stability for individual interlocks, most of which were not reinstated after the retirement or death of the directors who made them, the overall structure of the network showed great stability. This was in large part a result of the importance of primary interlocks, which tended to express relatively enduring intercorporate relationships (van der Knoop *et al.* 1984; see also Rutges 1984). The major multinationals, however, remained as peripheral to this network as they had been earlier in the century (Stokman *et al.* 1985). Unlike the German economy, where the universal banks had close relationships with most large industrials, the Dutch banks were very close only to the domestic industrials, having little connection with the Dutch multinational industrial enterprises. Although ABN and AMRO spheres of influence could be identified, the main structural characteristic of the Dutch economy was a sharp separation between a dense domestic network and the large multinationals on its periphery. The hegemony of financial intermediaries in the mobilization of capital did not extend to those multinationals that had access to international sources of finance.

Corporate Webs: The Latin Pattern

The Latin pattern has some parallels with the German system (as well as with the Japanese system, described below); but it is nevertheless marked by distinct structures of capital mobilization that can be termed 'corporate webs'. This pattern is most clearly apparent in Belgium, though it is also found in the French and Italian economies and in Latin America.

Industrialization in Belgium and France began earlier and proceeded more slowly than it did in Germany. The Belgian economy experienced very little growth until the rapid development of coal and iron during the 1860s and 1870s, and industrial development in France was erratic until the 1860 tariff reforms opened up greater opportunities for domestic industry (Fohlen 1970). Economic growth in both countries faltered after 1870, when agricultural stagnation had a particularly stultifying effect in economies that were dominated by backward peasant farming, and the French economy was further weakened by the loss of Alsace after the Franco-Prussian war.

Industrial growth in both countries was entrepreneurial in form. The French stock exchange was too weak to support autonomous

capital formation, and the limited capital requirements of the entrepreneurs did not stimulate the kind of banking development that
occurred in Germany. The collapse of the innovatory *Crédit Mobilier*
in 1867 meant that long-term banking capital played no significant
role in the French economy, although some of the older private
banks had begun to adopt a more positive approach towards industrial finance (Gerschenkron 1962: 12–13; Kindleberger 1984: 108–9).
These banks took small shareholdings in industrial enterprises, but
they regarded these as adjuncts to family capital and, following the
industrial failures of the 1870s, they withdrew completely from long-
term industrial finance. Until the 1830s, when Dutch political control ended, the *Société Générale de Belgique* had pursued a very
conservative banking policy. After this, however, the SGB and the
Banque de Belgique became more actively involved in industrial development through the provision of loans to family enterprises in coal,
iron, and steel. The Belgian banks, like the *Crédit Mobilier*, were not
'universal' banks of the German type: they were barely involved in
deposit banking, and were not able to finance rapid industrialization.
They did, nevertheless, take small strategic investments, and by 1860
the SGB owned about one-fifth of Belgian corporate capital. In both
France and Belgium, then, banks and business families played complementary and supportive roles in a system that failed to generate a
rapid industrial take-off. The maintenance of family control was the
overriding goal of entrepreneurs in both countries even more than it
was in Britain, and families turned to the banks only for small supportive investments. Industrialists made no significant demand for
long-term finance, and the banks were, in any case, unable to supply
it (Milward and Saul 1977: 118; Gille 1970: 280–1; Palmade 1961).

In addition to providing overdraft finance and mobilizing loan
capital through savings banks, the SGB acted as an underwriter for
Belgian family firms that sought to form joint stock companies. It
protected its investments in these enterprises by taking share participations and by placing its representatives on the new corporate
boards. It also formed subsidiary investment and holding companies
that extended its role in capital mobilization by enabling other interests to participate indirectly in industry. The investment-holding
companies spread their risks by taking a large number of small
stakes, though these stakes were often crucial for the funding of particular enterprises. Families spread their risks by investing in the
holding companies as well as in the banks. Sometimes a number of
banks would join forces to establish a joint holding-company and to

take larger stakes in railway, tramway, and electricity companies (Milward and Saul 1977: 178). This chain of family and investment holding-company participations created the corporate webs that are so characteristic of the Belgian economy.

The Belgian investment companies enlarged the pool of capital, but they did not become agents of direct control over particular enterprises. Their own capital was owned by intersecting bank and family shareholders, and wealthy families retained stakes in the various enterprises in which the investment companies also invested. The SGB and the *Banque de Belgique* did, nevertheless, become important forces in the control of Belgian companies by building up a massive system of share participations in numerous enterprises (Morrison 1967; Dhondt and Bruwier 1970). Family enterprises that wished to expand without the support of the SGB—without having to share control over their businesses—were forced to accommodate to an economic environment that was shaped by the SGB and its methods. Thus, some industrial entrepreneurs, such as Solvay, formed their own investment banks to participate in the capital of smaller family firms, so giving them access to outside capital while maximizing their autonomy from the SGB (Gille 1970: 285). Through the system of '*holdings*', industrial development occurred under the aegis of loose interest groups that combined enterprises in a range of business activities, tying them together through reciprocal shareholdings and interlocking directorships into extensive corporate webs. There thus emerged a differentiation between the sphere of the corporate webs, dominated by the holdings of the SGB, and the small capital sector of autonomous family-owned firms.

In France, the Parisian private banks—*haute banques* such as Rothschild, Mallet, Mirabaud, and Vernes—were concerned principally with state finance and foreign trade, while the deposit banks formed in the 1850s and 1860s were unwilling to commit their funds to long-term industrial ventures. During the 1870s and 1880s, however, French banking was transformed by the rise of 'mobilier' investment banks that mobilized available savings for use as industrial capital and operated like their Belgian counterparts. Their use of the holding-system of share participations and interlocks enabled their associated enterprises to expand more easily than could other enterprises. In response to the increasing power of investment banks, the private banks began to take industrial participations and to form holding systems of their own. As in Belgium, family firms wishing to expand had to ally themselves with existing bank groups or to form rival groups of their own. The *mobilier* and investment banks were, however, weaker than their Belgian counterparts, largely because of the greater size of the French economy and the lateness of their development. There was not, then, such great pressure on French manufacturers to expand, and many family firms could choose to protect family control by restricting the growth of their businesses. This 'entrepreneurial failure' slowed down the pace of French industrialization (Gille 1970: 280–1; Palmade 1961; Fohlen 1978).

The corporate-web system arose in France and Belgium because of the weakness of their stock exchanges, the absence of any significant state involvement in industrial investment, and, most importantly, the peculiarities of their banking systems (Chandler and Daems 1974: 10; Daems and van der Wee 1974). The French and Belgian investment banks did not draw their funds from deposit banking, and so could not operate as German-style universal banks. Capital was mobilized through the shareholdings of outsiders in investment and holding companies, not through mass savings in bank deposits; and bank funds were not directly tied up in long-term investments. The monetary base from which such a system could draw was narrower than it was in Germany, and the funds that could be mobilized were correspondingly less. Co-operation among banks and alliances among enterprises were, therefore, that much more necessary, and the complex corporate-web system arose as a consequence of this. The system was at its strongest in mining, heavy industry, utilities, and transport. Outside these sectors, where growth was not pursued, small- and medium-sized entrepreneurial firms could persist.

In the massive industrial reconstruction that took place in Belgium after the First World War, the corporate webs extended their influence and banks became more closely involved with industry. Banking failures in the depression of the 1930s, however, resulted in a law of 1935 that made direct bank investment in industry illegal. This reasserted the organizational separation of banking companies from investment holding companies, and the depressed level of share prices enabled the holding companies to buy devalued shares in large numbers (Readman *et al.* 1973: 96). In consequence the relationship between banks and their holding companies was restructured: instead of banks controlling holding companies, the latter became the principal shareholders in banks. In this way, the corporate webs became centred on holding companies and were consolidated as the dominant feature of the Belgian economy (Daems 1978: 10–12).

In France, the expansion of holding companies occurred as industrialists took the lead in building financial enterprises in order to
compensate for the failings of the banking system as a source of
investment (Levy-Leboyer 1980: 124). This was especially marked
during the 1920s, when many enterprises became involved in the
joint financing of ventures using specialized credit and banking subsidiaries set up for the purpose. Large enterprises in chemicals, automobiles, electrical engineering, and metallurgy grew by establishing
subsidiaries that drew on outside capital and so had great autonomy.
Parent enterprises came more and more to resemble investment-
holding companies rather than operating industrial companies, as
more of their activities were hived off to subsidiaries and joint ventures: 'The holding of securities was left with the parent firm, but the
financing of their issue became a separate function carried on by different institutions' (Levy-Leboyer 1980: 146). Loose groups were
formed within which the profits of any one enterprise could be redis-
tributed to support the expansion of others; though the group structure did not completely squeeze out smaller family firms.

Corporate webs centre on the investment-holding companies.
Although the phrase 'holding company' is widely used in law and
social science to describe the parent company of an enterprise, it is
used in a different sense in discussions of Belgium and France to designate a specific type of company with a web of affiliated companies.
Unlike an investment trust or investment company, such a holding
company is explicitly organized around the attempt to control or
influence other companies without taking full ownership of them.
Such a holding company is structured through the pyramiding of
majority and minority shareholdings in operating enterprises and
sub-holding companies. Though linked through shareholdings,
indebtedness, and interlocks, the companies that are brought
together in this way are only loosely co-ordinated, their finances are
not consolidated into a single set of accounts, they do not pursue a
single corporate strategy, and only rarely do they have a common
corporate identity (Daems 1978: 2–3, 34–5; Allard et al. 1978: 6–7).

The constituent enterprises of a corporate web retain a measure
of autonomy from the holding company, and the corporate web
must be seen as a mechanism of intercorporate co-ordination that is
stronger than a mere community of interest but looser than a combine (Scott and Griff 1984: Fig. 1.1). The arena in which this co-
ordination is effected may be the board of the main holding company, or it may be a central committee that is formally separate from

any of the constituent enterprises. In Britain and the United States, corporate webs were formed in transport and utilities during the first thirty years of the twentieth century, but they were not widespread outside these sectors. Even where the webs were important, they were not dominant. The transport sector in Britain in the interwar years, for example, was dominated by the big four railway companies, which participated in some of the corporate webs that had been formed in road and air transport, but which were themselves large, unified, and centralized enterprises. In France and Belgium, on the other hand, corporate webs were central to their economies, giving them a granular, group structure. Economic activity has been concentrated into the hands of a number of rival webs, each of which has subsidiaries and associates operating in the leading sectors of the economy.

This system has undergone a partial transformation during the post-war years. The structure of the webs has tightened, especially in France, and many have become combines or have amalgamated their constituent companies into a single enterprise (Levy-Leboyer 1980: 118–19). In both countries the webs have taken over many enterprises that were formerly subject to family control, while the surviving small enterprises have become increasingly dependent upon them. The investment banks and holding companies have continued to dominate the flow of capital to other business enterprises: two-thirds of investment funding in France in the period 1967–71 was from internal sources, but most external funding came through the banking system. Insurance companies and pension funds, however, play no great role in the capital market and, as shares tend to be closely held within the corporate webs, the stock exchange remains unimportant in the mobilization of capital. Indeed, about one-quarter of stock-exchange transactions in Belgium involve the shares of just one company, Petrofina.

A further transformation occurred in France as the state expanded its role through the acquisition of the big three deposit banks in the 1950s (*Banque Nationale de Paris*, *Crédit Lyonnais*, and *Société Générale*), and private-sector banking was restructured around the investment and private banks that had escaped nationalization. Originally oriented towards overseas investment, the two largest banks, *Suez* and *Paribas*, took over a number of other banks and their holding companies, and enlarged their links with the industrial sector. These two banks became the leading forces in the private sector, and they became key agents in industrial reorganization. The role of the investment banks was enhanced after 1967 when changes in banking legislation allowed them to set up deposit networks in competition with the traditional deposit banks (Carrington and Edwards 1979: 149; Readman *et al.* 1973: chs. 4 and 7). The public-sector financial institutions also became more involved in industry during the 1950s in support of a political strategy aimed at post-war reconstruction and at combating the *défi américaine*—the 'American challenge'—posed by the marketing and investment strategies of the expanding American multinationals. The state and capital, but not labour, were allied into a statist planning system. A number of recent studies have shown the implications of these trends for patterns of ownership and control prior to the further enlargement of the French public sector in 1981.

Table 42. Strategic control in the 200 largest French industrial enterprises (1971)

Mode of control	Type of controller					
	Family	Corporate	State	Foreign	Cooperative	Totals
Majority ownership	38	6	7	41	1	93
Exclusive minority control	43	13	1	9	0	66
Relative minority control	19	11	0	6	0	36
Internal control	–	5	–	–	–	5
Totals	100	35	8	56	1	200

Source: Adapted from Morin (1974a: 65, Table 9).
Note: 'Relative minority control' refers to the situation where a minority controller is subjected to influence from other groups. Morin misleadingly allocates the five 'internal' (i.e. management)-controlled companies to the column for corporate controllers.

Table 42 shows that, in 1971, half the top 200 French enterprises were family-controlled, most families having majority or exclusive minority control. In those that are described as subject to 'relative minority control', the former family controllers are subject to challenge from outside industrial or financial interests and their control is limited by the countervailing power of these other large shareholders. Thus family control has tended to become diluted, and it often involves the sharing of power with outside interests (Bleton

Table 43. Strategic control in the 500 largest French non-financial enterprises (1976)

Mode of control	Type of controller					
	Family	State	Technocratic	Foreign	Other	Totals
Exclusive majority	94	40	23	88	–	245
Exclusive minority	112	13	43	21	–	189
Predominant influence	6	0	4	0	–	20
Mutual	–	–	–	–	20	20
Joint	–	–	–	–	36	36
Totals	212	53	70	109	56	500

Source: Adapted from Morin (1977: 38, Table 18).
Note: The heading 'other' refers to those situations where there is no single controller. All jointly controlled enterprises have been allocated to this category, and no distinction is made between majority and minority holdings.

1966: 135–42; Bauer and Bertin-Mourot 1987).The top 500 enterprises of 1976 (see Table 43) show a similar pattern, indicating that family enterprises varied quite considerably in size. Morin (1974a) classified just under one-fifth of the largest enterprises in his 1971 study as subject to control by corporate shareholders, and in a later work (1977; see also Swartz 1986) he classified these as being subject to 'technocratic control'. Morin introduced this term to describe the situation where a number of large, predominantly corporate, shareholders prevent any one shareholder from achieving dominance, and where the board of directors is recruited from internal executives and from external groups such as retired civil servants (Morin 1974b: 6–7).[3] Technocratic control is

the situation in which it becomes impossible to determine control on the basis of economic property. Too dispersed and/or too heterogeneous in its nature (banks, state, insurance, family) and its strategies, economic property cannot confer control directly to any of the holders. Control is there-

---

[3] For a criticism of Morin (1974b) see Bleton (1976a). This debate was extended in Morin (1976) and Bleton (1976b). Though critical of Morin, Bleton gives considerable support to the notion of technocratic control.

fore delegated to the agents which exercise it without being holders themselves, in any significant sense, of economic property. (Morin 1977: 33)

This situation of 'technocratic control' results from the interweaving of share participations in a structure of impersonal possession. It has some similarities to control through a constellation of interests, though the shareholders that participate in control are not only financial institutions but also the investment-holding companies. The close association of investment-holding companies with other enterprises in their corporate webs means that enterprises have largely been protected from hostile takeover bids from outside their web. Similarly, almost a quarter of the forty-one large Belgian enterprises studied by De Vroey (1973) were controlled through intercorporate holdings (see Table 44). The shareholding interests that comprised these 'technocratic' controlling blocks were the elements of the corporate webs and combines that dominate the French and Belgian economies.

Table 44. Strategic control in forty-one large Belgian non-financial enterprises (1972)

Proportion of shares held by principal owners	Type of controller				
	Family	Corporate	Foreign	Mixed	Totals
0–25	0	0	0	1.5	1.5
25–49	0	4	1	1	6
50–74	2	2	1	3	8
75–99	5	2	3	2	12
100	0	0	11	0.5	11.5
Not known	–	–	–	–	2
Totals	7	8	16	8	41

Source: De Vroey (1973: 119–20).
Note: The firm of Agfa-Gevaert was a union of a minority-controlled company and a wholly owned company, and so De Vroey allocated half to each category.

The contours of the intercorporate networks of capital relations show how the major webs are tied together through interweaving shareholdings. De Vroey's researches confirmed that the biggest corporate shareholder in Belgium was the SGB. In 1969 this holding company controlled twenty-five of the top 115 Belgian enterprises and it shared control in a further eight. All eight of the enterprises classified as subject to corporate control in Table 44 were, in fact, controlled by the SGB, which also had minority participations in two of the family enterprises (De Vroey 1973: 112 ff.; 1975b: 7–8). The SGB, and its associated holding companies such as SOFINA, controlled about half of Belgian industry, and was especially strong in steel, metals, mining, and the financial sector. Other important holding companies, operating on a smaller scale, included Lambert, BRUFINA, Empain, Electrobel, and Cobepa, the Belgian subsidiary of the French Paribas group (CRISP 1962; Cuyvers and Meeusen 1976; 1978). Most of the leading financial institutions are linked to a corporate web and do not act independently of this. For this reason, 108 of the 141 largest listed companies in 1990 had a majority of their shares held by a single holder or by a closely connected web of shareholders (Wymeersch 1993: 8). De Vroey shows that 10 per cent of the shares in SGB are owned by enterprises under the control of the SGB itself (1973: 145–6, 157; see also Daems 1980). While the SGB has influence and minority control in a number of other enterprises, it is itself controlled through interweaving corporate and family interests (Readman 1973: 98). Cuyvers and Meeusen (1985) have described this as 'managerialism within finance capitalism', a particularly tight form of interweaving that forms the basis of the corporate web system.

Morin (1974a; 1977) reported that the largest French investment banks, Suez and Paribas, directly controlled twenty-three of the top 200 enterprises in 1971, and that they had a major influence in five others. The *Banque d'Indochine*, which was absorbed by Suez a year later, controlled two enterprises and influenced five others. In ten of the enterprises that were subject to relative minority control, family power was shared with one of these investment banks. Although a number of smaller investment banks, such as Worms, Lazard, Rothschild, Dreyfus, and Schlumberger were controlled by families or other dominant shareholders, the largest investment banks were subject to a similar pattern of circular control to that found in the SGB. 'In-house' holdings of 17 per cent in Suez in 1974 were buttressed by holdings of 10 per cent by the nationalized savings banks and insurance companies, 9 per cent by an American insurance company, and 10 per cent by the British government (Bleton 1974, 26–7).[4]

---

[4] The British government holding dates from the formation of the original Suez Canal company, when the Rothschilds arranged the purchase of a holding for Disraeli's Conservative government.

The circularity in Paribas was more clear-cut, with fewer large blocks held by companies that were unconnected with the group (Allard *et al.* 1978), though it has subsequently come under the partial control of a rival enterprise that it had itself tried to acquire. In 1991, its top five shareholders held 40 per cent of the votes (Charkham 1994: 128).

SGB in Belgium, and Suez and Paribas in France, have long been at the heart of their national economies; and each of these enterprises stood not only at the centre of its own web, but also at the heart of larger extended webs or *ensembles*—federations centred on a dominant group (Allard *et al.* 1978: 9).[5] Thus Paribas is seen as the basis of an *ensemble* that incorporated the BSN-Gervais-Danone, SCOA, Poliet et Chausson, DNEL, and other webs. The dominance in the French economy of the webs of enterprises around Suez and Paribas is such that their *ensembles* are popularly referred to as '*les deux galaxies*'. These webs of associated enterprises had been much enlarged during the 1950s and 1960s as part of the restructuring of the French economy to meet the American challenge. Paribas came to be identified with the 'modernist' wing of finance capital, supporting state intervention and being involved in a number of large industrial mergers; while Suez was a 'traditionalist' that has been more wary of state intervention and direction (Morin 1974b: 9–10; Allard *et al.* 1978: 10). Alongside the two big *ensembles* in France were to be found the huge webs of Rothschild and Empain-Schneider,[6] and below these were a number of large webs controlled by families (Willott, Dassault, Cartier-Bresson, Michelin, Chegaray, Bettencourt, and Peugeot), foreign enterprises (Chrysler, Honeywell, Hoechst, Fiat, IBM, ITT, and Nestlé), and the state (Allard *et al.* 1978; Bleton 1974; 1976a; Citoleux *et al.* 1977). Outside this corporate-web system of big business was a still-strong sphere of family capital that remained of great importance as new entrepreneurial capitalists rose to replace those that disappeared (Bleton 1966: 135–42). Bauer and Bertin-Mourot (1987) have shown that many of the leading participants in the control of the corporate webs have the characteristics of entrepreneurial capitalists, rentier capitalists, *and* finance capitalists. Although they often have a base in a particular enterprise, they have

[5] The technical problems of defining 'groups' and *ensembles* are discussed in Bellon (1977).

[6] Empain is Belgian and Schneider is French, the two being linked through holdings and joint ventures.

diversified investments that stretch beyond the corporate webs in which they are involved, and they fill the board-rooms of the major banks and insurance companies. The Seydoux, Rothschild, and David-Weill families epitomize this mixture of types.

The fact that the large *ensembles* overlapped with one another and incorporated a number of semi-autonomous webs points to the important fact that capital relations tied most of the large French enterprises into a single network. The formation of combines and the survival of the corporate webs did not lead to a completely frag-mented structuring of the economy, as the various groups had cross-holdings linking them together. Suez and its associates invested in enterprises that were part of the Paribas web, for example, and state enterprises were important investors in numerous large companies. The major *ensembles* appear as central clusters within the intercor-porate network, federations of interests with a higher density of link-ages than the surrounding network of which they form a part. The key banks held peak positions in the network because they were more active than 'institutional' investors in the use of their holdings for purposes of control, and they were also involved in the provision of loans to the enterprises in which they invested. Even within their *ensembles*, however, Suez and Paribas were frequently only minority shareholders, with equal or larger holdings retained by families such as Gervais, Gillet, Hachette, and Fabre.

This pattern of shareholdings was reflected in the structure of interlocking directorships. Table 40 shows that the distribution of directorships in the top 250 enterprises of 1976 was very similar in the two countries. Enterprises in Belgium had slightly larger boards than those in France, but the number of multiple directors and the proportion of directorships that they held were almost identical. The Belgian network, however, because of the dominance of a single group and its extended web, was highly centralized through a mass of interlocks that had their focus on the boards of the SGB and its associates (Cuyvers and Meeusen 1985; see also Daems 1978: 69–84).[7] By contrast, the French network was polarized around the rivalry of the Suez and Paribas *ensembles*, with the density of the interlocks between the two being far lower than their internal den-sities. The state enterprises themselves had few interlocks with any of the private groups, and were marginal to the network as a whole (Swartz 1985). SGB, Suez, and Paribas have become inextricably

---

[7] See Daems (1980: 210) for a comparison of Belgium and Japan.

linked at the international level following the acquisition by Suez of two-thirds of the capital of SGB.

Some changes to the structure of ownership and control in France occurred after 1981, when the newly elected socialist government began the implementation of a policy of nationalization. The whole of the banking system, including Suez and Paribas, was to be nationalized in order to give the state control over the extensive share participations that the banks had built up, but the policy was only falteringly introduced and some deregulation has since been introduced. Through its holdings in financial institutions, the state controlled between one-fifth and a quarter of share capital. Little change to the basic pattern of the corporate webs seems to have occurred, and a study for 1986 showed that 79 per cent of large French companies still had a dominant shareholder with 25 per cent or more of their shares (Meyer 1993: Graph 3). The distribution of shareholdings in France is difficult to assess, as they consist mainly of bearer-shares that are not registered in particular names, but deposited with custodians such as SICOVAM. It has been estimated, however, that just over a third of shares by market value were held by individuals in the late 1980s, and one-fifth were held by institutions. The data for 1989 in Table 37, p. 145, calculated on a slightly different basis, show that individuals held just under a quarter and that banks and financial institutions held less than 10 per cent. In 1988, the proportion of external funding provided as bank loans had fallen, and finance for investment depended far more on bank willingness to buy shares than it had in the 1970s (Milgram and Roberts 1992: 489–90; Wymeersch 1993: Table 1.1, 7).

Italy shows a variant of this Latin pattern. Although French capital was involved in the formation of investment banks in Italy in the 1860s, these banks invested mainly in the railways. Italian industrialization was also inhibited by the policies pursued by the state. Not until German, Austrian, and Swiss banks formed Italian associates in the last part of the nineteenth century did any significant industrial development take place. These universal banks were especially important in the newer electrical and chemical industries, but a series of banking crises prevented the establishment of the close and continuous relationship of banking and industry that had developed in Germany. In the older industries, entrepreneurial families remained important, the scale of production was much smaller, and the rate of growth was even lower than in the new industries (Cafagna 1971; Gershenkron 1962: ch. 4). In consequence, the stock exchange and financial institutions did not become important sources of industrial finance.

The weakness of the Italian state meant that state activity was of limited importance in the economy. State intervention did, however, take on significant proportions during the fascist period, and it was extended after the Second World War. The state holding company, IRI, was set up to rescue three of the failed universal banks in 1929, and it acquired their industrial participations along with their banking operations. Since that time IRI has set up a number of associated holding companies in various sectors, and two new and separate state holding companies have been set up in electricity and oil. In this and other ways, state activity helped to offset some of the dislocations that resulted from a failure to modernize Italian industry in the immediate post-war period. The 1950s and 1960s were, however, a period of industrial growth and reconstruction, as they were in France; and by the 1970s most long-term industrial finance was provided by state banks and credit agencies. State intervention, therefore, has transformed a chronically disabled system of bank hegemony into a state-regulated corporate-web system.

Unlike the French state holdings, those in Italy did not originate in pre-existing private holding companies, but were forged from the industrial participations of the universal banks and from subsequent extensions in public ownership. An early study showed the importance of private holding companies in the electricity industry in the 1920s (Zorzini 1925). Also outside the state holding system, a number of wealthy entrepreneurial families such as Agnelli, Pirelli, and Pesenti have established holding companies and webs of their own. The Agnellis, for example, operate through one principal and two associated investment-holding companies, through which they participate in the control of Fiat and various enterprises in tourism, food, engineering, and property, including stakes in French companies such as BSN and Worms. Although Table 40 shows the distribution of interlocks in Italy in 1976 to be similar to that found in Belgium, a more detailed investigation showed that there was a sharp split between a 'state pole' and a 'private pole' in the Italian network (Chiesi 1985). Each part of the network had a dense pattern of interlocks, but the state and private worlds were only loosely connected with one another. Nevertheless, a group of directors based in financial enterprises did bridge the two sectors, the main links running through IRI and the Falck and Pesenti groups (Chiesi 1982: Fig.

1). Although some state holdings have been privatized during the 1980s, Italy's state sector remains one of the largest in Europe (Segnana 1993).

The major economies of Latin America—Mexico, Brazil, Argentina, and Chile—have followed a variant of the Latin pattern of capital mobilization. In these economies, however, the transition from personal possession to more impersonal forms is only in its very early stages. Strong states have sponsored private-sector industrialization, leading to a shift from commercial production to more industrialized economies between the 1930s and the 1950s. The agents of capitalist development were entrepreneurial capitalists and their corporate webs, these being organized around *financieras*— private banks and other financial enterprises—that mobilized capital for the associated enterprises. These corporate webs were strengthened in the late 1970s as the economies expanded further (Johnson 1985*a*: 186; 1985*b*). In Mexico, for example, Diaz encouraged foreign investment from 1876, this investment coming mainly from the United States, Britain, and France and going into mines, oil, railways, and electric power. This ended with the revolution of 1910, and it was not until 1940 that industry took off, again with state sponsorship. Indigenous entrepreneurs in Monterrey and certain other areas formed diverse groupings around extended kinship groups, running their enterprises through subordinate managers (Derossi 1971: 57; Cordero and Santin 1982). More than half the large enterprises in the 1960s had relatives of the founder among their directors and top executives, and in many cases there were fewer than twelve shareholders altogether (ibid.: 101).

The best-studied Latin American economy, paradoxically, is Chile, one of its least industrialized. Zeitlin and his associates studied patterns of control in the top 37 non-financial enterprises and the big six banks of 1964–6, showing the importance of intercorporate holdings centred on extended kinship groups (Zeitlin 1984; Zeitlin and Ratcliff 1988). Levels of majority control were correspondingly very low: Table 45 shows that just six non-financials and two banks were controlled in this way. While thirteen enterprises had less than 10 per cent of their capital held by their twenty largest shareholders, only one enterprise had the degree of share dispersal that would warrant the designation 'management-controlled'. In the remaining enterprises, the large shareholders were usually allied with one another in webs of intercorporate minority relations. The Edwards family, descendants of English settler capitalists, controlled three

Table 45. Strategic control in large Chilean enterprises (1964–1966)

	Top 37 non-financials	Top 6 banks
Wholly owned	1	
Private	4	
Other majority	1	2
Exclusive minority (20% or more)[a]	6	1
Exclusive minority (10%–19%)	6	1
State/Corporate shared minority	2	
Limited minority	5	2
Intercorporate	11	
Management	1	
Totals	37	6

Source: Calculated from textual information in Zeitlin and Ratcliff (1988: 45), reporting changes to their Table 1.3 (1988: 40), and from the full data listing in Table 1.5 (1988: 46–9).
[a] includes some controlled by associated and intermarried families.

enterprises and participated in the control of a further three large enterprises, as well as controlling their own bank.

Chilean banks operate alongside insurance companies in a well-developed stock exchange, and have been a major source of corporate finance. Over half the directors of the big banks were also directors of the top 37 non-financials of 1964–6. As a result, these enterprises were connected together into an extensive network of interlocking directorships: 52 of the 165 directors held two or more directorships, and 16 of them held three or more (Zeitlin and Ratcliff 1988: Table 2.5, 105).

Corporate Collusions: The Post-Communist Pattern

While the Anglo-American, German, and Latin patterns are the result of long-lasting processes of capitalist development, the emergent 'post-Communist' pattern results from the transformation of an existing industrial system into a new economic framework. The post-Communist systems are not, however, creations completely *de novo*. The collapse of the Communist systems of the former Soviet Union and Eastern Europe left the controllers of their industrial enterprises with the critical problem of evolving methods for raising the capital that would allow them to continue their operations. In doing so, they have drawn on the heritage of both the Communist and the pre-Communist periods.[8]

Before the rise of Communism, the German pattern of bank-led industrialization spread through much of central and eastern Europe. In Germany itself, in the Austro-Hungarian Empire, and in their adjacent and dependent territories, industry was shaped by the availability of long-term banking capital. The areas of what are now the Czech Republic, Hungary, eastern Germany, and Russia all showed this pattern. Indeed, Bohemia and Moravia were the most valuable industrial areas in the Austro-Hungarian Empire, and when they were incorporated into the new state of Czechoslovakia, in 1918, it became the tenth most powerful economy in the world. This industrial success was largely due to German capital, which had been of critical importance in developing the engineering and armaments industries and light industry in north and west Bohemia, Prague, Brno, and northern Moravia, only Slovakia remaining predominantly an agricultural region.

In Russia, industrialization had been initiated by the state, but the extreme backwardness of its economy had seriously limited any possibility of an indigenous industrial take-off. Despite the great strides that were made in heavy industry and in oil during the 1890s, most industrial undertakings were very small in scale, and the economy remained largely agricultural: by 1914, wage-earners in industry, transport, mining, and construction amounted to only just over 10 per cent of the employed population (Rigby 1990: 116; Gerschenkron 1962: ch. 6; Nove 1969: ch. 1). Foreign investment was encouraged to hasten the pace of development, and by 1913 about one-third of its capital came from foreign investors, mainly from Britain, France, and Belgium. Much of this foreign capital was channelled through a nascent domestic banking system that was attempting to organize domestic industry into cartels, and the growth of universal banking encouraged the state to begin to

---

[8] In this discussion I concentrate on the industrial economies of the Czech Republic, Hungary, Poland, and Russia. The Baltic and Balkan states cannot yet be considered as 'industrial' in the same sense. While Yugoslavia did achieve a relatively high level of industrialization—and a very distinctive form of worker self-management—it too had a large and backward agricultural sector, and its political fragmentation into a state of civil war during the 1990s makes the future of its industrial districts highly uncertain.

withdraw from its role in industrial promotion (Gerschenkron 1962: 135–6). It was perhaps this German-style banking system that made Hilferding's (1910) account appear so plausible to Lenin (1916) as a general model for capitalist development. Further development in a 'German' direction was prevented by the First World War and the 1917 Revolution, however; though it is doubtful whether Russia's heavy dependence on foreign capital would have allowed a truly 'German' pattern to develop.[9]

Following the Revolution, Russian industrialization was set on a radically different course. Industry and banking were nationalized, and a mechanism of central planning was established. All factories, mines, workshops, and other units of production and distribution were operated as nationalized units of a single state entity, with the central ministry—the *Vesenkha*, or Supreme Council of National Economy—organizing production through its various divisions or sections (*glavki*). The domestic banks were nationalized and were merged into the People's Bank, the forerunner of *Gosbank*, and the role of foreign capital was curtailed. The nationalized banking system employed some of the same mechanisms that had been used by the universal banks, but it operated as a direct arm of the mono-organizational state apparatus and its planning system. Bank credit was not offered on a commercial basis, but only in relation to centrally specified production targets. All industrial undertakings were allocated to a specific state bank, which handled all their credit requirements. The economic operations of plants and industrial undertakings were specified in great detail in the state plans, and bank credit was freely available to them for the implementation of these plans. *Gosbank* itself was the directive centre of state industrial finance, and while it did operate consumer monetary transfers and manage the money supply, it cannot be said that the Soviet Union ever had a true money market or capital market (Zwass 1979; Garvey 1977). Russian industry was massively developed under this planning system, though the Soviet authorities concentrated on the rapid development of producer goods in heavy industry. The basic unit of economic activity was the 'concern' (*predpriyatiya*), which comprised a single plant, farm, or establishment—often extremely large—and had a recognized legal identity as an economic agent.

---

[9] Indeed, it must be recognized that the very nature of Russian industrialization contributed to the genesis of the 1917 Revolution.

Despite this legal identity, however, it differed markedly from the capitalist business enterprise.[10]

When the Soviet concerns were accorded their separate legal status, in 1921, they were also grouped into 'trusts' that were made the fundamental units of accounting and within which the production of a particular product in a specific locality was undertaken. The Baku oil-producing concerns, for example, were organized into the largest trust in the Union. Concerns were largely subordinate to their 'parent' trust during the period of the NEP, though the trusts did have some autonomy in raising capital through negotiation with the banks and the ministerial *glavki*. Some private shareholdings were even allowed in the specialist credit banks set up by *Gosbank* in this period. After 1929, the powers of the trusts and banks were reduced as they came to be seen as organs of unwieldy controls over concerns. There was, however, no real increase in autonomy for the concerns, and the *glavki* were replaced by 'associations' (*obyedineniya*) that operated as central purchasing and co-ordinating agencies for the various concerns (Nove 1969: 212). These associations had little autonomy from their ministries, and under Stalin's rule they were incorporated fully into the ministerial structure and re-named as *glavki*. This remained the basic system of economic administration until 1957.

Following the Communist takeover of power in Czechoslovakia, Hungary, Poland, and other countries of central and eastern Europe in the 1940s, their economies were organized along similar Stalinist lines. In East Germany, for example, many concerns (VEB) were grouped into vertically integrated combines (VEK) of a kind not found elsewhere in the Soviet bloc, and it was the VEK that took the leading economic role of allocating planning targets among the constituent concerns. The largest of the VEK—such as the Carl–Zeiss–Jena combine—were comparable in scale and scope to large integrated capitalist enterprises, though they operated without a significant market mechanism and without the mechanisms of control characteristic of the capitalist enterprise (Melzer 1981).

From 1957, the Soviet Union introduced a degree of regionalism into its industrial structure and there were attempts to group concerns and to give them greater autonomy from the ministerial *glavki*.

[10] It is for this reason that I have used the word 'concern' rather than 'enterprise', which is often used to translate *predpriyatiya*. 'Enterprise', in the capitalist sense, seems to be the principal characteristic that all observers agree was lacking in the Soviet economic undertaking.

These attempts were advanced more rapidly under the Kosygin reforms of 1965, and multi-plant groups of concerns were formed to merge their independent operations into larger and, it was intended, more efficient units. These groupings were termed 'firms' (*firmy*) or, if vertically integrated on the East German model, 'combines'. The previously autonomous powers of the merged concerns were transferred to the firms and combines, and by 1971 there were 650 of them in the Soviet Union. These firms and combines contained 2,700 concerns and accounted for 8.5 per cent of total industrial employment.

This increasing autonomy for firms and combines led Bettelheim to argue that the 1965 reforms heralded the restoration of capitalism in the Soviet Union. The managers and directors of concerns and the officials of the planning system, he argued, had connived in the subversion of planning principles to commodity relations, and they had to be seen as a 'state bourgeoisie' running a system of 'state capitalism' (Bettelheim 1970; 1968). These directors and officials had transformed the system of state property into their own collective property, had usurped state power, and had subordinated the planning system to the needs of the concerns. Firms, combines, and concerns became true 'economic subjects', loci of the crucial economic decisions on which the development of the economy depended. The principal difficulty with Bettelheim's argument—clearly seen in retrospect—is that he overstated the degree to which directors and economic officials had subordinated the state and established the autonomy of concerns. Hindess (1970: 20–1) has added the further important point that collectivized private property cannot be the basis of true *capitalist* ownership. An economy that is dominated by a single unit of private property is not a capitalist system at all, as capitalism presupposes the existence of relations between separate and competing units of private property that must be units of ownership and control.

The modern capitalist enterprise involves what can be termed a duality of possession: it is the *subject* of possession, in that it is the legal owner of the assets that it uses, and it is the *object* of possession, in that its joint stock form allows it to become involved in a structure of proprietary control. It is through this duality of possession that the capitalist enterprise is constituted as an economic agent. Its legal existence is defined by the duality of possession and by a whole cluster of associated legal relations (contract, agency, employment, and so on). The Soviet concern was neither the subject nor the object of

possession. Its assets were elements in a framework of state ownership, and its legal status was somewhere between that of a public corporation and a public authority. It had few of the legal rights
associated with the duality of possession that are characteristic of
capitalist enterprises, and it must be seen as an integral part of the
state apparatus. It is a plant or establishment legally constituted as an
agency of autonomous but limited economic action within a strictly
defined framework of centralized planning and direction.

It is 'the effective break-up of state property, whether or not the
legal form of state ownership is maintained, which constitutes the
decisive moment in the restoration of capitalism' (Hindess 1976: 21),
and this was not to occur until the 1990s. Until then, the state
remained, *de jure* and *de facto*, the focus of relations of ownership and
a major constraint on the ability of concerns to act as capitalist enterprises (see also Konrad and Szelényi 1974: 50–1).

More radical moves in the direction of economic autonomy had
been undertaken outside the Soviet Union. Concerns in Czechoslovakia had been amalgamated into associations with some
autonomous decision-making powers in the late 1950s, and in 1967
these were, briefly, accorded almost full autonomy: directive planning was virtually abandoned and banks were permitted to make
autonomous investment decisions (Rychetnik 1981). In Poland, the
Gomulka reforms of 1956–7 increased the autonomy of industrial
concerns for a while, but it was not until the early 1970s that major
reforms gave associations (WOGs) enhanced powers. By 1974, 100
WOGs accounted for almost 50 per cent of industry (Nuti 1981). The
most radical and long-lasting changes occurred in Hungary, where
the reforms of 1968 gave autonomy to associations of concerns to
operate in a market framework without centrally planned targets.
Despite this move towards a more 'guided market economy', the
concerns were not given any rights to transfer their assets or to alter
their legal structure, and their links to the political centre remained
of crucial importance. Hungarian concerns could gain funds for
investment, for example, only if they could persuade planners to
include the concern's own production targets in the national plan, so
allowing them a preferential position within the command system
(Radice 1981).

In the Soviet Union, the final elements of the old *glavki* system
were not abandoned until 1973, when new associations (renamed
obyedineniya) were introduced. These replaced some of the firms and
combines, but they also acted as autonomous economic units. The

powers that had been given to concerns in the 1965 reforms were transferred to the associations (Gorlin 1974). By the 1980s, the associations contained about half of all concerns, accounting for over 40 per cent of sales and industrial employment (Nove 1981). While the concerns retained powers of operational administration, the associations and the ministries shared the powers of strategic control.

By the 1980s, then, there were signs of movement, to varying degrees and at varying speeds, towards greater autonomy for concerns and associations throughout the Soviet bloc. Despite these changes, the Communist systems remained highly centralized systems of economic organization. Zaslavskaya (1990: 64) has aptly characterized the Soviet economy of the Brezhnev period as 'an economy of bargaining and deals'. Central planners had neither the knowledge nor the ability to monitor the activities of the concerns and associations, and so they resorted to negotiations with their managers. Planners bargained over their ability to make credit available, to set prices, and to offer incentives, while concern managers bargained over their ability to control the actual production process. The structure of bargaining extended also to the relations among concerns, which resorted to barter relations involving, for example, the exchange of surplus labour and machinery, and the direct bartering of output. Political reforms did, however, lead to further changes in the structure of economic administration during the 1980s.

From 1986 a series of legal changes in Russia altered the ownership and employment relations within which production took place, and by 1989 specifically capitalist forms of enterprise had effectively been legalized, and the joint stock company became a feature of the Soviet system (Pomorski 1991). Concerns and associations were permitted to determine their production in relation to direct orders, and they were required to compete for these orders. Wage-levels were to be determined according to the profitability of the concern. Concerns were also required to move to a system of 'full-cost accounting' under which they had to cover all their costs from revenue and, correspondingly, to pay less of their surplus to the state. In these ways, the 'concern' came closer to being a true 'enterprise'. Private-business-ownership was fully legalized in 1990, and Gorbachev persuaded parliament to pass proposals for the privatization of state enterprises.

Changes in Poland and Hungary were even more radical, as their Communist systems rapidly crumbled in a process of 'negotiated transition' (Szablowski and Derlein 1993). In Hungary, joint stock companies (*Részvéntársaság*) were permitted and increased rapidly in number, and in Poland the introduction of a shareholding system for concerns was associated with the encouragement of Polish *émigré* capital to return to the country, 'reclaim' nationalized assets, and invest in the development of Polish industry. In 1987 a private sector of 683 such 'Polonia' enterprises and half a million small businesses accounted for 7 per cent of GNP, and a whole 'second economy' of illegal economic activity was flourishing (Kolankiewicz and Lewis 1988).

The anti-Gorbachev coup in 1991 stalled the liberalization process in the Soviet Union, and the Yeltsin government's economic policies undermined the viability of many private enterprises. Because of the pressing need to raise funds, and as a result of pressure from the directors and managers of state enterprises, the government decided, nevertheless, to proceed with the privatization policy. The privatization of state enterprises had become widespread through-out Eastern Europe, as the Communist systems collapsed and these economies began their faltering move away from centralized state socialism to market systems of production and distribution. The officially stated aim has generally been to encourage private enterprise and popular share-ownership of the kind that is assumed to exist in Western economies, and 'privatization' in many East European economies has been an essential element in attracting or retaining IMF and World Bank funds for economic reconstruction (see Cox 1994*a*; 1994*b*). In practice, however, the pattern of privatization and of continuing public enterprise has shown considerable continuity with the old Communist system of economic administration. Even in the more reformed economies of the Czech Republic, Hungary, and Poland, the entrenched dominant strata of the old system have sought to adapt emergent capitalist forms of enterprise to their own vested interests (Staniszkis 1991*a* and *b*; Hankiss 1990).

Much of the privatization that took place in Hungary after 1989 has been financed by foreign capital, so increasing the significance of foreign ownership in the Hungarian economy. Concern over this transfer of state assets to foreign capital led to a shift in policy in 1992, the government aiming to increase opportunities for domestic capital. A study of the top 225 Hungarian enterprises of 1993 found that 36 were majority-owned by foreign interests (Stark 1996: 1002). Many of the remaining enterprises were controlled by the State Property Agency or the State Holding Company, but 87 were tied together through intercorporate holdings taken by other Hungarian enterprises. A flourishing small-business sector and 'second economy' of workers and peasants in supplementary small-scale production and trading completed the emergent framework of Hungarian capitalism (Szelényi 1989; Roman 1989).

In other former Communist countries the pace of privatization has been slow; but some large concerns have been privatized in the Czech Republic and in Russia since 1992. Moves towards privatization in Poland were slowed down by the return of a Communist government in 1993, but a beginning was made in 1995. The Czech privatization programme, after the split with Slovakia, was intended by its government to lead the economy towards what was called a 'Swedish' corporatist model of capitalist development.[11] To aid this process, the government encouraged the rapid development of an investment-banking system to spearhead industrial reconstruction, and there was a rash of bank formation. Following the collapse of some of these ill-organized banks and a wider restructuring of the banking system, the Czech financial system became effectively dominated by two massive banks, *Ceska Sporiteilna* and *Komercni Banka*. Almost two-thirds of the Czech population hold shares in privatized enterprises or in investment funds. Many of the investment funds are closely linked to, or owned by, the banks, which are important lenders to the enterprises in which the investment funds have their holdings. Through the strong links between the banks and the state, and because of the continuing significance of public sector industry, the Czech Republic does indeed seem to have introduced some of the elements of a Swedish or Austrian-style corporatist system. There are also signs of a similar development in Hungary, where tripartite corporatist organizations have come to play a leading role in the economy (Cox and Vass 1994).

Most privatization programmes have used the system of 'insider privatization', a system in which the managers and workers in an enterprise are entitled to acquire a majority of the shares (Cox 1994a: 398–9; 1994b). This has allowed the existing directors and managers to become the effective controllers of the privatized businesses. Where shares in an enterprise are directly transferred from the state to the workers, the directors and managers have generally been made trustees of the shares and they are able to use manipulatory

---

[11] The Czech Republic and Slovakia ended their federal structure in 1993. The Czech districts of Czechoslovakia had been the primary focus of industrial development.

methods to secure voting control over shares that are nominally owned by the labour force as a whole. The issuing of 'vouchers' or certificates exchangeable for shares has also buttressed existing management. Rudimentary financial information, the slow pace of privatization, and economic uncertainty have all conspired against the exchange of vouchers through an effective stock market. Instead, workers have tended to exchange their vouchers for hard cash or for shares in their own enterprises. In all these ways, the existing management acquire controlling majority and minority holdings, and this control allows them to secure credit, supplies, and outlets by entering into liaison shareholdings with other enterprises and agencies that are strategically located in their business environment (Clarke 1992: 14; Cox 1994a: 399).

In all the post-Communist economies under consideration, the industrial *nomenklatura* of former Communist officials have been involved in illegal and semi-legal privatizations as well as benefiting from official privatization policies. In many cases, control over state assets has been usurped through processes of 'spontaneous privatization'. Under this practice, the managers of an enterprise may lease the business to a new private enterprise that is under their ownership, and the undertaking is able to continue under new legal relations and privatized control. More extreme forms of spontaneous privatization have involved the liquidation and asset-stripping of concerns, to the benefit of new enterprises owned by the industrial *nomenklatura*. In either case, *de facto* managerial buy-outs take place (Ray 1994).

These management powers have been supplemented by the growing importance of external investment funds set up by former *nomenklatura*. These funds have accumulated vouchers in exchange for their own shares, and have built up strategic stakes in privatized enterprises. Three-quarters of all voucher-holders in Czechoslovakia allowed investment funds to purchase and manage shares on their behalf. Although investment funds are limited by law to a maximum 10-per-cent holding in any one company, the setting-up of subsidiaries and associate companies that can each take up to 10 per cent allows an investment group to mobilize large controlling blocks. The fifteen biggest funds in 1995 held a total of 40 per cent of privatized share capital, a higher level of share-concentration than in either Britain or the United States. In Poland, special investment funds have been set up to act as investment trusts, and vouchers exchangeable for shares in the investment funds have been offered to the public.

The disintegration of the command system has left the new

'enterprises' disconnected from the central agencies that formerly structured their relations with one another. Nevertheless, the industrial *nomenklatura* have retained day-to-day control of many enterprises, just as they did when they were 'concerns'. The collapse of the old system of state control did not mean that a completely new beginning had to be made, and the *nomenklatura* have sought to secure their advantages and interests, along with the economic viability of their enterprises, by adapting old practices to the new circumstances in which they find themselves. Faced with the 'persistence of routines and practices, organizational forms and social ties, that can become assets, resources, and the basis for credible commitments and coordinated actions' (Stark 1996: 995), the former *nomenklatura* continue to rely on the tried-and-tested practices of bargaining with public agencies, and on the inter-enterprise bartering that they have always had to employ. This now occurs, however, without any overarching framework of state planning or central enforcement. In consequence, relatively more 'anarchic' structures of bargaining and barter have developed (Burawoy and Krotov 1992), and capital mobilization can be said to involve a 'truck mechanism' of corporate collusion.[12] In such a system, access to capital and investment opportunities depends upon the making of bargains, especially those that involve barter or negotiation rather than straightforward commercial exchange. Access to bank credit, supplies, and outlets depends upon the bargaining abilities of directors and managers, and not on the commercial viability of particular projects. The mobilization of formal and informal social networks supersedes commercial criteria as enterprises collude with one another, with banks, and with the state.

These practices have encouraged a great deal of illegal racketeering and black market activity. Some of the new 'entrepreneurs', especially those who have emerged from the 'second economy' and black market of the Communist system, are, in fact, more heavily involved in racketeering, financial manipulation, and organized crime than they are in legitimate business activity, and close links exist between the industrial *nomenklatura* and the racketeers.[13] Those who control

---

[12] Burawoy and Krotov (1992) term the system 'merchant capitalism', but this term fails to emphasize the non-market elements of bargaining. Clarke (1992) makes the further point that specifically 'capitalist' mechanisms are not yet dominant in the Russian economy.

[13] The racketeers are often misleadingly termed 'mafia', though they are very different from the Sicilian and American mafia.

the necessary resources have been in a strong position to demand a role in corporate governance in return for making them available to the new enterprises, and the loosening of state control over the economy has allowed organized criminal networks to play a major part in the co-ordination of enterprises. It has been estimated that at least 70 per cent of privatized enterprises have criminal connections, and that 80 per cent of their voting shares are in criminal hands (Nelson and Kuzes 1995). Indeed, it has been suggested that the vast majority of privatized enterprises in Russia are paying up to half their profits, on top of dividend payments, to racketeers (Brummer 1994).

In all the post-Communist industrial economies, then, capital mobilization occurs through a network of corporate collusions that links together the large enterprises that are controlled by the industrial *nomenklatura*. In the Czech Republic, Hungary, and Poland, this has been supplemented by the growing influence of foreign and *émigré* capital. The formerly Communist state apparatuses remain crucial to the whole process of capital mobilization, and the continuing significance of public enterprise and state intervention through close links between the industrial and the political *nomenklatura* provides the potential for a corporatist structuring of their economies. Much may yet change in the post-Communist economies, but they seem set on a new path of capitalist development.

Corporate Sets: The Japanese Pattern

Through most of the Tokugawa period, from 1600 to 1868, there was little industry in Japan other than small-scale handicraft production. Some of these factories—especially those in cotton and silk production, rice-wine brewing, and sesame-oil making—had numerous employees and a division of labour, but they showed only a limited commercial development. Commercial undertakings proper were limited to the activities of large urban merchants (*shonin*) who achieved some considerable power in the domestic market. The closure of the country to foreign trade and influence meant that these merchants had no overseas interests until the enforced 'opening' of Japan to trade by the Western powers. Despite this restriction, there was a growth in mercantile power, especially in the south-eastern domains of Satsuma (Kagoshima) and Chosu (Yamaguchi), that progressively destabilized the Tokugawa regime. These powerful mercantile interests were a major factor behind the so-called imperial 'restoration' of 1868, and the restoration of the formal authority of the Meiji monarchy in fact marked the rise to power of conservative modernizers who sought to use the power of the state to build up the industrial base of the economy (Noguchi 1984: ch. 1). The Meiji modernizers saw state power as a way to offset the problems posed by the limited scale of indigenous entrepreneurial capital and the low level of technological development. To this end they set up strategic economic and military enterprises and supported private capital accumulation in railways, shipping, communications, and manufacturing (Westney 1979; Yazawa 1963; Clark 1979: 29–31). A number of aggressive tycoons such as Yasuda, Asano, and Okura took advantage of the opening of the ports for foreign trade, and they were joined by government protégés such as Mitsui and Iwasaki, and by other entrepreneurs such as Shibusawa, in the construction of a new foundation for the Japanese economy (Hirschmeier and Yui 1975; see also Yasuoka 1977; Nakagawa 1977; Morikawa 1977).

State-led industrialization, however, proved prohibitively expensive, largely because of poor management and the accumulation of debts, and the government was forced into a policy of divestment from the 1880s. This privatization of state assets enabled nascent businesses to expand even further through the acquisition of state factories (Clark 1979: ch. 1). This was explicitly intended to encourage the formation of strong and autonomous business groups that would provide a mechanism of capital accumulation capable of sustaining rapid industrialization and consolidating Japan's position as a major world power (Allen 1972; Lockwood 1968; Hirschmeier 1964).

Central to the new business groups were the wealthy merchants. Dynastic merchant families such as Mitsui had long been organized as corporate bodies using the legal form of the 'house', in which there was a unity of the enterprise and the family household (Clark 1979: 14; Allen 1972). The traditional family of the Japanese merchants and landowners is what Le Play (1871) called the 'stem family' (see Todd 1985). The Japanese stem family, traditionally termed the *ie*, was a corporate group subject to the authority of a male 'head' who had power over family members in all spheres of life. The family perpetuated itself as an entity from one generation to the next, and its headship passed through inheritance to a new head. A strong vertical link between the head and his sons was the central organizing principle of the family, as the head was responsible for managing the family property and for ensuring that the patrimony was passed on intact to the next generation (Befu 1971). Only one son would be able to inherit the family property and become its head. Undivided inheritance of the main family property allowed merchants to expand their activities on a scale that would not have been possible if inheritance had been fragmented. Non-inheriting sons had to leave the main family and form their own 'branch' families, though they would remain subject to the authority of the head of the senior line. An extended kinship group—the *dozoku*—consisted of several stem families organized into a hierarchical grouping dominated by the *honke* or main line of the family. Businesses were organized along family lines, and businesses run by branch families would generally be run as affiliates of the main family business.

In the Meiji period, merchant and other entrepreneurial families, with the encouragement of the state, formed and acquired enterprises in a wide range of industries and began to construct large business groups. These groups found joint stock organization a useful support for their economic expansion. The joint stock form enabled each family business to be formed as a separate corporation but, at the same time, it enabled them to be subjected to common control. It was also ideally geared to the Japanese form of family enterprise, as it allowed the main and branch families to take varying shares in the family enterprise without undermining the unity of the business.

Wealthy families built extensive industrial groupings. The old Mitsui family trading-house became a major industrial group under delegated management, and newer entrepreneurs such as Iwasaki (of Mitsubishi) and Yasuda formed similar groups. The largest of the business groups that emerged in the period leading up to the First World War—particularly Mitsui, Mitsubishi, Yasuda, and Sumitomo—came to be known by their opponents as *zaibatsu*, a word that means 'financial clique', 'estate of wealth', or, more colloquially, 'money trust'. Initially used as a critical term, the word was taken up by the wealthy controlling families themselves as a description of the form of business enterprise that produced their wealth. While there is some controversy—and even more confusion—about the definition of *zaibatsu*, the term may most usefully be employed to designate a specific structure of large-scale enterprise that involves tight family control over sets of legally separate enterprises co-ordinated as single units of capital. The companies that made up each *zaibatsu* operated in diverse industrial sectors and were clustered together into hierarchical sets through their links to the controlling family, through reciprocal trading arrangements, and through banking activities. These *zaibatsu* were especially strong in finance, overseas trade, mining, shipping, and heavy industry, but joint stock companies run by independent entrepreneurs were important in cotton textiles, light machinery, agricultural products, and various other sectors (Morikawa 1992: chs. 1 and 2; Noguchi 1984: ch. 3).

Although encouraged by the state, the corporate clustering from which the *zaibatsu* form of group organization sprung had as its main purpose the maintenance of family control over a diverse range of enterprises. The business leaders who took advantage of the economic environment created by state policies aimed to do so in a way that maintained the kind of cohesion that had been possible in the integrated merchant-houses. Wealthy families sought 'a device to assure that they would not be interfered with by outsiders in their efforts to keep the closed character of the business' (Yasuoka 1977: 94). The practice of pyramiding shareholdings within the group, with direct family holdings being limited to a parent holding-company, allowed external funds to be raised by the subsidiary operating companies without family control being undermined. The key to the whole structure was the so-called 'holding company'. This was not an investment holding-company of the kind found in France and Belgium, but nor was it simply a parent-holding company of the kind found in Britain and the United States. It was, in fact, generally a partnership, trust, or unlimited company that served to regulate and co-ordinate the family rather than the businesses.[14] It was concerned with such things as regulating family property and allocating income to family members in a situation where family interests were being diversified (Fruin 1983; Hirschmeier and Yui 1975). These holding-partnerships, as they may be called, acted primarily as 'family offices', but did, nevertheless, also function as effective 'head offices' for the *zaibatsu*. Such legal forms were essential for maintaining the unity and control of the *zaibatsu* families and their enterprises. The Mitsui *zaibatsu*, for example, had experienced great financial problems in the early Meiji period, and had delegated the task of reconstruction to a non-family manager, Minomura. Under his leadership, the group was strengthened and enlarged, and the Mitsui family re-established their control after his death by establishing a family partnership (*dozokukai*) to regulate the affairs of the eleven branches of the family and to co-ordinate the activities of the

---

[14] The names of these partnerships varied, but they were generally described by such terms as *omotokata* or *honsha* and their variants.

group. In a further reconstruction the partnership was abolished and its affairs were reorganized into an unlimited company (*gomeikaisha*) in 1909. During the 1920s the corporate structures of the *zaibatsu* were further tightened, the central partnerships becoming the bases for more centralized co-ordination of the groups.

The general pattern of control within a *zaibatsu* was for a family council to set up a holding partnership that co-ordinated the activities of the operating joint stock companies that were its 'subsidiaries'. Techniques of control that were used by the families to co-ordinate their sets were ties of share-ownership, the use of the group bank to make credit available to group enterprises, the centralization of commercial relations within the group, and the careful appointment of directors and executives to subsidiaries. Trading links within a set involved a common orientation to a trading company that undertook centralized marketing for the whole group, though there was little or no technical integration of production among the group enterprises. Shareholdings within a *zaibatsu* were used for control rather than for investment or finance, and capital for expansion continued to come from associated banks, the largest *zaibatsu* including banks among their constituent enterprises. These banks operated very differently from the German universal banks, as they were barely involved in savings or deposit business and concentrated almost exclusively on the corporate sector (Yamamura 1978: 241–2). Instead, a *zaibatsu* bank mobilized surplus funds from within its set and made these available for expanding the group's activities in existing or in new ventures. The core businesses within the group provided the surplus for investment in other areas of activity, and banks were the means through which this capital could be mobilized. The banks, then, were important elements in promoting the internal, autonomous growth of the *zaibatsu* (Tominomori 1979), though they were by no means as integral to industrial development as the German banks had been. In all these ways, *zaibatsu* families could retain control over massive operations on the basis of relatively small personal shareholdings. Control over such large groups would not have been possible if their constituent companies had been amalgamated into giant unified enterprises.

During the period from 1910 to 1920 the number of *zaibatsu* increased considerably, and the founding generation of industrial entrepreneurs were preparing to hand over to their successors and began to consolidate their diverse interests into more unified groups under parent holding-companies (Allen 1972: ch. 8; Lockwood 1968:

214–22). A number of the smaller, newer *zaibatsu* were groups grown from enterprises that had copied the techniques already employed by the established *zaibatsu* (Tsuchiya 1977). In the 1930s, when their power in the economy was at its peak, there were ten major *zaibatsu*: the big four of Mitsui, Mitsubishi, Yasuda, and Sumitomo, and the smaller groups of Asano, Furukawa, Nakajima, Nissan (Ayukawa), Nomura, and Okura. Each *zaibatsu* was organized as a strict hierarchy, generally headed by a family-owned holding company that owned a number of banking, commercial, and manufacturing subsidiaries that, in turn, owned smaller subsidiaries (Halliday 1975: 53–60; Hadley 1970: 20–4; Noguchi 1973: 85). Independent enterprises that were legally separate from the *zaibatsu* had some importance in the economy, but they had little real independence as they were generally tied through commercial relations to particular *zaibatsu*.

Table 46. Strategic control in the 200 largest Japanese nonfinancial enterprises (1936–1966)

	Number of enterprises		
Mode of control	1936	1956	1966
Wholly owned	12	0	0
Majority control	13	4	4
Minority control	93	64	76
No dominant interest	82	132	120
Totals	200	200	200

Source: Kiyonari and Nakamura (1977: 268, Table 4).
Note: A 10-per-cent cutoff point was used for minority control. The original source contains a misprint in the 1966 data and this has been corrected.

Table 46 shows how this corporate clustering was reflected in the control of the top 200 Japanese enterprises of 1936. As in the United States at that time, only a small number of large enterprises were subject to majority control, though rather more were wholly owned. The major difference between the United States and Japan, however, is to be found in the composition of the 'minority control' category. In Japan this category included not only enterprises that were minority-controlled by entrepreneurs and their families, but also those that were tied through intercorporate minority participations into *zaibatsu*. Similarly, many of those enterprises in which there appeared to be no single dominant interest were, in fact, subject to a system of intercorporate control (Hadley 1970: 66–7; Lockwood 1968). The existence of these reciprocal intercorporate holdings means that the usual categories of control are of little use in understanding the control of *zaibatsu* members. Although this intercorporate network has certain similarities with those that developed in the Anglo-American economies, the *zaibatsu* enterprises cannot be described as controlled through constellations of interests. Intercorporate shareholdings were not institutional holdings, and they were contained within corporate sets that were controlled, at their pinnacles, by the *zaibatsu* families.

The intercorporate holdings within the Mitsubishi group, for example, were a means of buttressing the control of the Iwasaki family over the whole group. In 1940, following the conversion of its holding partnership into a joint stock company and the sale of some of its shares to employees and affiliated companies, the Iwasaki family held 47.5 per cent of the new Mitsubishi holding company. Other companies controlled by this holding company and its subsidiaries held, in turn, a further 11.9 per cent of the holding company's capital (Yasuoka 1977: 97). An enterprise that by conventional procedures might be classified as minority-controlled by a family in fact had a majority of its shares held by associated shareholders. Furthermore, each of the associated corporate shareholders had a similar pattern of control. As a result of this circularity of shareholdings, the precise control status of any one enterprise can be determined only when the control status of all others is known. This indeterminacy at the level of immediate control, however, is counterbalanced by the clarity with which the *zaibatsu* families appear as the ultimate controllers.

The power of the *zaibatsu* in Japan had initially been challenged during the 1930s with the rise to power of the army, but the corporate sets were so necessary for its militaristic policies that they soon regained their lost ground (Allen 1940) and the pattern of capital mobilization through vertically structured clustering persisted until the end of the Second World War. The massive demands of production for this war forced most of the controlling families to incorporate their holding partnerships into joint stock companies in order to seek outside capital, and in this way their tight organization began to loosen and family control was somewhat weakened (Yasuoka 1977: 93; Tominomori 1971: 25–7). Not until the post-war American occupation, however, were the vertical sets fatally damaged.

The occupying authorities attempted to break the economic power of the *zaibatsu* through a policy of 'dissolution'. The various holding partnerships and leading companies were all designated as 'holding companies'. They were required to hand over their shareholdings to the Holding Company Liquidation Commission and they were then dissolved. Fifty-six members of designated *zaibatsu* families had their personal assets transferred to the Commission, which compensated them with rapidly devaluing government bonds, and the shares formerly owned by the families and their partnerships were put on the market (Morikawa 1992: 237–9). The stated American aim was to destroy the corporate sets and to force their constituent companies to operate independently of one another. While some of the largest operating companies were indeed broken up, this policy had only limited success by the end of the occupation. The former *zaibatsu* enterprises, with the encouragement of the Japanese state, began to re-establish their connections with one another as soon as business conditions improved. The big banks were the main sources of funds for post-war recovery and modernization, and the enterprises that benefited most from recovery were those that had been most closely allied to the banks. These were, naturally, the former *zaibatsu* enterprises, and the members of the largest pre-war groups tended to gravitate towards their group bank. The banks themselves changed their practices, becoming more involved in the mobilization of savings from the growing economy in order to make these available to their associated enterprises.

The Ministry of International Trade and Industry (MITI) positively encouraged the establishment of these links to help ensure the rapid reconstruction and development of key industries in the postwar years (Johnson 1982). This allowed the corporate sets to reform themselves, though on a different basis (Hadley 1970; Livingston *et al.* 1973*b*: part 2). During the 1950s, enterprises began to acquire large numbers of shares in those other enterprises with which they had formerly been grouped in the *zaibatsu* and with which they still had strong trading links. Internal executives rose to fill the managerial gaps created by the removal of the controlling families, but this did not involve share dispersal or management control. Instead, a restructured form of intercorporate control was established (Kiyonari and Nakamura 1977).

Critical to this regrouping was the spread of what may be called 'aligned participations'. As there were no longer any holding companies or controlling families, the corporate sets re-emerged with more decentralized structures of ownership. Associated enterprises took reciprocal shareholdings in one another's capital, and the core of tightly connected companies would jointly invest in other companies. The corporate sets comprised dense thickets of cross-holdings that were reinforced by trading links, banking links, and interlocking directorships. Enterprises within the sets are not controlled through constellations of interests, but through *coalitions of aligned interests*, a situation which has been described as 'corporate capitalism' to distinguish it from the 'institutional capitalism' of the Anglo-American economies. Institutional capitalism is a system in which financial institutions are central to the structure of impersonal possession. In a system of corporate capitalism, on the other hand, non-financial corporations join with banks and insurance companies to hold shares in other non-financials with the explicit aim of creating a structure of aligned group control (Okumura 1984; Futatsugi 1986).

It can be seen from Table 47 that the proportion of shares in companies listed on the Japanese stock exchanges that were owned by persons fell during the post-war period, much as it did in Britain and the United States, although the proportion remains higher than in either of those societies. By 1990, banks and insurance companies owned the great bulk of all publicly traded shares, and individuals owned less than a quarter (Gerlach 1992: 129). While the proportion of shares owned by financials has increased, the most obvious trend is the marked increase in the proportion owned by non-financial

Table 47. Beneficial ownership of Japanese company shares (1950–1980)

Type of holder	% of corporate shares held by each category				
	1950	1960	1970	1980	1990
Government, public sector	3.2	0.2	0.3	0.2	0.6
Financial companies	24.5	34.3	33.5	40.5	47.0
Non-financial companies	11.0	17.8	23.1	26.0	25.2
Foreign companies	0	1.1	3.0	4.0	4.2
Persons	61.3	46.6	40.1	29.3	23.1

Source: Ohtani (1984: 50, Table 8) and Charkham (1994: 105, Table 3.11). See also Miyazaki (1973: 304, Table 3) and Okumura (1975, cited in Clark 1979: 101–2).

Table 48. Strategic control in large Japanese enterprises (1966)

Mode of control		Type of control				
		Family	Corporate	Government	Intercorporate	Totals
Majority	90%+	3	5	1	13	22
control	50%–90%	7	4	4	27	42
Minority	30%–50%	12	3	1	22	38
control	10%–30%	42	11	3	77	133
Limited minority control		18	0	0	21	39
No dominant interest		–	–	–	191	191
Totals		82	23	9	351	465

Source: Miyazaki (1973: 312–13, Table 6).
Note: Limited minority control has been used to describe Miyazaki's category of minority control with a holding between 3 per cent and 10 per cent. The figures are based on the top 492
companies, of which twenty-seven were mutuals, public enterprises, or other special situations.
The data consisted of the ten largest holders in each company.

enterprises. During the 1960s, holdings by non-financials began to
grow at the expense of those of the financial intermediaries, and over
one-quarter of all shares in quoted companies are now owned by
domestic non-financials. During the 1980s, the figures for ownership
by financials seems to have stabilized at around two fifths, and that
for ownership by non-financials stabilized at a quarter. Table 46 and
Table 48 suggest that most of the large enterprises of 1966 that could
be classified into the categories of majority or minority control or of
'no dominant interest' were, in fact, controlled through aligned participations. There were 24 cases of majority control and 90 cases of
minority control where a single interest was unambiguously in control, but 191 enterprises were subject to varying levels of control by
coalitions of aligned interests or, in a few cases, by true constellations
of interests (Kiyonari and Nakamura 1977: 267; Caves and Uekusa
1976: 10).[15] The ten largest holders in Mitsubishi bank, for example,

[15] In those cases of control through a constellation of interests, there were a
larger number of holdings by other non-financials than is typically the case in Britain
or the United States.

held 30.6 per cent of its shares, and six of these (with a total of 19.8 per cent) were themselves members of the Mitsubishi set (Dodwell 1980). The predominant mode of control, then, was control through the coalitions of aligned interests that tied the enterprises into tightly co-ordinated corporate sets.

Table 49. Capital, commercial, and personal relations in Japan (1980 and 1986)

Group	Bank loans[a]	Shares[b]	Directors[c]	Trading ptrs[d]
	Percentage held in-house			
Mitsui	39.5	51.4	48.0	14.3
Mitsubishi	42.8	63.4	60.4	15.2
Sumitomo	42.4	63.9	67.1	12.8
Fuji	26.6	38.1	25.9	8.4
Sanwa	32.2	28.0	36.2	6.4
DKB	23.3	31.6	38.7	13.2

Source: Gerlach (1992: Tables 4.1, 4.2, 4.4, and 4.7, on 122, 126, 139, 145).
Notes: [a] % of capital provided by 10 biggest lenders that comes from own group bank. Top 200 (1986).
   [b] % of capital held by top 10 shareholders that is held by other group companies. Top 250 (1986).
   [c] % of directors coming from another company in same group. Top 250 (1980).
   [d] % of trade with other companies in the same group.

Table 49 shows the extent of the capital, commercial, and personal relations among the big six *kigyoshudan* during the 1980s (see also Ueda 1990; Scott 1986; Prowse 1992). The older groups remain far tighter than the new groups, and this is particularly apparent when relations between groups are considered. Mitsui and Mitsubishi companies draw 10 to 11 per cent of their loan capital from independent banks or from other groups, while Sumitomo companies draw just 3.9 per cent. In the three newer groups, on the other hand, companies averaged over 20 per cent of their loans from non-group banks (Miyazaki 1973: 312–3). In terms of shareholdings, the three older groups had over half their capital held 'in-house', while the figures for the newer groups ranged from a quarter to just over one-third.

Clearly, the group structure of aligned participations is central to an understanding of the Japanese economy; and while the contemporary situation has some similarities with that which existed before the war, there are a number of fundamental differences.[16] The large corporate sets that dominate the Japanese economy are generally termed *kigyoshudan* by Japanese commentators to distinguish them from the family-dominated *zaibatsu* (Okumura 1984; 1983; see also Lockwood 1965a, 495–7; Hadley 1970, 299). These 'enterprise groups' are relatively decentralized federations of aligned enterprises, and they are the basis of an 'insider' system of corporate control that is radically different from that found in Germany. Tominomori (1979) and Shinoda (1987) have argued that the 'dehumanization' of capital through a structure of intercorporate holdings creates an exclusionary structure in which the top executives of a group are defended from any attempt at control from outside the group. The stability of intra-group shareholdings creates a stable and protected pattern of intra-group control.

Three enterprise groups have their origins in the former *zaibatsu* sets of Mitsui, Mitsubishi, and Sumitomo, and though each embraces a range of banking, insurance, commercial, and manufacturing enterprises they are particularly strong in heavy industry and chemicals. The main basis for unity is provided by the reciprocal share participations that run among the group enterprises. During the post-war period, and especially since the 1960s, these groups have been increasing their reciprocal holdings, and have tended to become tighter in structure (Miyazaki 1973: 55; Bieda 1970: 210 ff.; Caves and Uekusa 1976: ch. 4).

Three other corporate sets join these three to make up the 'big six' groups. These are the Sanwa, Fuyo, and Daiichi Kangyo (DKB) combines. Each of these is based around a bank, and each incorporates the remnants of some of the smaller pre-war *zaibatsu*. Fuyo and Sanwa are centred around banking hubs and have fewer cross-holdings than is the case in the big three: links tend to run from the bank to the other enterprises, rather than among the enterprises themselves (Futatsugi 1969: 81; Futatsugi 1986). DKB, on the other hand, has a financial core that links two semi-autonomous industrial groups—Kawasaki and Furukawa—each of which have a high degree of internal cohesion but are linked together mainly through group financials.[17] The newer members of these groups joined dur-

---

[16]   The following description draws on Dodwell (1980), Clark (1979: 73 ff.), Bieda (1970), and Okumura (1983).

[17]   DKB was formed as a merger in 1971, Furukawa and Kawasaki being former *zaibatsu*. Fuyo is based around the former Yasuda *zaibatsu* and includes newer clients of the Fuji Bank (formerly Yasuda Bank). Sanwa Bank was formed in the 1930s

ing the 1950s and 1960s, as the big city banks built up shareholdings among their clients so as to counter the inroads of foreign capital.

Of all the countries considered in this book, Japan shows the strongest evidence for the existence of the rival financial-interest groups that were depicted in the theory of capitalist society and its model of finance capital. Members of the corporate sets are linked through reciprocal capital, commercial, and personal relations; they engage in preferential trading, joint ventures, and technical integration; and their aligned participations are reinforced by preferential loans supplied by the group bank and by funds from the trust and insurance companies within the group (Okumura 1991; Sheard 1994). *Kigyoshudan* are diversified internally through a policy of 'one set-ism' (Miyazaki 1967; Futatsugi 1986: 56 ff.) through which each group aims to internalize a complete 'set' of complementary industrial and financial enterprises. As in Germany, long-term bank funding has created a multiplier effect on industrial investment, and the level of internal funding has been lower than in Britain or the United States (Clark 1979: 69 ff.; Adams and Hoshi 1972; Thompson 1977: 60; Halliday 1975: 273). In 1980 bank loans accounted for 64 per cent of all external funding. While this figure fell somewhat over the 1980s as a result of the deregulation of Japanese financial markets, it rose again during the 1990s (Gerlach 1992: 127–8). In 1992, the 188 large enterprises that were members of *kigyoshudan* accounted for 17 per cent of the capital of all quoted companies, 19 per cent of their assets, and 16 per cent of their sales (Charkham 1994: 76).

Ueda (1983 and 1989) has shown that strong and weak interlocks are much more closely associated together in Japan than in the United States, but the overall level of interlocking is lower. Most directors are executives, though these executives were sometimes also large shareholders, and in the majority of enterprises the executives formed a majority on the board. Interlocking directorships in Japan are largely confined to the big *kigyoshudan* and are not involved in the creation of an extensive national network. The overall network density of interlocking directorships among the big six groups of 1980 was 0.041 (Gerlach 1992: 158). Most interlocks are carried by executives, and they are largely contained within the corporate sets. Steven (1983: 52) has shown that directors of the big enterprise

and built up a new group in the 1960s. A further industrial group with an important role in the economy is that of the Industrial Bank of Japan, which specializes in rescue operations, and has a number of dependent clients, but has no central policy-making forum for the group.

groups in 1980 held 47 per cent of all directorships in quoted companies. In 1983, a half of all interlocks among 1,795 quoted companies were primary interlocks. Executives who sat as monitors of other companies—Ueda terms them 'part-time auditors'—accounted for a further one in five (Ueda 1991).

These intra-group directorships are an important source of unity for the corporate sets, though corporate strategy is largely worked out in each group's 'presidents' council' (shacho kai). The origins of the presidents' councils are in the councils of the zaibatsu that brought together the family directors of the holding company and the top managers of its first-line subsidiaries, and these bodies were restructured during the 1950s and 1960s to meet the needs of the reorganized sets. The presidents' council of a group brings together the chief executives of the core enterprises, and provides a forum in which they can discuss matters of mutual concern. Although a council typically holds voting rights in all the shares held by group companies, it is not so much a command centre as a focus of group identity and coherence that stands at the apex of a nexus of formal and informal committees and gatherings, in which managers at various levels of the group enterprises are involved (Okumura 1984: 172–3, 180). The kigyoshudan, it has been said, comprises 'a layered set of personnel connections', culminating in the presidents' club (Gerlach 1992: 104).

Around the kigyoshudan and their smaller affiliated sets there circulate a number of large industrial enterprises with varying degrees of attachment to the big corporate sets. Hitachi, Nissan, Toyota, Nippon Steel, Matsushita, Sony, and certain others have financial links with the big combines and are often members of one or more of the presidents' councils, but they are autonomous decision-making centres that are organized in a similar way to large enterprises in the Anglo-American economies.[18] They are somewhat less centralized, as their subsidiaries are not always wholly owned, but the parent company is invariably a majority or large minority shareholder, and inter-group holdings are less common. Okumura (1984: 9–10) terms them groups linked through 'vertical alignments' rather than through the reciprocal alignments of the kigyoshudan. They are

---

[18]   Toyota split from Mitsui in the post-war dissolution and became independent, but it moved closer to that combine in the 1970s. Nissan is the remnant of a zaibatsu which originally included the now-independent Hitachi.

often seen as parent-associate groups (*keiretsu*).[19] While the *kigyoshu-dan* comprise companies controlled through coalitions of aligned interests, the parents of the autonomous *keiretsu* enterprises are controlled by families or by constellations of interests: in 1986, for example, Nissan was controlled by a twenty-member constellation that held 54 per cent of the shares, and Sony was controlled by the Morita family with 9.6 per cent. The major difference between the Anglo-American constellations and those in Japan is that the latter include more individuals and industrials, and that the total pool from which the interests are drawn is far smaller in Japan.

Below the *kigyoshudan* and the autonomous enterprises are a mass of small- and medium-sized enterprises that are heavily dependent on the activities of the large enterprises and combines, and that often act as subcontractors to them. Japan has a very large proportion of small firms (Caves and Uekusa 1976: 3), and in 1982 about two-thirds of all small- and medium-sized enterprises were subcontractors to large enterprises (Okumura 1984). Although frequently described as a 'dualistic' economy, involving a division between monopoly capital and a dependent non-monopoly sector (Broadbridge 1966), the Japanese economy is best seen as hierarchical, with a continuous gradation from the big three *kigyoshudan* to the small subcontractors (Clark 1979: 64). There is a division between hegemonic and subordinate enterprises, but financials *per se* are not hegemonic. The big six corporate sets are effectively self-controlling through aligned participations, and they stand as hegemonic groups, alongside some other financials, in relation to the smaller sets and the autonomous enterprises. This oligarchic structure of hegemony is a system in which the big sets have tight control over the flow of capital and so dominate the structure of business activity in major areas of the economy.

Korea shares many of the characteristics of the Japanese pattern, though it has not moved so far beyond the pattern of personal possession. The state in pre-industrial Korea had a more centralized bureaucratic structure than did Japan, and the country had only a very weak mercantile system until it was annexed to Japan in 1905 (Whitley 1992). Korea entered into the world economy as an adjunct to Japanese national expansion, and industrial enterprises were set up by the colonial power as integral elements of the Japanese

---

[19] *Kigyoshudan* translates as 'industrial group', while *keiretsu* translates as 'line of affiliation'. This distinction between horizontal and vertical alignments is, unfortunately, not always observed in the English-language literature on Japanese business.

zaibatsu (Kim 1991). This colonial system was broken up in 1945 by the American military authorities, and it was only then that Korean industry developed in legal independence from foreign capital. The partition of Korea into northern and southern states meant, however, that South Korea developed with American aid and in heavy dependence on the American economy. This was nevertheless the basis of a rapid industrial expansion during the 1960s and 1970s, when industrial enterprises were organized into *chaebol*, vertically structured and family-owned corporate sets modelled on the pre-war Japanese *zaibatsu*.[20] The South Korean state has encouraged the formation of these *chaebol*, according them special legal privileges, and it has employed planning, fiscal, and banking mechanisms to regulate their activities and to sponsor strategic industries (Hamilton and Biggart 1988: Steers *et al.* 1989; Kim 1991; Zeile 1991). This close alliance between the strong state and the *chaebol* has been the driving force in Korean industrialization.

Families typically have minority stakes of around 14 per cent in the central holding companies of the *chaebol*, with a further 50 per cent of the shares being held by the various enterprises that they control (Janelli 1993: 84). The largest of these *chaebol* are Hyundai, Samsung, Lucky-Goldstar, Daewoo, and Sunkyung (Kim 1991: 283). They differ from the *zaibatsu*, crucially, by the absence of group banks and by the correspondingly stronger role of the state in corporate finance. The economy of South Korea, then, shows a looser variant of the Japanese system of vertical corporate sets.

Corporate Co-operation: The Chinese Pattern

What I call the 'Chinese' pattern of capital mobilization is found in the overseas Chinese economies of Taiwan, Singapore, Malaysia, and Hong Kong, and it is re-emerging in mainland China. It is one in which rapid industrialization has been grounded in long-established mechanisms of capital mobilization that, during the 1960s and 1970s, were sponsored and encouraged by strong facilitative states (Castells 1992).[21] Central to this pattern have been certain features of the

[20] *Chaebol* and *zaibatsu* are direct linguistic equivalents of one another and are written with the same Chinese characters in both languages.

[21] Hamilton *et al.* (1988) have contrasted the 'strong state' of South Korea with the 'strong society' of Taiwan. This characterization tends to play down the

Chinese family system and the historical experience of migration. In the traditional Chinese family, inheritance involved a division of wealth among all the sons of the family, and in merchant families each son would have a right to a share in the business along with his brothers. This fraternal division of property sets definite limits to the possibilities for capital accumulation, as businesses tend to fragment on the death of their founders. While the inheriting brothers might continue to co-operate with one another, the unity of the original enterprise would be lost.

Fraternal inheritance means that businesses tend to develop, at best, into loose co-operating groups of firms that are linked through personal rather than capital relations. Some businesses can grow in the short and medium term if conditions are right, but the death or retirement of the principal owner of a constituent firm makes the fragmenting effects of the family system felt once more. The practice of equal inheritance, then, results in cyclical expansion and fragmentation in business (Wong 1985); and business growth in the Chinese economies depended on personal relations of kinship. Within these relations, a framework of 'trust' could be established, and business ventures with those outside the family would occur only if this framework of trust could be enlarged. Trade developed in traditional China only on its southern periphery, principally in Fujian and Guandong; it was accorded low social status, and the country was virtually closed to outside contact. Merchant families, therefore, migrated in pursuit of trade, and this migration became especially marked under the Qing Empire. As a result, Chinese trading settlements were established throughout the Far East (Pan 1990; Redding 1990: 19 ff.). While a framework of trust among merchants could be established in their localities on the mainland, this was not so easy in the overseas settlements. Dispersed among these various settlements and denied support by their government, Chinese merchants faced serious problems of trust. Businesses could expand beyond their fraternal base only if merchants felt that they could trust their potential business partners. In these circumstances, trust was placed in those of a similar provenance (S. L. Wong 1991). Teochius merchants, for example, felt that they could rely on fellow Teochius, but not on Hakka, and those who originated in the same mainland village or district were especially important in business

strength of the state in the Chinese societies, and I prefer to contrast the strong *facilitative* state of Taiwan with the strong *interventionist* state of Korea. Both correspond to the type that Castells has called the *developmental* state.

partnerships. This reliance on common ethnicity allowed for greater co-operation among separate family-based ventures, a personalized structure of business reinforced by Confucian culture, which stressed familism, filial piety, and respect for authority (Redding 1990).[22] Common provenance, then, supplemented kinship, but it did not replace it as the preferred basis for business undertakings; and business co-operation was, in the long term, undermined from within by the fragmenting effects of the system of family inheritance.

The co-operation of loosely allied family enterprises was the basis of Chinese business in the overseas communities and in the southern parts of the mainland, and this set the context for the economic development of these areas in the nineteenth century. On the mainland, merchants and foreign traders involved in overseas trade were restricted by law to the city of Guangzhou, and Chinese merchants in the city adopted a 'comprador' role as agents or middlemen for Spanish, Dutch, and British traders. With the forcible opening of China to Western influence in the early part of the nineteenth century, however, the British acquired Hong Kong by treaty, the cities of Guangzhou, Xiamen, Fuzhou, Ningbo, and Shanghai were opened to foreign trade, and further treaties allowed foreign penetration of the south-western provinces. Where the Meiji reformers in Japan had sought to make their country a strong and independent power by 'learning' from the West, the Chinese government rejected economic development and found itself facing terminal collapse. The disintegration of the political system worsened the economic situation of indigenous merchants, and accelerated the rate of migration to the overseas Chinese communities.

The nationalist government did begin to build railways, telegraphs, and a merchant navy, but there was little attempt to promote any significant industrial development and much commercial activity resulted from foreign initiative and capital. Industrial and commercial development was encouraged by the nationalist government at the beginning of the twentieth century, but this was severely circumscribed by the political instability of Chinese society, coming to a sharp end with the Second World War and the subsequent Communist seizure of power. Private business development on the mainland was put rapidly into reverse as capitalist development was abandoned: foreign businesses were expelled, indigenous

[22] On the wider issue of cultural support for Chinese business practices see Hamilton (1991a; 1984; 1990).

businesses were closed down, and there was a massive exodus of business families to Hong Kong and elsewhere (Wong 1988).

Taiwan (Formosa) became the base for nationalist opposition to the Communist state, and the Guomindang leadership began to build a strong economy around a powerful state-party sector of business.[23] Co-operating family-based firms using fraternal-provenance mechanisms of capital mobilization had prospered (Tong 1991; Cohen 1976), but the core of the state sector comprised former Japanese imperial *zaibatsu* companies that had been nationalized after the Second World War. This state sector extended through much of the banking system and into key industrial monopolies. Together with Guomindang-owned enterprises, the state-party sector now accounts for about half of all corporate assets in Taiwan. State banks alone control the bulk of the assets of the top 50 financials (Bello and Rosenfeld 1990: 232). Large private businesses have been built up through the established fraternal-provenance mechanisms of business trust (Kao 1991; Hamilton and Kao 1990), and both 'mainlander' and indigenous Taiwanese businesses have been closely allied with the state-party sector to form a dominant and monopolistic economic sector (Numazaki 1986, 1991, 1992; Hamilton *et al.*, 1987; Sillin 1976). Smaller enterprises, organized along traditional 'Chinese' lines, are mainly owned by indigenous Taiwanese and receive little financial support from the state. These small enterprises have prospered only as subcontractors to the state monopolies and to foreign capital.

The development of Taiwan was shaped by a particular relationship between a strong nationalist state and Chinese family enterprise. The activities of the strong state have been essential in preventing the fragmenting consequences of family enterprise from undermining economic expansion. As a result the country has experienced rapid economic growth since the 1960s. Economic development in the other overseas Chinese communities proved equally dynamic when strong states could adopt a similarly supportive role. The Singaporean state, for example, sought to encourage foreign investment that would, it believed, allow a firm base of subcontracting for local enterprises. Failure to establish economic protectionism, however, meant that multinational enterprises dominated the economy and domestic entrepreneurs were marginalized, their role being limited by powerful foreign capital (Bello and Rosenfeld 1990:

[23] The Guomindang is the nationalist party, originally formed in China and now the dominant force in Taiwanese politics.

294–7; Tan 1991). A study of the 120 largest non-foreign-owned enterprises in Singapore in 1991 found that 104 were interlocked with one another, and that interlocking was especially important among the smaller, family-owned enterprises (Zang 1995). Similarly in Malaysia, levels of both foreign ownership and family ownership were high, with the largest enterprises structured into intersecting chains and, in the foreign sector, into corporate webs (Lim 1981: 27–8, 41).

In Hong Kong the dominant force has long been foreign capital, most notably the colonial trading houses controlled by descendants of their founding families and that had extended their control into the growing economy. The British colonial state concentrated on establishing a political and legal framework that would allow private (British-owned) financial and commercial enterprises to prosper. This dominance of expatriate British business limited the opportunities for expansion on the part of Chinese businesses, which relied on fraternal-provenance mechanisms of capital mobilization. This situation began to change after the 1960s, when wealthy Chinese families were able to use profits from urban property development to enlarge their businesses through stock-exchange flotations and through the takeover of former colonial companies (G. Wong 1991). These families used fraternal-provenance mechanisms to take advantage of their unanticipated property earnings and build large structures based on corporate co-operation, and they have successfully dented the stranglehold of foreign capital.

Table 50 shows that seven of the ten largest family business groups in Hong Kong were owned by ethnic Chinese, all of them being first-generation businesses. Just three of the old colonial families survived as an important element in the Hong Kong economy. It is uncertain whether the Chinese enterprises will avoid eventual fragmentation as their growing scale and the effects of inheritance make corporate co-operation more difficult. Nevertheless, their rapid growth has led to considerable change in the structure of inter-corporate relations. The network of interlocking directorships connecting the top 125 Hong Kong companies became both more extensive and more inclusive during the 1980s, but it also became less cohesive and less centralized (G. Wong, 1991). The business network had become differentiated into a clustering of separate business groups, most of which were controlled by Chinese families. This break-up of the old colonial pattern, then, has involved a move towards the pattern of private business found in Taiwan, although

Table 50. The largest family groups in Hong Kong (1988)

Family	Main business
1 K. S. Li	Hutchison Whampoa
2 Swire*	Swire Pacific, Cathay Pacific
3 Keswick*	Jardine Matheson, Hong Kong Land
4 Kadoorie*	China Light and Power
5 Y. K. Pao	World International
6 T. S. Kwok	property, hotels, development
7 S. K. Lee	property, hotels, development
8 Y. T. Cheng	property, hotels, development
9 T. H. Chan	property, hotels, development
10 R. R. Shaw	Bond Corporation

Source: Redding (1990: 152–3).
* colonial families.

the future of Hong Kong business depends critically on the policy of the Chinese government after 1997.[24]

In mainland China itself, industrial concerns had followed the Stalinist model from the 1950s to 1978. They were mere elements in a centralized planning system and had no budgetary autonomy. In 1978, however, experiments in decentralized decision-making and a degree of market-orientation were made in Sichuan and were then allowed elsewhere (Chong 1986; Henley and Nyaw 1986). Deng's economic reforms established 'special economic zones' and 'open cities' along China's south and east coast, in Guangdong, and Fujian,[25] and the Shanghai stock exchange has become an important focus for industrial development, supported by foreign capital from Hong Kong, Taiwan, Korea, and Japan. The first joint stock company since the Communist takeover was set up in 1983, the state owning all its shares. By 1991 there were many companies, but fewer than 100 had issued shares to the public.[26] Private and municipal businesses continue to be subject to central control through state

---

[24] I have benefited greatly from discussion with Gilbert Wong on a number of issues raised in this section.

[25] These pockets of capitalism were in precisely those parts of the country where Deng's Qing predecessors had tolerated their mercantile counterparts.

[26] Shares have not, in general, been risk-bearing equity, but have been closer in form to bonds. Share capital rarely accounts for more than a half of a company's total capital.

contracting and official regulations, but the establishment of capitalist enclaves and the extension of this principle to the rest of the country during 1992 involved a strategy of combining an increasingly capitalist economy with a centralized and authoritarian state. The conscious and explicit model has been Taiwan, where a strong state facilitated both economic growth and consumer affluence.

So far, private business in China, as in the other 'Chinese' economies, has barely moved beyond personal possession and limited corporate co-operation. It is only where a strong and supportive state sector has existed that businesses have been able to prosper and expand. The Chinese government seems intent on establishing such a system in mainland China—supported by its policy of economic integration with Taiwan and Hong Kong—thereby allowing the development of more impersonal forms of possession. A crucial question is whether this strategy will require the eventual abandonment of Communist ideology and the introduction of a limited democratization of the political system, or whether it will result in the collapse of the whole political system.

In this and the preceding chapters, I have tried to show the variety of forms of capitalist enterprise that have existed in the transition from the personal possession characteristic of liberal capitalism, to the impersonal possession associated with disorganized capitalism. In the Anglo-American economies there has been a move from personal, entrepreneurial forms of control to control through a constellation of interests and polyarchic financial hegemony, and it is this particular pattern of capitalist development that was discussed in Chapters 4 and 5. Outside the Anglo-American world, countries with differing starting-points have pursued varying routes of capitalist development. Variations in legal systems, banking systems, state strategies, and private wealth have combined with cultural differences to produce oligarchic bank hegemony with corporate filiations, intersecting corporate webs, and corporate sets of aligned enterprises. In the economies of Eastern Europe and the Far East, different patterns again have emerged. In all the economies discussed, small- and medium-sized firms exist alongside, and dependent upon, the big-business sector of large monopolistic enterprises. At the same time, however, family enterprise has not been confined to these smaller enterprises. Even in the United States, entrepreneurial capitalists remain an important force in the economy. The salaried executives emphasized by managerialist theory have, of course, enhanced opportunities wherever owner-control is diluted, but no evidence has been found for a general move towards management control. In each economy, finance capitalists play an increasingly important role on the boards of the large enterprises, and especially in the banks, and as the formulators of corporate strategy and co-ordinators of corporate affairs. Little evidence has been found, however, to support the Marxist idea that capitalist economies have become internally structured into rival 'financial empires'. Only in Japan has the corporate pattern been at all close to this model. Nevertheless, by virtue of their pre-eminence on the boards of the hegemonic enterprises in all the major capitalist economies, finance capitalists have increasingly become the dominant elements in the interplay of finance capitalists, executive capitalists, and entrepreneurial capitalists that structures patterns of corporate development within the capitalist world-system.

7

MANAGERS, NETWORKS, AND HIERARCHIES

Discussions of corporate strategy have often taken a rather simplistic view of markets, seeing enterprise behaviour in terms of the interaction of supply and demand. Very little attention has been given to the role of 'non-market' factors in structuring commercial relations. The capitalist developments that I have documented in this book, however, have meant that both the nature of the market and the causal impact of market forces have altered in directions that were unforeseen by most managerialists. This was recognized, rather paradoxically, by one of the founders of managerialist theory in a report to the American *National Resources Committee* in the 1930s. In this report, Means showed that the relative importance of commercial market relations and of 'non-market controls' had altered. The increasing autonomy of large enterprises within their markets, he argued, made market forces a weaker influence on corporate behaviour: 'Where policies with respect to the use of resources are only limited and not dominated by market controls, the non-market controls become a significant factor making for more or less effective use of resources' (Means *et al.* 1939: 154).[1] This view suggested the need to move away from abstract models of markets and to build a more comprehensive understanding of business organization.

The early works of Commons (1924) and Coase (1937) followed a similar line in attempting to set out a more 'realistic' account of enterprise behaviour than had been provided by marginalist eco-

---

[1] An extract from the report was reprinted in the first edition of Bendix and Lipset's textbook, *Class, Status and Power* (1953), but was deleted from the second and more widely cited 1967 edition.

nomics. Their aim was to show that rational actions within markets are shaped by partial information and by the need to monitor and enforce contractual agreements. Non-market structures, generally, though rather misleadingly, termed 'institutions', are built and sustained whenever the benefits that they yield are greater than the 'transaction costs'—the costs of searching, negotiating, and contracting—that are incurred in creating and sustaining them.[2] Thus, enterprises will seek to grow through mergers that internalize transactions, for example, whenever the costs of doing so are lower than the costs of maintaining market relations with their merger partners. Williamson (1975; 1985; Williamson and Ouchi 1980) has built on these insights to present a view of changing organizational forms as resulting from attempts to minimize transaction costs. In Williamson's terms, corporate 'hierarchies' are likely to be formed when market relations involve long-term contracts (rather than immediate 'spot' contracts), where price and quality are uncertain or unpredictable, and where barriers to entry by alternative suppliers are high. According to Williamson, this is a deliberate and calculative process on the part of business leaders, though Nelson and Winter (1982; Winter 1967) have followed the pioneering work of Alchian (1950) and have emphasized processes of variation and selective retention that are responsible for organizational evolution (see also Grossman and Hart 1987). The central contention of these writers, then, is that 'hierarchy' relations within large enterprises are an alternative to 'market' relations among smaller enterprises.[3]

More recently, further refinements have been added to the argument about non-market factors by those who have focused on 'networks' of relations that exist 'between' market and hierarchy (see Powell 1990 and the discussions in Thompson et al., 1991). In its most general sense, the environment of the large business enterprise consists of a complex intercorporate network of capital, commercial, and personal relations that comprise a mixture of both 'market'

[2] The so-called 'institutionalist' economics to which this gave rise has recently been replaced by an approach to organizational life that is more strictly 'institutional' in character by virtue of its focus on frameworks of norms and values that structure economic action. See Powell and DiMaggio (1991). This whole approach draws on Granovetter (1985).

[3] There are numerous debates among writers in this broad area. One particular dispute concerns the question of whether enterprise 'hierarchy' is to be seen in terms of authority or contract. While Williamson stresses authority, Alchian and Demsetz (1972; Demsetz 1967; 1985) have stressed contractual relations and consequent problems of 'agency'. See the critical discussion in Parkinson (1993).

forces of supply and demand and 'non-market' forces of power and influence (Scott and Griff 1984: ch. 1). This intercorporate network, the basis of the new 'invisible handshake' of finance capital, has become a crucial determinant of corporate behaviour. What recent writers have emphasized, however, is the fact that intercorporate relations may be formed into informal relations of reciprocity and influence that link specific enterprises together into larger units. These larger units are not integrated enterprises, and so cannot be reduced to 'hierarchies', but neither can they merely be reduced to 'market' relations. It is these structures that many writers have described as 'networks', but this term is rather misleading as it equates specific groupings with the wider intercorporate networks in which they are located. Typical of such groupings are the corporate sets, corporate webs, and similar structures that I have considered in this book, and Teubner has usefully proposed that such groupings be called 'polycorporate collectives' (1993: 43). It is these 'polycorporate collectives' that may exist between market and hierarchy.[4]

It is from this standpoint that the exercise of corporate rule and the formulation of corporate strategy must be understood. While managerialist writers recognized the growing autonomy of large enterprises from market constraints, they have generally failed to appreciate the growing importance of non-market relations. For 'sectional managerialists' such as Marris (1964) and the early Williamson (1964), the separation of ownership from control allows managers to pursue their own goals and career prospects untrammelled by any considerations of shareholder interests. As I have shown, however, there is no evidence of any significant separation of ownership from control in the sense implied by managerialism. While corporate rulers—executives, financiers, and shareholders— do have a degree of autonomy in the strategic decisions that they make (Child 1972), they are constrained by the interplay of market and non-market relations.

---

[4] Teubner adds that polycorporate collectives do not strictly occur 'between' markets and hierarchies. Rather, they result from the 're-entry' of relations into both markets and hierarchies. The commonly accepted term 'between' does, however, serve to illustrate the distinctiveness of these phenomena.

Corporate Boards and Corporate Rule

The dominant coalition of corporate rulers in each enterprise is constrained by the network of intercorporate relations in which their enterprise is embedded and, beyond this, by the actions of the state and other political agencies and by the organized and unorganized actions of their employees (Child 1969a: 14; Wood 1980: 59). As members of the dominant coalition may seek to protect or enhance their conflicting interests, the dominant coalition will be marked by internal conflicts as well as by conflicts with outside interests that may seek to influence it. Corporate strategy, then, is the result of a continual, though generally latent, struggle for dominance.

Table 51. Board composition in thirty-five large US non-financial enterprises (1935)

	Number of directors					
	Executives	Commercial bankers	Investment bankers	Large shareholders	Others	Total
25 large industrials	191	29	27	69	56	372
5 large utilities	22	14	4	11	25	76
5 large railways	13	8	7	19	31	78
Totals	226	51	38	99	112	526

Source: Gordon (1945: 122–3).

The focus of corporate rule in an enterprise is its board of directors, and the composition of the board reflects its mode of control. In the Anglo-American economies, board composition reflects the gradually increasing importance of control through a constellation of interests. Table 51 shows that those who sat on the boards of thirty-five large American non-financial enterprises in 1935 fell into three categories: executives made up just under half, while financiers and large shareholders made up just under one-fifth each. Allowing for the fact that a number of the executives would also have been shareholders—perhaps substantial—these data give a clear picture of the major forces involved in the struggle for control at that time.[5] Of particular importance is the fact that financiers were the group most likely to hold two or more directorships, and that the thirty-five boards had an average of 2.5 bankers among their directors. Many of the 'other' directors were retired executives and bankers. Table 52 shows that the executives formed an almost identical proportion of the top 100 directorate of 1972 to that of their counterparts in the large enterprises of 1935, though it can be assumed that fewer would have had substantial shareholdings in their company. Herman's breakdown of the 'other' category in Table 52 refers only to the number of directorships held and to the characteristics of companies, but he does add that a related study for 1972 discovered that there were three main groups in this category: bank and financial executives, executives of smaller non-financials, and lawyers (Herman 1981: 43).

Table 52. Primary interests of directors of the top 100 US industrial enterprises (1972)

Primary interest	Number	%
Executive in top 100	633	44.0
Retired employee in top 100	80	5.6
Other	725	50.4
Totals	1438	100

Source: Herman (1981: 39, Table 2.5).
Note: Unfortunately, the breakdown of the 'other' category that Herman gives is not particularly useful.

Barratt Brown (see Table 14, p. 81) reported that the directorate of the top 120 British enterprises in 1966 consisted of about one-third entrepreneurial capitalists, one-third executive capitalists, and just under a half finance capitalists; and Table 53 shows the primary interests of multiple directors ten years later. Multiple directors made up 10.5 per cent of the total directorate of the top 250 enterprises, and two-thirds of these multiple directors were executives in

---

[5] Evidence on directors' shareholdings can be found in Chapter 9.

one of the top 250 enterprises. A further 11 per cent had their primary business interest—as shareholder, member of the dominant family, or holder of an important internal role—in one of these top enterprises. Financial executives contributed disproportionately to this group: financial enterprises contributed an average of 1.9 of their 'insiders' to other boards, while non-financials contributed an average of 0.6 insiders. A substantial number of the multiple directors had retired from an executive position in the top 250, or had their primary interest, as shareholder or executive, in smaller enterprises. Indeed, many finance-capitalist directors were former chief executives or managing directors, and they continued to be active participants in corporate rule after their retirement from these executive positions (Scott and Griff 1985: 230). A study for 1992 found that the posts of Chairman and Chief Executive were combined in a quarter of the top 1,000 enterprises, and in many other enterprises the chairman was a former chief executive (Charkham 1994: 264). Table 54 shows that there has been a substantial increase in the proportion of non-executive directors on the boards of large enterprises, this growth being greatest among enterprises with smaller boards. Non-executive directors, then, have become a more important element in corporate rule.

The roles of directors in enterprises controlled through constellations of interests has been explored by Hill (1995). The core members of a board, he found, were the chairman, chief executive, and

Table 53. Primary interests of multiple directors of the top 250 British enterprises (1976)

Primary interest	Number	%
Top 50 financials	97	34.4
Top 200 non-financials	112	39.7
Retired from top 50 financials	7	2.5
Retired from top 200 non-financials	17	6.0
Other financial	14	5.0
Other industrial	13	4.6
Other	22	7.8
Totals	282	100.0

Source: Scott and Griff (1985: Table 12.5).
Note: The enterprises analysed are those described in Table 16 and elsewhere.

Table 54. Board composition in the top 1000 British enterprises (1988 and 1993)

	Proportion of non-executive directors	
Board size	1988	1993
0–6	26.8	36.1
7–8	34.2	41.4
9–10	42.2	42.9
11–12	41.3	45.5
13 or more	44.6	47.9
All	36.0	41.4

Source: From Conyon (1994: 93, Table 2).
Note: The table relates to the top 1000 of 1992 and reports on their board composition in each of the two benchmark years.

finance director, all of whom had full-time or near-full-time involvement in the enterprise. Executive directors were subordinates of the chief executive and played a supportive role as the key 'insiders'. The task of a board, Hill argues, is to monitor performance through setting financial targets, but these targets are arrived at on the basis of proposals shaped by operational managers and presented to the chief executive by other top executives. A particular consideration for executives is to prevent any major disagreements over operational matters coming to the board, and so such disagreements are resolved informally and at pre-board meetings. Non-executive directors are regarded as sounding boards and counterbalances to the core group, and do not seek to become involved in operational matters (Pahl and Winkler 1974). They are seen as bringing 'an independent voice' into the internal deliberations of the enterprise, their extensive involvements in the wider business community being an important source of their ability to 'scan' the corporate environment and draw on their expertise to deal with potential external difficulties (see also Pettigrew and McNulty 1995). They are, however, important as guarantors of the interests of the financial institutions, even when they are not their direct representatives:

The selection by the chairman of appropriate individuals who are acceptable to the owners but are not their representatives is important for their peace of mind, given the reluctance of institutions to appoint their own

nominee directors, the possible difficulty of getting the members of a constellation to act in concert and the resistance of management to outside
interference. (Hill 1995: 266)

In the words of Pettigrew and McNulty (1995), the chief executive
runs the company but the chairman runs the board. The board—in
the top ten British enterprises of 1992 it averaged sixteen members
and held a full meeting once a month—brings together non-
executive and executive directors. The directors jointly receive,
reformulate, and co-ordinate executive plans and form them into a
coherent corporate strategy from which financial targets for the various parts of the business can be derived. The dominant coalition and
its core group attempts to balance internal corporate requirements
and the interests of the controlling constellations, through a balance
between executive and non-executive directors. For this reason, the
power of non-executive directors is especially great in times of crisis
and transition when, as Glasberg (1989) has shown for the United
States, banks and financial institutions play an especially important
role.

Outside the Anglo-American economies directors act in similar
ways, though subject to the different forms of impersonal possession
in which they are involved. Stokman and Wasseur (1985: Table 2.7)
have reported that the proportion of executives in the directorates of
the top 250 enterprises in the major European countries varied from
less than one in five in France and Belgium, to one in four in Italy,
and to one in three in Austria, Germany, the Netherlands, and
Switzerland. This finding is clearly related to variations in board systems and corporate structure. Those countries with a 'German' two-
board system showed a high proportion of executive directors, while
those countries which developed through the corporate webs had a
low proportion of executives. Bauer and Bertin-Mourot (1991)
report that chief executives (or their equivalents) in French and
German enterprises were typically appointed at age 48 or 49, having
worked in the enterprise for about ten years. Although entrepreneurial chief executives were important in both countries, French
chief executives were particularly likely to have *pantouflé*—moved
sideways—from the state administration, while two-thirds of
German chief executives had pursued an executive career in their
firm (see Table 55). The German system, then, is an 'insider' system,
reflecting the tight control exercised by the banks in their corporate
filiations. In the same way, the structure of the corporate sets in

Table 55. Chief executives in the top 200
French and German enterprises (1988)

	% of top 200 of 1988	
	France	Germany
State assets	44.53	7.96
Capital assets	33.59	26.55
Career assets	21.88	65.49

Source: Bauer and Bertin-Mourot (1991: 40–1).

Japan ensures that executives are the most numerous members of
the boards and the presidents' councils (Ueda 1991).

Profits and Performance

Those who participate in corporate rule may seek to shape corporate strategy in relation to their particular interests. Executives may
strive to benefit themselves through salaries, fees, share options,
and pensions; dominant shareholders may attempt to increase the
dividend payment on their shares or the capital value of their holdings; and bankers may attempt to increase the indebtedness of the
enterprise and hence the interest which it must pay. I have shown
in the previous chapters, however, that the pursuit of such interests
is far from straightforward, and all participants will share a concern
to maintain the financial well-being and cashflow of the enterprises
with which they are associated. The impact of the various participants on corporate behaviour might be expected to vary, however,
with the mode of control, and this has led many researchers to
hypothesize that mode of control and measures of economic performance would be statistically associated. Although the measured
size and the rate of profits that are earned by enterprises depend on
their accounting practices, and may not provide strictly comparable
yardsticks (Jones 1995), many investigations have attempted to
relate control to profit measures. In some cases this has been combined with other measures of performance, such as capital appreciation and the dividend pay-out ratio. Such measures are, however,

difficult to use with any certainty. The arbitrariness of profit measures is especially clear in the case of wholly owned or majority-controlled subsidiaries. Transfers of goods and services between such subsidiaries do not pass through the external market and so can be priced on criteria that are internal to the enterprise. Purely notional prices enter into the accounts of subsidiaries, and their 'profits' and 'losses' become equally notional, as losses in one part of a large enterprise can be offset against profits in another. Even in enterprises linked through relations of minority control, there is scope for non-market factors to influence the calculation—and the pursuit—of profit. The *Temporary National Economic Committee* investigators argued that this was the case in family-interest groups that were held together through majority and minority shareholdings:

> While all of these concerns are independent enterprises, with complete freedom to determine their own policies, it seems hardly likely, in view of the extent to which they are owned by the same people, that anyone of them would pursue a course which was prejudicial to the interests of the others. (Anderson *et al.* 1941: 24)

Despite these technical problems, many observers have suggested strong links between control and profitability. It has been claimed, for example, that enterprises with family or other personal-majority owners will pursue strategies of long-term growth and capital appreciation as a way of maintaining the value of the capital invested, while enterprises controlled by financial institutions will have to make high dividend pay-outs in order to meet the pension and insurance commitments of their leading shareholders (Wilson Report 1977: 22; Pahl 1977a: 15). Fitch held that relatively small shareholdings by banks, when backed up by interlocking directorships, could be the basis for 'reciprocity' within bank-interest groups in which each enterprise is subordinated to the profitability of its controlling bank (1972: 126; Fitch and Oppenheimer 1970c: 77, 81). As I showed in Chapter 5, there are limits to the extent to which any bank could depress the profitability of an enterprise with which it seeks a *continuing* relationship. If a bank forced reciprocal dealings to such an extent that some of its associated enterprises began to make losses, the bank might be forced to intervene with financial support to prevent the enterprise from going out of business (O'Connor 1971). The fact remains, however, that enterprises may be constrained by non-market factors to follow strategies that do not bring them as

high a profit as might have been earned, but that are profitable enough to allow them to continue in business.

Attempts to investigate these hypotheses have generally produced only very weak results. Investigations carried out in the United States during the 1960s found that 'owner-controlled' enterprises tended to be more profitable and to show a better return on capital than those without a dominant ownership interest. Ownership was not, however, the most important influence on profitability, which was found to be more strongly associated with the size of the enterprise and the existence of obstacles to market competition (Kamerschen 1968; Monsen *et al.* 1968; Larner 1970; Palmer 1973).[6] Zeitlin and Norich (1979) confirmed this picture in their examination of the relationship between ownership and profitability in the top 300 American industrials of 1964. Comparing the results from an investigation based on the definitions and methods of Palmer (1973) and one based on the definitions of Burch (1972), they found that neither method yielded any significant result.[7] An investigation of eighty-nine large British enterprises over the period 1957–67 found that owner-controlled enterprises had higher profit and growth-rates than those without dominant ownership interests, but this seems to reflect an inverse association between size and profitability: owner-controlled enterprises tended to be smaller, and smaller enterprises tended to be more profitable (Radice 1971: 558–61; see also Steer and Cable 1978). In a careful summary of the available research, Lawriwsky (1984) set out a number of broad conclusions. 'Owner-controlled' enterprises seem to be more profitable than those without a dominant ownership interest, but this has not generally been a statistically significant result.[8] There was also weak evidence that owner-controlled enterprises have faster growth-rates, a lower dividend pay-out ratio, and more risky patterns of investment.

In Britain and the United States, then, there is a slight association between the degree of owner-control and the level of profitability, though ownership is far from being the most important determinant of profits. One of the few studies undertaken outside the Anglo-

[6] See Stano (1976) and Kania and McKean (1976). The latter are criticized in McEachern (1978) and reply in Kania and McKean (1978).

[7] They did discover a significant relationship between 'rate of exploitation' (measured by census of production figures showing 'man-hour' equivalents of value added, wages, etc.) and rate of return on capital.

[8] It could be argued that tests of significance are not the appropriate measure where the study involves no sampling and the assumption of normally distributed measures is unlikely.

American economies also demonstrates the complexity of the relationship between control and profitability. In a study of the long-term growth of French enterprises, Savage (1979) found that enterprises in which the chief executive was not a major shareholder had a better growth record than those run by family heirs. He holds that this reflects the different patterns of growth found in family-controlled and other enterprises. Owner-controlled enterprises, he argues, have a high growth-rate under their founders and then stagnate when the heirs take over. Enterprises without dominant owners, on the other hand, followed a more sustained growth and profit pattern (Savage 1979: 10–11).[9]

The weakness of these results reflects the fact that any effect of control on performance is likely to be small. Profits result from a surplus of revenues over costs, and as the total surplus is always small in relation to revenues and costs, behaviour that is aimed at marginally altering the size of the surplus is unlikely to produce any significant variations between broad classes of enterprise (Peterson 1965; Lieberson and O'Connor 1972). This is exacerbated by the fact, already discussed, that measures of profit reflect accounting practices and internal corporate transactions and are not an unambiguous and objective measure of performance or efficiency.

It must also be recognized that the definitions of 'control' used in these studies have generally been inadequate. Typically a contrast has been drawn between 'owner control' and 'management control', with the division between the two being based on arbitrary and variable percentage shareholdings. As has been fully demonstrated in earlier chapters, such an approach fails to grasp the realities of corporate control and corporate rule. Even the more sophisticated classifications have tended to ignore differences between control by personal and control by corporate owners, and virtually all studies have failed to explore the implications of share-ownership by financial institutions and the role of polycorporate collectives (Reeder 1975). If the influence of an owner is assessed in terms of the presence or absence of shareholdings above a particular level—and some studies have used a 5-per-cent cutoff point for identifying 'owner control'—poor results must be expected. Such a definition includes in the same category not only cases of majority and minority control by both corporations and persons, but also many cases of control through a constellation of interests.

[9] Additional studies are Jacquemin and Gellinck (1980) on France and Thonet and Poensgen (1979) on Germany.

This is exacerbated when researchers have an inadequate understanding of the mechanisms through which the mode of control in
an enterprise may have a causal effect on corporate performance.
Indeed, Lawriwsky (1984) has argued that the causal complexity is
such that we should not expect to find any straightforward correla-
tion between mode of control and performance. Economic performance is affected by the internal organization of the enterprise, by
the product and capital markets in which it operates, by the general
economic climate, and by a whole range of other factors. The mode
of control comprises a non-market context through which these
other factors operate. An adequate understanding of the interdependence of these various mechanisms has to take account of the
interests that different types of corporate controllers have in maintaining their control. Lawriwsky argues, for example, that owners
may perceive the need to make a trade-off between higher profits
and retaining control: a strategy of growth that is aimed at securing
the highest profits may dilute the controlling shareholding to the
point at which it becomes too small to ensure continued control
(Lawriwsky 1984: 27–30; Reder 1947; see also Pitelis and Sugden
1983). Similarly, an enterprise without a dominant shareholding
interest and that seeks to avoid becoming the target of a takeover bid
may choose a strategy of growth in order to forestall such bids. The
same enterprise may, however, depart from growth if the dominant
coalition feel that the chance of a possible takeover is slim (Holl 1977;
1980; Lawriwsky 1980).

Although the influence of control on performance is variable, it
varies within certain limits, and each mode of control will be associated with a *range* of performance values. This is clear from the work
of Lawriwsky, who investigated large Australian enterprises that
were classified into three categories: private ownership control,
company control, and dispersed ownership. Enterprises subject to
majority or minority control by private individuals showed a
growth-rate that was strongly and negatively associated with the size
of the controlling holding: the larger the size of the shareholding, the
lower the growth-rate. These same enterprises also showed a lower
profitability and a higher retention rate, and Lawriwsky interprets
these findings as demonstrating a striving to maintain control (1984:
116). In enterprises where a controlling block was held by another
enterprise there was no determinate pattern of performance, and
Lawriwsky argues that this was because the performance of subsidiaries and associates depends upon the circumstances of their par-

ents (ibid.: 126). Finally, enterprises with dispersed ownership—those controlled through constellations of interests—showed patterns of performance that varied according to whether families or institutions were dominant within the constellation. In enterprises where a family participated in the controlling constellation and was represented on the board there was higher profitability and higher retention, though such enterprises were invariably smaller. In enterprises where financial institutions collectively held a high proportion of the shares there were higher growth-rates as their controllers sought to avoid takeover (ibid.: 133–5). Lawriwsky's study, therefore, came up with strong and unambiguous findings and, while it is possible to question some of his interpretations, he has certainly established his case. Mode of control, understood as a set of non-market controls, does have an impact on corporate performance, but its causal impact is mediated through other factors, is exercised alongside other mechanisms, and must be understood as setting limits for economic performance rather than determining a specific corporate strategy.

The mode of control in an enterprise is a determinant of the limits and opportunities available to the participants in business leadership in their struggle for control over corporate strategy. It is to be expected, therefore, that economic performance will also be associated with the balance of power and interests in the dominant coalition and with the resources of capital and information that its members are able to mobilize on behalf of the enterprise. The availability of these resources is determined by the network of capital, commercial, and personal relations in which an enterprise is involved and that constitute the enterprise's environment of action. 'Mode of control' as conventionally defined grasps one aspect of this network of intercorporate relations. It grasps those capital relations that involve ownership of share capital, holding of the associated voting rights, and the opportunities that these present for making further capital available. There has been far less research on the impact of interlocks or of other personal relations on economic performance, but the results have generally been conclusive. Burt (1980) for the United States and Ziegler (1982) for Austria and Germany have shown that interlocking within product markets occurs as an attempt to reduce uncertainty and enhance profit-seeking, though there was little evidence that these strategies of horizontal co-optation were successful. On the other hand, Pennings (1980) and Carrington (1981) have shown that profitability is positively associated with bank interlocks in both the United States and in Canada. Meeusen and Cuyvers (1985) confirmed this in their study of interlocks in the top 250 Belgian and Dutch enterprises of 1976. They discovered that the profitability of non-financial enterprises was significantly associated with the number of bank interlocks that they had, but that this relationship did not hold for interlocks with the Belgian holding companies. Enterprises interlocked with the holding companies performed less well than others, suggesting that the holding companies did indeed use non-market controls to enhance their own profitability and depress the performance of their associates.

The discussion so far has assumed that large enterprises are unproblematically committed to the making of profits, but this is precisely one of the assumptions of classical economic theory that has been questioned by many managerialist writers. Non-sectionalist managerialists, for example, have seen the autonomy of the large enterprise as a basis for its pursuit of 'soulful' strategies geared to social responsibility and public welfare. I have shown, however, that the structure of non-market controls is such that a large number of factors—and not simply managerial motives—will shape corporate strategy. An enterprise that pursues a strategy that departs from profitability will, eventually, be forced out of business, and so the various non-market controls must operate within these market constraints. This point has particularly been emphasized by Alchian (1950) in his 'natural selection' model of corporate behaviour (see also Becker 1962). According to Alchian, the market is a selective device, and only those enterprises that are successful in the market will survive. In order to survive, an enterprise must earn sufficient profits to meet its current commitments; and in order to prosper, it must do better than its competitors. There is, however, no way in which business leaders can evolve a corporate strategy that will ensure them either survival or prosperity. In the long run, surviving enterprises will be found to be those that have actually succeeded in the search for profits; but this is a consequence of market conditions and not of the foresight of business leaders.

The problem for business leaders, then, is to formulate strategies that permit them to survive. Contrary to the assumptions of classical economic theory, however, this search for profits may not involve profit maximization (Winter 1967; Nelson and Winter 1982). Simon (1945) has developed a particularly powerful approach to this matter, arguing that business leaders formulate strategies on the basis of their knowledge of the economic environment as they perceive it. They evolve a definition of the situation (Simon 1945: 67) that suggests a range of alternative possible actions from which they have to choose a specific course of action to follow (Marris 1964: 47; Karpik 1972). Traditional economic theory assumed that enterprises would choose the course of action that would maximize their profits, but Simon argues that the uncertainty of outcomes that is inherent in imperfect knowledge means that no action can guarantee maximization. Business leaders can never be sure that they have chosen the optimal course of action; all they can do is establish decision criteria that seem to ensure them 'satisfactory' outcomes. The 'satisficing' behaviour of the large enterprise involves the search for those courses of action that will generate sufficient profits for them to survive over the long term.

On this point there is a surprising degree of agreement between sophisticated managerialists and Marxists. While they employ the language of 'maximization', Baran and Sweezy recognized that the pursuit of profits is a long-term rather than a short-term process. Large enterprises, they argue, are involved in a 'systematic temporal search for highest practicable profits' (1966: 37). In a given market situation, they argue, this level of profit is generally the greatest increase that will not ruin later opportunities for profit. Short-term profit-maximization, even if it were predictably possible, would involve 'a reckless and wholly irrational pursuit of immediately realizable profit, regardless of any longer-term consideration' (Miliband 1968: 54). Similarly, Mandel has argued that the modern enterprise eschews such 'reckless' hedonism:

In conditions of monopolistic competition short-term maximization is a completely senseless goal. Company strategy aims at long-term profit maximization, in which factors such as domination of the market, share of the market, brand familiarity, future ability to meet demand, safeguarding of opportunities for innovation, i.e., for growth, become more important than the selling price which can be obtained immediately or the profit margin which this represents. (Mandel 1972: 232; Baran and Sweezy 1966: 51; Aaronovitch and Sawyer 1976: 42ff.)

This Marxist position can be compared with the managerialist view of Peterson:

The compelling constraint . . . is that the firm's health, indeed its survival depend on the relation within it of revenues and costs. . . . Pursuit of profit does not mean that management spends much of its time contemplating profit as such but that its time is spent on decisions regarding the planning, providing, pricing, and selling of products, which govern revenue, and the organizing, equipping, and carrying on of production, together with the purchase of labour, supplies, and other requirements, which govern costs. . . . This is the essence of profit-seeking and of capitalist behaviour in employing resources. (Peterson 1965: 9; Baumol 1962; Marris 1964: 59, 107ff.)

The large enterprise, then, is a long-term 'profit seeker' rather than a short-term 'profit maximizer', and corporate rulers will attempt to evolve decision criteria that give the greatest chance of achieving a ratio of revenue to costs that is likely to give it the best chance of survival and prosperity in the market. The imperatives of the market ensure that unprofitable enterprises will not survive, and the dominant coalitions are constrained by these market forces in the formulation of their corporate strategies. Business leaders must strive to pursue policies that will allow them to earn a rate of profit that does not fall too far below the average. Enterprises that depart from these principles of long-term profitability will face problems of bankruptcy or decline. Far from undermining the pursuit of long-term profitability, the creation of extensive hierarchies of professional managers in the large enterprises can be seen as reinforcing it. Professional managers have more effective means of accumulating the technical knowledge and information-processing capacity that is required to interpret market constraints. The various techniques of modern business management and corporate planning serve to reduce the market uncertainty facing the large enterprise and enable it to more effectively pursue long-term profitability (Baran and Sweezy 1966: 40, 58; Mandel 1972: 233; Pahl and Winkler 1974, 118).

Corporate Strategy and Corporate Hierarchies

Modern large enterprises are profit-seekers, whose corporate rulers formulate strategies for market survival within a framework of non-market controls. These strategies are implemented by managerial hierarchies that are geared towards effective operations in the market, and which are possibly involved in intercorporate networks structured into various types of polycorporate collectives. The relationship between corporate strategy and managerial hierarchies has been influentially explored in the work of Chandler (1962; 1976; 1977) and his followers and, with some reservations, this can be seen as a useful approach for understanding corporate development.

Chandler sees the American pattern of corporate development from liberal to contemporary capitalism as prototypical for capitalist societies. Liberal capitalism was structured around the single-unit entrepreneurial firm, while contemporary capitalism is organized around large-scale divisional enterprises. In these two forms of enterprise the relationship between corporate strategy and operational management differs significantly. Corporate strategy concerns the long-term goals and objectives of an enterprise in relation to investment, corporate organization, and executive recruitment. The exercise of strategic control has been seen as participation in the processes of corporate rule through which corporate strategy is formulated. These strategic issues have been distinguished from the lower-level processes of decision-making that concern the operational administration of an enterprise within the financial constraints set by its corporate strategy. These lower-level processes are, in one sense, equally 'strategic', as they involve a deliberate instrumental manœuvring for tactical advantage. Considerable confusion arises, however, if they are not distinguished from the formulation and pursuit of a long-term corporate strategy. The 'strategic' aspects of operational administration are the outcome of a continuing series of short-term decisions in which middle managers respond in *ad hoc* and pragmatic ways to the pressing demands of those higher up the corporate hierarchy. Corporate strategy, by contrast, typically involves a more conscious and deliberate process of decision-making, in which long-term planning and the monitoring of the consequences of decisions play a central part.

The entrepreneurial firm of the nineteenth century was based around a close fusion of strategic decision-making and operational management in the person of the entrepreneur. Production took place exclusively at one location; the plant was small enough for an owner to supervise production personally; and it was also geared to local markets, which meant that the owner-manager could also oversee the sales of the enterprise's products. Strategy and operations were not distinguished, and there were few 'managers' separate from the entrepreneur, although 'clerks' were employed to undertake office work such as book-keeping and correspondence (Lockwood 1958).

Towards the turn of the century the scale of industrial production had increased to meet the needs of a national market. Through internal growth and through mergers, systems of mass production were established and the new large enterprises had to evolve systems of management that were capable of co-ordinating their new range of activities. The big banks, as I have shown, were central to the process of merger, amalgamation, and expansion, and their involvement in the development of the railways suggested that the system of railway administration could be transformed into a system of management appropriate to large-scale industrial production. Railway operations were spread over a large number of locations and took place on a distinctively national scale. It was in the railways, then, that new forms of management had to be developed. This involved the building of an extensive managerial hierarchy and a division of management into 'line' and 'staff' branches. Line management was concerned with the enterprise's main operations—the movement of passengers and freight by train— while staff management was concerned with specialist tasks such as accounting and equipment supplies.

The introduction of these new systems of administration to industrial enterprises was the basis of what Chandler calls the 'functional' system of departmental administration, and what Williamson (1975) has described as the unitary or 'U-form' enterprise. It was in these large enterprises that the organizational and technological principles of 'Fordist' systems of production were set up (Sabel 1982: 33; Lash and Urry 1987). Each function (production, sales, and so forth) is assigned to a separate head-office department, each department being co-ordinated by a head-office management team. The constituent departments, then, have virtually no decision-making autonomy, and it is at head-office level that strategic issues are concentrated. The corporate rulers and their subordinate executives formulated corporate strategy and recruited large numbers of salaried managers to run the business operations (Ehrenreich and Ehrenreich 1979).

It was through these centralized 'functional' enterprises and their unitary, 'manufacturing' systems of administration (Fligstein 1990: ch. 3) that organized capitalism took shape in the United States, and by the First World War many businesses were organized in this way. Their development was, however, uneven, and many large enterprises—especially those in which bankers played little part—were simply loose federations of firms under a parent 'holding company' that acted mainly as a central selling-agency or market-sharing device.[10] These federal enterprises were often amalgamations of separate family enterprises, each of which sought to maintain a maximum autonomy while reaping the benefits of centralized sales in the national market. Most strategic issues in these enterprises were decided at the level of the constituent firms, and not on the boards of the holding companies. Even where the parent board sought to determine an overall group strategy, the decentralized system of strategic management rarely allowed the formulation or implementation of a coherent strategy. By the end of the First World War big business in the United States was divided between a majority of 'functional enterprises', such as Du Pont and General Electric, and a minority of 'holding companies', of which the main examples were General Motors and Standard Oil. By 1929, 73 of the top 100 non-financial enterprises had adopted the unitary, functional form of organization (see Table 56).

Table 56. Administrative structure in the top 100 US enterprises (1919–1979)

	Percentage of corporations						
	1919	1929	1939	1948	1959	1969	1979
Holding	31	25	16	5	5	7	4
Unitary/functional	69	73	75	75	43	20	10
Multidivisional	0	2	9	20	52	73	86
	100	100	100	100	100	100	100
Multinational	41	53	65	67	77	87	93

Source: Fligstein (1990: 336, Table C.3).

The main stimulus to the creation of large enterprises of the functional and the federal type was the desire to internalize the transaction costs faced by the separate enterprises. A non-market 'reciprocity' of transactions administered through a management hierarchy was seen by corporate leaders as likely to result in lower

[10] The concept of 'holding company' used by Chandler refers neither to the Franco-Belgian investment-holding system described in Chapter 5, nor to the mere 'parent' company, though it is related to both. As will be apparent from the discussion, it refers to a specific form of federal management. For a definition and justification of this usage see Simons (1927).

prices than would be the case in a system of market exchange. But the advantages of a system of internalized transactions could only be fully achieved in those enterprises that had already established a managerial hierarchy capable of co-ordinating and planning the internalized transactions. In the federal-holding-company form of organization no effective managerial system existed, and they were unable to secure the full range of lower costs that the functional enterprises enjoyed. In neither type of enterprise, argued Chandler, was there a full separation of strategy from operations; the holding company combined aspects of both at the subsidiary level, while the functional enterprise combined them at head-office level. In both cases, therefore, long-term planning was inhibited by the continued involvement of top managers and directors in the details of day-to-day operations.

In Britain, France, and Germany, the holding-company form of organization became far more widespread than was the case in the United States. Holding companies in Britain were the characteristic form of business amalgamation in the late nineteenth and early twentieth centuries, and they continued to be widely used throughout the inter-war years (Hannah 1976b, 1980; Gospel 1983a and 1983b). Holding-company boards were arenas in which rival families struggled with one another, and there was little attempt to recruit professional managers or to engage in long-term strategic planning. Managers occupied weak and subordinate positions and were recruited through internal labour markets rather than on the basis of transferable skills or credentials. Only in ICI and Unilever was there any significant move away from this form of organization before the Second World War (Hannah 1974; 1976c: ch. 6; Chandler 1977: 499; Pollard 1965). In France, this federal structure of administration was an integral part of the corporate webs, and, in consequence, management structures were even weaker than in Britain.

Morikawa's (1977) study of management in the Japanese *zaibatsu* showed that the established family-trading house of Mitsui had, by the 1890s, adopted a federal structure, while the newer entrepreneur-led Mitsubishi had created a more centralized, functional organization. After 1917, however, Mitsubishi was reorganized as a federal organization—the classic organizational form of the *zaibatsu*—as the vertically structured corporate sets were consolidated in the Japanese economy. In Japan, however, the structure of the corporate sets allowed the controlling families to build systems of delegated managerial administration. This was due to the particularly rapid pace of industrialization in Japan, which created both the need and the opportunity for managerial hierarchies. The fact that the Japanese holding partnership established centralized family control at the level of the parent company, and that the latter controlled its subsidiaries through majority and minority holdings rather than by owning the whole of their share capital, gave them unique opportunities for delegating operational management. Each subsidiary was headed by a 'President', who had a status superior to that of the subordinate manager in more centralized enterprises. At the same time, top managers in a subsidiary could be permitted to acquire shares in the subsidiary company without this threatening either the parent's control of the subsidiary or the family's control of the corporate set. Managers could be retained within a *zaibatsu* through these rewards of status and share-ownership (Morikawa 1977: 59–60; Mishima 1977). In the post-war period, the federal structure has remained the predominant form of business organization in Japan, and the 'presidents' councils' of the new *kigyoshudan* have become the meeting-places at which the presidents of the constituent enterprises evolve group strategy.[11] The economic success of the *kigyoshudan* organization has meant that the major groups have faced few pressures to modify their internal management structures. The federal organization is an integral part of Japanese 'corporate capitalism'.

In other economies, the failure to fully separate strategic control from operational administration caused grave problems of inefficiency in the flow of resources in both the functional and the federal structures of administration. In an expanding economy, such as that of the United States prior to the First World War, these weaknesses were less obvious and could often be swept to one side. In the post-war depression, however, they became acute and could no longer be ignored. In response to these problems, Chandler argues, American enterprises began to seek alternative structures of corporate management in which centralized strategic control was combined with decentralized operational administration. In the case of a centralized, functional enterprise, this involved the building of autonomous operating units. In the case of the federal enterprise it involved the creation of a general office and general staff. It was through these changes that the so-called 'divisional', or 'multidivisional' form of

[11] Holding companies *per se*, it will be recalled, were made illegal after the Second World War, but the same organizational structure exists whether an operating company is an effective parent or there is a central presidents' council.

organization—Williamson's 'M-form enterprise'—was introduced. The operational units in the increasingly diversified enterprises came to be structured as 'product divisions', each of which contained its own functional specialists and was responsible directly to the general office (Chandler 1976: 27–8). Head office itself became more concerned with general, enterprise-wide strategic issues and with the financial control of the various divisions. It is for this reason that Fligstein (1990: ch. 7) holds that these enterprises are organized around a 'financial conception of control' in which the corporate rulers are concerned with the short-term profitability of each division.

Williamson suggests that such enterprises take a diversified or conglomerate form whenever each unit of production is better able to acquire capital than it could as a separate enterprise. By setting up product divisions as profit centres, the divisional enterprise establishes an internal system of capital mobilization for its various divisions. Perrow (1990; see also 1986: ch. 7) has argued, however, that the costs of this kind of administrative provision can be higher than market costs, especially where pricing becomes a matter of bargaining within the enterprise and new integrated accounting and financial systems have to be established. Efficiency, he claims, is an uncertain consequence of hierarchy, and hierarchical forms are more likely to be shaped by the possibility of appropriating the profit-flow of other enterprises than it is by any attempt to internalize costs.

A key part in the restructuring of enterprises was played by accountants. The economic difficulties of the early 1920s had exposed the need to identify and control costs more closely, and leading accountants began to propose that the auditing techniques that were used to regulate relations among enterprises, and between them and the state, could also be applied to the internal management of enterprises (Armstrong 1984). Accountants introduced techniques of central budgeting that permitted head offices to exercise control over their autonomous operating-divisions. In the divisional form of organization, head office concentrated on the task of strategic planning, and accounting and budgetary principles were used to co-ordinate the operational units. This occupational strategy was available to accountants in the United States and, later, in Britain, because the stock-exchange system of industrial finance had already given them a major role in the financial activities of joint stock companies (Johnson 1982). In those countries where bank funding was more important than the stock exchange, the legal requirements of company reporting differed and the role of professional accountants was far more limited. For this reason, accountants in Germany were not able to tie their own occupational interests to the establishment of divisional organization (Lawrence 1980).

During the inter-war years, divisional organization rapidly became the typical form of administration among large American enterprises, resulting in an almost complete separation of strategy from operational management in the big-business sector. Table 56 shows that over half the top 100 enterprises had adopted this form by 1959, and that the proportion had risen to three-quarters by 1969. In these enterprises the corporate headquarters housed the top executives and their large advisory and financial staffs, who were responsible for planning the long-term strategy of the enterprise as a whole and co-ordinating, monitoring, and evaluating divisional performance. The dispersed operating divisions, on the other hand, were responsible for the production and distribution of a product line in a specific market, and had complete autonomy within the financial targets and limits set by head office. The concerns of the operational division were with materials and labour management, with the senior operational managers co-ordinating materials and labour not in terms of physical quantities but in terms of the financial values used in the budgets produced by head office.

In Britain and other European countries, the federal system of administration did not begin to give way to the divisional form until after the Second World War. The stimulus for this restructuring of management was provided by the competitive pressure of those American multinational enterprises that had already adopted the divisional form of organization and that were expanding profitably into European markets. Table 57 presents the results of a study by Channon (1973) of the top 100 manufacturers of 1970 and their corporate structures in earlier decades. Just 12 per cent of these enterprises had adopted multidivisional organization by 1950, and even in 1960 less than one-third had made this move. Only four of the twelve pioneers were fully British-owned, while eight were foreign or binational, mainly American subsidiaries.[12] By 1970, largely because of American success and the influence of American management consultants, more than two-thirds of the top 100 were multidivisional enterprises.

[12] These four were Smiths Industries, Spillers, British-American Tobacco, and ICI. Unilever was treated as part-foreign.

Table 57. Administrative structure in the top 100 British, French, and German non-financial enterprises (1950–1970)

Administrative structure	Britain			France			Germany		
	1950	1960	1970	1950	1960	1970	1950	1960	1970
Holding company	28	40	20	20	18	12	15	14	12
Functional	52	22	8	50	32	14	36	21	20
Functional/ holding	–	–	–	24	29	20	43	48	18
Multidivisional	12	30	68	6	21	54	5	15	50
No information	8	8	4	0	0	0	1	1	0
Totals	100	100	100	100	100	100	100	100	100

Source: Calculated from Channon (1973: 72 and 74, Tables 3.3 and 3.4); Dyas and Thanheiser (1976, 72 and 184, Table 6.5 and Fig. 12.2).

Table 57 also shows clearly the pattern of corporate development in Britain. In the first decade after the War many of the enterprises which had adopted a centralized functional administration moved over to a holding-company organization, and in the second decade the large number of holding companies built their divisional structures. That is to say, the holding-company form was retained by those enterprises that had adopted it before the War, and was employed as a transitional form of decentralized administration by those that had not. In similar studies for France and Germany, Dyas and Thanheiser (1976) introduced the category of 'functional/holding' organization to refer to the transitional form adopted in these countries, where the main pattern of corporate development was from functional, to functional/holding, to multidivisional. It can be seen from Table 57 that the number of functional/holding enterprises in France in 1970 was high, reflecting the legacy of the French investment holding system which was described in Chapter 6.

While overseas investment and overseas trading has a long history, multinational production is a fairly recent phenomenon. The multinational enterprise has been defined by Vernon as 'a cluster of corporations of different nationalities that are joined together through bonds of common ownership, that respond to a common strategy, and that draw on a common pool of human and financial resources' (Vernon 1971*b*: 694; 1971*a*: 11–15). In an extension of the Chandler thesis, Vernon has claimed that geographical diversification is impelled by the same mechanisms as product diversification. Routinization of activity within a market after initial entry and innovation results in a weakening of the barriers to entry and a fall in profitability. In order to protect its chances of survival and prosperity, therefore, the large enterprise is impelled to seek new markets where competitors cannot match the scale and complexity of the technology required, and where, in consequence, the profits are higher (Vernon 1971*a*: 26–7; 1977: ch. 5; Kurth 1975; Michalet 1976: 106 ff.). Geographical expansion is an alternative to product diversification, and in this way enterprises progress from the local to regional and national and, eventually, to international level. Thus the rise of the multinational enterprise is 'a change in degree, not kind, from the world of very large expansive enterprises still contained within national borders' (Heilbronner 1976: 73; Papandreou 1973: 109; Hymer 1972).

For some time, American multinational enterprises continued to be organized along federal lines. Until the 1960s and 1970s, domestic and substantial overseas businesses were internally structured as divisional organizations, but the international structure itself took the form of a holding company. American overseas subsidiaries, therefore, had a high degree of autonomy from their parent companies and were often majority-controlled with share participations and board representation from the financial institutions of the overseas country. European multinationals adopted an even looser structure than their American counterparts, reflecting the predominance of the federal form in their national economies. As European enterprises began to adopt multidivisional organization, so European multinationals from the 1970s on began to organize their foreign operations into a 'matrix' in which the product-division structure of the group as a whole was cross-cut by separate national subsidiaries that co-ordinated all group activities within their particular country. Only since the middle of the 1970s has there been any significant move towards the creation of international product divisions co-ordinated by the head office (Francko 1976). Table 58 shows some of the consequences of these differences for ownership patterns of multinational subsidiaries. In 1970 almost three-quarters of American foreign subsidiaries were wholly owned, while this was true for only a half of European subsidiaries and one-third of Japanese subsidiaries.

Table 58. Ownership status of foreign subsidiaries in industrial economies (1970)

Ownership	180 US companies		135 European companies		61 Japanese companies	
	No.	(%)	No.	(%)	No.	(%)
Wholly owned	2612	(72.5)	1788	(55.8)	6	(13.0)
Majority-controlled	657	(18.2)	802	(25.0)	8	(17.4)
Minority-controlled	302	(8.4)	404	(12.6)	30	(65.2)
Unknown	32	(0.9)	213	(6.6)	2	(4.4)
Totals	3603	(100)	3207	(100)	46	(100)

Source: Calculated from Vernon (1977: 34, Table 4).
Note: Subsidiaries outside the core capitalist economies are not included. This distorts the picture for Japan, as most of its subsidiaries are in Asia (Weinstein 1976).

Japanese multinationals operated mainly through minority participations, reflecting a translation of the structure of aligned participations from the national to the international scale.

Many American multinational enterprises, by contrast, adopted a thoroughgoing multidivisional structure during the 1960s. Minority and majority shareholdings were increasingly transformed into the whole-ownership of subsidiaries, and lines of communication between overseas divisional executives and parent headquarters were strengthened. Divisional executives of American enterprises in Europe, for example, increasingly filled the board seats of the American subsidiaries, so tying them into a cohesive group that was isolated from or peripheral to the European national networks of interlocking directorships (Fennema and Schijf 1985).

The changing forms of corporate administration are related to variations in patterns of ownership and control between countries. Chandler (1962) saw the presumed change from private ownership to 'management control' in the United States as the economic basis for the transition from entrepreneurial firms to functional and multidivisional enterprises. Changes in ownership, he argued, lead to changes in strategy that, in turn, produce changes in administrative structure. I have already shown, however, that management control occurred only for a relatively short time in the very largest American enterprises as they underwent a transition from family ownership to control through a constellation of interests. There is little evidence that management control ever had any real significance in Britain. It is in this light that Chandler's secondary explanation of the emergence of centralized administration becomes more important. He suggested, it will be recalled, that the merger activities undertaken by the big financiers of the 'Money Trust' were essential for the creation of large enterprises and for building managerial hierarchies. Although rather undeveloped, this argument is clearly compatible with that presented in the earlier chapters of this book. Centralized administration in the United States was largely the result of the control that banking interests achieved around the turn of the century, as they forged the new structures of organized capitalism. This centralized administration was transformed into divisional forms of administration as this control weakened and gave way to the control through a constellation of interests that characterizes patterns of impersonal possession in disorganized capitalism.

The separation of City and industry in Britain meant that banks did not achieve the same kind of control over industry as did their American counterparts before the First World War—and high levels of family ownership persisted for much longer than was the case in the United States. The close relationship of City and industry that came about during the inter-war years was a response to the specific economic difficulties faced by leading enterprises in heavy industry, and it was not associated with any significant administrative restructuring. As a result, many federal enterprises survived into the post-war period. The growth of institutional shareholdings and of control through a constellation of interests was an important precondition for the transition from holding company to divisional organization during the 1950s and 1960s, when the inroads of American enterprises highlighted the inadequacies of British management organization, and initiated the transformation of Fordist organization and production systems that culminated in the post-Fordist regimes of flexible specialization (Piore and Sabel 1984; Offe 1984). The post-war American penetration of the French economy was similarly a stimulus to managerial restructuring in that country, but the predominance of corporate webs led to the emergence of the hybrid 'functional/holding' organization. The relative weakness of control through a constellation of interests in France and Japan is associated with the smaller proportion of enterprises with divisional organization and their long traditions of corporate webs and aligned participations.[13]

[13] More general discussions of differing trajectories of organizational structures can be found in Lammers and Hickson (1979a) and Hofstede (1980).

Careers and Compensation

The expansion of corporate hierarchies through the functional, fed-eral, and divisional forms has led to a massive growth in the numbers of those employed to fill positions of bureaucratic command. As managerial tasks grew in scale and scope, so managers with a wider range of more specialist skills were recruited, and layers of subordi-nate clerical workers were added. In this way, those in 'service-class' situations (Renner 1953; Goldthorpe 1982) were linked with routine white-collar workers in the formation of large 'middle classes'.

It has often been claimed that it is the increase in the number of salaried managers and of those involved in bureaucratic administra-tion that has altered the prevailing pattern of motivation among business leaders and so has had an influence on the behaviour of large enterprises. Dahrendorf (1959: 46), for example, has argued, 'Never has the imputation of a profit motive been further from the real motives of men than it is for the modern bureaucratic manager'; and Shonfield (1965: 377) states that 'the manager, who is not the owner, is neither driven into automatic responses by the forces of the market place nor guided by the exclusive desire to make the maxi-mum profit on behalf of his shareholders'. Changes in patterns of control are held to create the conditions under which management may exercise a certain amount of discretion and so may move away from an exclusive concern with profit. Monsen and Downs (1965), for example, argue that, while the shareholders of a company look for a steady dividend income and capital gains, managers seek to maximize their lifetime incomes.

I have already shown why such conclusions are unfounded, and I have suggested that modern corporate managers might be better equipped to seek profits than were old-style capitalist entrepreneurs. It is important, nevertheless, to show how it is that managerial moti-vation becomes an integral part of the profit-seeking activities of business enterprises. The key to this lies in the nature of the corpo-rate hierarchies that have been built in the large enterprises, hierar-chies which are central to the 'career' structures that have shaped managerial work for most of the present century.

To the extent that managers share expectations concerning the legitimacy of their occupational advancement through a bureau-cratic hierarchy and of the role of their superiors in securing this advancement for them, the idea of a 'career' will be an important

control over their actions (Thomas 1981). Both actual and anticipated advancement, through promotion or job transfer, reinforces
their commitment to their current employer and their current position. Furthermore, the identity of 'management' as a distinct group
within an enterprise is strengthened by the exclusion of other workers from these same prospects of advancement. The career-structur-
ing of work is a means of social differentiation within the workforce;
but at the same time it fragments the management group itself,
encouraging managers to seek individual solutions (such as promotion and job change) to their shared interests. The autonomy of
managers in their work situations is a consequence of the absence of
close surveillance and technical control, and is expressed in the 'high-
trust' characteristics of managerial work (Fox 1974).[14] Managers are
'high-trust' workers, controlling 'low-trust' clerical and manual
workers but controlled themselves through the very concepts of
career and discretion which differentiate them from those they control. During the 1980s, the idea of a managerial 'career' has become
less salient for many, as large organizations respond to recession and
the introduction of computer technology by 'downsizing' their managerial workforces. This has mainly affected lower-level and middle
managers, whose work can more easily be replaced by information-
processing technologies or can be contracted-out to 'consultants'.
Even among the senior managers in the corporate head offices, however, there have been considerable staffing reductions, leaving operational managers with greater autonomy to work within the
strategic plans drawn up by the slimmer head-office teams (Useem
1993: ch. 3). Senior managers, then, are more precarious, less secure
in their careers; but the effect of this is to reinforce even more
strongly the need to be successful (Pahl 1995).

Corporate careers depend upon a manager making an effective
contribution to the success of the enterprise, and managers tend to
become subjectively committed to this through the 'selective and
moulding effects of institutions on the personnel that operates them'
(Baran and Sweezy 1966: 49).[15] Through business-school training
and through the general corporate culture, managers are imbued
with prevailing conceptions of business practice, which are, in turn,

[14] Friedmann (1977) describes this as 'responsible autonomy'. Trends in management thought are discussed in Child (1969b). For a study of ambivalence in
career commitment of British managers see Pahl and Pahl (1971).

[15] For more general statements of this thesis see Bourdieu (1974) and Gerth and
Mills (1954: 165 ff.).

selected through an evolutionary process. It is those managers who have the appropriate orientation to business practice that 'survive' and are successful (Fligstein and Brantley 1992). Marxist and non-Marxist writers are agreed on the point that the corporate goals of size, strength, and growth through profits 'become the subjective aims of the business world because they are the objective requirements of the system' (ibid.: 53; Parsons 1940).

Managers are committed because they are locked in to a structure of material rewards and incentives that reinforce commitment to the system. Salaries, share options, and other fringe benefits are all geared to the maintenance of career commitment. McEachern (1975) has argued that managerial salaries and other rewards will vary with the mode of control in an enterprise and, in particular, with the existence of a dominant shareholder and the representation of this shareholder on the board. Dominant shareholders, he argues, structure managerial incentives in such a way as to constrain managers to act in their interests. In a study of forty-eight industrials for 1969–72, it was discovered that enterprises with a dominant shareholder had systems of management compensation that geared managers to profits and to the market value of shares, and McEachern shows that this resulted in these enterprises showing a higher rate of return on capital (McEachern 1975: 112–13). In a larger study of 218 industrials for 1975–6 Allen (1981) argued that the power of the chief executive was the most important intervening variable between mode of control and managerial compensation, and he demonstrated that the level of compensation was inversely associated with mode of control. Allen argues that a chief executive's power is highest if he or she is the dominant shareholder; it is lowest if the chief executive has a negligible shareholding and has to contend with substantial shareholders on the board. Even after allowing for size and performance, chief executives who were low in power were also low in compensation. But this relationship was not unilinear, as the most powerful chief executives were found to have the lowest rates of compensation. Allen suggests that this was a deliberate tactic on the part of these executives to divert any criticisms that they were using their power for their own benefit, and he claims that they were, in any case, able to offset their low salary with their high dividend income.

Although managers are constrained to pursue long-term profitability by the structuring of careers and compensation in bureaucratic hierarchies, a number of studies have produced evidence that their subjective commitments may not be unambiguous. Nichols (1969) and Francis (1980b) both found evidence that managers expressed a belief in long-term financial goals, most frequently maximizing the growth of total profits and maximizing the rate of return on capital; but there was a tendency for these goals to be allied with the notions of 'social responsibility' and 'community service' that appear in non-sectionalist managerialist theory. These ideas were reconciled through their belief in an underlying harmony of interests in the business enterprise. Fidler (1981: ch. 5) found that chief executives in large British enterprises espoused a 'balancing of interests ethos', seeing their occupational role as involving an attempt to balance the varying short-term interests of shareholders, workers, and customers with the long-term interest in profitability that they were all assumed to have in common. This system of beliefs, argues Fidler, is fundamental to what Fox (1973; 1974) has called the 'unitary' viewpoint of British management. Managers believe that, because of the underlying harmony of interests, there should be a unified hierarchy of authority, with managers having 'the right to manage' unchallenged by trades unions or other forms of worker resistance (Storey 1980: 41–2; 1983: ch. 6). This unitary view is grounded in conceptions of the rights of property ownership—managers seeing themselves as the trustees of the mass of shareholders—and the requirements of economic efficiency, and it involves the belief that managers must secure compliance from workers who lack the detailed information that would enable them to perceive the underlying harmony of interests. Industrial conflict is seen as due to poor communication between managers and workers, the action of union 'militants', or outside interference, and it is seen as soluble through good management. At the same time, most senior executives have little contact with employees other than other managers and their own secretaries (Winkler 1974). Industrial relations, that is to say, is regarded as an operational matter rather than as something that should figure directly in corporate strategy; and personnel managers in the operating divisions must secure pay settlements that enable their division to meet the budgetary targets set by headquarters.

The subjective beliefs of managers must be seen as aspects of the legitimation of control, rather than as direct influences on corporate behaviour. Market forces, as mediated through corporate hierarchies and shaped by non-market controls, lead managers to specify levels of effort and production among the workforce that require a

degree of consent from their employees.[16] Conceptions of 'human-
ization', 'participation', and 'enrichment', no less than the espousal
of 'social responsibility', are social meanings upon which managers
draw to justify the acceptance of a system in which they perceive
themselves and their subordinates as having little choice (Bendix
1956). The role of such vocabularies of motive (Mills 1940) is to legitimate both the corporate structure and the position of managers
within it.

Dore (1987: 54; see also Dore 1973; Smith 1983) contrasts the
'company-law' model of managerial legitimacy found in the Anglo-
American economies with what he terms the Japanese 'community
model' of the business enterprises. Japanese managers present themselves as leading figures in a unified collectivity in which shareholders are seen in the same way as customers, as one of the 'external'
interests that need to be satisfied by the operations of the enterprise.
Within this structure, a 'high-trust' orientation towards full-time
workers can be maintained. Such an orientation would be unsus-
tainable in the Anglo-American economies, as it is the structure of
share-ownership in Japan that insulates Japanese enterprises from
direct external intervention.

The strategy formulated by a dominant coalition within an enterprise is constrained by the operation of market forces. Corporate
rulers, nevertheless, have a degree of choice about the ways in which
they respond to these forces. They have absolute choice, of course, as
to whether to observe the requirements at all; though failure to do so
for any period of time is likely to result in the collapse of an enterprise. The way in which corporate rulers exercise this choice depends
on the various non-market factors that constrain them. These
include, most notably, the network of intercorporate capital and personal relations that shape modes of control and the internal hierarchies through which managerial careers are structured. It is through
the integration of the subjective motivation of managers with the
objective structures of hierarchies and intercorporate relations that
enterprises engage in the long-term search for profitability.

[16] Littler and Salaman (1984) call this the 'dual nature' of the capital–labour relation. See also Littler (1982).

8

DISORGANIZATION, DISARTICULATION, AND DEREGULATION

I T seems natural to describe economic activity as focused around national economies. Indeed, much of my discussion so far has referred to forms of ownership and control, of corporate rule and of corporate structure, 'in' Britain, the United States, Germany, Japan, and elsewhere. These national economies have, indeed, been foci of economic activity since at least the seventeenth century, but they have never existed as isolated and self-contained entities. In this chapter, attention turns to the relationship between national economies and the wider international processes in which they are embedded. I have, so far, written of liberal capitalism, organized capitalism, and disorganized capitalism as if they were unproblematic terms for describing national economies. In this chapter, these will be examined more thoroughly as stages in the development of an increasingly globalized economic system.

The Capitalist World-Economy

Wallerstein (1974a, 1980, 1989; see also Chase-Dunn 1989; Shannon 1989) has emphasized the need to move analytically beyond the national economy to the broader economic units in which national economies are embedded. The true units of economic analysis, he argues, are, and have been for thousands of years (Frank and Gills 1993a), 'world systems'. A world system is an economic unit with 'a single division of labour and multiple cultural systems' (Wallerstein 1974b: 5). That is, it is a network of economic transactions that encompasses a diversity of ethnic and other cultural groups based in a large number of territories and having a wide—though not necessarily global—extent. For much of human history, world systems have taken the form of 'world-empires', world systems with single, unifying political centres. The early Chinese and Roman imperial systems are examples of such world-empires. Until the fifteenth century, north-west Europe formed a marginal part of the remnants of the old Roman Empire; it had become 'feudalized' in its structure, and was surrounded by the hostile or indifferent empires of Byzantium, India, and China. Feudal Europe was united by the cultural framework of Christianity and its particular form of 'civilization', but in economic and political terms it was weak. Between the fifteenth and the seventeenth centuries, however, medieval Europe gave rise to a distinctively modern world system, structured as a 'world-economy' rather than a world-empire. In a world-economy there exist a multiplicity of political units, and in modern Europe these began to form themselves into nation-states, whose territories constituted the national economies within the overarching and specifically *capitalist* world-economy:

over a large geographical area going from Poland in the north east westwards and southwards throughout Europe and including large parts of the Western Hemisphere as well, there grew up a world economy with a single division of labour within which there was a world market, for which men (*sic*) produced largely agricultural products for sale and profit. (Wallerstein 1974b: 16)

This was, then, a system of agrarian and commercial capitalism, its core lying in the Hanseatic and Flanders trading-centres of northwest Europe and in northern Italy. In these core areas, capitalist merchants accumulated resources on a massive scale and established autonomous bases of power in the major towns and cities. These 'bourgeois' merchants stood at the heart of the system of trade that constituted the nascent world-economy, its reach spreading through eastern Europe, the Atlantic islands, and the Americas. Their resources came not only from the local and 'national' economies in which they were based, but from the peripheral, exploited regions of eastern Europe and the Americas that were forced to provide the inhabitants of the core areas with grain, gold, silver, cotton, and sugar on terms of unequal exchange (Frank 1969). Portuguese expansion to the West—to the West Indies and the Americas—was followed by Spanish expansion and by similar colonial sorties from other European states. Intermediate between core and peripheral regions in the world-economy were the semi-peripheral regions of Mediterranean Europe, later joined by the declining areas of Spain and Italy (Wallerstein 1974a; Emmanuel 1972). In the national economies of the core—the nation-states of England, the Netherlands, and northern France—social classes of capitalist merchants achieved a strong position. It was in these national economies, and in England in particular, that the capitalist industrial take-off occurred. Between 1750 and 1870, England rose to dominance as the 'hegemonic' power within the world-economy, establishing a position for itself as the pivot of a liberal, free-trade system of 'international' economic relations. Commercial and industrial growth was the basis for the territorial expansion of this system of 'liberal capitalism' into areas of the globe that previously lay outside the capitalist world-economy.

The capitalist world-economy was surrounded by world-empires in varying states of expansion and decay. The Ottoman and Russian empires posed perhaps the greatest challenges to the capitalist world-economy, while China and India more readily succumbed to capitalist expansion. As the system expanded, the Russian empire declined and was incorporated into the world-economy as a part of its semi-periphery, while the non-imperial areas of Asia and Africa were incorporated into its periphery. The East Asian empires of China and Japan had shut themselves off from foreign influences when European expansion began to make itself felt in the sixteenth and seventeenth centuries, and it was only in the mid-nineteenth century that they began to be incorporated into the capitalist world system. China retained some economic and political autonomy until the 1890s, but the political and military collapse of the empire led rapidly to its peripheral incorporation into the capitalist system. The Meiji leadership in Japan sought to avoid China's fate, and state-led industrialization was seen as an essential step towards an autonomous economic and political position in the world-economy. By protecting its markets from foreign domination, Japan entered the world-economy as a semi-peripheral, rather than a peripheral economy.

The development of the capitalist world-economy helped to shape the variations in ownership and control that have been described in earlier chapters. The transition from personal to impersonal possession has been a feature of the world-economy as a whole, though it has taken varying forms in the national economies that make up this system. Liberal capitalism was a specific phase in the development of the capitalist world-economy, a phase in which economic activity was undertaken in national economies by national, capitalist classes of merchants and industrialists. National economies themselves were structured into small-scale business enterprises that were subject to the personal possession of entrepreneurial capitalists and that entered into relations of atomistic competition in their domestic markets. International economic relations involved, for the most part, the trading of commodities that were produced within particular national economies, with merchants and bankers playing a key role in this international system.

British hegemony came under challenge from the 1870s as industrial take-off occurred in many areas that felt under threat from British capital. 'Late' industrialization in the United States, Germany, and Japan transformed the world system, moving economic activity in a more 'organized' direction. Banks played a leading role in the promotion of new, large-scale enterprises and in the amalgamation of family enterprises. The growing fusion of banking and industrial capital into 'finance capital' was paralleled by the growing intervention of nation states in economic activity, whether as supports or promoters of private enterprise. In this stage of 'organized capitalism', economic activity came increasingly under the control of 'finance capitalists', and entrepreneurial capitalists had to rely on the more indirect forms of personal possession that Berle and Means (1932) called 'majority control' and 'minority control'. The enterprises that the finance capitalists and entrepreneurial capitalists controlled operated in more concentrated and less-competitive national markets: capital came to be organized on a national scale within the various industrial sectors. International economic relations of commodity exchange were supplemented by the growth of overseas investment, as capitalists from the various national economies invested in bonds and shares in other national economies.

The core of the capitalist world-economy in the stage of organized capitalism comprised Western Europe and the United States, the late-industrializing economies of Germany and the United States joining the more established core economies of Britain, France, Belgium, and the Netherlands. In a semi-peripheral location were the Central and Eastern European regions of the Austro-Hungarian and Russian empires, Spain, Italy, and Japan, all of which were late but 'backward' industrializers (Gershenkron 1962). Peripheral areas in the capitalist world-economy at this time were the Balkans, the Middle East, Asia, Africa, and South America. The Communist seizure of power in China in 1949 effectively removed China from the capitalist world-economy and began its move in the radically different economic direction of socialist industrialization, from which it has only recently diverged (So and Chiu 1995).

American hegemony characterized the capitalist world-economy from the end of the First World War until at least the 1960s. American enterprises expanded across the world, these 'multinational' enterprises putting pressure on the less-efficient enterprises of Europe and forcing them to restructure their own activities. Japan rose from semi-periphery to core in this period, as the United States sought to reconstruct the Japanese economy as a bulwark against the threat of the Chinese Communist state. Multinational enterprises operated on an international rather than a national scale, and production itself began to take on an international dimension. As multinationals came to shape the international division of labour and flow of funds, so they began to undermine the powers of nation states. As a result, national economies became increasingly 'disarticulated' or 'disorganized', and it became increasingly unrealistic to think in terms of integrated national economies, nationally cohesive capitalist classes, or powerful nation states. Through the post-war period, then, the growth of impersonal possession in the core economies was associated with a process of disarticulation that has been seen as involving a transition from organized capitalism to 'disorganized capitalism'.

These processes of transition—from liberal capitalism to organized capitalism, and from organized capitalism to disorganized capitalism—have developed unevenly across the world-economy. In Britain, where the industrial take-off was early, the 'organization' of capitalism occurred slowly and had weaker roots. In late-industrializing, strong state economies such as Germany and Japan, on the other hand, the organization of capitalism was more rapid and more deeply rooted. In these more organized forms of capitalism, the 'disorganization' of capitalism has been later and slower than it was in weakly organized economies such as Britain (Lash and Urry 1987: 5, 7; See also Aglietta 1979: 222–3).

Global Strategies and Economic Disarticulation
....

The capitalist world-economy, I have argued, developed from the fifteenth century onwards as a system of trading relations among individuals and enterprises in its constituent local economies. Most of the businesses involved in this trade were very small, and corporate organization was unimportant, but some of the earliest capitalist enterprises were giant international traders that were organized as joint stock companies. Such enterprises as the British East Africa Company, the East India Company, and the Hudson's Bay Company, for example, had large share capitals and were ruled by boards of directors. International economic relations were almost exclusively commercial transactions that involved the buying and selling of raw materials and of finished products. While the large trading companies operated through overseas offices and trading-posts in peripheral economies, most international trading relations took place among merchants indigenous to the various national economies. Not until the early nineteenth century were these trading relations supplemented by any significant overseas investment by capitalists from one country in the economy of another; but from this time on, capitalists from the core economies—and most notably from Britain—began to invest in mines, railways, ranches, and other enterprises in the primary and agrarian sectors of the peripheral and semi-peripheral economies of the United States, Canada, Argentina, and Australia. Using principles of portfolio investment, individual capitalists would take shares or make loans to investment and mortgage companies that provided funds to overseas undertakings, and their funds were also used to form banks that specialized in the financing of these activities.

Britain's hegemonic position in the world-economy meant that it held a central position in the flow of international trading and investment relations. The growth of overseas investment was remarkable, and by 1855 it amounted to £230m. Declining domestic investment opportunities after the 1870s led to a massive export of capital, and the volume of British overseas investment rose to £4,000m by 1914 (Cottrell 1975; Cairncross 1953; Kennedy 1976). At the heart of this growth were the enterprises of the City of London, which diversified from trading and public finance activities into the management of overseas investment (Chapman 1984: 189 ff.). The City had evolved alongside the growth of British trade, and its banks and merchants became the central agents in an international monetary system in which the currencies of the leading trading countries were freely convertible, at fixed exchange rates, into sterling and gold (Ingham 1984). The Bank of England was central to the City and became a central bank with major responsibilities for maintaining both currency exchange rates and the domestic money supply. Closely allied with the British state, whose power underpinned the expansion of British economic interests across the globe, the City became the focus of the international economy, and sterling became the *de facto* world currency. Similar developments took place in the other core economies, though these developments were nowhere as strong as in Britain. By the end of the nineteenth century the capitalist world-economy was thoroughly structured around the national economies of the core, which were linked to one another through an international financial and commercial system operated by central banks and government departments. It was this particular pattern of international economic relations that underpinned the emergence of organized capitalism and the system of finance capital.

Through the nineteenth century and up to the First World War, overseas investment was overwhelmingly portfolio investment, though some American investment took a more direct form. In 'direct investment', manufacturing enterprises set up subsidiaries to operate directly in overseas markets, these locally registered and managed subsidiaries being integral elements in the operations of their parent enterprises. This form of investment grew considerably after the First World War, and it rapidly became a major element in the development of Canada, South America, and many parts of Europe (see Table 59). From the 1930s, the scale of direct investment overtook that of portfolio investment, this growth reflecting the transformation in corporate structures described in Chapter 7.

With the world-wide expansion of American enterprises after the Second World War, there was a significant shift in the direction of American foreign investment, as shown in Table 59, the shift being particularly marked during the 1960s. About one-third of all American overseas investment has been in Canada—a level slightly higher than before the War—but there was a substantial shift in investment from Latin America to Europe. The rate of increase of American investment in Europe in the post-war period was twice that in Canada. By the early 1970s, American investment in Britain amounted to $7,158m from its total overseas investment of $67,702m.; that in West Germany was $4,252m (Vernon 1971a: 19;

Table 59. US direct foreign investment (1929–1968)

Area	% of total investment stake in			
	1929	1949	1959	1968
Europe	19	14	16	30
Canada	25	31	33	33
Latin America	33	39	35	17
Other	23	15	16	20
Totals	100	100	100	100

Source: Adapted from Barratt Brown (1974: 208–9, Table 20).

Hughes 1973: 161). Early multinational enterprises tended to invest in those areas where they obtained their raw materials or where the cost of labour was cheapest. With the increased salience of marketing in corporate strategies, however, enterprises have tended to invest in or near their main markets. As a result, the most favoured sites for American investment in the post-war period have been other advanced industrial economies (Magdoff 1970; Williams *et al.* 1983: 30–1). This has not been an exclusively one-way process. Since 1960, for example, Canadian enterprises have invested on a greater scale in the United States, partially countering the earlier growth of American investment in Canada (Carroll 1985: 46). Increasingly, foreign direct investment has established an interchange of capital relations among the advanced capitalist economies, and it has been estimated that about a half of all their capital exports are to one another (Barratt Brown 1974; Dunning 1970: 49–50; Hood and Young 1979).

The challenge posed to European industry by this growth in American direct investment (Servan-Schreiber 1967) forced European enterprises to modify their own practices in response. By 1970, virtually all of the largest European manufacturers had overseas operations, and three-quarters of the top 85 operated in six or more countries. It was difficult for European enterprises to break into the American market, where large and efficient American enterprises had established themselves, and much of the expansion of European enterprises was within Europe itself. Total British foreign investment in the 1960s was equivalent to just under 10 per cent of net domestic investment, and the foreign assets of British companies were divided equally between the advanced capitalist economies and the less-developed nations. Showing a similar trend to that shown by American direct investment, British investment in Europe was growing more rapidly than it was anywhere else. American enterprises, however, remained a potent force in many of the key European industries, reflecting a concentration of direct investment in those industries where American enterprises held a strategic advantage. By the early 1970s, 85 per cent of total American investment in Europe was in four industrial sectors (vehicles, chemicals, mechanical engineering, and electrical and electronic engineering), and 40 per cent of American investment in Britain, Germany, and France was undertaken by General Motors, Ford, and Exxon (Hughes 1973: 162–4; Turner 1970; Hodges 1974: 53). By contrast, American enterprises in Europe accounted for just 6 per cent of all sales in manufacturing (Vernon 1971a: 21). The hegemony of American enterprises in the core of the world-economy, then, was expressed in their dominance in specific industries that are highly concentrated and that involve the use of advanced technology:

The more narrowly one chooses to define an 'industry', the more commonly one encounters extreme rates of US participation. In Italy, during the 1960s, US enterprises were reported as controlling 100 per cent of the ball-bearing industry and most of the heavy electric industry; in Great Britain, more than 75 per cent of the carbon black industry, more than 40 per cent of the computer industry; in France, more than 90 per cent of the carbon black output, more than 40 per cent of the telegraph and telephone equipment and more than 35 per cent of the tractor and agricultural machinery output. (Vernon 1971a: 24; Steuer et al. 1973)

Japan has also experienced American direct investment, though there have been big obstacles to its expansion, and Japanese enterprises have been able to counter the American challenge by making an effective marketing thrust into the United States and Europe. While the Japanese zaibatsu had set up subsidiary enterprises in Japanese colonial territories, this ended with the Japanese defeat in the Second World War and, despite the post-war American occupation, there was very little inward or outward foreign investment until the 1960s. While British overseas investment amounted to 20 per cent of GNP in 1969, the corresponding figure for Japan was just 1.6 per cent (Halliday and McCormack 1973: 33). Most Japanese investment has been in south-east Asia and the economies of the Pacific rim that comprised its main trading partners: Indonesia, Hong

Kong, Taiwan, and, above all, South Korea. Britain's entry into the EEC forced Australia to move into closer contact with Japan as part of a policy of Pacific realignment. Since the 1970s, however, Japan has increased the level of its investment in Europe, at the same time as European and American enterprises have begun to invest in Japan. Japanese overseas investment has been especially marked in the electrical and electronic industries, in automobiles, and in banking and finance (Dunning 1994). Most Japanese-owned operations in Europe are subsidiaries of enterprises outside the big *kigyoshudan*, though Mitsubishi and Sumitomo have had significant levels of European direct investment. Those enterprises with large numbers of European subsidiaries have tended also to have large numbers of American subsidiaries (Gittelman and Graham 1994: 145, 148). In 1989 there were 501 Japanese manufacturing subsidiaries operating in Europe and about twice this number operating in the United States (Hawawini and Schill 1994: 239; Yamawaki 1994: 93).

By contrast, foreign enterprises have found it far more difficult to set up subsidiaries within Japan. In 1970, 83 of the top 200 American industrials had Japanese operations, mainly in the electrical, oil, and chemical industries where IBM and Standard Oil were major forces (Halliday and McCormack 1973: 5–6). While American investment has benefited greatly from Japan's role as an American military base in the Far East, it has not had a great influence on the economy and it has been limited mainly to small subsidiaries or to minority holdings in joint ventures with Japanese partners (Okumura 1983). A major obstacle to foreign investment in Japan has been the shareholding structure of the corporate sets, as the aligned shareholdings can be used by members of the sets to prevent the growth of any hostile foreign ownership. There has, as a result, been no example of the successful takeover of a Japanese enterprise by foreign interests.

The patterns of ownership and control in the world's largest enterprises naturally reflect the predominance of American enterprises. In 1972, 90 manufacturing enterprises had 40,000 or more employees. British and American enterprises dominated this group, amounting to 30 and 19 enterprises respectively, while French and German enterprises (12 of each) were much less significant (Prais 1976: 221–3).[1] Among European enterprises, those from Britain, France and Germany predominate. Forty-four of the top 100 European enterprises in 1981 were British, 22 were German, and 12

---

[1] This study excluded steelmakers and Japanese enterprises.

were French. Apart from these countries, only Switzerland and Sweden had 5 or more of their enterprises among the top 100 European enterprises (*Financial Times* 1982; see also George and Ward 1975: 55; Jacquemin and de Jong 1977: 98). A study of the 487 largest enterprises in the world (Grou 1983) found that 237 were from the United States. These enterprises—as I showed in Chapter 4—were predominantly controlled through constellations of interests, and accounted for the bulk of the world's largest enterprises that were without dominant ownership interest (see Table 60). Grou (1983) discovered that the percentage of shares held, though not the number of enterprises controlled, by financial institutions increased substantially between 1965 and 1978, largely at the expense of family ownership. The proportion of the world's largest enterprises that were family-controlled declined from 39 to 20 per cent, a growth in both state and foreign ownership contributing to this decline: between 1965 and 1978 state control increased from 4 to 10 per cent, and foreign control increased from 3 to 9 per cent. Thus, the enterprises that dominated the world economy fell into four main categories: multinational enterprises controlled through constellations of interests and owning subsidiaries in a number of countries; family enterprises based in various countries; British, French, and German state-controlled enterprises; and French, Belgian, and Japanese enterprises controlled through aligned participations and interweaving shareholdings. These enterprises had achieved powerful positions within their base national economies, and their power was strengthened by the growth of international intercorporate relations among them.

The dominance of British and American enterprises was less marked in world banking than it was in industry. Although the two largest banks in the world were American, the 20 largest banks of 1981 included 6 from Japan and 4 from France. Britain and the United States supplied 3 each and Germany provided 2 (*Financial Times* 1982).[2] In 1991, 8 of the world's 10 largest banks were Japanese and 2 were French. Other financial sectors showed less increase in Japanese dominance. The 10 largest bond underwriters, for example, included three Swiss enterprises, three American, two Japanese, one German and one French (Hawawini and Schill 1994: 236–7).

Growth in overseas investment has also resulted in a growth in international commercial, capital, and personal relations. These

---

[2] The remaining two were from Canada and Brazil.

Table 60. Strategic control in the world's 487 largest non-financial enterprises (1978)

Mode of control	Type of controller						Totals
	Family	Corporate	Bank	State	Foreign	None	
Majority control	25	9	1	38	26	–	99
Minority control	72	33	124	9	16	–	254
No dominant interest	–	–	–	–	–	134	134
Totals	97	42	125	47	42	134	134

Source: Grou (1983: 45).
Note: Because some binational and other enterprises appeared on two or more of the lists consulted by Grou, the total number of independent enterprises was reduced from 500 to 487. The cutoff point for minority control was 5 per cent.

commercial relations of international trade, capital relations of foreign ownership, and personal relations of interlocking directorships have tied the world's largest enterprises into a web of international connections. Through shareholdings, for example, the economies of the capitalist core have become more closely integrated with one another (Rowthorn 1971). Thus in 1976, the 250 largest American enterprises held majority control in 116 of the 2,000 largest European enterprises. Although these same European enterprises had only two such controlling holdings in the United States, there were numerous controlling holdings that connected the various European economies with one another.[3] Those countries with the highest levels of foreign ownership among their top 250 enterprises were Belgium, with seventy-two foreign subsidiaries (thirty-two of them American), Germany, with twenty-seven, and Britain and Austria, with twenty-five each. The United States, Britain, France, and the Netherlands were the economies in which most of the foreign parents were based.

A study of the largest enterprises in thirteen countries in 1970 reported that bonds of ownership were reinforced and extended through an international network of interlocking directorships.

---

[3] The discussion which follows draws heavily on Fennema (1981) and Fennema and Schijf (1985). The latter draws on data from various national economies collected for the research reported in Table 40. See also Grou (1983: 51).

Banks were especially important in this international network, reflecting their centrality in national economies. While Japanese enterprises had no international interlocks and were separated from this network, American and European enterprises had numerous interconnections. Britain and the United States were especially well-connected internationally, as were Canada and the Netherlands (Fennema 1981). These interlocks reflected the broad international orientation of Britain, the United States, and the Netherlands, as well as American investment in Canada. Reflecting on this evidence, Fennema and Schijf (1985) suggested that there is a social division between Anglo-American and continental European directors. The continental European economies did not form a tightly integrated bloc, however, and German enterprises in particular had few international interlocks. The German enterprises that did have international connections were those that had intense links with a small number of Dutch enterprises. Indeed, continental European directors tended mainly to link neighbouring national economies, largely following linguistic divisions: Belgium was linked with France, Germany with the Netherlands, and, to a lesser extent, Germany with Switzerland and Italy with Switzerland. All of the continental economies had weaker links to Britain and the United States, which were linked to one another through their common links with Canadian enterprises (Carroll 1985).

Through the international network of intercorporate commercial, capital, and personal relations, multinational enterprises have transferred the 'visible hands' of capital—along with their 'invisible handshakes'—to the international level. Corporate strategies in the multinational enterprises have become 'global strategies' that are relatively unconstrained by national boundaries. As a result, the capitalist world-economy is driven towards ever greater levels of 'globalization'. Multinational enterprises mutually co-ordinate their activities on a global scale, and questions of national interest play only a minor part in their calculations and strategies (Sklair 1995a: 116; see also Ross and Trachte 1990; Howells and Wood 1993).

Non-market administrative controls within the multinational enterprises allow them to internalize market transactions to a greater extent than is possible in a purely national enterprise. This power of multinational enterprises to override market-pricing considerations in their internal transactions means that foreign subsidiaries do not necessarily behave in the same way as locally owned enterprises:

Although the multinational system as a whole must make a profit in order to survive, each of the affiliates in the system does not independently have to meet that test. Moreover, the price in any given transaction between a pair of affiliates need not be tested against competing offers in the open market. (Vernon 1977: 128; Brooke and Remmers 1970: 68–76)

Through transfer pricing and the allocation of investment funding, the constituent subsidiaries of a multinational enterprise subsidize one another and allow the overarching divisional profit centres to meet their targets. It is the profitability of the divisions and, thereby, of the multinational enterprise as a whole that is the overriding concern of a global strategy (Brooke and Remmers 1972: 30 ff.; 1970: 72 ff.; Hughes 1973: 172–3; Hood and Young 1979: 122; House 1977).[4] As a result of the differential behaviour of foreign subsidiaries and domestic enterprises in a national economy, many critical decisions are removed from the sphere of national decision-making. In a globalized economy, areas of economic activity become locked in to international circuits of commercial, capital, and personal relations rather than into purely national ones. The powers of nation states and of indigenous capitalist interests are increasingly countered by the powers of foreign corporate interests; and the powers of those who manage branch plants and subsidiaries are limited by the powers of the international corporate rulers in the parent companies.

The largest enterprises, operating on a global scale, are the central agents in the capitalist world system, and their actions constrain the possibilities that are open to those in its constituent economies. Economic decisions that shape the development of particular economies are increasingly taken in the board-rooms of enterprises that are based in other countries. As a result, each of the advanced capitalist societies now experiences two contradictory tendencies: the declining national autonomy of its economy, and the growing power of its own multinationals to act in ways that undermine the autonomy of other national economies. The declining autonomy of distinctively 'national' economies increases the disorder of the world economic system, so creating greater unpredictability for national decision-makers. The development of the British or Canadian economies, for example, depends to an ever greater extent on investment decisions that are taken by powerful American and German

---

[4] Detailed accounts of particular multinational enterprises can be found in Sampson (1973; 1975) and Cronjé et al. (1976).

enterprises. While the United States and Germany themselves, as strong and powerful economies, have retained a relatively higher level of national integration than have the weaker economies of the capitalist core, they are also affected by the activities of multinational enterprises based outside their national boundaries. Only the Japanese economy has, until recently, been able to withstand the 'disorganizing' effects of globalized commercial, capital, and personal relations. In Europe, with its complex interweaving of international capital movements, the development of each national economy is now significantly influenced by the operation of foreign multinationals based in the United States and in other European countries.

Capital accumulation in any one economy occurs as the unintended consequence of the intersecting global strategies of multinational enterprises, and it becomes increasingly difficult for nation states to pursue distinctively 'national' economic policies:

The capacity of any government to command a particular firm to take a specified task in support of public policy, such as settling in a backward region or holding down a key price, has been reduced; large firms now have a capacity that they never had before for choice between competing nations. (Vernon 1977: 63)

Cross-border flows of capital are co-ordinated by 'transnational practices' that are beyond the control of individual nation states (Sklair 1995a). These states are therefore unable to use conventional policy measures to control activities within their own boundaries. This is not to say, of course, that nation states are completely unable to shape economic development. Any state with sufficient resources, appropriate information, and the will to act can have an effect. Most actual states, however, are dependent on private business for their resources and information, and so fail to develop the will to act against the interests of private capital. Because of their dependence on the global political economy, any state that does not formulate a will to act in this way is likely to face serious unintended consequences as multinational enterprises shift their activities and resources in response. By facilitating and supporting the activities of private enterprises, both domestic and overseas, nation states actually reduce their capacity to influence the direction of development in their national economies.

The growth of foreign direct investment by multinational enterprises operating on a global scale involves a growing 'disarticulation' of national economies. This has been especially apparent in peripheral economies, such as those of Latin America (Frank 1969). Enterprises are simply juxtaposed rather than being highly integrated among themselves, and each is separately and strongly integrated into multinational enterprises 'whose centres of gravity lie in the centres of the capitalist world' (Amin 1971: 289; 1973: 237). Now the economies of the capitalist core themselves have become more and more disarticulated. The growth of mutual inward investment in Europe, for example, has meant that the external linkages of industries dominated by foreign capital become more important than their linkages to other industries within their economy. The networks of capital, commercial, and personal relations within particular national economies become less dense and more fragmented; and the various fragments become tied into close capital, commercial, and personal relations with global enterprises based outside their boundaries. The expansion of one sector or market has far less impact on the development of other sectors within the same economy, and the development of the economy as a whole becomes increasingly uneven. In the face of this disarticulation, it becomes difficult to identify coherent national economies. Circuits of capital flow on a global scale and no longer overlap with one another; and through this disarticulation of capital within particular economies, each economy is decentred.

Central to the growing disarticulation of national economies has been the transformation of the world financial system. Since the 1970s, money and capital markets have been globalized through the expanding international branch networks of American, Japanese, and European banks, the establishment of multinational banking corporations and banking groups and, above all, the growth of new money markets in 'Euro-dollars' and other 'Euro' currencies unregulated by any government or central agency. The latter has been made possible by the application of new technologies to financial and commercial practices. With the rise of new forms of electronic data storage and communication using computers and satellites, financial transactions take place at an ever-increasing pace.[5] They become, to all intents and purposes, instantaneous. Dealing in currencies is supplemented by the dealing in financial 'futures' and other 'derivatives', a form of trading based on expectations of the future prices of commodities and securities. The enterprises that are involved in this flow of information and funds are drawn into

---

[5] Baker (1984) and Thrift (1995) have both argued that face-to-face interaction remains an essential support for computerized global trading.

transnational economic practices that are increasingly detached from the process of production itself.

The City of London has remained an important financial centre within the globalized financial system, though its activities are closely geared to those of the money and capital markets of New York and Tokyo. The City now functions as a European financial centre, concerned especially with the mark rather than with sterling, and it is the focus of the circulation of the mark, dollar, and yen. Between 1979 and 1986 the proportion of pension and insurance capital invested overseas doubled (Lash and Urry 1994: 20), and the relaxation of exchange and capital controls, together with the removal of domestic banking and credit controls during the 1980s, has meant that the British state has increasingly lost control of exchange-rate and interest-rate changes in the British economy. The centrality of the City to the global financial system makes the British economy peculiarly exposed to the disarticulating effects of globalization: overseas competition, inward direct investment, and overseas borrowing have all expanded massively without any significant hindrance, and the 'integrity' of the economy has become almost non-existent. While British overseas assets amount to 30 per cent of GDP, this is matched by a similar total of short-term liabilities to foreigners. There is, as a result, a 'growing territorial non-coincidence between extending capital and its domestic state' (Murray 1971: 96):

There is . . . a tendency for the process of internationalization to increase the potential economic instability in the world economy at the same time as decreasing the power of national governments to control economic activity even within their own borders. (Murray 1971: 102–3; Picciotto and Radice 1973: 63; Mandel 1972: 316; 1970)

Banking and industry 'have been internationalized as separate and relatively uncoordinated circuits of capital. So they are de-synchronized and in no sense come together at the boundaries of individual nation states' (Lash and Urry 1994: 286). In the face of such disarticulation, states have sought to increase the level of their political integration with one another through international bodies such as the International Monetary Fund, the World Bank, the European Community, and so on (Held 1991a). There is no longer any territorial coincidence between the political forms of states, the flow of economic transactions, and the cultural and communal boundaries of 'societies'. The capitalist-world system becomes an increasingly fragmented political and social system (Lash and Urry 1994: 279 ff.; Ray and Reed 1995).

The implications of economic disarticulation in the core economies have been particularly well-studied in relation to the development of the Canadian and Australian economies in the face of British and American direct investment. Canada developed as a British colony, British portfolio and direct investment being a major force in the economy. Although the level of foreign ownership in Canadian business declined from 38 per cent before the Second World War to 32 per cent in 1954, this same period saw a rise in the level of American ownership from 19 per cent to 25 per cent. While British investment had been especially strong in the commercial and financial sectors, the strength of American investment was in the manufacturing sector; and by 1959 more than a half of all Canadian manufacturing assets were foreign-owned. American investment was especially strong in the automobile, chemical, oil, and electrical industries (Drache 1970: 24–5; Porter 1965: 267; Safarian 1966: 14; Aitken 1959a: 7–8; Blyth and Carty 1956). The circuits of financial and industrial capital were globalized through interpenetrating investments, and the development of the Canadian economy was locked-in to the international capital markets. This growth in capital relations between the United States and Canada was matched by closer commercial relations: by the mid-1950s, the United States bought 60 per cent of Canadian exports and provided 75 per cent of Canadian imports.

Similar trends to these are apparent in Australia, where over half of all foreign investment in 1964 came from Britain, and a further third came from the United States (Encel 1970: 337; Brash 1970). Wheelwright and Miskelly (1967) estimated that 36 per cent of the share capital of the top 200 Australian companies in the 1960s was owned from abroad. British portfolio and direct investment in Australia, still channelled through the City of London, was concentrated in petroleum, chemicals, non-ferrous metals, iron and steel, food processing, textiles, and electrical engineering, while American capital was concentrated in petrol, chemicals, metals, and food but was equally strong in motor vehicles and agricultural equipment (Lawriwsky 1982).

The development of the Canadian and Australian economies reflects 'the imperatives of more advanced areas' (Aitken 1959a: 3), their patterns of capital accumulation being subordinate to those of multinational enterprises based in Britain and the United States

(Porter 1965: 269; Gonick 1970; Aitken 1959b). Managers in foreign-owned subsidiaries are largely excluded from any significant participation in strategic control. Their responsibilities are limited to operational matters and to meeting external financial targets set by those who rule the parent enterprises (Levitt 1970: 77). As I have shown in Chapters 4 and 5, however, the rulers of enterprises that are owned and controlled from within Canada and Australia are an important force in strategic control. These indigenous capitalists have been able to exercise some influence over the operations of foreign subsidiaries because of their dominance of the banking and insurance system, and the maintenance of an autonomous financial system has been an important factor in helping to offset economic disarticulation. Evidence from Scotland (Scott and Griff 1984: ch. 3) supports this argument. Although English and foreign investment has considerably reduced Scotland's economic autonomy, the maintenance of a separate banking and investment system in Edinburgh served as a focus for Scottish capitalist interests and prevented the complete loss of all economic decision-making powers.[6] The deregulation of financial markets in all the leading capitalist economies during the 1980s, however, has opened them up to foreign competition, and indigenous capitalists have found it more difficult to sustain their position and power within their economies.

Concentration and Economic Disorganization

The theory of capitalist society predicted a gradual and inexorable rise in the level of economic concentration in all national economies. Markets would become more concentrated as producers became monopoly suppliers, and whole economies would become more concentrated as enterprises began to operate across a range of markets and the circuits of industrial and financial capital became more closely integrated. While it is clear that national economies vary considerably in their level of concentration, and it is far from certain that these levels do inexorably rise in quite the way that the theory suggests, even critics of Marxism have highlighted the consequences of growing concentration. What is common to both Marxism and its

---

[6] The argument that Scotland has become a 'branch plant economy' can be found in Firn (1975). Similar evidence for Wales is provided in Tomkins and Lovering (1973).

critics is a view of economic concentration as the outcome of two distinct processes. There is, first, the formation of large enterprises that come to act as the 'visible hands' of capital. Formed through amalgamation and merger, generally diversified and operating through large-scale units of production and distribution, the rulers and managers of the corporate hierarchies become the ever more visible agents whose decisions directly shape opportunities in the capital, commodity, and labour markets.

The operation of the visible hands is supplemented and partly superseded, however, by the 'invisible handshakes' through which separate enterprises mutually influence one another. This second process of concentration occurs through the growth of commercial, capital, and personal relations that fall short of full merger, but tie enterprises together into extensive networks of intercorporate relations. A national economy in which large enterprises are connected through a dense network of intercorporate relations has a higher level of concentration than a similar economy with a less dense network. This second process of concentration has been inadequately explored in studies of economic concentration, which have generally limited their attention to such intercorporate relations as the formation of 'cartels' and similar commercial arrangements.

Conventional economic theories of market behaviour assumed the existence of 'perfect' competition. Enterprises were assumed to be too small to have any appreciable power to determine market prices. These prices, it was argued, resulted from the competitive forces of supply and demand that were the outcome of *aggregate* effects of enterprise behaviour. As far as each individual enterprise was concerned, prices were 'given' and decisions about levels of production had to be matched to these given prices. Early theorists of 'imperfect' and 'monopolistic' competition, such as Robinson (1933) and Chamberlin (1933), recognized that the formation of large enterprises undermined these assumptions: while they may have provided a reasonable description of market behaviour in the stage of liberal capitalism, they were no longer appropriate to the more organized forms of capitalism that had developed during the twentieth century. Managerialist theory was a great stimulus to the attempt to formulate a viable alternative to the neo-classical model of perfect competition, leading to new models of market 'oligopoly' that were premised on the enhanced market power of large enterprises.

Although I have challenged many of the assumptions of managerialist theory, I have suggested in Chapter 7 that there have been important changes in the market behaviour of large enterprises. The large capitalist enterprise is a long-term profit-seeker operating under market constraints, but its scope for choice within these constraints is much greater than was the case for the small entrepreneurial firm. In concentrated markets the enterprise can become a 'price maker', rather than simply a 'price taker'. Large enterprises have greater information about market conditions and can formulate more accurate expectations about the likely behaviour of their competitors, and they are able to enter into tacit or overt price-fixing arrangements with other enterprises. Baran and Sweezy suggested that the growth of intercorporate alliances permitted enterprises to co-operate on monopoly pricing policies and then to compete more vigorously in non-price areas, such as advertising, to determine the distribution of the monopoly profits among themselves (Baran and Sweezy 1966: 68; see also Baran 1957: 196 ff.). Through such means they can reduce the uncertainty or 'anarchy' of the market mechanism: markets become more 'organized', more 'regulated'.

What is the evidence for this? Merger activity in the United States led to a massive increase in the level of concentration over the period between 1890 and 1904, under the aegis of the 'Money Trust' (Bunting 1986: 36; 1974). This was reinforced by the accumulation of large numbers of directorships by the investment bankers who were responsible for many of the largest amalgamations. The percentage of assets concentrated in the top 100 enterprises remained at around 40 per cent over the period from 1899 to 1929, but had risen to 44 per cent by 1939 (Bunting 1986: 70). The level of concentration under this 'Money Trust' continued to increase until the early 1930s. The share of the top 100 enterprises in total assets also declined during the latter part of the inter-war years, and it was not until the early 1950s that the level of concentration began to level off. Table 61 shows that the level of asset concentration in the top 100 enterprises for 1975 was lower than that achieved fifty years before. Figures on the proportion of total value produced by the top 200 manufacturers suggest that the fall in the overall level of concentration may have been somewhat less than Herman's data suggest, with the figure for the mid-1960s being somewhat higher than that for 1929 (Means 1964: 15; Chandler 1969: 278; Bunting 1986: 70). The top 200 enterprises of 1987 accounted for 43 per cent of total value-added. The inter-war years saw a fall in the level of interlocking among large enterprises as the financial power of the investment bankers declined. Putting these trends together, it is clear that the level of

Table 61. Share of the top 100 US non-financial enterprises in net assets (1909–1975)

	1909	1929	1933	1975
% of assets	33	49	57	35

Source: Herman (1981: 191, Table 6.2).

Table 62. Diversification in the top 100 US non-financial enterprises (1909–1960)

	Number of enterprises					
	1909	1919	1929	1935	1948	1960
10 or more	3	4	7	16	24	33
3–9	29	43	43	50	43	45
2	20	8	9	4	4	8
1	29	33	23	12	12	4
No information and non-manufacturers	19	12	18	18	17	10
	100	100	100	100	100	100

Source: Calculated from Chandler (1969: 290–8, Table 2).
Note: The original lists related to the top 100 non-financials, but Chandler gives information only on those involved in manufacturing industry.

'organization' in the American economy had begun to fall back: the economy was beginning a process of 'disorganization'.

Table 62 shows that the concentration of economic activity in the United States was associated with a considerable diversification of enterprise activity. The number of large manufacturers operating in only one or two industries declined substantially between 1909 and 1935, as it did again during the 1950s. Conversely, the number of enterprises operating in ten or more industries increased substantially after 1929. By 1960, most large American enterprises were operating in five or more industries. Because large enterprises had subsidiaries in many markets, the changing trend of concentration in aggregate economic activity was associated with a continuous increase in concentration at the level of particular markets (Chandler

1969: 257). Despite the growth of 'conglomerate' mergers during the 1980s and the popularity of 'demerger' in the 1990s, a high degree of diversification remains the norm for large enterprises.

In Britain, economic concentration increased steadily from the 1870s until the Second World War, though it never achieved the level of organization that the American economy achieved under the Money Trust. The amalgamation of family enterprises into large units prior to the First World War was associated with the creation of defensive cartels and trusts that aimed to control sales and output, but it also resulted in a considerable concentration of economic activity (Pollard 1962). Hannah (1976c) has claimed that an organized corporate economy had been established in the heartland of the British economy by 1914, and a contemporary observer remarked that

While . . . a greater part of our industrial system still continues to be competitive, the area of the power of capitalist combination is growing and the effective protection furnished by competition to the consumer is diminishing. (Hobson 1906: 215)

There was a particularly rapid increase in concentration during the merger boom of 1919–20. Table 63 shows that the 100 largest manufacturers of 1909 accounted for 15 per cent of total output—less than in the United States—and that by 1930 their share had risen to 26 per cent, a level comparable to that in the United States at that time. Over this same period, as I showed in Chapter 5, the density and intensity of interlocking directorships among the top manufacturers was also increasing: by the 1930s a large proportion of national output was accounted for by large enterprises that were closely connected with one another through a network of capital, commercial, and personal relations. As a result, a big-business sector in which competitive relations were contained within an extensive intercorporate network had been formed. The enterprises of the big-business sector in Britain before the First World War came disproportionately from textiles and brewing, though non-manufacturers that operated on a national scale included the railways, the banks, and insurance companies. By the Second World War, 'big business' had become a more diverse and more powerful sector of activity, and it was increasingly shaping the conditions under which smaller enterprises had to operate. These small- and medium-sized businesses still operated under more competitive conditions and were often dependent suppliers to the large enterprises.

Table 63. Share of the top 100 British manufacturers in net output (1909–68)

	1909	1919	1930	1939	1948	1958	1968
% of output	15	17	26	23	21	33	42

Source: Hannah (1976*c*: 216, Table A.2).

From the late 1930s until the late 1940s the level of concentration fell back slightly, but through the 1950s and 1960s it once again increased, as the inroads of American enterprises stimulated defensive mergers and takeovers. As a result of the massive increase in concentration in Britain during the 1960s, the top 100 manufacturers in Britain accounted for 42 per cent of output and 65 per cent of corporate assets in 1968, while those in the United States accounted for just 33 per cent of output (Jewkes 1977: 15; Meeks and Whittington 1975; 1976; Prais 1977). The British economy, then, had not followed the American trajectory of 'disorganization', but had continued to show an increasing level of 'organization' until the 1960s. Only from the 1970s did the British economy begin to show the effects of 'disorganization' in its level of concentration.

The concentration of markets and of the national economy was not, in Britain, associated with any substantial reorganization of plant-level production. Mergers brought together large numbers of small factories, but these were not rationalized into larger, integrated operations at the technical level. The top 100 manufacturers of 1904 had an average of six plants each, those of 1958 had an average of twenty-seven plants, and those of 1972 had an average of seventy-two plants. Although the concentration of economic activity into a small number of enterprises was greater than in any other country in the world at this time, the proportion of the labour force employed in large plants had remained constant since the inter-war years. Mergers and concentration had occurred at the financial level, resulting in concentrated strategic control but fragmented operations. Most British workers in private employment worked for large enterprises, but they did not necessarily work in large plants (Utton 1982: 22).

This was not the case in the United States, where average plant size has been considerably higher than in many other countries. The proportion of the labour force employed in establishments with more than 1,000 employees varies from high levels of 28 to 30 per cent in the United States, Germany, and the Netherlands, to low levels of 13 to 17 per cent in Italy, France, and Japan (Morvan 1972: 221). Among European countries, only in Germany has there been any significant association between economic concentration and technical reorganization at the plant level (George and Ward 1975: 44; Daems and van der Wee 1974).

Table 64. Share of the big four groups in Japanese capital (1937–1966)

	% of capital by big four groups in					
Industrial sector	1937	1941	1946	1955	1960	1966
Heavy and chemical industries	12.1	16.5	33.3	18.4	23.8	25.4
Other primary and secondary industries	11.6	13.7	17.8	15.4	13.5	19.2
Finance, distribution, and communications	9.2	8.2	17.3	6.7	8.9	12.0

Source: Miyazaki (1973: 326–9, Table 10).

The concentration of economic activity in a small number of large enterprises is far less marked in Japan than it is in Britain, the top 100 Japanese manufacturers of 1967–8 accounting for 29.2 per cent of total sales (Caves and Uekusa 1976: 18). This comparison does not, however, take account of the capital, commercial, and personal relations that tie these enterprises together. The pattern of aligned participations that underpins the large corporate sets has resulted in a level of overall concentration much higher than that in Britain. Within the corporate sets there has been a massive fusion of capital in manufacturing, mining, banking, and insurance, creating giant units of finance capital that dominate the major sectors of the Japanese economy. As Table 64 shows, this is no recent phenomenon. The proportion of capital controlled by the big four *zaibatsu* and their descendants increased substantially between 1937 and 1966. The massive increase that took place during the 1940s was abruptly ended by the post-war *zaibatsu* dissolution programme, but the level of concentration began to increase as these controls were relaxed. The big six *kigyoshudan* in 1981 accounted for 5 per cent of business employment and held 26 per cent of business assets

(Okumura 1983: 14). Table 65 shows that the big six groups that controlled so many of the large enterprises accounted for over a half of industrial turnover and insurance income, and they were responsible for over 40 per cent of all bank lending. While there was some loosening in the organization of the big corporate sets during the 1980s, this now seems to have stabilized and, in some respects, to have tightened (Nakata 1995).

Table 65. Share of the big six groups in Japanese industry, banking, and insurance (1974)

Group	% of industrial turnover	% of bank lending	% of insurance premium income
Mitsubishi	13.2	8.5	8.3
Mitsui	10.0	6.0	6.0
Sumitomo	10.1	7.9	11.0
DKB	9.1	6.0	7.8
Fuyo	8.5	7.0	–
Sanwa	8.5	6.4	20.8
Totals	59.4	41.8	53.9

Source: Stokes (n.d.: 76, 77). The original source was Dodwell (1975).
Note: No insurance figures were given for Fuyo, which was unimportant in this sector.

State Intervention and Deregulation

In recognizing the crucial part played by nation states in maintaining the integrity of national economies and in enhancing the international power of their multinational enterprises, Marxist theory posited a growing integration between the state and finance capital. As economies became more monopolized, so the level of state intervention and regulation, it argued, would increase. The political form of organized capitalism was described as 'state monopoly capitalism'. Whatever may have been the truth of this as a depiction of organized capitalism, I have suggested that the contemporary disarticulation of national economies has been associated with the declining economic powers of nation states and with an economic 'disorganization' of capitalist societies.

The growing power of nation states with the 'organization' of capitalist societies, and their subsequent declining power with the 'disorganization' of these societies, are paralleled by changes in the volume and pattern of state expenditure. In purely quantitative terms the volume of state expenditure has increased massively in all the major capitalist societies. Although the level of spending by the British state reached an all-time high of 75 per cent of GNP during the Second World War, high levels of peacetime expenditure have also been achieved. State expenditure increased steadily from the 1920s to reach a figure of over 50 per cent of GNP by the 1960s (Gough 1975: 61). Britain, France, West Germany, and Italy showed remarkably similar high levels of state expenditure during the 1970s, though levels of public expenditure were somewhat lower in the United States and were considerably lower in Japan. Indeed, state expenditure in Japan, expressed as a percentage of GNP, was only half as high as in Europe (Gough 1975: 59).

This quantitative growth in state expenditure reflects the increased provision by the state of those activities that cannot be met by private capitalist enterprise but are essential for the reproduction of capitalist activity. Public provision of posts and telecommunications, police and military activities, education, welfare, transport, and housing required a shift from merely facilitative to more supportive and interventionist policies, and this was central to the transition from liberal to organized capitalism (Pahl 1977b). In a system of facilitative mediation, state provision is limited to those conditions that facilitate the market regulation of competitive economic activity. Facilitative state policies are concerned only with such economic matters as property and commercial law, currency, and taxation. As economic activity became more concentrated, so states were impelled to become more 'supportive' of private capital, undertaking the provision of educational and welfare facilities that private capital was unable to provide for itself (Winkler 1976; 1977; Cawson and Saunders 1983). Weak and unprofitable sectors of the economy were targeted for public ownership, regulation, or subsidy as means of solving their difficulties. The unprecedented depression of the inter-war years was critical in driving supportive states in ever more interventionist directions. In all the core economies, state-sponsored economic reforms were undertaken with the intention of restructuring private capital (Yaffe 1973: 216–17; Fine and Harris 1976: 107; Westergaard 1977; Booth 1982). From the early 1960s, interventionist mediation by many states involved an extension of the kinds of indicative planning that had been pioneered in France and Japan. Although this trend was common to all the advanced capitalist economies, Germany and the United States were the last to adopt systems of long-term planning. By promoting mergers and joint ventures, by extending state ownership, by restructuring whole industries, and by selective taxation and incomes policies, governments attempted to ensure that private capital contributed to the goals of public policy, which was, in turn, oriented towards the promotion of private-sector profitability (Shonfield 1965; Warren 1972; Causer 1978; Halliday 1975: 53–60; Lockwood 1965a: 501 ff.).[7]

The disorganization of capitalist production began to make itself felt at the political level from the late 1970s, and nation states began to dismantle their interventionist and planning structures and to introduce policies for the 'deregulation' of many areas of economic activity. Paradoxically, this deregulation involved much 'reregulation', especially in relation to such areas as the environment, public health, and the utilities. By contrast with direct state regulation, however, these newer forms of regulation involve the delegation of regulatory powers to autonomous bodies and agencies, many of them having closer links to the private sector than to the state apparatus. These trends were not, of course, a mechanical response to economic disarticulation, although they were significantly furthered by it. The changing role of the state was, at least initially, a response to the accumulating effects of the growth of state intervention. While intervention grew in response to problems of private profitability, expenditure that improves the position of private capital in the long term can, in the short term, produce effects that undermine private capital. In order to finance their expenditure on collective provision, states must borrow money or raise taxation. Either strategy will reduce the funds that are available to the private sector, and so the productivity of capital must be sufficient to meet both the immediate needs of capital and the needs of the state. Even if state expenditure in the past has led to an increase in the productivity of capital, a portion of this increased productivity will be required to finance current and future state expenditure; and unless private productivity grows along with the growth of state expenditure there will be a decline in the rate of capital accumulation. The financing of state expenditure, then, is always problematic. State intervention becomes a necessary support for private capital that nevertheless

---

[7] Marxist views can be found in Habermas (1973: 33–4) and Miliband (1968), while a related, but distinctly non-Marxist view can be found in Berle (1955: 23).

poses problems for private profitability and so makes further public expenditure more difficult to finance. O'Connor, on whom this argument draws, concluded, 'The socialisation of costs and the private appropriation of profits creates a fiscal crisis or "structural gap", between state expenditures and state revenues' (O'Connor 1973: 9, 40; see also Yaffe 1973: 225; Fine and Harris 1976: 102–5; Rowthorn 1976: 66–7).

The growth of collective provision and of state intervention leads to political dislocations within the state itself. In Habermas's words, underlying economic 'crisis tendencies' do not disappear as a result of growing intervention, but are displaced into the structure of the state itself (Habermas 1973: 39–40, 47). States may attempt to accommodate to their budgetary problems through 'stop-go' policies and the introduction of systems of regulation, co-ordination, and planning, but there are structural limits to their power to achieve this. In a private-enterprise system, then, there are determinate limits to state power. Ownership of business enterprises remains largely a private matter, governments have only limited information about private investment plans, and public planning authorities do not have sufficient control over production to make their plans effective. If states seek to build up more comprehensive bodies of information about corporate plans and intentions as a way of buttressing their interventionist role, they must evolve mechanisms of information-gathering that will help them to pursue their goals. To do this, they must establish structures of representation and policy-formation that enable them to secure the information required, and to feed it into the policy-making process. This information can be obtained only from capitalist enterprises, which are likely to use any links that they have with particular state agencies and departments as instruments of competition with their rivals. Competition among monopoly enterprises is as a result partly displaced into conflict and inadequate co-ordination among the various sections of the state apparatus (Habermas 1973: 62; Mandel 1972: 233, 235–6; Miliband 1977: 96). Rather than securing an independent and autonomous policy or one that is in the 'general interests' of capital, states are likely to pursue policies that reflect a balance of power among the various capitalist interests represented within their agencies. Consensual state policies, to the extent that they occur, are consequences of the dominance of particular fractions of capital within the state apparatus.

This trend from facilitative to interventionist and then to deregulatory state activity has taken a different form in the various capitalist economies. With some simplification, it can be suggested that the Anglo-American economies have adopted looser forms of intervention and have found deregulation and subsequent reregulation a correspondingly easier policy to adopt, while the German economies have adopted tighter forms of intervention and have made correspondingly slower moves towards deregulation. Jopperson and Meyer (1991: 217) have identified a contrast between 'liberal', 'statist', and 'corporatist' systems in advanced Western economies. In the liberal system, which they see as characteristic of Britain, the United States, Australia, and other Anglo-American economies, considerable autonomy is accorded to private organizations and associations, and there is a low level of institutionalization of public functions by their states. In the statist systems, on the other hand, autonomous private organizations are countered by an active state that undertakes numerous public functions. Such systems characterize the Latin economies of France, Belgium, and Italy. Corporatist systems, however, combine an active state with the incorporation of private-sector organizations into a formal apparatus of political decision-making, and so allow a high level of concertation in economic activity. Such systems have been found in the German economies (Germany, Austria, and Switzerland) and in Scandinavia.

Business interests in the United States, then, have tended to operate in a 'liberal' way. They have been only loosely organized into representative bodies, and their members have typically attempted to influence government through lobbying political parties and representatives, by supporting candidates with donations, by sitting on advisory bodies, and by employing other methods of pressure-group politics (Anker *et al.* 1987; Mizruchi 1992; Wilson 1982). Useem has emphasized the role of those he terms, following Lundberg (1937) and Zeitlin (1974), the 'inner circle' of the capitalist class.[8] He argues that their position in the intercorporate network gives them access to a wide spread of business information, and that this leads them to adopt a standpoint in business affairs that 'discourages the specific and fosters the general' (1984: 55). Over and above their participation in the strategic control of particular enterprises, members of the inner circle have a role in 'consensus building' in the sphere of business opinion, and act as the 'leading edge' of the capitalist class in

---

[8] In Useem (1978) this group is called the 'inner group', the term employed by Zeitlin (1974), and in Useem (1982) they were called the 'dominant segment'.

matters of general business policy (see also Lundberg 1969: 302 ff.). Through their membership of commissions and advisory bodies such as the Business Round Table, the Committee for Economic Development, and the Council on Foreign Relations, they can construct a degree of unity and formulate long-term policy orientations that promote the interests of business within the state and so ensure that the political rulers are responsive to them (Domhoff 1971).

Commentators on Britain have identified a move towards 'bargained corporatism' (Crouch 1977) or 'corporate bias' (Middlemas 1979), a slightly more organized version of the American 'liberal' system that arose in response to the concentration of the economy in the first decades of the century. The Liberal government of the years immediately following the First World War built on the corporatist practices that had been introduced by the wartime coalition, and established a system in which business leaders became a central force in political decision-making. The transition from facilitative to more interventionist practices, however, was a result of private rather than public initiative throughout the inter-war years. The predominance of business leaders in government—rather than, as in France, the predominance of civil servants in big business—meant that government policies directly reflected the wishes of a particular section of capital. This section of capital was big business, and at its heart were the banks of the City of London and those industrialists who sat on bank boards. It was these people who oversaw the introduction of interventionist practices of 'rationalization' in the slump years of the 1920s (Hannah 1979c: ch. 3). Politicians supported such policies, but they did not seek to become actively involved as independent agents of public intervention. The banks, whose capital was tied up in overdrafts to the ailing industrial giants, were seen as the most appropriate agents of economic change, and the banks connived in this limitation of autonomous state power. 'The City' dominated strategies of industrial reconstruction, with the Bank of England playing the role of co-ordinator and spokesman for City interests (Booth 1982). Instead of a state-led system of corporatism, Britain established a bank-led system of 'corporate bias'.

Through all the subsequent vicissitudes of intervention and deregulation the City viewpoint has remained central to British industrial and economic policy. This City view of economic affairs is based around a commitment to Britain's international trading position and the international role of sterling through restrictions on

public expenditure and on growth in the money supply.[9] City interests have been represented in the state through informal and personal mechanisms, not through formal corporatist institutions. This
has given the British system its characteristic looseness. Whereas the
American liberal system has stressed the mechanisms of pressure-
group politics, the smaller scale of the British economy has allowed
it to operate through informal channels. The kinship and friendship
links that tie members of the City into the established social orders
have been central to this (Moran 1983: 52–5; Longstreth 1979b; see
also Scott and Griff 1984: ch. 4; Lupton and Wilson 1959). The Bank
of England was, until the 1960s, virtually the only formal channel of
communication that existed between the City and the state, but it
stood at the heart of a system of personal and informal links to both
the Treasury and the other financial institutions of the City.

In the post-war period the dominance of the City viewpoint was
an essential element in a 'post-war settlement', a consensus over the
broad aims of economic management and social reform in which
governments of either party could depend upon the support of both
business and working-class organizations in a strengthened variant
of the corporate bias (Jessop 1980; Lazar 1990: 135). 'Keynesian' economic policies and practices aimed to secure full employment without any significant departure from 'normal' market mechanisms.
Changes in the level of government spending were geared towards
counteracting cyclical booms and slumps in private economic activity so as to ensure a constant level of aggregate expenditure. Officials
in the Treasury and the Bank of England had the task of designing
and implementing a policy that would receive the support of City
interests and other business leaders and that would also be elec-
torally successful.

Keynesianism began to crumble in the late 1950s as a decay in 'traditional' respect for authority reinforced the growing willingness of
workers to use their organized powers to the full in order to achieve
greater wage increases (Skidelsky 1979). Such traditional attitudes
had underpinned the informality, consensus, and overlap of personnel between City and government, and the 'de-traditionalization' of
British institutions meant that these could no longer be relied upon,
as the whole 'establishment' crumbled (Scott 1991b). The concen-

---

[9] It should be clear from the argument of Chapter 5 that the City is not a separate and distinct fraction of capital, but a sector of economic activity, well-integrated with others, whose hegemonic enterprises have been able to ensure that its
commercial practices are a major influence on business opinion.

tration of economic activity in the post-war period created major strains for the system of interest representation. From the early 1960s, governments falteringly established corporatist institutions of tripartite consultation among government, business, and trades unions to reinforce a move towards economic planning and greater state intervention. The state began to encroach on areas formerly left to City self-regulation, the Bank of England came to be regarded more and more as a department of the state,[10] new agencies of industrial reconstruction were formed (Young and Lowe 1974; Hague and Wilkinson 1983), and the Confederation of British Industry became an increasingly powerful forum of business opinion (Grant and Marsh 1977; Blank 1973).[11] As the state began to adopt more formal means of consultation with the CBI and the trades unions, the direct influence of a distinctively 'City' viewpoint became somewhat weaker.

The City was itself under pressure, as family ownership of the merchant banks was weakened by the increased scale of banking activities, by the adoption of divisional organization and by the increasing globalization of financial markets. This restructuring of City enterprises occurred in response to the inroads of American and other overseas enterprises in the British financial system and the growth of rival financial centres in the United States, Europe, and the Far East (Channon 1977; Moran 1983: 58). City enterprises began to transform old trade associations into effective lobbying organizations, formed themselves into new organizations—such as the institutional shareholders' committees—and became members of the CBI. Though it retained its role as a central business forum, the Bank of England was increasingly bypassed by these organizations, and could no longer be seen as a spokesman for the City. While financial institutions have achieved enhanced economic power, 'the City' as a bloc of opinion has become of declining significance: 'In place of the old cohesive City is left a series of separate sectors displaying varying levels of organized cohesion and effectiveness' (Moran 1983: 67; Moran 1991). The CBI, dominated by the big private and public enterprises in both finance and industry, became the effective representative body of finance capital, though its fragmentation and lack of co-ordination prevented it from acting as a corporatist 'peak organization' within a system of concertation (Strinati 1982). Its role was,

[10] The Bank had, in fact, been nationalized in 1946.

[11] For a general analysis of business power see Finer (1955 and 1956), Judge (1990), and Marsh and Locksley (1983).

in any case, being transformed by the move away from interventionism and towards deregulation that was taking place during the 1980s. The various financial markets had been opened up to global competition, and the City became a disarticulated element in a disarticulated national economy. At the same time the state was disengaging itself from its responsibility for full employment and shifted from demand-oriented to supply-oriented policies (Offe 1982: 61–2; Grant 1993).

This move was common to all the Anglo-American economies. In the United States, for example, business interests mobilized around a more conservative agenda of politics instead of the corporate liberalism that had hitherto dominated business affairs. This agenda, from the early 1970s, was the basis of the eventual electoral success of Reagan in 1980, and 'Reaganism', like 'Thatcherism', gave voice to the deregulation of the economy (Clawson and Clawson 1987).

Austria, on the other hand, epitomizes the 'corporatist' representation that its government had adopted as a deliberate constitutional innovation in the 1930s, reflecting the highly 'organized' character of Austrian capitalism and the growth of nationalized enterprise. This system was expanded by the Conservative-Socialist coalition that held power from the Second World War until 1966, and it remained characteristic of Austrian policy through the 1970s and 1980s. The state sector became a dominant element in the Austrian economy, and directorships were filled in such a way as to maintain a party balance. The business interests of Austria, then, were formed into a strong 'corporatist' system (Ziegler *et al.* 1985. For a useful review of the general debate on corporatism see Schmitter 1974, 1977, 1981, 1982; and Lehmbruch 1982).

From the beginnings of German industrialization the state endeavoured to link business with national goals and to adopt a degree of planning, and this strategy was pushed further during the 1920s and the Nazi era (Feldman 1981; Schmitter 1974; see also Neuman 1944). While the Communist takeover in East Germany led to the adoption of Soviet-type structures, the Federal Republic combined considerable state intervention with an absence of economic planning. The partition of Germany had reduced the size of the market for West German enterprises, which were therefore forced to expand abroad in order to maintain the scale of their operations. Because the German banks had produced a highly concentrated economy, the Federal state was able to intervene in key areas and to adopt Keynesian incomes policies without the need for any significant extensions of the state machinery itself. KFW, a reconstruction bank formed under the Marshall Plan, was underwritten by the federal government as a plank in its policy of industrial support. This bank, which pays no dividends, lends to other banks in order that they can lend to industrial enterprises. The state has therefore both supported and legitimated the actions of the banks in reconstructing an economy in which they held central positions in the mobilization of capital (Hirsch 1980: 121). During the 1960s there was a strengthening of the planning apparatus as part of the 'social market' economy (Offe 1981; Streeck 1982),[12] but the policies of the 1980s and 1990s have reverted to more deregulated business practices.

In Sweden corporatist institutions were associated with an attempt during the 1970s to establish shareholding funds controlled by employees as part of a centralized incomes policy (von Otter 1980; Korpi 1978; Lash 1984). Only slightly less corporatist in character has been Japan, where an alliance of business and government has been strengthened by the paternalistic incorporation of labour (Lehmbruch 1982: 25). Intermediate between the statist and the corporatist cases is the Netherlands, where formal corporatist institutions have been well-established and combined with a degree of concertation in planning (De Vries 1978: 73; Fennema 1988).

Statist systems emerged in Italy and in Latin America.[13] In Italy, this developed from attempts to create enduring corporatist structures. Corporatist policies and public enterprise were employed in the 1920s in response to Italian dependence on foreign capital and to the highly uneven development of the economy, and under fascism a corporatist strategy was adopted as a matter of deliberate policy. These instruments of intervention were refined after the War by the governing Christian Democrats, but this superficially strong development of state regulation was countered by the loose federal structure of the Italian state and the fragmented structure of the corporate webs, which together ensured that only a limited and unstable concertation of the competing corporate groups was possible. Different groups within Italian capital allied themselves with distinct branches and agencies of the state. State action was, as a result, ineffective and poorly co-ordinated, depending on 'arrangement and illicit practices' in a statist structure (Donolo 1980: 168; Regini 1982).

---

[12] The situation in Switzerland is described in Kriesi (1982).

[13] Jopperson and Meyer (1991), however, suggest that the Latin American economies can be characterized by what they call a 'segmental' system.

The centralized practices of the French state predisposed it to a statist response to the American challenge of the post-war years. Planning and nationalization have been directed towards the restructuring of the economy in order to promote its international competitiveness. Gaullism established a government/civil-service axis that reduced the role of parliament and parties in national decision-making and allowed appointed officials to act in economic matters in what was presented as a 'technical' rather than a 'sectional' party way. This stance was reinforced and legitimated through the education that staff received in the École Nationale d'Administration, which encouraged the view that the civil service was the voice of business (Suleiman 1986). Civil servants 'retired' from government positions into private-sector directorships, becoming a central force in corporate rule;[14] but it was only during the 1970s that this became a two-way interchange of personnel between business and politics. Thus, French business organizations only belatedly came into close contact with the economic machinery of the state, and their incorporation was not associated with any real attempt to use the state to concert private interests (Birnbaum 1980).

While they have often aimed at establishing Scandinavian-style 'corporatism', the post-Communist societies of Russia and Eastern Europe have in fact established statist systems. Private enterprises have been accorded high levels of autonomy and, in Russia in particular, the state has been too weak to incorporate the new business interests into corporatist institutions. In Hungary, for example, incorporated business associations and organizations that were formed under the Communist regime from the 1970s were accorded greater autonomy after 1988, so limiting the possibility of establishing a properly corporatist structure (Cox and Vass 1994: 156; see also Reutter 1995 and Ornstein 1994). This was further limited by the centralization of corporate debt. Banks were encouraged to take on the debts of industrial enterprises, while the banks themselves were acquired by the state. As the state was unwilling to use its control of the banking system as a mechanism of economic restructuring, the net result has been a bailing-out of the private sector and a debt-ridden state whose fiscal problems have led it to resort to cuts in health, welfare, education, and public sector salaries (Oberschall 1996: 1040). In mainland China and in the overseas Chinese societies too, statist policies have been pursued. Powerful states and powerful

---

[14] This was central to what Morin (1974) refers to as 'technocratic' control.

private enterprises have characterized the rapid economic growth of Taiwan and Singapore in particular, and statism proved a highly successful development strategy (Appelbaum and Henderson 1992).

The post-war period in all countries of the capitalist world-economy has seen regular shifts in economic policy, largely as a result of changes in governing parties. The nation state is central to the maintenance of a national economy in the face of tendencies towards its disarticulation, and to ensure this the nation state has had to both support private capital and intervene in its reconstruction. The 'displacement' into the state of the economic dislocations produced by concentration and internationalization might be expected to make state policies contradictory and shifting, but an enhanced role for the state cannot be avoided. While there has been a move away from the high levels of intervention characteristic of organized capitalism, the stage of disorganized capitalism still involves a higher level of state activity than characterized the facilitative state.

9

THE CORPORATION AND CAPITALIST CLASSES

....

THE changing structure of ownership and control, no matter how misunderstood it has been, has been widely seen as leading to the disappearance of the class of capitalist property-owners whose personal wealth and power were produced by the business conditions of nineteenth-century liberal capitalism. One of the earliest formulations of this idea was that of Burnham, a former Marxist, who held that the orthodox Marxist theory of capitalist society had been undermined by the economic transformations that had taken place between the 1880s and the 1930s. The finance capitalists identified by Hilferding were seen by Burnham as a mere transitional feature of the shift from the family capitalism of the nineteenth century to an emergent 'managerial society'. The managers who carry out the 'technical direction and co-ordination of the process of production' (Burnham 1941: 70) become technically indispensable to the new industrial system, and so are destined to replace the finance capitalists, just as they had ousted the entrepreneurial capitalists. By merging individual enterprises and rationalizing the organization of production, the finance capitalists had created the basis from which the internal executive managers, who 'are in no way dependent upon the maintenance of capitalist property and economic relations' (ibid.: 80), could rise to power in their place and become a new ruling class.

This view of the replacement of a capitalist class by a managerial class has been stated most forcefully by advocates of the theory of industrial society. What, for Burnham, was a scenario for the future, they have seen as a fully established state of affairs. Daniel Bell, for example, saw entrepreneurial capitalists as having been drawn into the turn-of-the-century system of 'finance capitalism' that he saw, like Burnham, as being a brief prelude to the final demise of family capitalists. Similarly for Berle, 'the transformation of property from an active role to passive wealth has so operated that the wealthy stratum no longer has power' (Berle 1963: 53). As family inheritance and control over property became less important in business, the old propertied class of family entrepreneurs would completely disappear. The possession of wealth is no longer a route to economic power, and social inequality becomes more closely geared to occupational status and occupational earnings (Bell 1957: 40–1; 1958: 50 ff.; Parsons 1954a: 431). It is in this new social structure that the technically indispensable managers have become a new class, dependent on their salaries rather than property.

I have thoroughly reviewed the evidence concerning the supposed separation of ownership from control that is held to underpin managerial power in business enterprises, and I have shown that the economic development of capitalism, in all the countries that I have considered, has been radically different from the picture painted by the managerialists. If capitalist societies have not changed in the direction anticipated by managerialism, it is the case, nevertheless, that their class structures have been transformed. The transition from personal to impersonal possession has transformed, but not eliminated, the capitalist class. As Zeitlin concluded, 'News of the demise of the capitalist classes . . . is, I suspect, somewhat premature' (Zeitlin 1974: 46).

Capital, Class, and Possession

'Class' is a much misused word. For many people it is merely a matter of accent, style of dress, or social standing. A society is seen as 'class-ridden' when its members identify one another in these terms and adopt attitudes of approval and disapproval towards one another. A society is 'classless', on the other hand, when these kinds of attitudes are weak or non-existent and when people's opportunities are unrestricted by others' judgements of their 'class'. Such views ignore what most sociologists aim to highlight with the term 'class'. They concentrate, in fact, on what Weber called 'status', which he distinguished clearly and systematically from 'class' (1914; 1920). According to Weber, 'status' was a matter of social standing or prestige, while 'class' was a matter of economic power rooted in market and property relations. This distinction between class and status is fundamental to my concerns in this chapter, where I firmly link 'class' to relations of possession (see also Scott 1996a). For Weber, class relations were economic relations. They were those aspects of the social distribution of power that arose from structured alignments of interests in the property and labour markets.[1] Marx showed that such structured relations resulted from the possession or non-possession of the means of production, and that changing forms of class relations reflected changing forms of possession.

Weber distinguished 'class situations' from 'social classes'. Where class situations are structurally defined locations within the property and labour markets, social classes are large-scale collectivities of households that stand in definite relations to one another in a hier-archical structure of advantaged and disadvantaged life-chances. The formation of a social class involves the clustering together of class situations on the basis of circulation and interaction, and these demographic processes establish real social boundaries and the basis for social solidarity. 'Circulation' occurs through the intergenerational and career mobility of individuals, their multi-occupancy of class situations, and through household formation. 'Interaction' or association involves informal and intimate relations, such as living together, eating together, sociability, and so on. Marriage relations have been central mechanisms of both circulation and interaction, bringing together different generations of individuals involved in various class situations, and creating a network of kinship relations that are important bases of informal and intimate interaction. It is through these processes of circulation and interaction that the boundaries of social classes are defined. Weber sees a social class, then, as a cluster of class situations among which mobility is easy and typical (Weber 1920: 302). The intergenerational and lifetime mobility of individuals among different class situations links them into the same social class, separating them from those class situations with which there is less interchange or circulation.[2]

Social classes are the result of complex structuring processes and do not, therefore, have sharply defined boundaries. While the core members of a social class may be easily distinguished from those of

---

[1] Weber identified what he called 'constellations of interests' in market relations, and my use of the term 'control through a constellation of interests' derives from this more general account of domination.

[2] This argument is set out at greater length in Scott (1996a).

other classes, those on its fringes will have many characteristics in common with those on the fringes of adjacent social classes. As Cole has argued, social classes

are not sharply definable groups whose precise numbers can be determined by gathering in enough information about every individual. They are rather aggregates of persons round a number of central nuclei, in such a way that it can be said with confidence of those nearer each centre that they are members of a particular class, but that those further from a centre can be assigned to the class it represents only with increasing uncertainty. (Cole 1955: 1; Sweezy 1951)

Using Weber's concepts, we may say that a *capitalist social class* exists whenever distinctively *capitalist class situations* are closely interconnected through circulation and interaction. In these circumstances, a capitalist class exists as a demographically bounded collectivity. The capitalist social class in contemporary capitalism consists of those households whose life-chances are determined by their occupancy of capitalist class situations.

These class situations are defined by relations of possession, the actual relations of effective control associated with particular legal forms of ownership. Marx saw bourgeois or capitalist class situations as rooted in legal relations of private property that give their occupants personal possession of the means of production. Personal possession is seen most clearly in the individual capitalist entrepreneur, who has a direct and immediate control over productive assets. Capitalist class situations are those of people whose personal wealth allows them to benefit from the labour of those they employ to work in their factories, shops, and offices. Weber added that these benefits take the form of advantaged life-chances: superior incomes, greater security, better education and health, and so on.

The spread of the joint stock company transformed the legal context in which capitalist entrepreneurs operate, and it opened up the basis for a transformation in their class situation. Where an individual or family holds all or a majority of the shares in a company, the use of the joint stock form merely results in a shift from direct personal possession to indirect personal possession. Instead of owning the business assets directly, the entrepreneur owns shares in a company that is the legal owner of the assets. The further development of large-scale business enterprise, however, leads to more complex alterations in class relations. The differentiation of 'shareholders' from 'directors' and top executives separates—at least in a formal sense—relations of possession from the relations of command or authority through which the relations of possession are made effective within the enterprise. While shareholders retain personal possession of the capital embodied in company shares, the powers of command over business assets rest with the directors. In many cases, of course, the shareholders and the directors are the same people, but in larger enterprises they may be different people. Indirect personal possession is not possible when an individual or family owns less than a majority of the shares and the directors and top executives achieve a greater autonomy from particular shareholders. When the great bulk of company shares are not owned by individuals but by institutions or other corporations, the resulting system of impersonal possession transforms class situations once more. Individual shareholders become purely 'rentier' shareholders, and they are completely dissociated from top executives. Rentiers have stakes in a large number of companies and controlling blocks in none, while executives occupy salaried class situations and hold key command situations in the large enterprises.

There are, then, four capitalist class situations in contemporary capitalism. There are, first, the surviving entrepreneurial capitalist situations, occupied by the majority and minority controllers of large enterprises who now operate through indirect personal possession rather than the direct personal possession that was possible for their early- and mid-Victorian counterparts. Such entrepreneurial capitalists survive, to a greater or lesser extent, in all the capitalist economies that have been considered in this book. Second, there are the rentier capitalist situations occupied by those with diversified portfolios of shareholdings in a large number of enterprises who depend upon the dividend incomes from their holdings. Rentiers benefit from the ways in which their wealth is used in the corporate system, and they remain important elements in the capital markets. These class situations have grown with the expansion of the stock exchange, which has allowed erstwhile entrepreneurs to detach themselves from particular enterprises and to spread their financial risks. The third capitalist class situation is that of the executive or director who is a salaried employee of the enterprise, and who exercises authority over subordinate managers and the mass of workers. These class situations have grown with impersonal possession and the consequent bureaucratization of administration in large enterprises (Wright 1979: 3–4; 1980: 328–9. See also Wright et al. 1982). Executive capitalists hold collective powers of command in relation to what Carchedi (1975; 1983) has called the 'global function of capital'. As Wright puts it, 'They may not personally possess the means of production as individuals, but they are members of collectivities that do possess those means of production' (Wright 1980: 338; see also McDermott 1991: 78).

Finally, it is possible to add the class situation of the finance capitalist, who holds multiple directorships or executive positions in a number of separate enterprises. As Hilferding (1910) first indicated, such class situations have grown along with the fusion of finance and industry. The finance capitalists and executive capitalists are those who most clearly epitomize the system of impersonal possession, as they are most closely involved in the positions of corporate rule through which effective control is exercised. Rentier capitalists increased in number as controlling family holdings have declined in size, and they form the core of the large personal shareholders in major companies. Entrepreneurial capitalists have remained an important element in most capitalist societies, running their enterprises through majority or minority control.[3]

A capitalist social class, then, is formed wherever capitalist class situations are demographically clustered through processes of circulation and interaction. The class is unified to the extent that its members, in their own lifetimes or across the generations, can move freely from one class situation to another and associate regularly with those in these same class situations. Thus, for example, a rentier capitalist may also be a finance capitalist, the son of an entrepreneurial capitalist may become an executive capitalist, the daughter of a rentier capitalist may marry an entrepreneurial capitalist, and an executive capitalist may regularly play golf with a finance capitalist (Soref and Zeitlin 1988).

This capitalist social class may, however, stretch beyond its core class-situations to encompass those who depend upon property ownership or executive positions, but whose property or involvement in strategic control is not sufficient to ensure them the security of life-chances enjoyed by those in the core. This will be the case

[3] Abercrombie and Urry (1983) have misleadingly seen them as the only true capitalists. Personal ownership of the means of production, they argue, is the defining characteristic of capitalist economic locations, and so a distinctly 'capitalist' class becomes more and more restricted to those small enterprises in which such personal ownership is possible. It should be clear from my argument, however, that the transformation of property leads to the new capitalist-class situations of impersonal possession.

wherever mobility and interaction is great enough to connect them to the core. So long as there is 'easy and typical' circulation around these class situations, and so long as there is informal and intimate interaction among their occupants, they will form a part of the same social class. A capitalist social class as a whole is dependent on the success of the business system which produces its wealth. It is a 'propertied class' or 'business class' in as much as its members are dependent on the capitalist private-property business system for their advantaged life-chances (Scott 1982b: ch. 6).

A capitalist business class is rooted in the large enterprises that constitute the system of impersonal possession, along with the entrepreneurial capitalists whose large personal shareholdings give them a continuing role in the business system. A 'petty bourgeoisie', on the other hand, is a social class whose members are the owners or principal shareholders in small- and medium-sized enterprises and whose activities are increasingly dependent on the operations of big business (Scase 1982). Where there is little circulation or interaction among those in capitalist and in petty-bourgeois class situations, they will comprise distinct social classes. A capitalist class can also be distinguished from a 'service class' that may be formed from those in levels of management and expertise below that of the top executives and directors (Goldthorpe 1982).[4] These subordinate managers and administrators have been characterized by Wright as occupying 'contradictory' class situations. They are workers who are excluded from participation in strategic control over money capital, but who participate in the operational control of production and labour. Their class situations are contradictory because 'they share class interests with two different classes but have interests identical to neither' (Wright 1980: 331). In Carchedi's terms, they participate in the performance of some aspects of the 'global function of capital', while at the same time engaging in the work of the 'collective labourer' (Carchedi 1975).[5] Their class situations involve a high degree of trust and autonomy in the exercise of delegated authority, and, as I showed in Chapter 7, they have been based in bureaucratic hierarchies in which recruitment and promotion is organized through career expectations (Abercrombie and Urry 1983: 118 ff.; Goldthorpe 1982: 168; Ehrenreich and Ehrenreich 1979).

---

[4] See also Bechhofer *et al.* (1978) and Goldthorpe (1978). The concept of the service class was first introduced by Karl Renner (1953).

[5] See also Mackenzie (1982).

The core of a service class would comprise those households whose life-chances are rooted in the progress of one or more of their members through a career in service locations. They have no substantial wealth, other than modest domestic property, and so are dependent solely on their occupational salaries and 'fringe benefits'. The service class is rooted firmly 'in the middle' of the class hierarchy, though it may stretch a considerable distance, from households dependent on the earnings of a junior manager to households whose members have reached peak career positions and may be on the verge of a capitalist class situation.[6]

My discussion so far has concentrated on the social class hierarchy and its basis in the class situations of households, but it is also important to recognize the analytically distinct contribution to life-chances made by the structures that Weber described as comprising status situations. While class situations involve the determination of life-chances through the material consequences of property ownership and economic location in a market, status situations involve their determination through communal solidarity and shared values. More specifically, status situations are determined by the 'social estimation of honour' (Weber 1914: 932). Social honour, Weber argued, is estimated on the evidence offered of a person's life style: specific styles of life are expected of those occupying particular social positions, and the outward trappings of life style tend to become the observable attributes in terms of which individuals are 'placed' by others in a status hierarchy. It is when individuals regard one another as status equals that they are especially likely to marry one another, to engage in informal and intimate interaction, and to exclude from such interaction those whom they regard as their status inferiors. Status equals, that is to say, tend to establish a social closure around themselves (Parkin 1979: 44–5).

Class and status are analytically distinct from one another, though they interpenetrate in concrete situations to form complex patterns of stratification. In some circumstances status will correspond to and legitimate class differences, reinforcing the effects of material circumstances on circulation and interaction and so reinforcing the formation of social classes. In other circumstances, however, status evaluations may run counter to the effects of class and so obscure

---

[6] Strictly speaking, it is necessary to refer to both 'class situations' and 'command situations' in corporate hierarchies. As these tend to be closely associated, I have not explicitly drawn the distinction except where it would cause confusion not to do so. The argument is developed at length in Scott (1996a: chs. 6 and 7).

class relations under a veil of status considerations. Weber illustrated this well in the case of property ownership, which, he argued, has distinct class and status implications. Those with property may claim a superior status, though it is rarely the case that property *per se* guarantees such honour: in a reference to the status disadvantages of the *nouveau riche*, Weber argued that the status evaluation of property 'normally' stands in sharp opposition to the pretensions of sheer property' (1914: 932): 'old' wealth is superior to 'mere' wealth. Nevertheless, he recognized that those for whom property ownership is significant will often assert their distinctive social status (Weber 1920: 307).

Inequalities of Income and Wealth

Having set out these conceptual clarifications, it is now possible to explore the actual patterns of capitalist class formation that can be found in contemporary capitalist societies. A provisional view of this can be gained from evidence on the distribution of income and wealth, among the most important structured differentials in life chances that result from differences in class situation. The top income- and wealth-recipients in a society—defined as a statistical category such as the top 0.5 per cent, top 1 per cent, or whatever—do not, of course, constitute a social class. They form a purely nominal category that includes those from various class situations whose level of income and wealth happens to be similar. Nevertheless, distributional studies can show the broad contours of the social inequalities that arise from property ownership in capitalist societies.

The top 10 per cent of income recipients in the United States received a more or less constant share of around one-third of all income before tax throughout the first half of this century (Kolko 1962: 15, 24, 37; Kuznets 1953). Although an increase in the concentration of income within this category took place prior to 1919, this was partially reversed during the Depression and the Second World War. The share of the top 1 per cent in income, for example, fell from 14 per cent to 10 per cent during the 1930s and 1940s. By the late 1950s the share of the top 1 per cent of families stood at 8 per cent (Domhoff 1967: 41; Birnbaum 1971; Bottomore 1965: 44; Miller 1966: 113). The picture in Britain is remarkably similar. While the share of the top 10 per cent of income recipients in before-tax income seems to have remained in the region of one-third, the proportion received by the top 1 per cent fell from 16.6 per cent in 1938 to 11.2 per cent in 1949 and to 6.2 per cent in 1974 (Nicholson 1967: 42; Lydall 1959; Solgow 1968; Scott 1994b: 106).[7] The reduction in the share received by the top 1 per cent in Britain occurred mainly between 1949 and 1957, the proportion then remaining constant until the late 1970s. The main causes of the post-war reduction in Britain were the policies of the post-war Labour government and the fact that from 1949 to 1957 earned incomes rose faster than income from other sources. After 1957, the most rapidly growing sources of income were rent, dividends, and interest (Nicholson 1967: 49). The trend in after-tax income has been slightly less marked, the share of the top 1 per cent being 6 per cent in the 1940s and 5 per cent in the 1950s and 1960s. Even the conservative estimates of Polanyi and Wood suggest that in 1970 the share of the top 1 per cent in after-tax income stood at 5 per cent (Polanyi and Wood 1974: 64). Noble (1975: 178, 199) showed that, while the share of the top 1 per cent before tax fell from 9 to 7 per cent, their share after tax fell from 5 to 4 per cent.

During the 1970s and 1980s, however, income inequality began to increase, largely as a result of Conservative government policies aimed at cutting back social provision and deregulating the economy. The share of the top 1 per cent of income recipients rose by almost a quarter (Rentoul 1987: 26). A major factor in the recent increase in income inequality has been the rising trend of top executive salaries. A quarter of chairmen and chief executives in 1986 had received an annual pay rise of 23 per cent, and one in ten had received a 42 per cent rise (Rentoul 1987: 30). Top salaries were further enhanced by share-option schemes that allowed executives to acquire substantial shareholdings in their companies, blurring the distinction between executive and rentier class situations.

With respect to wealth distribution, a major study of the United States by Lampman (1959; 1962) showed that the share of the top 1 per cent in personal wealth fell over the period between 1922 and 1949 and then rose again through the 1950s to stand at between a quarter and a third. The top 1 per cent of wealth holders owned about one-third of all wealth in the 1920s and 1930s, but by 1972 their share had fallen to 20.7 per cent (Rubinstein 1986: 147). It has been

---

[7] For comprehensive discussions of trends see Atkinson (1972), Diamond Report (1975a), and Scott (1994b). For problems with official statistics see Titmuss (1962), Meade (1964), and Atkinson (1975).

suggested that this share continued to rise through the 1960s (Smith and Calvert 1965; Domhoff 1967; Lundberg 1969). Lundberg's (1937) study of wealth holding claimed that there were 11,800 millionaires in the United States in 1937, this group including such families as the Morgans, Rockefellers, Du Ponts, and Fords. By 1972 there were 180,000 millionaires, though the falling value of money over the period has to be taken into account in comparing these figures (Jaher 1980: 221). Nevertheless, there were 3,413 people in 1969 who had wealth in excess of $10 million. There were 160 families with wealth of at least $200 million in 1986, the list including such well-known families as Du Pont, Ford, Getty, Rockefeller, and Mellon, together with lesser-known names such as Cargill, Dunforth, Deere, McGraw, Mars, Upjohn, Weyerhauser, and many others whose names are virtually unknown outside their immediate circles (Allen 1987: Appendix). The bases of their wealth were the financial and commercial enterprises of New York and the North-East, though regional enterprises also generated substantial wealth for the rentier and entrepreneurial families associated with them. Lampman argues that much of the reduction in concentration during the period between the World Wars can be explained in terms of a redistribution of wealth within families and that it does not, therefore, represent a significant change in the social distribution of wealth. Nearly half of the wealth held by the top 1 per cent in 1953 was held by the top 0.11 per cent of the population (about 113,300 people), and there is no evidence to suggest that the situation is any different today. Zeitlin (1989) showed for 1982 that 32,000 adults—less than 0.002 per cent of the adult population—had assets of $5 million or more.

Britain has a rather higher degree of wealth-concentration than does the United States. The share of the top 1 per cent fell from 69 per cent in 1911 to 55 per cent in 1938, 47 per cent in 1950, and then to about 30 per cent in the 1960s and 1970s (Atkinson 1983: 168; Rubinstein 1986: 95; Lydall and Tipping 1961: 253; Atkinson 1972: 21; Revell 1965). The proportion of wealth held by the top 5 per cent declined from 86 to 55 per cent over the same period, and Atkinson shows that, while the share of the top 1 per cent has declined by half, the wealth of the next 4 per cent remained constant or actually increased over the period. Atkinson draws the conclusion that this reflected redistribution within families aimed at the avoidance of estate duty (Atkinson 1972: 22–3; Polanyi and Wood 1974: 17). As in the United States, almost half the wealth now held by the top 1 per cent is held by the top 0.1 per cent.

The share of the top 1 per cent of wealth-holders did not rise during the 1980s, as was the case with income recipients. Indeed, by 1987 the share of the top 1 per cent had fallen to 18 per cent of total personal wealth, though they held three-quarters of all privately owned shares (Oppenheim 1990: 133). To qualify for membership in the top 1 per cent of wealth-holders a person had to own assets valued at £190,000 or more; but detailed research shows this category to be very diverse. 20,000 people, forming the top 0.05 per cent, were multi-millionaires, and 400 individuals held £20 million or more (Beresford 1990). It was at these highest levels of wealth distribution that the inheritance of property played an especially important part, and the very wealthy tended to hold their assets as company shares and other financial instruments rather than as domestic property.

Table 66. Large estates in Britain (1900–1977)

Size of estate (£)	Number of estates		
	1900–1901	1938–1939	1976–1977
250,000–500,000	51	98	n.a.
500,000–1 million	17	30	11
More than 1 million	9	4	21
Total	77	132	32

Source: Rubinstein (1981: 31–2, Tables 2.2 and 2.3); *Daily Mail Year Book* (1977).
Note: n.a. = not available. Net values of estates do not include value of land. For 1976–7 the band for medium-to-large estates was £700,000–£1,000,000.

The data in Table 66 show that the number of millionaires in Britain has declined since 1900. The decline is particularly marked in view of the changing value of money over that period. A millionaire of 1976 had equivalent purchasing power to a person with £65,000 in 1900, so clearly the absolute figures give a false impression.[8] The increase in the number of quarter-millionaires between 1900 and 1938 was at approximately the level that would be expected simply on the basis of changes in purchasing power, though the number of full millionaires shows a real decline on this same basis. Although the increase in the number of full millionaires between 1900 and

[8] Calculations of spending power are taken from Butler and Sloman (1979).

1976 was large, it was substantially lower than would be expected on the basis of constant purchasing power. This could indicate simply that wealthy people distribute the bulk of their wealth to members of their families prior to their own death in order to minimize their liability to estate duty, though Rubinstein suggests that it shows a real decline in wealth concentration over much of the period. Only from the 1950s, he argues, has there been any move back towards greater concentration as entrepreneurial capitalists began to make fortunes in property, consumer goods, and in some financial services (Rubinstein 1981: 61). Despite these 'new' fortunes at the top of the scale, however, there is considerable evidence that inheritance continues to play a major part in wealth distribution (Harbury and Hitchens 1979; see also Revell 1960; Harbury 1962; Harbury and McMahon 1974).

Although the two categories are not the same, large income-recipients tend also to be large wealth-holders, with the greatest contribution to real disposable income being made by that part of their wealth consisting of company shares. Investigations undertaken by the *Temporary National Economic Committee* showed that 7 per cent of the American population in 1937 held the whole of the 60 per cent of company shares that were owned by individuals. These same people were among the largest income recipients: the higher their income, the greater was the contribution to it from dividends. For individuals with annual incomes greater than $100,000, dividends accounted for 60 per cent of their income (Goldsmith and Parmelee 1940: 10–13). These people were also more likely to have diversified portfolios, investing in an average of twenty-five companies each. While the number of shareholders declined somewhat during the Depression and the Second World War, it began to increase again during the 1950s. Lundberg (1969: 28) discovered that 1.4 million families held 65 per cent of all investment assets in 1962, with fewer than a quarter of a million families holding almost a third of these assets. In the early 1980s only 19 per cent of families owned any corporate stock, while the top 1 per cent of individuals in 1982 held a half of all corporate stock. They also held virtually all assets in trust accounts, one-seventh of all cash and bank deposits, and one seventh of all real estate. In total, these individuals held a quarter of the total net worth in individual hands. Fuller figures for 1983 show that the top 0.5 per cent of families held 15.3 per cent of real estate, 46.5 per cent of corporate stock, and 77 per cent of all trust assets (Zeitlin 1989a: 145).

In Britain the highest rates of shareholding have been found among the wealthiest groups. The top 5 per cent of wealth-holders in 1961 held 96 per cent of all personally owned shares (Atkinson 1972: 30; 1975: 135; Westergaard and Resler 1975: 107 ff.). These shareholdings are an important source of income: the top 10 per cent of those in receipt of investment income in 1960 received 99 per cent of all income from this source (Blackburn 1967), and the top 1 per cent of income recipients in 1970 received 7 per cent of all income but 17 per cent of investment income (Noble 1975: 180). Despite the spread of shareholdings that occurred with the privatization of public enterprises, shareholdings remain highly concentrated. In 1979, 4.5 per cent of the population owned shares, but by 1995 around 17 per cent of adults owned shares, most of the new shareholders having bought shares only in the privatized enterprises (Saunders and Harris 1994: 4, 144). Saunders and Harris have estimated that the proportion of the population owning shares could be as high as one-quarter. Three-quarters of individual shareholders held shares in fewer than four different enterprises, and two-thirds had shares in just one company. This is hardly evidence for popular capitalism. Indeed, 'there is little evidence . . . to support the view that millions of ordinary people have begun to invest in shares to any significant extent' (Saunders and Harris 1994: 145).

There is also considerable evidence to support the argument that corporate directors and executives are disproportionately numbered among the large personal shareholders at the tops of the hierarchies of income and wealth. Directors and executives of the top 200 American enterprises in 1939 held 5.5 per cent of their shares, most of these being held by directors. Corporate management typically held less than 1 per cent of the shares of their own enterprises, though in a quarter of all enterprises management holdings amounted to 5 per cent or more (Goldsmith and Parmelee 1940: 56–60, 64–5; Gordon 1936; 1938). Kolko (1962: 57) estimated that directors owned an average of 9.9 per cent of the shares in the top industrials of 1957, though the figures presented in Table 67 suggest that, overall, the average size of the shareholding block held by directors in very large enterprises declined between 1939 and 1975 (see also Domhoff 1967: 58). Directors and managers in the top 10 American enterprises of 1975 held, on average, 2.1 per cent of their capital, though in the middle and lower ranks of the top 500 they held an average of 20 per cent (Demsetz 1983: 198). In Britain this is the case too, though many of the enterprises of 1976 in which

Table 67. Directors' shareholdings in Britain and the United States (1939–1976)

% of shares held by directors	United States			Britain	
	1939	1960	1975	1951	1976
Less than 1%	23	68	132	79	136
1–2%	} 42	45	15	} 87 } 26	
2–5%		43	25		
5–10%	17	39	8	25	5
More than 10%	33	37	20	42	33
Totals	115	232	200	233	200

Source: US data from Gordon (1945: 27), Villarejo (1961a: 51, Table X), Herman (1981: 87, Table 3.9). British data from Florence (1961: 90–1, Table IVc), Scott and Griff (1984: 103, Table 4.1).
Note: Data relate to non-financial enterprises, though the US data for 1939 are limited to industrials. The British data for 1951 relate to a selection of ninety-eight large non-financials and samples of smaller enterprises.

directors held less than 1 per cent were wholly owned subsidiaries or had a majority of their shares held by another enterprise.

Even where managers have a low percentage holding, their stakes nevertheless tend to be of great monetary value. Larner has calculated, for example, that the median value of shares held by executives in ninety-four large American enterprises in 1965 was $658,359, giving them a median dividend income of $23,605 (Larner 1970: 36–7, 66). A shareholding of 0.017 per cent held in General Motors held by its chairman in 1967 had a market value of nearly $4m (Miliband 1968: 52; Villarejo 1961b: 53; see also Burcke 1976). For Britain, Nichols (1969: 75) has shown that while the period from 1936 to 1951 saw a decline in the average holding of directors in their own companies, the actual wealth represented by these holdings remained extremely high. This finding was confirmed by Stanworth (1974: 255), who showed that 31.6 per cent of directors in the top seventy-five British companies of 1971 held shares in their own company worth £10,000 or more, and that 13.5 per cent held shares with a market value in excess of £100,000. Management shareholdings are encouraged by stock-option schemes and bonuses. In 1983 1.5 per cent of large enterprises had stock-option schemes for their directors; by 1990 the proportion had risen to 25.4 per cent (Useem 1993: 207). Income from shares can be six times as great as a manager's salary, though top executive salaries remain very high (Useem 1980: 48): the average chief executive salary in large British enterprises in 1992 was £140,000 plus bonuses, and in the very largest enterprises salaries averaged £387,904 (Charkham 1994: 265–6). Because a manager's total after-tax income is highly dependent on dividends, and hence on profits, a career orientation is by no means incompatible with a shareholder interest.

Income distribution at the upper levels is remarkably similar in the other major capitalist countries, despite variations in their systems of capital mobilization—though all tend to show greater inequality than Britain (Scott 1994b: ch. 5). The top 10 per cent of income recipients in France, Germany, Belgium, and the Netherlands received just over 30 per cent of income before tax in 1970, while the top 10 per cent in Italy received only just under 30 per cent (Lawson and George 1980: 236–7; Atkinson 1973a; Babeau and Strauss-Kahn 1977: 41 ff.; Daumard 1980; Zamagni 1980). A study of the 502 wealthiest German families in 1911 showed that over a quarter—more than in Britain at the time—were bankers and that 12.4 per cent came from heavy industry. Just under half had business involvements in large enterprises, generally as entrepreneurial or finance capitalists (Augustine 1994: 31). Comparable evidence for the contemporary period in Germany is not available, though both income and wealth remain highly unequal in their distribution. This is also the case in France, where the richest people in 1985—as shown in Table 68—were predominantly drawn from those active in business, and many were from rentier families. Post-communist Russia is characterized by growing inequality, though the full scale of this is difficult to assess. While its new business leaders have accumulated massive fortunes, the extent of their wealth seems still to remain low by international standards (Kryshtanovskaya 1993; 1994; Scott 1994b: 143). Mainland China has shown a growth in inequality as its economic reforms have made themselves felt, and the fastest-growing incomes have been found among those who are most centrally involved in market-oriented activities (Nee 1991).

The Japanese *zaibatsu* were foundations of major fortunes for their controlling families. Morioka has estimated that the annual income of the Iwasaki family—the controllers of Mitsubishi—amounted to more than ¥1 million in 1895 (see Table 69). The present situation is unclear, though there is evidence that Japan

Table 68. France's wealthiest individuals (1985)

Ranking		Wealth (millards of francs)
1	Marcel Dassault	7.0–7.5
2	Liliane Bettencourt	6.6–7.0
3	Marcel Bich	2.1–2.2
4	Edmond de Rothschild	2.0–2.5
5	Robert Hersant	2.0–2.2
6	Michel David-Weill	1.5–2.0
7	Geneviève Seydoux	1.5–1.6
8	Jean-Noel Bongrain	1.3–1.4
9	Sylvain Floirat	1.2–1.3
10	Philippe Rossillon	1.2–1.25
11	Jérôme Seydoux	1.1–1.2
12	Nicolas Seydoux	1.1–1.2
13	Anne Gruner-Schlumberger	1.1–1.2
14	Michel Seydoux	1.0–1.1
15	Francis Bouygues	1.0–1.1
16	Gustave Leven	1.0–1.1

Source: Bauer and Bertin-Mourot (1987: 99).

currently has a similar level of income inequality to that found in the United States (Atkinson 1983: 26). Unfortunately, material on inequality is sparse, and studies by Steven (1983) and Morioka (1989) overstate the size of the 'capitalist' elements at the top of the income hierarchies by including managers and small employers in this category.

It is difficult to draw sharp distinctions among the various coun-

Table 68. Wealthy *zaibatsu* families in Japan (1895)

Ranking	Family	Annual Income (¥000)
1	Iwasaki	1084
2	Mitsui	529
3	Sumitomo	156
4	Yasuda	94
5	Okura	65
6	Furukawa	62

Source: Morioka (1992: Table 1.1 on 25).
Note: ¥1000 = £217.71 at contemporary exchange rates.

tries that I have described. The 'Anglo-American' economies show varying levels of inequality: levels are highest in the United States and lowest in Britain and Australia, where there have been stronger frameworks of public welfare committed to reducing the level of inequality. The German and Latin economies, on the other hand, show relatively high levels of overall concentration, though they tend to have lower levels of poverty than are found in either Britain or the United States. These differences reflect, perhaps, the relative weakness of institutional capital in the German and Latin economies, the corporate-web system, in particular, providing opportunities for the accumulation of large fortunes. The Japanese economy is the basis of a relatively low level of inequality because of the highly depersonalized system of capital mobilization that has existed throughout the post-war period as a result of the American occupation authorities forcing wealthy *zaibatsu* families to sell their shareholdings. Nevertheless, a high level of concentration in share ownership has persisted, and corporate managers are among the leading individual shareholders. Individuals hold just under one-third of all shares in Japan, with the largest personal shareholdings being those of executives in their own enterprises (Steven 1983: 15; Komiya 1961).

Circulation and Class Formation

Managerialists, it will be recalled, claimed that the social class of capitalist entrepreneurs in all advanced industrial societies had dissolved. I have shown that specifically capitalist class situations do indeed exist—those of the entrepreneurial capitalists, rentier capitalists, finance capitalists, and executive capitalists—and I have outlined the conditions under which the occupants of these class situations might be forged through demographic processes of circulation and interaction into a capitalist social class. The evidence on inequality in income and wealth distributions has provided *prima facie* evidence for the existence of advantaged life-chances for those in capitalist class situations. It remains to be seen, however, whether these people are also formed into cohesive social classes and, if so, through what means. It is first necessary to look at the demographic processes of recruitment to capitalist class situations, and I will then turn to their consequences for the formation of capitalist social classes.

A persistent theme in managerialist writing has been the claim that the decline of personal possession as the basis of business recruitment has been associated with an increase in the importance of education. The attainment of diplomas and qualifications at schools, colleges, and universities has been seen as the means through which propertyless individuals have been able to pursue managerial careers and rise to top executive positions. Evidence from the United States does support the contention that higher levels of education are now required for business leaders than was the case for the nineteenth-century entrepreneurs, but this does not seem to be associated with any decline in the life-chances of those from entrepreneurial backgrounds. In 1928 58 per cent of American executives were recruited from families with a business background, only 13 per cent being upwardly mobile professional managers, and a college education was important for heirs and the mobile alike (Taussig and Joslyn 1932). The salience of education had increased by the post-war period, and a later study found that three-quarters of top corporate executives in 1952 had been to college. By the 1970s higher levels of education had become the norm. A study of chief executives in 1976 found that more than half had been to graduate school, mainly studying for the Master of Business Administration (MBA) or a law degree (Burcke 1976).[9] One-fifth of these executives had attended one of the top four universities (Yale, Harvard, Princeton, or Cornell), most typically the 'second-generation' sons of entrepreneurs and executives. The upwardly mobile managers had, for the most part, come through second-rank colleges and universities, especially the larger state and city universities (Warner 1959: 112, based on Warner and Abegglen 1955). These results suggest that entrepreneurs have ensured that their children have acquired the necessary training for success in a business career, and that they have also ensured that their children have received their education at the most prestigious institutions. This view has been confirmed by Allen (1978b: 517), who found that an increase in the proportion of college graduates among multiple directors between 1935 and 1970 was associated with a continuing high level of recruitment from the top private colleges.

Private schooling and attendance at one of the ancient universities

---

[9] Some sectoral variations have been discovered. Whitt (1981) found that the proportion of directors from top universities in 1970 was lower in the oil industry than the average for manufacturing industry.

have for long been an important factor in entry to the board-rooms of Britain's major enterprises (Perkin 1978; Heath 1981: 88, 96). More than half the directors in large British enterprises during the 1950s came from families with a business background—44 per cent having fathers who had been directors—and 58 per cent of the whole directorate had been educated at private schools. Among those with higher qualifications, those trained in law or accountancy tended to become multiple directors, while those with a technical training were found among the executive directors of engineering and chemical enterprises (Copeman 1955: 89, 92–5, 105, 120; Clements 1958: 173 ff.). Recruitment of bank directors has been narrower than that of industrial directors, and the proportion of former public-school boys who sat on the boards of the big clearing banks increased from 68.2 to 79.9 per cent over the period 1939 to 1970.[10] During this same period, the proportion of top bank directors recruited from Oxford and Cambridge increased from 45.3 to 60.4 per cent. Although recruitment from other universities also increased over this period, it remained at an extremely low level: in 1970 just 8.2 per cent of clearing-bank directors came from universities other than Oxford or Cambridge (Boyd 1973: 84, 92; Stanworth and Giddens 1974a: 89). Clearing-bank directors who had not come from a business background of entrepreneurial or rentier families were especially likely to have taken the private-school/Oxbridge route to the boardroom (ibid.: 96, 102, 110; see also Thomas 1978: 309). Useem found that the greater the number of directorships a person held, the more likely was that person to have attended one of the major public schools (1984: 68).[11]

Nichols (1969: 81–3, 93) found some evidence to suggest that professional management training was becoming more widespread among middle managers in Britain, a finding confirmed by Whitley et al. (1981). Directors of the largest enterprises, however, have rarely been recruited through the business schools. Instead, attendance at public schools and Oxbridge provided the social assets of contacts and connections that could be used to ease entry into the top board-rooms. The growth of student numbers on the MBA courses at the London and Manchester business schools in the period 1976–8 was mainly accounted for by those from a small business or middle man-

[10] Perkin (1978: 227) shows that, over the period 1880–1970, only one woman became chairman of one of the top 200 enterprises—Lady Pirrie, who succeeded her husband at Harland and Wolff.
[11] The British 'public schools' are, in fact, private schools.

agement background. Over half the students had attended a major public school (Whitley *et al.* 1981: 94) and the authors conclude that private education is used as a means of access to higher education and, thereby, to the business schools.

It appears that levels of both family continuity and technical education are higher in France than in either Britain or the United States. Indeed, Carré (1978) has stressed the 'familial' character of French capitalists. Nevertheless, education has been extremely important, especially for rentier families that cannot rely on the direct inheritance of business positions for their children. Almost three-quarters of chief executives in a sample of French enterprises in 1976 had attended one of the *Grandes Écoles*, the science schools such as the *École Polytechnique*, *École Centrale*, and *École des Mines* being especially popular; and many chief executives were drawn from a business background (Savage 1979: 119–21; Hall and De Bettignies 1968; Swartz 1986: 62: Hall *et al.* 1969; Granick 1962). About two-thirds of these chief executives were heirs to family businesses, the proportion being somewhat lower in the very largest enterprises. Nevertheless, the proportion of the top 100 chief executives who came from business families had increased from 39 to 46 per cent between 1952 and 1972 (Bourdieu and de St Martin 1978: 46, cited in Savage 1979: 132; see also Birnbaum *et al.* 1978). Attendance at a technical school had been especially important for those chief executives in large enterprises who had few family connections with business, their level of education being generally much higher than their entrepreneurial counterparts (Monjardet 1972: 139 ff.). Professionals and civil servants, for example, could enhance the business prospects of their sons by sending them to the private schools that could ensure them entry to the *Grandes Écoles*, where they would acquire the technical credentials required for a high-level business career. The ENA and the *École Polytechnique* were the most important sources of recruitment for all those who were chief executives in 1989. In most industrial sectors over half of all chief executives came through these schools, and in banking the figure was 80 per cent (Bauer *et al.* 1995: 70–1). Similarly, those who chose to enter the lower rungs of a managerial career through the acquisition of a business-school diploma found that their chances of successful entry to INSEAD were much greater if they had attended a private school (Whitley *et al.* 1981: 96; Marceau 1977: 133; Marceau 1989b).

The most senior business leaders in France combined business background with educational credentials. It was the post-war response to the 'American challenge', leading to planning and statist interventions, that brought about a closer alignment between the *Grandes Écoles* and the business world (Swartz 1986). Chairmen of enterprises subject to financial control or controlled through the corporate webs were especially likely to come from an exclusive social background and to possess technical diplomas, and many had arrived through *pantouflage* from administrative careers in the state.[12] The rate of *pantouflage* among graduates of the *École Nationale d'Administration* increased slowly from around 5 per cent in 1961 to 20 per cent in the late 1970s. From 1978, however, the rate increased markedly, and by 1989 it had reached 91 per cent (Bauer and Bertin-Mourot 1994: 4). This was due in part to the growth and establishment of the school itself over the period, and to the declining attractiveness of careers in the state. The particular increase in the 1980s, however, can be traced to the political changes of the period that resulted in an efflux of civil servants as governments changed.

Evidence on business recruitment in other European countries is rather sparse. Belgium and Italy show a similar pattern to France with respect to both family inheritance and technical qualifications, though education is not so hierarchically organized in either country as it is in France (Martinelli and Chiesi 1989). In Germany, top executives have been less highly educated than their counterparts in France. In her study of Wilhelmine business families, Augustine (1994: 51, 56) discovered that 45 per cent of the wealthiest businessmen of 1911 were the sons of big businessmen, and another 39 per cent were sons of those in smaller businesses. Of those for whom information was available, 107 attended university. This rate of university attendance was much higher than in Britain, and this national difference has persisted (Hall *et al.* 1969; see also Spohn and Boderman 1989). Family capitalists in the Netherlands during the 1980s show a lower educational level than do directors of non-family enterprises. Executive capitalists have especially high levels of education, being overwhelmingly economists and lawyers from top universities such as Amsterdam, Rotterdam, Leiden, Tilburg, and Utrecht, or engineers from Delft (Beckenkamp and Dronkers 1984). In both Spain and Italy, business is smaller in scale and family

---

[12] The term *pantouflage* is widely used in France to describe this practice. It literally means 'stepping into bedroom slippers' or 'putting one's feet up'.

Table 70. Social background of business leaders in Britain, the United States, and Japan (1952 and 1960)

Occupation of father	Britain (1952)	US (1952)	Japan (1960)
Professional and administrative	26	16	21.5
Executive, director, or owner of large business	32	31	22.0
Small business	19	18	21.5
Landlord or farmer	5	9	24.0
Other	18	26	11.0
Totals	100	100	100

Source: Mannari (1974: 61, Table 1.5). The British data derive from Copeman (1955) and the US data from Warner and Abegglen (1955).

enterprise has been correspondingly stronger, suggesting a lesser reliance on educational credentials (Gallino 1971: 101–3; Giner 1971: 151).[13]

Top executives in Japan have been highly educated but, as in France, have often been drawn from families with business connections. One-third of top executives in 1960 were the sons of entrepreneurial capitalists, just over 10 per cent were the sons of executives in large enterprises (most being the sons of bankers), and a further 17 per cent were the sons of landowners (Mannari 1974: 18, 20–1). Most of the entrepreneurs' sons were, in fact, heirs in the family business, but almost one-fifth of the executives' sons also worked for the same enterprise as their father had done. Table 70, while using data that may not be completely comparable, nevertheless suggests that, if 'openness' is measured by the degree of self-recruitment, there is a greater openness in Japanese board-rooms than in those of the United States and Britain. When recruitment from landed and industrial backgrounds are combined, however, Japanese board-rooms appear even more closed than those in Britain.[14] While the direct inheritance of positions is lower in Japan, the level of recruitment from among wealthy rentiers is higher. As in France, the wealthy had

---

[13] For fragmentary evidence on Canada and Australia see Porter (1965: 122, 246–7, 275–8), Clement (1975a: 192, 173–8), Smith and Tepperman (1974), and Encel (1970: 391–5).

[14] On land and industry in Germany see Koenig (1971: 284).

to ensure their entry to top business positions through the acquisition of a higher education. Specialist schools and universities provided 91 per cent of Japanese executives, one-third coming from Tokyo University and one-tenth each from Kyoto and Hitotsubashi. Just under half these executives had degrees in economics, while one-quarter were engineers and one-quarter had studied law or government (Mannari 1974: 65).

In terms of recruitment, then, education has played a greater role in all countries than in the past, though it has not had the particular significance ascribed to it by managerialist writers. It has, indeed, allowed some from non-capitalist class situations to enter the business world, though they have generally had to follow a privileged pattern of private schooling and attendance at the exclusive universities. It is these same educational channels that have buttressed the continuing participation of entrepreneurial and rentier capitalists in business and have allowed them to maximize their opportunities for entry to executive capitalist and finance-capitalist class situations. The circulation encouraged by educational systems, therefore, has ensured that mobility among the capitalist class situations has been both easy and frequent in all the advanced capitalist societies. It has been through this social circulation that the bases of large and cohesive capitalist social classes were built.

Integration and Class Formation

The capitalist class of liberal capitalism comprised families with direct personal possession of family enterprises. This system of 'family appropriation' (Grou 1983: 107) lasted in most capitalist societies until the First World War or, in some cases, into the inter-war years. In this system there was a close correspondence between family wealth and family enterprise, and business families were founding owners or inheriting owners. The transformation of private property in the joint stock company, and the emergence of indirect and impersonal forms of possession, have removed the direct and immediate linkage between personal-property owners and strategic control. Propertied households are now less likely to have the bulk of their property tied up in the majority ownership of a particular enterprise. To this extent, the theorists of industrial society have correctly pointed to a change in the basis of the capitalist class. I have shown in earlier chapters, however, that they have misunderstood the significance of these changes for the ownership and control of large enterprises, and it should not be surprising that they have also misunderstood their implications for class formation.

In the stage of organized capitalism, capitalist social classes were formed on a national basis. These national capitalist classes were large and cohesive collectivities organized around the ownership and control of private property in the business systems of national economies. Family enterprises were controlled through indirect personal possession, often by dynastic families, most of whose members were inheriting owners and were connected with rentier investors into an extensive, nationwide kinship system. In the stage of 'disorganized capitalism', national economies have become increasingly disarticulated and capitalist classes have altered accordingly. While their social identities continue to reflect their particular national cultures and their focus on particular nation states, their economic interests have become increasingly globalized. Capitalist families and capitalist enterprises alike are locked into globalized circuits of capital and investment that are no longer organized around distinctively national economies. As a result, some have suggested that national capitalist classes are themselves becoming progressively fragmented as class relations take on a more global form (Arrighi et al., 1989; van der Pijl 1984; 1989).

Berkowitz (1975) has shown that the rise of organized capitalism in the United States led to the formation of a nationally integrated capitalist class occurring in parallel with the changing structure of corporate control. In this process the growth and interweaving of economic relations was combined with the demographic integration of families and 'family compacts' into a nationwide structure of social relations. The foci of American mercantile capitalism from the seventeenth century to the 1820s were eastern-seaboard commercial centres such as Boston, Newburyport, New Haven, Philadelphia, Salem, and Providence. A patrician social class of mercantile families of Puritan descent dominated economic and civic affairs in each major town and city. Expansion in the scale of economic activity could be handled within a framework of family enterprise through co-operation among families. Mercantile families entered into joint business activities and partnerships in order to extend the capital base of their undertakings, and it was the combination of these business relations with relations of intermarriage and interaction that gave rise to the 'family compacts'. Family compacts were groups of loosely interconnected entrepreneurial families associated with particular enterprises in which kinship relations and capital mobilization reinforced one another.

After the revolution, these entrepreneurial capitalists expanded from commerce into insurance and banking, and their families began to enter the professions in great numbers. It was in this context that industrial development took place, and the system of liberal capitalism that emerged after 1820 consolidated the position of the patrician entrepreneurial classes and their family compacts. In Boston, for example, new entrepreneurs in cotton and in the railways merged with the old mercantile families, the city comprising a well-integrated system of interweaving shareholdings, directorships, and family firms (Jaher 1982; Farrell 1993). Similar developments took place in New York, whose trade completely overshadowed that of the other East-coast ports. New York became the principal money market for the whole of the United States, its investment banks, chartered banks, and stock exchange being central to industrial and railway development, as I have shown in Chapters 4 and 5.

The old patricians and the new entrepreneurs of finance and industry came to terms with one another under the aegis of the Morgans and the other powerful families of the 'Money Trust'. The New York financial system was also a means through which the family compacts and localized capitalist classes of New England were forged into tighter and more cohesive structures on a national basis. From the last third of the nineteenth century family enterprises in many industries, especially those in the South and the West, faced the problem of the succession from their first generation of founders to their second generation of heirs, and this occurred as their enterprises began to be merged into larger units by the New York financiers. Families became more dynastic, with wider circles of kin becoming involved in the control of the large family enterprises. The idea of the family became more important, its name constituting a 'symbolic estate' (Allen 1987: 102) that is inherited along with the material estate of family wealth. Such families stress the male lineage, and women frequently maintained their own name and identity after marriage—using their family name as a middle name—in order to emphasize the continuity of both family lines (see also Ostrander 1984).

Solidified family dynasties in which the 'family' and the 'firm' were structurally separated are the outcome of this process, and the economic basis for a national capitalist class emerged when external credit supplemented kinship as a source of capital. As a result, there is a partial dissociation of family fortunes from the profitability of specific family enterprises. Conversely, capital mobilization by enterprises no longer depends solely on the wealth of its directors (Berkowitz 1975: 208). An extensive kinship network was formed within which various dynastic 'cliques' can be identified around particular firms. Zeitlin has usefully characterized these dynastic families as 'kinecon groups':

The corporation is the legal unit of ownership of large-scale productive property. The set of interrelated kin who control the corporation through their combined ownership interests and strategic representation in management constitute the kinecon group. (Zeitlin *et al.* 1975: 110)

The development of organized capitalism, then, saw the emergence of a national capitalist class rooted in shared economic interests and a common schooling that provided the basis for geographical mobility among class situations. As Jaher argues:

Interrelationships expanded among Atlantic seaboard upper classes. The increased interaction centred in New York, the country's social and economic capital. The city's elites had cosmopolitan geographical roots and the children of its tycoons and aristocrats joined the younger generation of genteel Bostonians and Philadelphians at the same eastern boarding schools and Ivy League colleges. (Jaher 1982: 280)

In the South and West, in such cities as Chicago and Houston, newer, more brash industrialists had remained as somewhat distinct and localized capitalist classes of first generation entrepreneurs; but strong links to the eastern financial centres had been built by the early years of the twentieth century, and they became a fully integrated part of the national capitalist class (Marcus 1992).

Baltzell has shown that this national capitalist class formed an 'inter-city aristocracy' (1958; 1964), forged through status-exclusive patterns of circulation and interaction. The key institutions in its cohesion as a social class were the New England boarding-schools and universities such as Harvard, Yale, and Princeton, which socialized its members into the ways of the class and served as mechanisms of recruitment to large national enterprises. Education was regarded as a 'status investment' (Allen 1987: 248) that would sustain the privileges and advantages of family members. The capitalist class had become a nationally organized social class whose members were 'parts of interlocking social circles which perceive each other as equals, belong to the same clubs, interact frequently, and freely intermarry' (Domhoff 1974: 86; Mills 1956: 47, 62; Sweezy 1951).

With the inheritance of shareholdings in the dynastic kinecon groups, controlling blocks of shares became more dispersed among second and third generations of heirs who, in many cases, had little involvement in the affairs of the enterprises formed by their families. If family control was to persist, then the kinecon groups had to evolve new mechanisms for sustaining the link between a family and its enterprise. Complex legal forms were devised to integrate the dispersed ownership interests of family members. Trusts, foundations, family offices, and pyramidal structures of trusts and private companies functioned as 'surrogates' for direct personal possession, and lawyers and accountants were employed to manage the surrogate structures monitoring the relative holdings of the various branches of the family (Marcus 1992:15; Allen 1987: ch. 6). The surrogate structures not only solidified family control, they also allowed families to begin to detach themselves from dependence on a particular enterprise. Co-ordination of family shareholdings allowed minority control to be held by families whose individual members could reduce their holdings and invest in the released funds in a wider range of enterprises. Families diversified their interests and became, in greater numbers, rentier rather than entrepreneurial capitalists. By the 1930s the diversification of family wealth in the United States was well-advanced, and the corporate rich had become the owners of extensive investment portfolios (Goldsmith and Parmelee 1940: 115 ff.).

Family wealth showed a greater tendency to diversification as personal shareholdings in large enterprises became more dispersed with the development of impersonal possession. Wealthy families spread their investments on a system-wide basis: 'Family A does not own Company X while Family B owns Company Y, as it may have been in the past; instead, Family A and Family B both have large stockholdings in Companies X and Y, as does Family C, which used to be the sole owner of Company Z' (Domhoff 1967: 40; Bertaux 1977: 78). For many dynastic families the period after 1950 saw the transfer of shareholdings from the third generation to a fourth generation, and there was a massive increase in the numbers of those who derived an income from the enterprises founded by their great-grandparents. As a result, the average size of each individual holding within the family group fell, and disputes over income between different branches of the same family became more common. In these circumstances the surrogate structures come under such strain that the problem of co-ordinating the family holdings as a single block become insuperable. The dynastic families dissipate into myriad rentier families (Allen 1987: 100–7). Diversification of family investments and impersonal possession together result in a 'depersonalization' of property in large enterprises (Birnbaum 1969: 12) that underpins what Mills (1956: 147) termed the 'managerial reorganization of the propertied class':

The growth and interconnections of corporations . . . have meant the rise of a more sophisticated executive elite which now possesses a certain autonomy from any specific property interest. Its power is the power of property, but that property is not always or even usually of one coherent and narrow type. It is, in operating fact, class-wide property. (ibid.: 122; Domhoff 1967: 40)

This restructuring does not alter the basic features of the system, as the participants in corporate control constitute 'the most active and influential part of the propertied class' (Baran and Sweezy 1966; Sweezy 1951). Indeed, those who own company shares constitute a 'pool' from which directors and executives are recruited. Corporate managers and large personal shareholders are linked through the easy and typical circulation of individuals (Florence 1961: 93, 137; 1953: 200; Klein et al. 1956).

The most forceful statement of the thesis of the managerial reorganization of the propertied class is that of Zeitlin, who argues that capitalists participate as members of a single social class in the control of class-wide property:

Although the largest banks and corporations might conceivably develop a relative autonomy from particular proprietary interests, they would be limited by the general proprietary interests of the principal owners of capital. To the extent that the largest banks and corporations constitute a new form of class property . . . the 'inner group' . . . of interlocking officers and directors, and particularly the finance capitalists, become the leading organizers of this class-wide property. (Zeitlin 1976: 901)

This managerial reorganization of the capitalist class has occurred alongside a globalization of the economy that has strengthened the international interests of its members while weakening their national attachments. Growing international links 'disorganize' the capitalist class as a distinctively national one.

This process is, however, at a very early stage in the United States, and the pattern of social background described by Baltzell (1958: 7) has remained as an important source of national cohesion for the capitalist class. Research by Useem (1984: 68) found that about one in six multiple directors in the top 212 American enterprises of 1976 had attended exclusive boarding schools and that one in five were listed in the *Social Register*, the crucial indicator of social exclusivity. In their study of the top 250 enterprises of the same year, Bearden and Mintz (1987; see also Johnsen and Mintz 1989) found that those directors who predominated in the nationwide intercorporate network tended to be members of exclusive social clubs and to participate in policy-planning groups. Those who sat on the same board tended to be members of the same clubs, suggesting that clubs were important mechanisms of board recruitment. At the same time, however, the class was losing much of its specifically patrician or aristocratic character. In the new and expanding cities of Los Angeles, Dallas, and Houston, business leaders were far less patrician in character, and since the Second World War these cities have increased their financial power as that of New York has declined (Mintz 1989: 217–18). In these cities, associated with partially distinct regional business networks, exclusive social clubs were less important as foci of recruitment than they were for the more cosmopolitan New York-based network (Bearden and Mintz 1987).

Useem has particularly emphasized the part played in social class integration by members of the inner circle, the multiple directors who occupy key positions in the intercorporate network and whose connections generate a high degree of cohesion within the core of the class (Useem 1984: 61–2; see also Ratcliff 1987). On a number of measures, the inner circle were found to be drawn from a more exclusive social background than were those with a directorship in just one major enterprise: they were more likely to have attended a private school, more likely to be members of big-city clubs, and more likely to be mentioned in the Social Register (Useem 1984: 65, 68, 69; Soref 1976: 360).

Pluralist writers in the United States have claimed that business leaders form a loose coalition of sub-groupings with divergent interests, and that they exercise little influence over matters other than economic affairs (Rose 1967: 102–3; Presthus 1973). Against this position, however, it has been shown conclusively that the United States, like Britain, still has a strong business establishment. In a critical review, Burch (1983) concluded that a business establishment had emerged by the 1940s and that it became a major force in policy-making through its participation in advisory bodies such as the Business Round Table, the Business Council, the Council on Foreign

Relations, and the Tri-lateral Commission, and through donations to presidential and party campaigns (Burch 1983; Useem 1984: 73, 87; Domhoff 1975; Freitag 1975; Mintz 1975).

In Britain, dynastic business families were long characteristic of the City of London enterprises, but the rise of organized capitalism saw their emergence throughout the economy as central elements in a nationwide capitalist social class (Scott and Griff 1984: ch. 4; Allen 1982). Studies of class cohesion in Britain have shown that the integration and cohesion of this class was strengthened by the informality and frequency of interaction and by the similarity of attitudes and opinions that result from a common educational background. Directors of the major City financial institutions have particularly close kinship links with one another, and have interacted freely and easily in clubs and on the grouse moors as well as in board-rooms and on committees (Lupton and Wilson 1959; Whitley 1973; 1974; see also Stanworth and Giddens 1974a: 99 ff.; Rex 1974b; Thomas 1979; Lisle-Williams 1984). A common background and pattern of socialization, reinforced through intermarriage, residential propinquity, and other forms of interpersonal interaction, generated a community of feeling among the core members of the British capitalist class (Scott 1982b: 159–60; 1991b: ch. 5). Useem (1984) found that members of the inner circle were especially likely to be members of exclusive clubs and to hold a title. While 8.9 per cent of those with one directorship in 196 large enterprises of 1976 were members of one of the exclusive London clubs, 31.8 per cent of those with three or more directorships were members of these same clubs. Similarly, 3.6 per cent of those with one directorship had a title (a knighthood, baronetcy, or peerage), while 17.5 per cent of those with three or more directorships were titled (Useem 1984: 65, 69).[15]

These features defined the informality that characterized the City in its relation to big business up to and through the stage of organized capitalism. In the City, business leaders were oriented to one another in terms of their reputation within a face-to-face interactional status system in which maintenance of one's 'name' was all-

[15] Biographical measures of this kind are complicated by the fact that not all directors are listed in reference books. It is therefore possible to base estimates on either the proportion of those listed or the proportion of those in the data-set. Useem (1984: 65, 209) is inconsistent on which is likely to be closest to the actual figure, but it seems clear that what he calls the 'B' estimate (based on the proportion of those in the data-set) is the preferable figure. This is confirmed by a statement in Useem and McCormack (1981: 389).

important. City practices were largely unregulated by formal mechanisms as the informal mechanisms—rooted in traditional status and exclusivity—were so effective. With the growing scale of economic activity and its increasing globalization, this system became unviable. Traditional status ideals could no longer regulate its economic practices, and more aggressive moneymaking activities proliferated. The demise of traditional, informal regulation in the stage of disorganized capitalism is one important source of the growth in fraudulent and illegal activities that have led to an increase in formal regulation. The predominant trend in the City, however, has been the thorough deregulation of its markets and their operations, leaving the core elements of the capitalist social class less cohesive and well-integrated than before.

In Britain, the core of the capitalist class has formed an 'establishment', a dominant status group. The British establishment emerged during the last third of the nineteenth century as the newly powerful industrialists began to fuse with the already powerful financial and landed classes. A national capitalist class was forged in a cultural context in which traditional values were adapted to legitimate the new forms of corporate power (Abercrombie *et al.*, 1980: ch. 4). These values defined the status symbols of the establishment, the gentlemen of property who monopolized the major political positions and the key posts in the military, the Church, and the law (Scott 1982*b*: 104 ff.; 1991*b*: ch. 5). The inner circle of business leaders have consistently been drawn from this establishment, and they and their sons have been able to transfer from business to politics and the professions with ease. Since the Second World War, however, the establishment has crumbled as a political force and its status distinctiveness has lately declined (Finer 1956; Guttsman 1963; 1974; Johnson 1973; Miliband 1969).

The Japanese *zaibatsu* families had many similar characteristics to the dynastic kinecon groups (Yasuoka 1977: 84–5), and large-scale family-controlled businesses continue to have some of these features. The research of Hamabata (1990) has shown the critical nature of the collective or corporate character of the traditional family household. The continuity of the family household and its name is all-important, not merely the abstract rights, or the lack of them, that are possessed by particular family members. As Marcus showed for the United States, surrogate structures for personal possession are central to maintaining this unity. The 'lineage' is socially constructed so as to bring together real and fictive kin in a single extended family household that can provide the resources required for the family business and maintain its link with 'the family'. Hamabata has highlighted the central role of women in this process. While formal links within the business group are made and sustained by male members of the family, informal communal links among family members are sustained by its female members. Links through a woman's family of birth—despite the formal patrilineal character of business—were important elements in the whole structure of intercorporate relations through which family and business were connected.

Yanaga (1968) has argued that, as in the United States, Japanese business leaders influence state policy through their membership in various overlapping *batsu*. These 'cliques' or 'circles' reflect the high concentration of business influence, and the business cliques (*zaikai*) centred on the employers' association and chamber of commerce have ensured that the Liberal Democratic Party has been, in effect, the political arm of organized business. This is reinforced by the practice of '*amakudari*'—literally 'descent from heaven', a process whereby civil servants from various ministries in the state are able to take on business directorships when they retire. Many *amakudari* directors become powerful executives in the *kigyoshudan*. Charkham (1994: 96) traced 248 cases of such movement to top enterprises in 1992: 72 civil servants joined banks, 63 joined other financials, 50 joined major industrials, and others joined business agencies and organizations that comprise the *zaikai*. In the *zaikai*, argues Yanaga, business interests are discussed and negotiated in order to form a unified general viewpoint which can be conveyed to the government and other bodies as the consensus of the business community. As in Britain and the United States, the inner circle of Japanese business leaders constitutes the political leading edge of the capitalist class.

Clement has presented a similar picture of the Canadian capitalist class, pointing to the 'elite forums' that have provided exclusive locales for the interaction of those in capitalist class situations (1975a: 255 ff; see also Brym 1985a and 1989). He recognizes, however, that the division between the internationally oriented capitalists and those with purely domestic interests is an important source of segmentation (Clement 1975b; Marchak 1979), though I showed in Chapter 5 that the two sectors have close economic links with one another. A more important division in Canada, and one with implications for the degree of capitalist class cohesion, is that between Anglophones and Francophones. While the dominant status-group within the capitalist class is based in Toronto and Montreal and operates nationwide, the French Canadian businesses of Quebec operate on a somewhat smaller scale and recruit from within their own community (Niosi 1981). Evidence for other countries is more limited, but data from France (Bleton 1966, 134, 144; Landes 1951) and from Sweden (Commission on Concentration 1968, 37, 48; Therborn 1976) suggest that economies in which family enterprise is strongest show the persistence of dynastic kinecon groups. Business families in France, for example, comprised a cohesive '*patronat*' based around their common educational and familial background (Birnbaum *et al.* 1978; Marceau 1989*a*). In such circumstances, cultural assets and educational credentials have become especially important elements in class reproduction.

Van Hezewijk (1986) has looked at the participation of multiple directors in top business organizations in the Netherlands and at their club memberships, showing clear evidence for the existence of a business establishment. The Wilhelmine business establishment in Germany was tied together through strong bonds of intermarriage along regional and national lines, though it remained sharply separated from the landed aristocracy (Augustine 1994: 80). Many in the German establishment at this time were multiple directors, often with a primary base in a bank. Of the top 502 businessmen, 219 were active in one or more of the top 200 enterprises of 1913,[16] 101 being active in more than one enterprise and 22 being involved with five or more enterprises. The survival of many of these entrepreneurial, rentier, and finance capitalist families in Germany has occurred within a framework that is increasingly shaped by those in executive situations in banks and large industrial enterprises (Spohn and Bodemann 1989). Windolf and Beyer's work (1994: 21) broadens this picture, showing that the two top German business organizations of the 1990s, the BDI and the BDA, recruit their leadership principally from multiple directors in top enterprises.

The countries that are most difficult to assess from the standpoint of their class relations are the post-Communist societies and mainland China. The emergent class situations in the post-Communist societies reflect the simultaneous development of both direct and indirect personal possession, while forms of impersonal possession are barely beginning to be built. Alongside émigré groups and small-scale entrepreneurs, the principal class situations are those that

[16] Augustine's data actually relate to the 502 wealthiest people of 1911 and their involvement with the top 200 enterprises of 1913 or the top 100 industrials of 1907.

might be termed the 'nomenklatura capitalists' and the 'racketeer capitalists', both of which are involved, to a greater or lesser extent, in the illegal and shady activities that are encouraged by the ways that the system of corporate collusions operates (Róna-Tas 1994). Processes of social-class formation are remarkably weak, and there is little evidence yet that the kind of demographic relations that would make it possible to talk of a single social class have been established in any of the post-Communist societies (Kovacs and Maggord 1993).There are, at most, fractional social classes formed around the various distinct class situations.

In the overseas Chinese communities of east Asia, entrepreneurial capitalist situations predominate and the reproduction of social classes is still quite directly linked to the mechanisms of capital reproduction. The situation in mainland China, however, is rather different and its future is uncertain. The principal class situations include those of the new entrepreneurs, the party and state officials and expatriate 'red capitalists' (Sklair 1995a: 227 ff; see also Nee 1996, 1989).The state and party officials have some similarity with the post-Communist nomenklatura, though they still form part of a centralized command-system. These officials are involved in commercialized state activities that further their personal income and wealth, and they are major participants in 'corrupt' or semi-legitimate activities that arise from their monopoly of raw materials and other resources (Oberschall 1996: 1033). The expatriate red capitalists are the bankers, brokers, and merchants who live overseas as representatives of the Chinese state and private enterprises, and who are central to China's growing sector of transnational economic practices. The entrepreneurial capitalists of the mainland operate mainly through small family enterprises, though some large enterprises are emerging because of links with their overseas Chinese kin in Hong Kong, Singapore, Taiwan, and elsewhere (Chossudovsky 1986). As the drive towards capitalist industrialism has involved the intrusion of a significant amount of foreign capital, there is a possibility that entrepreneurial and other capitalist class situations in China may be tied to external interests in a 'comprador' structure. Sklair (1995a: 233–4) has shown that the three capitalist class situations in China are linked through kinship and joint business ventures—along 'traditional' Chinese lines—but that they are not yet formed into a single capitalist social class.

I have shown that capitalist social classes are shaped by demographic processes of circulation and integration that establish forms of social closure. These demographic relations, where they have formed, have reinforced commercial, capital, and personal relations of economic interaction among capitalist enterprises. In entrepreneurial and rentier capitalist households there has been a fusion of economic and familial concerns through the controls that have been exercised over inheritance. Marriage strategies, therefore, have been one of the most important mechanisms of class reproduction. The choice of a marriage partner is a strategy, intended or unintended, for ensuring the maintenance and accumulation of privilege. Marriage patterns reinforce the mechanisms of schooling, friendship, visiting, and commensality as well as the more organized unity fostered by membership of clubs and associations. These mechanisms ensure a similarity of background and attitudes and allow the formation of a social class whose members possess not merely equivalent life chances, but also a similarity of life style (Domhoff 1967: 3–4; 1971: 21–6, 77, 84; Tawney 1931: 53). Kinship and personal possession entwine to form a cohesive social class that stands at the head of a status hierarchy.

The transformation of property ownership breaks the direct link between kinship and control. Executive capitalists and finance capitalists cannot rely on personal possession, and so must ensure their recruitment to directorships and executive positions through alternative mechanisms. In particular, they have relied on access to educational credentials. Bourdieu and his colleagues have described this as a transition from a 'personal' mode of class domination, appropriate to the stage of liberal capitalism, to a 'structural' mode of domination that corresponds more closely to the requirements of impersonal possession. In these circumstances, executive and finance capitalists are less likely to define themselves as members of a specifically 'capitalist' class that—like managerialists—they see as a class of personal possessors, of entrepreneurial capitalists. Instead, they tend to define themselves as 'middle-class', drawing on the social imagery of those in service-class situations with whom they share their career orientation. Impersonal possession and the managerial reorganization of the capitalist class, then, has meant that capitalist social classes, to the extent that they are formed, are less likely to exhibit a shared class awareness, let alone a common class consciousness.

This does not mean, however, that they are unaware of their particular class interests or of how they differ from those in other class situations. When the selection and promotion of business leaders depend on educational credentials, the reproduction of a capitalist class comes to depend on its success in monopolizing the benefits that can be derived from the educational system. By ensuring that their sons and daughters are well-educated, members of capitalist households can ensure that they are well-placed at the start of the contest for corporate positions. In this way, they can offset the declining possibilities for the direct inheritance of positions of business leadership. If established families can monopolize access to the educational system, they can also ensure that those who are most qualified for controlling positions in the corporate system are none other than their own sons and daughters. Personal wealth—whether derived from salaries, dividends, or interest payments—allows the purchase of a privileged education and so allows wealthy families to 'convert' their economic assets into the cultural assets of educational certificates and accomplishments. These cultural assets become the means through which access to well-paid jobs in capitalist locations can be achieved, and so they can be 'reconverted' into further economic assets. Through such 'strategies of reconversion' wealthy families may reproduce and enhance their life-chances without having to transmit controlling blocks of corporate shares to the next generation (Bourdieu 1971: 73; Bourdieu and Passeron 1970). Where the personal mode of domination involved the 'direct transmission of social positions between the holder and the inheritor designated by the holder himself', the structural mode of domination operates in an indirect way at the level of the class as a whole. Transmission of capitalist class situations 'rests on the statistical aggregation of the isolated actions of individuals or collective agents who are subject to the same laws, those of the educational market' (Bourdieu et al. 1973: 83).[17]

This points to the need to recognize that the development of capitalism has led to a partial dissociation between mechanisms of capital reproduction and mechanisms of class reproduction. These mechanisms coincide in a system of direct personal possession, and there is an immediate and transparent relationship between control over capital and the life-chances of propertied families. There is no significant separation of the personal assets of households from the assets of businesses. In a system of indirect possession, on the other hand, there is a limited separation of the two mechanisms. This sep-

---

[17] Bourdieu and Boltanski (1978) seems to be a virtual translation of Bourdieu et al. (1973), though no indication of this fact is given.

aration is limited because individuals and families retain close links with enterprises that they control. Property-owners become more aware of the distinction between their stakes in a business and the wealth that this represents. In particular, they are drawn into using legal and financial devices (shares, trusts, and so on) through which the value of their wealth can be protected and passed on to succeeding generations, even if their involvement in running a business becomes even more attenuated. The entrepreneurial orientation towards the business, then, is tempered by a growing rentier orientation to their wealth.

In a system of impersonal possession, effective control rests with financial institutions and other corporate interests, and substantial property-holders diversify their investments on a system-wide basis. The limited separation of class reproduction from capital reproduction becomes an extended separation. The life-chances of wealthy individuals and families depend upon system-wide—and increasingly globalized—portfolios, but positions of corporate rule are filled through 'structural' rather than through personal mechanisms. Executive and finance capitalists occupy command situations that no longer flow directly from their ownership of controlling holdings. Personal wealth allows the purchase of education, and it ensures that a greater benefit is derived from education; and it is education and the social connections that it brings that are the key to a business career for executive and finance capitalists. The connection between property and privilege allows the connection between capital and class to be sustained, despite the extended separation that exists between the mechanisms responsible for them.

In many European countries there has been a growth in international integration through the establishment of international business schools. INSEAD, for example, opened in 1959 as the first business school in Europe and specifically aimed to create the 'international' managers needed for European multinational enterprises. Its students have come mainly from France, Germany, and Britain, with significant numbers also coming from Switzerland, Belgium, and the Scandinavian countries. Between a quarter and one-third of the intake has come from entrepreneurial families, but particular importance has been in providing a channel for those from professional and managerial backgrounds to acquire the educational credentials that would allow them to pursue an international business career (Marceau 1989b: 36, 98). Although many graduates have been employed as subordinate—service-class—managers, INSEAD and similar institutions have undoubtedly fostered a stronger international outlook among corporate rulers and have weakened their attachments to 'national' enterprises.

Along with the trends towards globalization and disarticulation that were discussed in Chapter 8, this points to the fact that national capitalist classes themselves are being increasingly fragmented along the lines of the globalized circuits of capital and investment that they are involved in. This has led some to suggest that contemporary capitalism exhibits the formation of 'transnational capitalist classes' that become detached from purely national class situations and tend to merge at the global level into an increasingly cohesive social class (Sklair 1995a: 71; 1995b). While capitalists in the various nation states are, indeed, involved in transnational economic practices and are adopting an increasingly global outlook, it is unclear whether it is yet possible to talk of a transnational capitalist class at the global level. This would be the case only if there were transnational demographic relations that tied the occupants of different national class situations into a single social class. For this to occur, demographic relations of circulation and association *between* nation states would have to be at least as important as those *within* nation states. In these circumstances, the members of the transnational capitalist class would have a global solidarity and cohesion, and could no longer be described as 'British', 'American', or 'German', for example, except by virtue of their residence or legal citizenship. Despite the evidence of internationalized education at leading business schools, there is little sign that such a global process of social-class formation has proceeded very far. Contemporary capitalist societies are characterized by fragmenting capitalist classes, but not yet by an integrated global capitalist class.

A capitalist class of propertied families owing their superior life-chances to the income and wealth that is generated by their possession and use of property can still be found at the head of the stratification systems of contemporary industrial capitalism. Far from having their privileges usurped by upwardly mobile career managers, they remain a potent economic and political force. The emergence of impersonal possession has resulted merely in a managerial reorganization of the propertied class. Wealthy families have diversified their income-earning assets, and many now participate in strategic control on the basis of mechanisms other than direct inheritance of a place in the family firm. In the stage of disorganized capitalism, however, the members of this class have become involved in the more extensive transnational economic practices that are disarticulating their national economies. National capitalist classes have themselves become more fragmented and 'disorganized', and their futures may—though this is, as yet, unclear—involve the formation of a global capitalist class.

Bibliography

Where the date of an English-language edition or a reprint differs from the date of first publication, this date is shown after the publisher's name.

Aaronovitch, S. (1955), *Monopoly: A Study of British Monopoly Capitalism* (London: Lawrence and Wishart).

—— (1961), *The Ruling Class* (London: Lawrence and Wishart).

—— and Sawyer, M. C. (1975), *Big Business* (London: Macmillan).

Abercrombie, N., Turner, B., and Hill, S. (1980), *The Dominant Ideology Thesis* (London: George Allen and Unwin).

—— and Urry, J. (1983), *Capital, Labour, and the Middle Classes* (London: George Allen and Unwin).

Adams, T. F. M., and Hoshi, I. (1972), *A Financial History of the New Japan* (Tokyo: Kodansha International).

Aglietta, M. (1979), *A Theory of Capitalist Regulation: The US Experience* (London: New Left Books).

Aitken, H. G. J. (1959*a*), 'The Changing Structure of the Canadian Economy', in Aitken (1959*b*).

—— (1959*b*), *The American Impact on Canada* (Cambridge: Cambridge University Press).

Alchian, A. A. (1950), 'Uncertainty, Evolution and Economic Theory', *Journal of Political Economy*, 58.

—— and Demsetz, H. (1972), 'Production, Information Cost and Economic Organisation', *American Economic Review*, 62.

Alexander, M., and Murray, G. (1992), 'Interlocking Directorships in the Top 250 Australian Companies: Comment on Carroll, Stening and Stening', *Companies and Securities Law Journal*, 10.

—— —— and Houghton, J. (1994), 'Business Power in Australia: The Concentration of Company Directorship Holdings Among the Top 250 Corporates', *Australian Journal of Political Science*, 29.

Alford, R., and Friedland, R. (1985), *Powers of Theory: Capitalism, The State and Democracy* (Cambridge: Cambridge University Press).

Allan, G. (1982), 'Property and Family Solidarity', in Hollowell (ed.) (1982).

Allard, P., Beaud, M., Bellon, B., Lévy, A.-M., and Lienart, S. (1978), *Dictionnaire des groupes industriels et financiers en France* (Paris: Éditions du Seuil).

Allen, G. C. (1940), 'The concentration of economic control', in Livingston *et al.* (eds.) (1973*a*).

—— (1972), *A Short Economic History of Modern Japan* (3rd edn., London: George Allen and Unwin).

Allen, M. P. (1974), 'The Structure of Interorganizational Elite Cooptation', *American Sociological Review*, 39.

—— (1976), 'Management Control in the Large Corporation', *American Journal of Sociology*, 81/4.

—— (1978*a*), 'Economic Interest Groups and the Corporate Elite', *Social Science Quarterly*, 58.

—— (1978*b*), 'Continuity and Change Within the Core Corporate Elite', *Sociological Quarterly*, 19.

—— (1981), 'Power and Privilege in the Large Corporation: Corporate Control and Managerial Compensation', *American Journal of Sociology*, 86.

—— (1987), *The Founding Fortunes: A New Anatomy of the Super-Rich Families in America* (New York: E. P. Dutton).

Amin, S. (1971), *Accumulation on a World Scale* (New York: Monthly Review Press, 1974).

—— (1973), *Unequal Development* (Sussex: Harvester Press, 1976).

Andersen, S. S., Midttun, A., and Sarfi, E. (1989), *The Articulation of Capital-Interests in Norway: Embeddedness and the Organisation of Capital* (Sandvika: Norwegian School of Management).

Anderson, D., *et al.* (1941), *Final Report to the Temporary National Economic Committee on the Concentration of Economic Power in the United States* (Washington: Government Printing Office for the US Senate).

Anderson, P. (1964), 'Origins of the Present Crisis', *New Left Review*, 23.

Andrews, J. A. Y. (1982), *The Interlocking Corporate Director: A Case Study in Conceptual Confusion* (MA dissertation, University of Chicago).

Anker, L., Seybold, P., and Schwartz, M. (1987), 'The Ties that Bind Business and Government', in Schwartz (ed.) (1987).

Ansoff, H. I. (1965), *Corporate Strategy* (New York: McGraw-Hill).

Antitrust Committee (1965), *Interlocks in Corporate Management* (Antitrust Subcommittee of the Committee on the Judiciary, House of Representatives, 89th Congress, 1st session, Washington: Government Printing Office).

Antoniou, A., and Rowley, R. (1986), 'The Ownership Structure of the Largest Canadian Corporations, 1979', *Canadian Journal of Sociology*, 11.

Aoki, M., and Dore, R. (eds.), (1994), *The Japanese Firm: The Sources of Competitive Strength* (Oxford: Oxford University Press).

Appelbaum, R. P and Henderson, J. (eds.) (1992), *States and Development in the Asian Pacific Region* (Beverly Hills, Sage).

Archer, M. S., and Giner, S. (eds.) (1971), *Contemporary Europe: Class, Status, and Power* (London: Routledge and Kegan Paul).

Armstrong, P. (1984), 'Management Control Strategies and Interprofessional Competition', Paper to UMIST-Aston Conference on the Labour Process, March.

Aron, R. (1960), 'Classe sociale, classe politique, classe dirigeante', *European Journal of Sociology*, 1.

—— (1967), *The Industrial Society* (London: Weidenfeld and Nicolson).

—— (1968), *Progress and Disillusion* (Harmondsworth: Penguin, 1972).

Arrighi, G., Hopkins, T., and Wallerstein, I. (1989), *Antisystemic Movements* (London: Verso).

Atkinson, A. B. (1972), *Unequal Shares* (Harmondsworth: Penguin, 1974).

—— (1973*a*), 'The Distribution of Income in Britain and the US', in Atkinson (ed.) (1973*b*).

—— (ed.) (1973*b*), *Wealth, Income and Inequality* (Harmondsworth: Penguin).

—— (1983), *The Economics of Inequality* (2nd edn., Oxford: Oxford University Press).

Augustine, D. L. (1994), *Patricians and Parvenus: Wealth and High Society in Wilhelmine Germany* (Oxford: Berg).

Babeau, A., and Strauss-Kahn, D. (1977), *La richesse des français* (Paris: Presses Universitaires de France).

Bachrach, P., and Baratz, M. S., (1962*a*), 'Two Faces of Power', *American Political Science Review*, 56; reprinted in Scott (1994*a*).

—— —— (1962*b*), 'Decisions and Nondecisions: An Analytical Framework', *American Political Science Review*, 57; reprinted in Scott (1994*a*).

Bacon, J., and Brown, J. K. (1977), *The Board of Directors: Perspectives and Practices in Nine Countries* (New York: The Conference Board).

Baker, W. (1984), 'The Social Structure of a National Securities Market', *American Journal of Sociology*, 89.

Baldamus, W. (1961), *Efficiency and Effort* (London: Tavistock).

Baltzell, E. D. (1958), *Philadelphia Gentlemen* (Glencoe, Ill.: Free Press).

—— (1964), *The Protestant Establishment: Aristocracy and Caste in America* (New York: Random House).

Bank of England (1979), 'Composition of Company Boards', *Bank of England Quarterly Review*, 14.

Banks, J. A. (1959), 'Veblen and Industrial Sociology', *British Journal of Sociology*, 10.

Baran, P. A. (1957), *The Political Economy of Growth* (Harmondsworth: Penguin).

—— and Sweezy, P. M. (1966), *Monopoly Capital* (Harmondsworth: Penguin, 1968).

Barratt Brown, M. (1968a), 'The Controllers of British Industry', in Coates (ed.) (1968).

—— (1968b), 'The Limits of the Welfare State', in Coates (ed.) (1968).

—— (1974), *The Economics of Imperialism* (Harmondsworth: Penguin).

Barry, B. (ed.) (1976), *Power and Political Theory* (London: Wiley).

Bauer, M., and Bertin-Mourot, B. (1987), *Les 200: Comment devient-on un grand patron?* (Paris: Éditions du Seuil).

—— —— (1991), *Les 200 en France et en Allemagne* (Paris: CNRS/ Heidrick and Struggles).

—— —— (1994), *L'ENA: Est-elle une Business School?* (Paris: CNRS/ Boyden).

—— —— and Thobois, P. (1995), *Les No. 1 des 200 plus grandes enterprises en France et en Grande-Bretagne* (Paris: CNRS/Boyden).

Baum, D. J., and Stiles, N. B. (1965), *The Silent Partners: Institutional Investors and Corporate Control* (Syracuse, NY: Syracuse University Press).

Baumol, W. J. (1959), *Business Behaviour* (New York: Macmillan).

—— (1962), 'On the Theory of Expansion of the Firm', *American Economic Review*, 52.

Baums, T. (1993a), 'Bank and Corporate Control in Germany', in McCahery et al. (eds.) (1993).

—— (1993b), 'Takeovers Versus Institutions in Corporate Governance in Germany', in Prentice and Holland (eds.) (1993).

Bearden, J. (1987), 'Financial Hegemony, Social Capital and Bank Boards of Directors', in Schwartz (ed.) (1987).

—— Atwood, W., Freitag, P., Hendricks, C., Mintz, B., and Schwartz, M. (1975), 'The Nature and Extent of Bank Centrality in Corporate Networks', paper to the American Sociological Association.

—— and Mintz, B. (1985), 'Regionality and Integration in the United States Interlock Network', in Stokman et al. (eds.) (1985).

—— —— (1987), 'The Structure of Class Cohesion: The Corporate Network and its Dual', in Mizruchi and Schwartz (eds.) (1987).

Bechhofer, F., Elliott, B., and McCrone, D. (1978), 'Structure, Consciousness and Action: A Sociological Profile of the British Middle Class', *British Journal of Sociology*, 29.

Beckenkamp, G. G., and Dronkers, J. (1984), 'Rotterdam, Delft, Leiden: De plaats van het onderwijs in de rekrutering van president-directeuren', in Dronkers and Stokman (eds.) (1984).

Becker, G. S. (1962), 'Irrational Behaviour and Economic Theory', *Journal of Political Economy*, 70.

Becker, L. C. (1977), *Property Rights* (London: Routledge and Kegan Paul).

Beed, C. S. (1966), 'The Separation of Ownership from Control', *Journal of Economic Studies*, 1.

Befu, H. (1971), *Japan: An Anthropological Introduction* (New York: Harper and Row).

Bell, D. (1957), 'The Breakup of Family Capitalism', in Bell (1961).

—— (1958), 'Is There a Ruling Class in America?', in Bell (1961).

—— (1961), *The End of Ideology* (New York: Collier-Macmillan).

—— (1973), *The Coming of Post-Industrial Society* (New York: Basic Books).

Bello, W., and Rosenfeld, S. (1990), *Dragons in Distress* (Harmondsworth, Penguin, 1992).

Bellon, B. (1977), 'Methodologie de delimitation et de reportage des ensembles financiers' (Working Paper, CERCA, Paris).

Bendix, R. (1956), *Work and Authority in Industry* (New York: Wiley).

—— and Lipset, S. M. (eds.) (1953), *Class, Status and Power* (Glencoe, Ill.: Free Press).

—— —— (eds.) (1967), *Class, Status and Power* (rev. edn., London: Routledge and Kegan Paul).

Beresford, P. (ed.) (1990), *The Sunday Times Book of the Rich* (London: Weidenfeld and Nicolson).

Berg, M. (1994), *The Age of the Manufacturers* (London: Routledge).

Berger, S. (ed.) (1981), *Organizing Interests in Western Europe* (Cambridge: Cambridge University Press).

Berkowitz, S. D. (1975), 'The Dynamics of Elite Structure' (Ph.D. thesis, Brandeis University).

—— (1982), *An Introduction to Structural Analysis* (Toronto: Butterworths).

Berle, A. A. (1955), *The Twentieth Century Capitalist Revolution* (London: Macmillan).

—— (1960), *Power Without Property* (New York: Harcourt Brace).

—— (1963), *The American Economic Republic* (London: Sidgwick and Jackson).

—— and Means, G. C. (1932), *The Modern Corporation and Private Property* (New York: Macmillan, 1947).

Bertaux, D. (1977), *Destins personnels et structure de classe* (Paris: Presses Universitaires de France).

Bettelheim, C. (1968), *The Transition to Socialist Economy* (Hassocks, Harvester Press, 1975).

—— (1970), *Economic Calculation and Forms of Property* (London: Routledge and Kegan Paul, 1976).

Bieda, K. (1970), *The Structure and Operation of the Japanese Economy* (Sydney: John Wiley).

Biehler, H. (1986), 'Die Kapitalverflechtung zwischen den größten Deutschen unternehmen des jahres 1981', *Soziale Welt*, 37.

Birnbaum, N. (1969), *The Crisis of Industrial Society* (Oxford: Oxford University Press).

Birnbaum, P. (1971), *La Structure du pouvoir aux États-Unis* (Paris: Presses Universitaires de France).

—— (1980), 'The State in Contemporary France', in Scase (ed.) (1980).

—— Barucq, C., Bellaiche, M., and Marie, A. (1978), *La Classe dirigeante française* (Paris: Presses Universitaires de France).

Blackburn, R. (1967), 'The Unequal Society', in Blackburn and Cockburn (eds.) (1967).

—— and Cockburn, A. (eds.) (1967), *The Incompatibles* (Harmondsworth: Penguin).

Blank, S. (1973), *Industry and Government in Britain* (Farnborough: Saxon House).

Bleton, P. (1966), *Le Capitalisme français* (Paris: Éditions Ouvrières).

—— (1974), 'L'Argent: pouvoir ambigu', *Economie et Humanisme*, 220.

—— (1976a), 'Le Capitalisme français à l'ombre de l'université', *Economie et Humanisme*, 229.

—— (1976b), 'Bons concepts et méchantes réalités', *Economie et Humanisme*, 229.

Blum, U., and Siegmund, J. (1993), 'Politics and Economics of Privatizing State Enterprises', in Derlien and Szablowski (eds.) (1993).

Blumberg, P. I. (1975), *The Megacorporation in American Society* (Englewood Cliffs, NJ: Prentice-Hall).

—— (1993), 'The American Law of Corporate Groups', in McCahery *et al.* (eds.) (1993).

Booth, A. (1982), 'Corporatism, Capitalism, and Depression in Twentieth Century Britain', *British Journal of Sociology*, 33.

Bottomore, T. B. (1965), *Classes in Modern Society* (London: George Allen and Unwin).

—— and Brym, R. J. (eds.) (1989), *The Capitalist Class: An International Study* (Hemel Hempstead: Harvester Wheatsheaf).

Bourdieu, P. (1971), 'Cultural Reproduction and Social Reproduction', in Brown (ed.) (1973).

—— (1974), 'Avenir de classe et causalité du probable', *Révue française de sociologie*, 15.

—— and Boltanski, L. (1978), 'Changes in Social Structure and Changes in the Demand for Education', in Giner and Archer (eds.) (1978).

—— and de St Martin, M. (1978), 'Le Patronat', *Actes de la Recherche en Sciences Sociales*, 20–1.

—— and Passeron, J. C. (1970), *Reproduction in Education: Society and Culture* (London: Sage, 1977).

—— *et al.* (1973), 'Les Strategies de reconversion: Les Classes sociales et le systeme d'enseignement', *Social Science Information*, 12.

Boyd, D. (1973), *Elites and their Education* (Windsor: NFER).

Bradley, C. (1993), 'Contracts, Trusts and Companies', in McCahery *et al.* (eds.) (1993).

Brandeis, L. D. (1914), *Other People's Money and How the Bankers Use It* (New York: Harper and Row, 1967).

Brash, D. T. (1970), 'Australia as Host to the International Corporation', in Kindleberger (ed.) (1970).

Braverman, H. (1974), *Labor and Monopoly Capital* (New York: Monthly Review Press).

Briston, R. J., and Dobbins, R. (1978), *The Growth and Impact of Institutional Investors* (London: Institute of Chartered Accountants).

Broadbridge, S. (1966), *Industrial Dualism in Japan* (London: Frank Cass).

Brooke, M. Z., and Remmers, A. L. (1970), *The Strategy of Multinational Enterprise* (London: Longman).

—— —— (1972), *The Multinational Corporation in Europe* (London: Longman).

Brown, G. (ed.) (1975), *The Red Paper on Scotland* (Edinburgh: Edinburgh University Student Publications Board).

Brown, P., and Crompton, R. (eds.) (1994), *Economic Restructuring and Social Exclusion* (London: UCL Press).

Brown, R. (ed.) (1973), *Knowledge, Education and Cultural Change* (London: Tavistock).

Brummer, A. (1994), 'The Other Side of the Coin', *The Guardian* (29 April).

Brym, R. J. (1985a), 'The Canadian Capitalist Class, 1965–85', in Brym (ed.) (1985b).

—— (ed.) (1985b), *The Structure of the Canadian Capitalist Class* (Toronto: Garamond Press).

—— (1989), 'Canada', in Bottomore and Brym (1989).

Bukharin, N. (1918), *Imperialism and World Economy* (London: Merlin Press, 1972).

—— and Preobrazhensky, E. (1920), *The ABC of Communism* (Harmondsworth: Penguin, 1962).

Bunting, D. (1974), *Statistical View of the Trusts* (Westport: Greenwood Press).

—— (1976), 'Corporate Interlocks', 1–4, *Directors and Boards*, 1.

—— (1983), 'Origins of the American Corporate Network', *Social Science History*, 7.

—— (1986), *The Rise of Large American Corporations, 1889–1919* (New York: Garland Publishing).

—— and Barbour, J. (1971), 'Interlocking Directorates in Large American Corporations, 1896–1964', *Business History Review*, 45.

Burawoy, M., and Krotov, P. (1992), 'The Soviet Transition from Socialism to Capitalism', *American Sociological Review*, 57.

Burch, P. H. (1972), *The Managerial Revolution Reassessed* (Massachusetts: Lexington Books).

—— (1983), 'The American Establishment: Its Historical Development and Major Economic Components', *Research in Political Economy*, 6.

Burcke, C. G. (1976), 'A Group Profile of the Fortune 500 Chief Executives', *Fortune*, 93.

Burnham, J. (1941), *The Managerial Revolution* (Harmondsworth: Penguin, 1945).

Burt, R. (1980), 'Corporate Profits and Cooptation: A Network Analysis of Market Constraints and Directorate Ties in the 1967 American Economy' (Working Paper, Survey Research Center: Department of Sociology, University of California at Berkeley).

Butler, D., and Sloman, A. (1979), *British Political Facts 1900–79* (London: Macmillan).

Cadbury, Sir A. (1992), *Report of the Committee on the Financial Aspects of Corporate Governance* (London: Gee).

Cafagna, L. (1971), 'Italy, 1830–1914', in Cipolla (ed.) (1973b).

Cairncross, A. K. (1953), *Home and Foreign Investment* (Cambridge: Cambridge University Press).

Carchedi, G. (1975), 'On the Economic Identification of the New Middle Class', *Economy and Society*, 4.

—— (1983), *Problems in Class Analysis* (London: Routledge and Kegan Paul).

Carosso, V. P. (1970), *Investment Banking in America* (Cambridge, Mass.: Harvard University Press).

Carré, B. (1978), *Le Pouvoir de l'élite familiale* (Paris: Presses Universitaires de France).

Carrington, J. C., and Edwards, G. T. (1979), *Financing Industrial Investment* (London: Macmillan).

Carrington, P. J. (1981), 'Anticompetitive Effects of Directorship Interlocks', Research Paper no. 27, Structural Analysis Programme, University of Toronto.

Carroll, R., Stening, B., and Stening, K. (1990), 'Interlocking Directorships and the Law in Australia', *Company and Securities Law Journal*.

Carroll, W. K (1982), 'The Canadian Corporate Elite: Financiers or Finance Capitalists', *Studies in Political Economy*, 8.

—— (1985), 'Dependency, Imperialism and the Capitalist Class in Canada', in Brym (ed.) (1985b).

—— (1986), *Corporate Power and Canadian Capitalism* (Vancouver: University of British Columbia Press).

Carroll, W. K (1989), 'Neoliberalism and the Restructuring of Canadian Finance Capitalism', *Capital and Class*, 38.

—— and Lewis, S. (1991), 'Restructuring Finance Capital: Changes in the Canadian Corporate Network, 1976–1986', *Sociology*, 25.

Castells, M. (1992), 'Four Asian Tigers with a Dragon Head', in Appelbaum and Henderson (eds.) (1992).

Causer, G (1978), 'Private Capital and the State in Western Europe', in Giner and Archer (eds.) (1978).

—— (1982), 'Some Aspects of Property Distribution and Class Structure', in Hollowell (ed.) (1982).

Caves, R. E., and Uekusa, M. (1976), *Industrial Organization in Japan* (Washington: Brookings Institution).

Cawson, A., and Saunders, P. (1983), 'Corporatism, Competitive Politics and Class Struggle', in King (ed.) (1983).

CDE (1980a), 'Banking and finance', *CDE Stock Ownership Directory*, 3 (New York: Corporate Data Exchange).

—— (1980b), *Banking and Finance: The Hidden Cost* (New York: Corporate Data Exchange).

—— (1981), *Fortune 500. CDE Stock Ownership Directory*, 5 (New York: Corporate Data Exchange).

Chamberlin, E. (1933), *The Theory of Monopolistic Competition* (Cambridge, Mass.: Harvard University Press).

Chandler, A. D. (1962), *Strategy and Structure* (Cambridge, Mass.: MIT Press).

—— (1969), 'The Structure of American Industry in the Twentieth Century: An Historical Overview', *Business History Review*, 43.

—— (1976), 'The Development of Modern Management Structure in the US and UK', in Hannah (1979).

—— (1977), *The Visible Hand* (Cambridge, Mass.: The Belknap Press of Harvard University Press).

—— (1990), *Scale and Scope* (Cambridge, Mass.: The Belknap Press of Harvard University Press).

—— and Daems, H. (1974), 'Introduction', in Daems and van der Wee (eds.) (1974).

—— —— (eds.) (1980), *Managerial Hierarchies* (Cambridge, Mass.: Harvard University Press).

Chandler, R. F. (1982), 'The Control and Accountability of New Zealand's Public Corporations', *New Zealand Journal of Business*, 4.

Channon, D. F. (1973), *The Strategy and Structure of British Enterprise* (London: Macmillan).

—— (1977), *British Banking Strategy and the International Challenge* (London: Macmillan).

Chapman, S. D. (1984), *The Rise of Merchant Banking* (London: Unwin Hyman).

Charkham, J. (1994), *Keeping Good Company: A Study Of Corporate Governance in Five Countries* (Oxford: Clarendon Press).

Chase-Dunn, C. (1989), *Global Formations* (Cambridge, Mass.: Blackwell).

Chevalier, J. M. (1969), 'The Problem of Control in Large American Corporations', *The Antitrust Bulletin*, 14.

—— (1970), *La Structure financière de l'Industrie americaine* (Paris: Cujas).

Chiesi, A. M. (1982), 'L'élite finanziaria Italiana', *Rassegna Italiana Di Sociologia*, 23.

—— (1985), 'Property, Capital, and Network Structure in the Italian Case', in Stokman *et al.* (eds.) (1985).

Child, J. (1969a), *The Business Enterprise in Modern Industrial Society* (London: Collier-Macmillan).

—— (1969b), *British Management Thought* (London: George Allen and Unwin).

—— (1972), 'Organisational Structure, Environment and Performance: The Role of Strategic Choice', *Sociology*, 6.

—— (1973), *Man and Organisation* (London: George Allen and Unwin).

Chong, L. E. (1986), 'The PRC's Managers Under the Self-Responsibility System' in Clegg *et al.* (eds.) (1986).

Chossudovsky, M. (1986), *Towards Capitalist Restoration? Chinese Socialism After Mao* (London: Macmillan).

Cipolla, C. (ed.) (1973a), *The Fontana Economic History of Europe*, iii (London: Fontana).

—— (ed.) (1973b), *The Fontana Economic History of Europe*, iv (London: Fontana).

Citoleux, Y., Encaoua, D., Franck, B., and Heon, M. (1977). 'Les Groupes de sociétés en 1974: une méthode d'analyse', *Economie et Statistique*, 87.

Clark, R. (1979), *The Japanese Company* (New Haven: Yale University Press).

Clarke, S. (1992), 'Privatisation and the Development of Capitalism in Russia', *New Left Review*, 196.

Clarke, T., and Pitelis, C. (eds.) (1993), *The Political Economy of Privatisation* (London: Routledge).

Clarke, W. (1889), 'Industrial (Basis of Socialism)', in Shaw (ed.) (1889).

Clarke, W. M. (1967), *The City in the World Economy* (Harmondsworth: Penguin).

Clawson, D., and Clawson, M. A. (1987), 'Reagan or Business: Foundations of the New Conservatism', in Schwartz (1987).

Clegg, S. R., Dunphy, D., and Redding, S. G. (eds.) (1986), *The Enterprise and Management in East Asia* (Hong Kong: Hong Kong University).

Clement, W. (1975a), *The Canadian Corporate Elite* (Toronto: McClelland and Stewart).

—— (1975b), *Continental Corporate Power* (Toronto: McClelland and Stewart).

Clements R. V. (1958), *Managers: A Study of their Careers in Industry* (London: George Allen and Unwin).

Coase, R. (1937), 'The Nature of the Firm', *Economica*, 4.

Coates, K. (ed.) (1968), *Can the Workers Run Industry?* (London: Sphere).

Cohen, M. L. (1976), *House United, House Divided: The Chinese Family in Taiwan* (New York: Columbia University Press).

Cole, G. D. H. (1948), *The Meaning of Marxism*. (Ann Arbor: University of Michigan Press 1964).

—— (1955), *Studies in Class Structure* (London: Routledge and Kegan Paul).

Collett, D., and Yarrow, G. (1976), 'The Size Distribution of Large Shareholdings in Some Leading British Companies', *Oxford Bulletin of Economics and Statistics*.

Commission on Concentration (1968), 'Ownership and Influence in the Economy' (Extract from Commission on Industrial and Economic Concentration, Stockholm: Government Publications Office, in Scase (ed.) (1976).

Commons, J. R. (1924), *The Legal Foundations of Capitalism* (New York: Macmillan).

Connell, R. (1976), *Ruling Class, Ruling Culture* (Cambridge: Cambridge University Press).

Conyers, M. J. (1994), 'Corporate Governance Changes in U.K. Companies between 1988 and 1993', *Corporate Governance*, 2.

Copeman, G. H. (1955), *Leaders of British Industry* (London: Gee).

Cordero, S., and Santin, R. (1982), *Los grupos industriales: una nueva organización económica in México* (Mexico: Colegio de México).

Cottrell, P. L. (1975), *British Overseas Investment in the Nineteenth Century* (London: Macmillan).

—— Lindgren, H., and Teichova, A. (eds.) (1992), *European Industry and Banking Between the Wars* (Leicester: Leicester University Press).

Cox, E. B. (1963), *Trends in the Distribution of Stock Ownership* (University of Pennsylvania Press).

Cox, T. (1994a), 'Privatization and Social Interests in Eastern Europe', *Journal of European Public Policy*, 1.

—— (1994b), 'Privatization, Class and Interest Formation in Eastern Europe', in Brown and Crompton (eds.) (1994).

—— and Vass, L. (1994), 'Civil Society and Interest Representation in Hungarian Political Development', *Journal of Communist Studies and Transition Politics*, 10.

Crewe, I. (ed.) (1974), *British Political Sociology Yearbook*, i (London: Croom Helm).

CRISP (1962), *Morphologie des groupes financiers belges* (Bruxelles: CRISP).

Cronjé, S. *et al.* (1976), *Lonrho* (Harmondsworth: Penguin).

Crosland, C. A. R. (1956), *The Future of Socialism* (London: Jonathan Cape).

—— (1962), *The Conservative Enemy* (London: Jonathan Cape).

Crouch, C. (1977), *Class Conflict and the Industrial Relations Crisis* (London: Heinemann).

—— (ed.) (1978), *British Political Sociology Yearbook*, v (London: Croom Helm).

—— (ed.) (1979), *State and Economy in Contemporary Capitalism* (London: Croom Helm).

Crough, G. (1980), 'Small is Beautiful but Disappearing: A Study of Share Ownership in Australia', *Journal of Australian Political Economy*, 8.

CSO (1991), *The Ownership of Company Shares: Share Register Survey Report at the End of 1989* (London: HMSO).

—— (1994), *Share Ownership '94: The Share Register Survey Report, End 1993* (London: HMSO).

Cubbin, J., and Leech, D. (1983), 'The Effect of Shareholder Dispersion on the Degree of Control in British Companies: Theory and Measurement', *Economic Journal*, 93.

Cutler, A. *et al.* (1977), *Marx's 'Capital' and Capitalism Today*, i (London: Routledge and Kegan Paul).

—— *et al.* (1978), *Marx's 'Capital' and Capitalism Today*, ii (London: Routledge and Kegan Paul).

Cuyvers, L., and Meeusen, W. (1976), 'The Structure of Personal Influence of the Belgian Holding Companies', *European Economic Review*, 8.

—— —— (1978), 'A Time-Series Analysis of Concentration in Belgian Banking and Holding Companies' (Paper to European Consortium for Political Research, Grenoble).

—— —— (1985), 'Financial Groups in the Belgian Network of Interlocking Directorships', in Stokman *et al.* (eds.) (1985).

Daems, H. (1978), *The Holding Company and Corporate Control* (Leiden: Martinus Nijhoff).

—— (1980), 'The Rise of the Modern Industrial Enterprise: A New Perspective', in Chandler and Daems (eds.) (1980).

—— and van der Wee, H. (eds.) (1974), *The Rise of Managerial Capitalism* (The Hague: Martinus Nijhoff).

Dahrendorf, R. (1959), *Class and Class Conflict in an Industrial Society* (London: Routledge and Kegan Paul).

Daumard, A. (1980), 'Wealth and Affluence in France Since the Beginning of the Nineteenth Century', in Rubinstein (ed.) (1980).

Davies, P. L. (1993), 'Institutional Investors in the UK', in Prentice and Holland (1993).

Davis, K., and Moore, W. E. (1945), 'Some Principles of Stratification', *American Sociological Review*, 10.

De Alessi, L. (1973), 'Private Property and Dispersion of Ownership in Large Corporations', *Journal of Finance*, 28.

Demsetz, H. (1967), 'Toward A Theory of Property Rights', in Demsetz (1988).

—— (1983), 'The Structure of Ownership and the Theory of the Firm', in Demsetz (1988).

—— (1988), *Ownership, Control and the Firm* (Oxford: Basil Blackwell).

Derlien, H.-U., and Szablowski, G. J. (eds.) (1993), *Regime Transitions, Elites and Bureaucracies in Eastern Europe*, special issue of *Governance* 6/3 (Oxford: Basil Blackwell).

Derossi, F. (1971), *The Mexican Entrepreneur* (Paris: OECD).

De Vries, J. (1978), *The Netherlands Economy in the Twentieth Century* (Assen: Van Gorcum).

De Vroey, M. (1973), *Propriété et Pouvoir dans les Grandes Enterprises* (Brussels: CRISP).

—— (1975a), 'The Separation of Ownership and Control in Large Corporations', *Review of Radical Political Economics*, 7.

—— (1975b), 'The Owners' Interventions in Decisionmaking in Large Corporations', *European Economic Review*.

—— (1976), 'The Measurement of Ownership and Control in Large Corporations: A Critical Review' (Document de travail no. 718, C.R.I.D.E.).

Department of Industry (1979), *The Ownership of Company Shares: A Survey for 1975* (London: HMSO for the Central Statistical Office).

Dhingra, H. L. (1983), 'Patterns of Ownership and Control in Canadian Industry: A Study of Large Non-Financial Private Corporations', *Canadian Journal of Sociology*, 8.

Dhondt, J., and Bruwier, M. (1970), 'The Low Countries, 1700–1914', in Cipolla (ed.) (1973b).

Diamond Report (1975a), *Royal Commission on the Distribution of Income and Wealth*, Report No. 1, Cmnd 6172 (London: HMSO).

—— (1975b), *Royal Commission on the Distribution of Income and Wealth*, Report No. 2, Cmnd 6173 (London: HMSO).

Di Donnata, D., Glasberg, D. S., Mintz, B., and Schwartz, M. (1988), 'Theories of Corporate Interlocks: A Social History', *Research in the Sociology of Organisations*, 6.

Dodwell (1975), *Industrial Groupings in Japan* (Tokyo: Dodwell).

—— (1980), *Industrial Groupings in Japan, 1980–81* (Tokyo: Dodwell).

Domhoff, G. W. (1967), *Who Rules America?* (Englewood Cliffs, NJ: Prentice-Hall).

—— (1971), *The Higher Circles: The Governing Class in America* (New York: Vintage Books).

—— (1974), *The Bohemian Grove* (New York: Harper and Row).

—— (1975), 'Social Clubs, Policy-Planning Groups and Corporations', *Insurgent Sociologist*, 5.

Donolo, C. (1980), 'Social Change and Transformation of the State in Italy', in Scase (ed.) (1980).

Dooley, P. C. (1969), 'The Interlocking Directorate', *American Economic Review*, 59.

Dore, R. (1973), *British Factory, Japanese Factory* (London: George Allen and Unwin).

—— (1987), *Taking Japan Seriously* (London: Athlone Press).

Drache, D. (1970), 'The Canadian Bourgeoisie and its National Consciousness', in Lumsden (ed.) (1970).

Dronkers, J., and Stokman, F. N. (eds.) (1984), *Nederlandse Elites in Beeld* (Deventer: van Loghum Slaterus).

Drucker, P. F. (1951), *The New Society: The Anatomy of the Industrial Order* (London: Heinemann).

Drucker, P. F. (1976), *The Unseen Revolution: How Pension Fund Socialism Came to America* (New York: Harper and Row).

Dunkerley, D., and Salaman, G. (eds.) (1979), *International Yearbook of Organisation Studies 1979* (London: Routledge and Kegan Paul).

—— —— (eds.) (1980), *International Yearbook of Organisation Studies 1980* (London: Routledge and Kegan Paul).

Dunning, J. H. (1970), *Studies in International Investment* (London: George Allen and Unwin).

—— (1994), 'The Strategy of Japanese and US Manufacturing Investment in Europe', in Mason and Encarnation (eds.) (1994).

Dyas, G. P., and Thanheiser, H. T. (1976), *The Emerging European Enterprise* (London: Macmillan).

Eaton, J. (1963), *Political Economy* (New York: International Publishers).

Edwards, G. W. (1938), *The Evolution of Finance Capitalism* (London: Longmans Green).

Edwards, J., and Fischer, K. (1994), *Banks, Finance and Investment in Germany* (Cambridge: Cambridge University Press).

Eigner, P. (1994), 'Interlocking Directorships Between Commercial Banks and Industry in Interwar Vienna', in Teichova *et al* (eds.) (1994).

Eisenberg, M. A. (1969), 'The Legal Roles of Shareholder and Management in Modern Corporate Decision-Making', *California Law Review*, 57.

Emmanuel, A. (1972), *Unequal Exchange* (New York: Monthly Review Press).

Encel, S. (1970), *Equality and Authority* (London: Tavistock).

Erritt, M. J., and Alexander, J. C. D. (1977), 'Ownership of Company Shares', *Economic Trends* (September).

Evely, R., and Little, I. M. D. (1960), *Concentration in British Industry* (Cambridge: Cambridge University Press).

Fama, E. F. (1980), 'Agency Problems and the Theory of the Firm', *Journal of Political Economy*, 88.

—— and Jensen, C. M. (1983), 'Agency Problems and Residual Claims', *Journal of Law and Economics*, 26.

Farrell, B. G. (1993), *Elite Families: Class and Power in Nineteenth Century Boston* (Albany, NY: State University of New York Press).

Fay, B. (1975), *Social Theory and Political Practice* (London: George Allen and Unwin).

Feldman, G. D. (1981), 'German Interest-Group Alliances in War and Inflation, 1914–23', in Berger (ed.) (1981).

Fennema, M. (1982), *International Networks of Banks and Industry* (The Hague: Martinus Nijhoff).

—— (1988), 'Post-War Reconstruction in the Netherlands: A Passive Revolution' (Amsterdam: Faculty of Political and Social Sciences, University of Amsterdam).

—— and Schijf, H. (1978), 'Analysing Interlocking Directorates', *Social Networks*.

—— —— (1985), 'The Transnational Network', in Stokman *et al.* (eds.) (1985).

Fidler, J. (1981), *The British Business Elite* (London: Routledge and Kegan Paul).

Field, F. (ed.) (1979), *The Wealth Report* (London: Routledge and Kegan Paul).

The Financial Times (1982), 'The F.T. European 500' (Supplement to *Financial Times*, 21 October).

Fine, B., and Harris, L. (1976), 'State Expenditure in Advanced Capitalism: A Critique', *New Left Review*, 98.

Finer, S. (1955), 'The Political Power of Private Capital', 1, *Sociological Review*, 3.

—— (1956), 'The Political Power of Private Capital', 2, *Sociological Review*, 4.

Firn, J. (1975), 'External Control and Regional Policy', in Brown (ed.) (1975).

Fitch, R. (1971), 'Reply to James O'Connor', *Socialist Revolution*, 7.

—— (1972), 'Sweezy and Corporate Fetishism', *Socialist Revolution*, 12.

—— and Oppenheimer, M. (1970a), 'Who Rules the Corporations?', I, *Socialist Revolution*, 4.

—— —— (1970b), 'Who Rules the Corporations?', II, *Socialist Revolution*, 5.

—— —— (1970c), 'Who Rules the Corporations?', III, *Socialist Revolution*, 6.

Fligstein, N. (1990), *The Transformation of Corporate Control* (Cambridge, Mass.: Harvard University Press).

—— and Brantley, P. (1992), 'Bank Control, Owner Control, or Organizational Dynamics: Who Controls the Large Modern Corporations?', *American Journal of Sociology*, 98.

—— and Froeland, R. (1995), 'Theoretical and Comparative Perspectives on Corporate Organisations', *Annual Review of Sociology*, 21.

Florence, P. S. (1947), 'The Statistical Analysis of Joint Stock Company Control', *Statistical Journal*, 1.

—— (1953), *The Logic of British and American Industry* (London: Routledge and Kegan Paul, rev. edn.).

—— (1961), *Ownership, Control, and Success of Large Companies* (London: Sweet and Maxwell).

Fogelberg, G. (1978), 'Changing Patterns of Shareownership in New Zealand's Largest Companies', Research Paper No 15 (University of Wellington: Department of Business Administration).

—— (1980), 'Ownership and Control in New Zealand's Largest Companies, 1962 and 1974', *New Zealand Journal of Business*, 2.

Fohlen, C. (1978), 'Entrepreneurship and Management in France in the Nineteenth Century', in Mathias and Postan (eds.) (1978a).

Fournier, P. (1978), *The Quebec Establishment* (Montreal: Black Rose Books).

Fox A. (1973), 'Industrial Relations: A Socialist Critique of Pluralist Ideology', in Child (ed.) (1973).

—— (1974), *Beyond Contract* (London: Faber and Faber).

Francis, A. (1980a), 'Families, Firms, and Finance Capital', *Sociology*, 14.

—— (1980b), 'Company Objectives, Managerial Motivations and the Behaviour of Large Firms', *Cambridge Journal of Economics*, 4.

Francko, L. G. (1976), *The European Multinationals* (London: Harper and Row).

Frank, A. G. (1969), *Capitalism and Underdevelopment in Latin America* (New York: Monthly Review Press).

—— and Gills, B. K. (1993a), 'The 5000-Year World System', in Frank and Gills (eds.) (1993b).

—— —— (eds.) (1993b), *The World System: Five Hundred Years or Five Thousand* (London: Routledge).

Frankel, H. (1970), *Capitalist Society and Modern Sociology* (London: Lawrence and Wishart).

Franks, J., and Mayer, C. (1992), 'Corporate Control: A Synthesis of the International Evidence' (unpublished paper, London Business School and University of Warwick).

Freitag, P. J. (1975), 'The Cabinet and Big Business: A Study of Interlocks', Social Problems, 23 / 2.

Friedmann, A. (1977), Industry and Labour (London: Macmillan).

Fruin, W. M. (1983), Kikkoman: Company, Clan and Community (Cambridge, Mass.: Harvard University Press).

Futatsugi, Y. (1969), 'The Measurement of Interfirm Relationships', Japanese Economic Studies, 1973.

—— (1986), Japanese Enterprise Groups (Monograph no. 4, School of Business Administration, Kobe University).

Galaskiewicz, J., and Wasserman, S. (1981), 'A Dynamic Study of Change in a Regional Corporate Network', American Sociological Review, 46.

Galbraith, J. K. (1952), American Capitalism (Massachusetts: Riverside Press).

—— (1954), The Great Crash (Harmondsworth: Penguin, 1961).

—— (1967), The New Industrial State (London: Hamish Hamilton).

Gallino, L. (1971), 'Italy', in Archer and Giner (eds.) (1971).

Garvy, G. (1977), Money, Financial Flows and Credit in the Soviet Union (Cambridge, Mass.: Ballinger Publishing).

George, K. D., and Ward, T. S. (1975), The Structure of Industry in the EEC (Cambridge: Cambridge University Press).

George, V., and Lawson, R. (eds.) (1980), Poverty and Inequality in Common Market Countries (London: Routledge and Kegan Paul).

Gerlach, M. L. (1992), Alliance Capitalism: The Social Organisation of Japanese Business (Berkeley: University of California Press).

Gershenkron, A. (1962), Economic Backwardness in Historical Perspective (Cambridge, Mass.: The Belknap Press of Harvard University Press).

Gerth, H., and Mills, C. W. (1954), Character and Social Structure (London: Routledge and Kegan Paul).

Gessell, G. A., and Howe, E. J. (1941), A Study of Legal Reserve Life Insurance Companies (Monographs of the Temporary National Economic Committee, no. 28, Washington: Government Printing Office for the US Senate).

Giddens, A. (1971), Capitalism and Modern Social Theory (Cambridge: Cambridge University Press).

—— (1973), The Class Structure of the Advanced Societies (London: Hutchinson).

—— (1976), 'Classical Social Theory and the Origins of Modern Sociology', American Journal of Sociology, 81.

—— (1984), The Constitution of Society (Cambridge: Polity Press).

—— and Mackenzie, G. (eds.) (1982), *Social Class and the Division of Labour* (Cambridge: Cambridge University Press).

Gille B. (1970), 'Banking and Industrialisation in Europe', in Cipolla (ed.) (1973a).

Giner, S. (1971), 'Spain', in Archer and Giner (eds.) (1971).

—— and Archer, M. S. (eds.) (1978), *Contemporary Europe: Social Structures and Cultural Patterns* (London: Routledge and Kegan Paul).

Gittelman, M., and Graham, E. (1994), 'The Performance and Structure of Japanese Affiliates in the European Community', in Mason and Encarnation (eds.) (1994).

Glasberg, D. S. (1981), 'Corporate Power and Control: The Case of Leasco Corporation and Chemical Bank', *Social Problems, 29.*

—— (1987), 'The Ties that Bind? Case Studies in the Significance of Corporate Board Interlocks with Financial Institutions', *Sociological Perspectives, 30.*

—— (1989), *The Power of Collective Purse Strings: The Effects of Bank Hegemony on Corporations and the State* (Berkeley: University of California Press).

—— and Schwartz, M. (1983), 'Ownership and Control of Corporations', *Annual Review of Sociology, 9.*

Gogel, R., and Koenig, T. (1981), 'Commercial Banks, Interlocking Directorates and Economic Power: An Analysis of the Primary Metals Industry', *Social Problems, 29.*

Goldsmith, R. W. (1958), *Financial Intermediaries in the American Economy since 1900* (Princeton: Princeton University Press).

—— and Parmelee, R. C. (1940), *The Distribution of Ownership in the 200 Largest Non-financial Corporations* (Monographs of the Temporary National Economic Committee, no. 29, Washington: Government Printing Office for the US Senate).

Goldthorpe J. H. (1964), 'Social Stratification in Industrial Societies', in Halmos (ed.) (1964).

—— (1972), 'Class, Status and Party in Modern Britain', *European Journal of Sociology, 13.*

—— (1974), 'Theories of Industrial Society', *European Journal of Sociology, 12.*

—— (1978), 'Comment', *British Journal of Sociology, 29.*

—— (1982), 'On the Service Class, its Formation and Future', in Giddens and Mackenzie (eds.) (1982).

—— Lockwood, D., Bechoffer, F., and Platt, J. (1968a), *The Affluent Worker: Industrial Attitudes and Behaviour* (Cambridge: Cambridge University Press).

———————— (1968b), *The Affluent Worker: Political Attitudes and Behaviour* (Cambridge: Cambridge University Press).

Goldthorpe J. H., Lockwood, D., Bechoffer, F., and Platt, J. (1969), *The Affluent Worker in the Class Structure* (Cambridge: Cambridge University Press).

Gollan, J. (1956), *The British Political System* (London: Lawrence and Wishart).

Gonick, C. W. (1970), 'Foreign Ownership and Political Decay', in Lumsden (ed.) (1970).

Gordon, R. A. (1936), 'Stockholdings of Officers and Directors in American Industrial Corporations', *Quarterly Journal of Economics*, 50.

—— (1938), 'Ownership by Management and Control Groups in the Large Corporations', *Quarterly Journal of Economics*, 52.

—— (1945), *Business Leadership in Large Corporations* (Washington: Brookings Institution).

Gorlin, A. C. (1974), 'The Soviet Economic Association', *Soviet Studies*, 26.

Gospel, H. (1983a), 'Management Structure and Strategies: An Introduction', in Gospel and Littler (eds.) (1983).

—— (1983b), 'The Development of Management Organisation in Industrial Relations', in Thurley and Wood (eds.) (1983).

—— and Littler, C. R. (eds.) (1983), *Management Strategy and Industrial Relations* (London: Heinemann).

Gough, I. (1975), 'State Expenditure in Advanced Capitalism', *New Left Review*, 92.

Granick, D. (1962), *The European Executive* (New York: Doubleday).

Granovetter, M. (1973), 'The Strength of Weak Ties', *American Journal of Sociology*, 78.

—— (1985), 'Economic Action and Social Structure: The Concept of Embeddedness', *American Journal of Sociology*, 80.

Grant, W. (1983), 'Representing Capital: The Role of the CBI', in King (ed.) (1983).

—— (1993), *Business and Politics in Britain* (2nd edn., London: Macmillan).

—— and Marsh, D. (1977), *The Confederation of British Industry* (London: Hodder and Stoughton).

Grønmo, S. (1995a), 'Structural Change During Deregulation and Crisis: The Position of Banks in the Norwegian Intercorporate Network', Paper to the International Social Network Conference (London, July 1995).

—— (1995b), 'Assessing the Centrality of Banks in Intercorporate Networks', Research On Banking, Capital and Society, Report No. 63 (Oslo: Research Council of Norway).

Grossfeld, B., and Ebke, W. (1978), 'Controlling the Modern Corporation: A Comparative View of Corporate Power in the US and Europe', *American Journal of Comparative Law*, 26.

Grossman, S. J., and Hart, O. (1987), 'The Costs and Benefits of Ownership: A Theory of Vertical and Lateral Integration', *Journal of Political Economy*, 94.

Grou, P. (1983), *La structure financière du capitalisme multinational* (Paris: Presses de la Fondation Nationale des Sciences Politiques).

Gustavsen, B. (1976), 'The Social Context of Investment Decisions', *Acta Sociologica*, 19.

Guttsman, W. L. (1963), *The British Political Elite* (London: McGibbon and Kee).

—— (1974), 'The British Political Elite and the Class Structure', in Stanworth and Giddens (eds.) (1974b).

Habermas, J. (1973), *Legitimation Crisis* (London: Hutchinson, 1976).

—— (1976), *Communication and the Evolution of Society* (London: Heinemann, 1979).

—— (1981a), *Theory of Communicative Action*, i (London: Heinemann 1984).

—— (1981b), *Theory of Communicative Action*, ii (London: Heinemann 1987).

Hadden, T. (1977), *Company Law and Capitalism* (London: Weidenfeld and Nicolson).

—— (1993), 'Regulating Corporate Groups: An International Perspective', in McCahery *et al.* (eds.) (1993).

Hadley, E. M. (1970), *Antitrust in Japan* (Princeton: Princeton University Press).

Hague, D. C., and Wilkinson, G. (1983), *The IRC: An Experiment in Industrial Intervention* (London: George Allen and Unwin).

Hall, D., and De Bettignies, H.-C. (1968), 'The French Business Elite', *European Business*, 3.

—— —— and Amado-Fischgrund, G. (1969). 'The European Business Elite', *European Business*, 4.

Hall, S. *et al.* (1957), 'The Insiders', *Universities and Left Review*, 1.

Halliday, J. (1975), *A Political History of Japanese Capitalism* (New York: Pantheon Books).

—— and McCormack, G. (1973), *Japanese Imperialism Today* (Harmondsworth: Penguin).

Halmos, P. (ed.) (1964), *The Development of Industrial Societies* (Sociological Review Monograph, no. 8).

Hambata, M. (1990), *The Crested Kimono: Power and Love in the Japanese Business Family* (Ithaca, NY: Cornell University Press).

Hamilton, G. C. (1984), 'Patriarchalism in Imperial China and Western Europe: A Revision of Weber's Sociology of Domination', *Theory and Society*, 13.

Hamilton, G. C. (1990), 'Patriarchy, Patrimonialism and Filial Piety: A Comparison of China and Western Europe', *British Journal of Sociology*, 41.

—— (1991a), 'The Organizational Foundations of Western and Chinese Commerce: A Historical and Comparative Analysis', in Hamilton (ed.) (1991b).

—— (ed.) (1991b), *Business Networks and Economic Development in East and South East Asia* (Hong Kong, University of Hong Kong).

—— and Biggart, N. (1988), 'Market, Culture and Authority: A Comparative Analysis of Management and Organisation in the Far East', *American Journal of Sociology*, 94, Supplement.

—— and Kao, C. S. (1990), 'The Institutional Foundations of Chinese Business: The Family Firm in Taiwan', *Comparative Social Research*, 12.

—— Orrú, M., and Biggart, N. (1987), 'Enterprise Groups in East Asia', *Shoken Keizai*, 161.

Hankiss, E. (1990), *East European Alternatives* (Oxford: Clarendon Press).

Hannah, L. (1974), 'Managerial Innovation and the Rise of the Large-Scale Company in Interwar Britain', *Economic History Review*, 27.

—— (ed.) (1976a), *Management Strategy and Business Development* (London: Macmillan).

—— (1976b), 'Strategy and Structure in the Manufacturing Sector', in Hannah (ed.) (1976a).

—— (1976c), *The Rise of the Corporate Economy* (London: Methuen).

—— (1980), 'Visible and Invisible Hands in Great Britain', in Chandler and Daems (eds.) (1980).

Harbury, C. D. (1962), 'Inheritance and the Distribution of Personal Wealth in Britain', in Atkinson (ed.) (1973b).

—— and Hitchens, D. M. W. N. (1979), *Inheritance and Wealth Inequality in Britain* (London: George Allen and Unwin).

—— and McMahon, P. C. (1974), 'Intergenerational Wealth Transmission and the Characteristics of Top Wealth Leavers in Britain', in Stanworth and Giddens (1974b).

Harvey, J., and Hood, K. (1958), *The British State* (London: Lawrence Wishart).

Hawawini, G., and Schill, M. (1994), 'The Japanese Presence in the European Financial Services Sector', in Mason and Encarnation (eds.) (1994).

Heath, A. (1981), *Social Mobility* (London: Fontana).

Heilbronner, R. L. (1976), *Business Civilization in Decline* (Harmondsworth: Penguin).

Heiskanen, I., and Johanson, E. (1985), 'Finnish Interlocking Directorships: Institutional Groups and their Evolving Integration', in Stokman et al. (eds.) (1985).

Held, D. (1991a), 'Democracy, the Nation State and the Global System', in Held (1991b).

—— (ed.) (1991b), *Political Theory Today* (Cambridge: Polity Press).

Helmers, H. M. *et al.* (1975), *Graven naar Macht* (Amsterdam: Van Gennep).

Henderson, W. O. (1961), *The Industrial Revolution in Europe* (Chicago: Quadrangle).

Henley, J. S., and Nyam, M. K. (1986), 'Developments in Managerial Decision-Making in Chinese Industrial Enterprise', in Clegg *et al.* (1986).

Herman, E. S. (1973), 'Do Bankers Control Corporations?', *Monthly Review*, 25.

—— (1981), *Corporate Control, Corporate Power* (Cambridge: Cambridge University Press).

Higley, J. *et al.* (1976), *Elite Structure and Ideology* (Oslo: Universitetsforlaget).

Hilferding, R. (1910), *Finance Capital* (London: Routledge and Kegan Paul, 1981).

Hill, S. (1995), 'The Social Organisation of Boards of Directors', *British Journal of Sociology*, 46.

Hindess, B. (1970), 'Introduction', in Bettelheim (1970).

Hirsch, J. (1980), 'Developments in the Political System of Western Germany since 1945', in Scase (ed.) (1980).

Hirschmeier, J. (1964), *The Origins of Entrepreneurship in Meiji Japan* (Cambridge, Mass.: Harvard University Press).

—— and Yui, S. (1975), *The Development of Japanese Business* (Cambridge, Mass.: Harvard University Press).

Hirst, P. (1979), *On Law and Ideology* (London: Macmillan).

Hobsbawm, E. J. (1968), *Industry and Empire* (Harmondsworth: Penguin, 1969).

Hobson, J. A. (1906), *The Evolution of Modern Capitalism* (London: George Allen and Unwin, 1926).

Hodges, M. (1974), *Multinational Corporations and National Government* (Farnborough: Saxon House).

Hofstede, G. (1980), *Culture's Consequences: International Differences in Work-Related Values* (Beverly Hills: Sage).

Holl, P. (1977), 'Control Type and the Market for Corporate Control in Large US Corporations', *Journal of Industrial Economics*, 25.

—— (1980), 'Control Type and the Market for Corporate Control: Reply', *Journal of Industrial Economics*, 28.

Hollowell, P. G. (1982a), 'On the Operationalisation of Property', in Hollowell (ed.) (1982b).

Hollowell, P. G. (ed.) (1982*b*), *Property and Social Relations* (London: Heinemann).

Hood, N., and Young, S. (1979), *The Economics of Multinational Enterprise* (London: Longman).

Hoogvelt, A. (1976), *The Sociology of the Developing Societies* (London: Macmillan).

Hoselitz, B. F. (1960), *Sociological Aspects of Economic Growth* (Glencoe, Ill.: Free Press).

—— and Moore, W. E. (1966), *Industrialisation and Society* (Paris: Mouton).

House, J. D. (1977), 'The Social Organisation of Multinational Corporations: Canadian Subsidiaries in the Oil Industry', *Canadian Review of Sociology and Anthropology*, 14.

Howells, J., and Wood, M. (1993), *The Globalisation of Production and Technology* (New York: Belhaven Press).

Hughes, M. D. (1973), 'American Investment in Britain', in Urry and Wakeford (eds.) (1973).

Hunt, A. (ed.) (1977), *Class and Class Structure* (London: Lawrence and Wishart).

Hussain, A. (1976), 'Hilferding's Finance Capital', *Bulletin of the Conference of Socialist Economists*, 13.

Hutton, W. (1995), *The State We're In* (London: Jonathan Cape).

Hymer, S. (1972), 'The Multinational Corporation and the Law of Uneven Development', in Radice (ed.) (1975).

Ingham, G. (1982), 'Divisions within the Dominant Class and British "Exceptionalism" ', in Giddens and Mackenzie (eds.) (1982).

—— (1984), *Capitalism Divided?* (London: Macmillan).

Jacquemin, A. P., and De Jong, H. W. (1977), *European Industrial Organisation* (London: Macmillan).

—— and Gellinck, E. de (1980), 'Familial Control, Size and Performance in the Largest French Firms', *European Economic Review*, 13.

Jaher, F. C. (1980), 'The Gilded Elite: American Multimillionaires, 1865 to the Present', in Rubinstein (ed.) (1980).

—— (1982), *The Urban Establishment: Upper Strata in Boston, New York, Charleston, Chicago and Los Angeles* (Urbana: University of Illinois Press).

James, H., Lindgren, H., and Teichova, A. (eds.), (1991), *The Role of Banks in the Interwar Economy* (Cambridge: Cambridge University Press).

Jancovici, E. (1972), 'Informatique et entreprise', *Sociologie du travail*, 14.

Janelli, Roger L. (1993), *Making Capitalism: The Social and Cultural Construction of a South Korean Conglomerate* (Stanford, Calif.: Stanford University Press).

Jeffries, I. (ed.) (1981), *The Industrial Enterprise in Eastern Europe* (Eastbourne: Praeger).

Jeidels, O. (1905), *Das Verhaltnis der deutschen Grossbanken zur Industrie mit besonderer Berucksichtigung der Eisenindustrie* (Leipzig: Duncker und Humbott).

Jensen, C. M., and Meckly, W. H. (1976), 'The Theory of the Firm: Managerial Behaviour, Agency Costs and Ownership Structure', *Journal of Financial Economics*, 3.

Jessop, B. (1980), 'The Transformation of the State in Post-War Britain', in Scase (ed.) (1980).

—— (1990), *State Theory* (Cambridge: Polity Press).

Jewkes, J. (1977), *Delusions of Dominance* (London: Institute of Economic Affairs).

Johnsen, E., and Mintz, B. (1989), 'Organizational Versus Class Components of Director Networks', in Perrucci and Potter (eds.) (1989).

Johnson, C. (1982), *MITI and the Japanese Miracle* (Stanford, Calif.: Stanford University Press).

Johnson, D. L. (1985*a*), 'The State as an Expression of Class Relations', in Johnson (ed.) (1985*c*).

—— (1985*b*), 'The Roots of Dictatorship in South America', in Johnson (ed.) (1985*c*).

—— (ed.) (1985*c*), *Middle Classes in Dependent Countries* (Beverly Hills: Sage).

Johnson, R. W. (1973), 'The British Political Elite, 1955–1972', *European Journal of Sociology*, 14.

Johnson, T. (1982), 'The State and the Professions: Peculiarities of the British', in Giddens and Mackenzie (eds.) (1982).

Jones, C. (1984), 'Corporate Social Accounting: The Conflict Between Theory and Practice' (unpub. paper, Department of Economics and Social Science, Bristol Polytechnic).

—— (1995), *Accounting and the Enterprise: A Social Analysis* (London: Routledge).

Jones, K. (1982), *Law and Economy* (London: Academic Press).

Jopperson, R. L., and Meyer, J. W. (1991), 'The Public Order and the Construction of Formal Organisations', in Powell and Di Maggio (eds.) (1991).

Judge, D. (1990), *Parliament and Industry* (Aldershot: Dartmouth).

Juran, J., and Louden, J. K. (1966), *The Corporate Director* (New York: American Management Association).

Kamerschen, D. R. (1968), 'The Influence of Ownership and Control on Profit Rates', *American Economic Review*, 58.

Kania, J. J., and McKean, J. R. (1976), 'Ownership, Control and the Contemporary Corporation', *Kyklos*, 29.

Kania, J. J., and McKean, J. R. (1978), 'Ownership, Control, and the Contemporary Corporation: A Reply', *Kyklos*, 31.

Kao, C. S. (1991), ' "Personal Trust" in the Large Businesses in Taiwan', in Hamilton (ed.) (1991b).

Karpik, L. (1972), 'Les Politiques et les logiques d'action de la grande entreprise industrielle', *Sociologie du travail*, 14.

Kautsky, K. (1902), *The Social Revolution* (New York: Dial Press, 1925).

Kaysen, C. (1957), 'The Social Significance of the Modern Corporation', *American Economic Review*, 47.

Keller, S. (1963), *Beyond the Ruling Class* (New York: Random House).

Kennedy, W. P. (1976), 'Institutional Responses to Economic Growth: Capital Markets in Britain to 1814', in Hannah (1976a).

—— (1987), *Industrial Structure, Capital Markets and the Origins of British Economic Decline* (Cambridge: Cambridge University Press).

Kerr, C. *et al.* (1960), *Industrialism and Industrial Man* (Harmondsworth: Penguin, 1973).

Kiernan, V. G. (1974), *Marxism and Imperialism* (London: Edward Arnold).

Kim, E. M. (1991), 'The Industrial Organization and Growth of the Korean *Chaebol*: Integrating Development and Organizational Theories', in Hamilton (ed.) (1991b).

Kindleberger, C. P. (ed.) (1970), *The International Corporation* (Massachusetts: MIT Press).

—— (1984), *A Financial History of Western Europe* (London: George Allen and Unwin).

King, R. (ed.) (1983), *Capital and Politics* (London: Routledge and Kegan Paul).

Kinsey, R. (1983), 'Karl Renner on Socialist Legality', in Sugarman (1983).

Kitahara, I. (1980), 'Ownership and Control in the Large Corporation', *Keio Economic Studies*, 17.

—— (1985), *Gendai Shihonshugi ni Okeru Shoyu to Kettei* (Tokyo: Iwanami Shoten).

Kiyonari, T., and Nakamura, H. (1977), 'The Establishment of the Big Business System', in Sato (ed.) (1980).

Klein, L. R. *et al.* (1956), 'Savings and Finances of the Upper Income Classes', *Oxford Institute of Statistics Bulletin*, 18.

Knowles, J. C. (1973), 'The Rockefeller Financial Group', *MSS Modular Publications*, Module 343.

Kocka, J. (1978), 'Entrepreneurs and Managers in German Industrialisation', in Mathias and Postan (eds.) (1978a).

—— (1980), 'The Rise of the Modern Industrial Enterprise in Germany', in Chandler and Daems (eds.) (1980).

Koenig, R. (1971), 'Western Germany', in Archer and Giner (eds.) (1971).

Koenig, T., and Gogel, R. (1981), 'Interlocking Corporate Directorships as a Social Network', *American Journal of Economics and Sociology*, 40.

—— —— and Sonquist, J. (1979), 'Models of the Significance of Interlocking Corporate Directorates', *American Journal of Economics and Sociology*, 38.

Kolankiewicz, G., and Lewis, P. G. (1988), *Poland* (London, Pinter Publishers).

Kolko, G. (1962), *Wealth and Power in America* (London: Thames and Hudson).

Komiya, R. (1961), ' "Monopoly capital" and income redistribution policy', in Sato (ed.) (1980).

Konrad, G., and Szelényi, I. (1974), *The Intellectuals on the Road to Class Power* (Brighton: Harvester Press, 1979).

Korpi, W. (1978), *The Working Class in Welfare Capitalism* (London: Routledge and Kegan Paul).

Kotz, D. M. (1978), *Bank Control of Large Corporations in the United States* (Berkeley: University of California Press).

Kovacs, D., and Maggard, S. W. (1993), 'The Human Face of Political, Economic and Social Change in Eastern Europe', *East European Quarterly*, 27.

Krejci, J. (1976), *Social Structure in Divided Germany* (London: Croom Helm).

Kriesi, H. (1982), 'The Structure of the Swiss Political System', in Lehmbruch and Schmitter (eds.) (1982).

Kryshatanovskaya, O. (1993), ' The Emerging Business Elite', in Lane (ed.) (1993).

—— (1994), 'Rich and Poor in Post-Communist Russia', *Journal of Communist Studies and Transition Politics*, 10.

Kumar, K. (1978), *Prophecy and Progress* (Harmondsworth: Penguin).

Kurth, J. R. (1975), 'The International Politics of Post-Industrial Societies', in Lindberg (ed.) (1975).

Kuusinen, O. V. et al. (eds.) (1959), *Fundamentals of Marxism-Leninism* (New York: Crowell-Collier and Macmillan, n.d).

Kuznets, S. (1953), *Shares of Upper Income Groups in Incomes and Savings* (New York: National Bureau of Economic Research).

—— (1961), *Capital in the American Economy* (Princeton: Princeton University Press).

Lammers, C. J., and Hickson, D. J. (1979a), 'A Cross-National and Cross-Institutional Typology of Organisations', in Lammers and Hickson (eds.) (1979b).

—— —— (eds,), (1979b), *Organisations Alike and Unlike* (London: Routledge and Kegan Paul).

Lampman, R. (1959), 'The Share of Top Wealth Holders in the United States', in Atkinson (ed.) (1973*b*).

—— (1962), *The Share of Top Wealth Holders in National Wealth* (Princeton: Princeton University Press).

Landes, D. S. (1951), 'French Business and the Businessman: A Social and Cultural Analysis' (Bobbs Merrill Reprint no. 159).

Lane, D. S. (1993), *Russia in Flux* (Cheltenham: Edward Elgar).

Larner, R. J. (1966), 'Ownership and Control in the 200 Largest Non-Financial Corporations: 1929 and 1963', *American Economic Review*, 56.

—— (1970), *Management Control and the Large Corporation* (New York: Dunellen).

Larsson, M. (1991), 'State, Banks and Industry in Sweden with Some Reference to the Scandinavian Countries', in James *et al.* (eds.) (1991).

Lash, S. (1984), 'The End of Neo-Corporatism?: The Breakdown of Centralised Bargaining in Sweden' (paper presented to ESRC Seminar on Social Stratification, University of Cambridge, September).

—— and Urry, J. (1987), *The End of Organised Capitalism* (Cambridge: Polity Press).

—— —— (1994), *Economies of Signs and Spaces* (London: Sage).

Lawrence, P. A. (1980), *Managers and Management in West Germany* (London: Croom Helm).

Lawriwsky, M. L. (1980), 'Control Type and the Market for Corporate Control: A Note', *Journal of Industrial Economics*, 28.

—— (1982), 'Some Issues in Foreign Relations and the Control of Australia's Mineral Resources', *Australian Quarterly*.

—— (1984), *Corporate Structure and Performance* (London: Croom Helm).

Lawson, R., and George, V. (1980), 'An Assessment', in George and Lawson (eds.) (1980).

Leech, D. (1987*a*), 'Corporate Ownership and Control: A New Look at the Evidence of Berle and Means', *Oxford Economic Papers*, 39.

—— (1987*b*), 'Ownership Concentration and Control in Large US Corporations in the 1930s: An Analysis of the TNEC sample', *Journal of Industrial Economics*, 35.

Lehmbruch, G. (1982), 'Introduction: Neo-Corporatism in Comparative Perspective', in Lehmbruch and Schmitter (eds) (1982).

—— and Schmitter, P. C. (eds.) (1982), *Patterns of Corporatist Policy Making* (Beverly Hills: Sage Publications).

Leinhardt, S. (ed.) (1977), *Symposium on Social Networks* (New York: Academic Press).

Lenin, V. I. (1917*a*), *Imperialism: The Highest Stage of Capitalism* (Moscow: Progress Publishers, 1966).

—— (1917b), *The State and Revolution* (Moscow: Progress 1969).

Lenski, G. (1966), *Power and Privilege* (New York: McGraw-Hill).

Le Play, F. (1871), *L'Organisation de la famille* (Tours: Mame).

Levine, J. (1972), 'Spheres of Influence', *American Sociological Review*, 37.

—— (1978), 'The Theory of Bank Control: Comment on Mariolis's Test of the Theory', *Social Science Quarterly*, 58.

—— and Roy, W. S. (1977), 'A Study of Interlocking Directorates', in Leinhardt (ed.) (1977).

Levitt, K. (1970), *Silent Surrender: The Multinational Corporation in Canada* (Toronto: Macmillan).

Levy, A. B. (1950), *Private Corporations and their Control* (London: Routledge and Kegan Paul).

Levy-Leboyer, M. (1980), 'The Large Corporation in Modern France', in Chandler and Daems (eds.) (1980).

Lieberson, S., and O'Connor, J. R. (1972), 'Leadership and Organizational Performance: A Study of Large Corporations', *American Sociological Review*, 37.

Lim, M. H. (1981), *Ownership and Control in the One Hundred Largest Corporations in Malaysia* (Singapore: Oxford University Press).

Lindberg, L. *et al.* (1975), *Stress and Contradiction in Modern Capitalism* (London: D. C. Heath).

Lindenberg, S. M., and Schrender, H. (eds.) (1993), *Interdisciplinary Perspectives on Organization Studies* (Oxford: Pergamon).

Lintner, J. (1959), 'The Financing of Corporations', in Mason (ed.) (1959).

Lipset, S. M. (1960), *Political Man* (London: Heinemann).

Lisle-Williams, M. (1984), 'Beyond the Market: The Survival of Family Capitalism in the English Merchant Banks', *British Journal of Sociology*, 35.

Livingston, J., Moore, J., and Oldfather, F. (eds.) (1973a and b), *The Japan Reader*, i and ii (Harmondsworth: Penguin, 1976).

Lockwood, D. (1958), *The Blackcoated Worker* (London: George Allen and Unwin).

Lockwood, W. W. (1965a), 'Japan's "new capitalism" ', in Lockwood (1965b).

—— (1965b), *The State and Economic Enterprise in Japan* (Princeton: Princeton University Press).

—— (1968), *The Economic Development of Japan* (Princeton: Princeton University Press).

Longstreth, F. (1979), 'The City, Industry and the State', in Crouch (ed.) (1979).

Lukes, S. (1974), *Power: A Radical View* (London: Macmillan). Reprinted in Scott (1994a).

Lumsden, I. (ed.) (1970), *Close the 49th Parallel: The Americanization of Canada* (Toronto: University of Toronto Press).

Lundberg, F. (1937), *America's Sixty Families* (New York: Vanguard Press).

—— (1969), *The Rich and the Super Rich* (London: Nelson).

Lupton, C., and Wilson, C. (1959), 'The Social Background and Connections of Top Decision-Makers', in Urry and Wakeford (eds.) (1973).

Luxemburg, R. (1913), *The Accumulation of Capital* (London: Routledge and Kegan Paul, 1951).

Lydall, H. F. (1959), 'The Long-Term Trend in the Size Distribution of Income', *Journal of the Royal Statistical Society*, Series A, 122.

—— and Tipping, D. G. (1961), 'The Distribution of Personal Wealth in Britain', in Atkinson (ed.) (1973b).

McCahery, J., Picciotto, S., and Scott, C. (eds.) (1993), *Corporate Control and Accountability: Changing Structures and the Dynamics of Regulation* (Oxford: Clarendon Press).

McClelland, D. C. (1961), *The Achieving Society* (New York: Van Nostrand).

McDermott, J. (1991), *Corporate Society: Class, Property, and Contemporary Capitalism* (Boulder, Colo.: Westview Press).

McEachern, W. A. (1975), *Managerial Control and Performance* (Lexington: Lexington Books).

—— (1978), 'Corporate Control and Growth: An Alternative', *Kyklos*, 31.

Mace, M. L. (1971), *Directors: Myth and Reality* (Cambridge: Harvard University Press).

Mackenzie, G. (1982), 'Class Boundaries and the Labour Process', in Giddens and Mackenzie (eds.) (1982).

Macpherson, C. B. (1973), *Democratic Theory* (Oxford: Clarendon Press).

Macrosty, H. W. (1901), *Trusts and the State* (Fabian Series no. 1, London: Grant Richards).

Mallin, C. (1995), *Voting: The Role of Institutional Investors in Corporate Governance* (London: Institute of Chartered Accountants in England and Wales).

Mandel, E. (1970), *Europe Versus America* (London: New Left Books).

—— (1972), *Late Capitalism* (London: New Left Books, 1975).

Mankoff, M. (ed.) (1972), *The Poverty of Progress* (New York: Holt, Rinehart and Winston).

Mannari, H. (1974), *The Japanese Business Leaders* (Tokyo: University of Tokyo Press).

Manne, H. (1965), 'Managers and the Market for Corporate Control', *Journal of Political Economy*, 73.

Marceau, J. (1977), *Class and Status in France* (Oxford: Oxford University Press).

—— (1989a), 'France', in Bottomore and Brym (eds.) (1989).

—— (1989b), A Family Business? The Making of an International Business Elite (Cambridge: Cambridge University Press).

March, J. G., and Simon, H. A. (1963), Organizations (New York: John Wiley).

Marchak, P. (1979), In Whose Interest (Toronto: McClelland and Stewart).

Marcus, G. E. (1992), Lives in Trust (Boulder, Colo.: Westview Press).

Marcuse, H. (1964), One Dimensional Man (London: Sphere Books, 1968).

Mariolis, P. (1975), 'Interlocking Directorates and Control of Corporations', Social Science Quarterly, 56.

—— (1978), 'Type of Corporation, Size of Firm, and Interlocking Directorates: A Reply to Levine', Social Science Quarterly, 58.

Marris, R. (1964), The Economic Theory of 'Managerial' Capitalism (London: Macmillan).

Marsh, D., and Locksley, G. (1983), 'Capital in Britain: Its Structural Power and Influence Over Policy', West European Politics, 6.

Martinelli, A., and Chiesi, A. M. (1989), 'Italy', in Bottomore and Brym (eds.) (1989).

Marx, K. (1857), 'Introduction' to Grundrisse (Harmondsworth: Penguin, 1973).

—— (1865–7), Capital, iii (London: Lawrence and Wishart, 1959).

—— (1864–6), Capital, ii (London: Lawrence and Wishart, 1974).

Mason, E. S. (ed.) (1959), The Corporation in Modern Society (New York: Atheneum Press).

Mason, M., and Encarnation, D. (eds.) (1994), Does Ownership Matter? (Oxford: Clarendon Press).

Mathias, P. (1969), The First Industrial Nation (London: Methuen).

—— and Postan, M. M. (1978a and b), Cambridge Economic History of Europe, vii and viii (Cambridge: Cambridge University Press).

Maw, N., Lord Lane, and Craig-Cowper, Sir M. (1994), Maw on Corporate Governance (Aldershot: Dartmouth).

Mayer, C. (1993), 'Ownership' (Inaugural Lecture, unpublished paper, Coventry: University of Warwick).

Mayo, E. (1949), The Social Problems of an Industrial Civilization (London: Routledge and Kegan Paul).

Meade, J. E. (1964), Efficiency, Equality, and the Ownership of Property (London: George Allen and Unwin).

Means, G. C. (1964), 'Economic Concentration', Report to Senate Hearings, in Zeitlin (ed.) (1970).

—— et al. (1939), 'The Structure of Controls', Chapter 9 in The Structure of the American Economy (National Resources Committee of the US Senate, Washington: Government Printing Office).

Meeks, G., and Whittington, G. (1975), 'Giant Companies in the United Kingdom', *Economic Journal*, 85.

—— —— (1976), *The Financing of Quoted Companies* (Background Paper no. 1, Royal Commission on the Distribution of Income and Wealth, London: HMSO).

Meeusen, W., and Cuyvers, L. (1985), 'The Interaction Between Interlocking Directorships and the Economic Behaviour of Companies', in Stokman *et al.* (eds.) (1985).

Melzer, M. (1981), 'Combine Formation and the Role of the Enterprise in East German Industry', in Jeffries (ed.) (1981).

Menshikov, S. (1969), *Millionaires and Managers* (Moscow: Progress Publishers).

Michalet, C. A. (1976), *Le capitalisme mondial* (Paris: Presses Universitaires de France).

Middlemas, K. (1979), *Politics in Industrial Society* (London: André Deutsch).

Milgrom, P., and Roberts, J. (1992), *Economics, Organization and Management* (Englewood Cliffs, NJ: Prentice-Hall).

Miliband, R. (1968), 'Professor Galbraith and American Capitalism', in Mankoff (ed.) (1972).

—— (1969), *The State in Capitalist Society* (London: Weidenfeld and Nicolson).

—— (1970), 'The Capitalist State', *New Left Review*, 59.

—— (1973), 'Poulantzas and the Capitalist State', *New Left Review*, 82.

—— (1977), *Marxism and Politics* (Oxford: Oxford University Press).

Miller, H. P. (1966), 'Income Distribution in the United States', in Atkinson (ed.) (1973b).

Mills, C. W. (1940), 'Situated Actions and Vocabularies of Motive', *American Sociological Review*, 5.

—— (1956), *The Power Elite* (New York: Oxford University Press).

Millward, A. S., and Saul, B. S. (1977), *The Development of the Economies of Central Europe, 1850–1914* (London: George Allen and Unwin).

Minns, R. (1980), *Pension Funds and British Capitalism* (London: Heinemann).

—— (1982), 'Management of Shareholdings in Large Manufacturing Companies' (Social Science Working Papers, Milton Keynes: The Open University).

Mintz, B. (1975), 'The President's Cabinet, 1897–1972', *Insurgent Sociologist*, 5.

—— (1989), 'United States of America', in Bottomore and Brym (eds.) (1989).

—— and Schwartz, M. (1981a), 'Interlocking Directorates and Interest Group Formation', *American Sociological Review*, 46.

―― ―― (1981b), 'The Structure of Intercorporate Unity in American Business', *Social Problems*, 29.

―― ―― (1983), 'Financial Interest Groups and Interlocking Directorates', *Social Science History*, 7.

―― ―― (1985), *The Power Structure of American Business* (Chicago: University of Chicago Press).

―― ―― (1986), 'Capital Flows and the Process of Financial Hegemony', *Theory and Society*, 15.

Mishima, Y. (1977), 'Comments [on Morikawa]', in Nakagawa (ed.), (n.d.).

Miyazaki, Y. (1967), 'Excessive Competition and the Formation of Keiretsu', in Sato (ed.) (1980).

―― (1973), 'The Japanese-Type Structure of Big Business', in Sato (ed.) (1980).

Mizruchi, M. S. (1982), *The American Corporate Network, 1900–74* (London: Sage).

―― (1983a), 'Relations Among Large American Corporations, 1904–74', *Social Science History*, 7.

―― (1983b), 'Who Controls Whom? An Examination of the Relation Between Management and Boards of Directors in Large American Corporations', *Academy of Management Review*, 8.

―― (1987), 'Managerialism: Another Reassessment', in Schwartz (ed.) (1987).

―― (1992), *The Structure of Corporate Political Action: Interfirm Relations and Their Consequences* (Cambridge, Mass.: Harvard University Press).

―― and Schwartz, M. (eds.) (1988), *Intercorporate Relations: The Structural Analysis of Business* (New York: Cambridge University Press).

Mokken, R. J., and Stokman, F. N. (1974), 'Interlocking Directorates Between Large Corporations' (paper to European Consortium for Political Research, Strasbourg).

―― ―― (1976), 'Power and Influence as Political Phenomena', in Barry (ed.) (1976).

Monjardet, D. (1972), 'Carrière des dirigeants et contrôle de l'entreprise', *Sociologie du travail*, 14.

Monsen, R. J., and Downs, A. (1965), 'A Theory of Large Managerial Firms', *Journal of Political Economy*, 73.

―― Chiu, J. S., and Cooley, D. E. (1968), 'The Effect of Separation of Ownership and Control on the Performance of the Large Firm', *Quarterly Journal of Economics*, 82.

Moody, J. (1904), *The Truth About the Trusts* (Chicago: Moody Publishing).

―― (1919), *The Masters of Capital* (New Haven: Yale University Press).

Moran, M. (1983), 'Power, Policy and the City of London', in King (ed.) (1983).

—— (1984), *The Politics of Banking* (London: Macmillan).

—— (1991), *The Politics of the Financial Services Revolution* (London: Macmillan).

Morikawa, H (1971), 'Managerial Structure and Control Devices for Diversified *Zaibatsu* Business', in Nakagawa (ed.) (n.d.).

—— (1992), *Zaibatsu: The Rise and Fall of Family Enterprise in Japan* (Tokyo: University of Tokyo Press).

Morin, F. (1974a), *La Structure financière du capitalisme français* (Paris: Calmann-Levy).

—— (1974b), 'Qui detient le pouvoir financier en France?', *Economie et Humanisme*, 220.

—— (1976), 'Ombres et lumières du capitalisme français', *Economie et Humanisme*, 229.

—— (1977), *La banque et les groupes industriels a l'heure des nationalisations* (Paris: Calmann-Levy).

Morioka, K. (1989), 'Japan', in Bottomore and Brym (eds.) (1989).

Morrison, R. J. (1967), 'Financial Intermediaries and Economic Development: the Belgian Case', *Scandinavian Economic History Review*, 15.

Morvan, Y. (1972), *La Concentration de l'industrie en France* (Paris: Librairie Armand Colin).

Mullins, N. (1973), *Theory and Theory Groups in Contemporary American Sociology* (New York: Harper and Row).

Murray, R. (1971), 'The Internationalization of Capital and the Nation State', in R. Murray, *Multinational Companies and Nation States* (Nottingham: Spokesman Books).

Nairn, T. (1972), *The Left Against Europe* (Harmondsworth: Penguin, 1973).

—— (1977), *The Breakup of Britain* (London: New Left Books).

Nakagawa, K. (ed.) (n.d.) (1977), *Strategy and Structure of Big Business* (University of Tokyo Press).

—— (1977), 'Business Strategy and Industrial Structure in Pre-World War II Japan', in Nakagawa (ed.) (n.d.).

Nakata, M. (1995), 'Ownership and Control of the Large Corporation in contemporary Japan' (paper to Inaugural Seminar of School of East Asian Studies, University of Sheffield).

Nelson, L. D., and Kuzes, I. Y. (1995), *Radical Reform in Yeltsin's Russia* (Armonk: M. E. Sharpe).

Nelson, R., and Winter, S. (1982), *An Evolutionary Theory of Economic Change* (Cambridge, Mass.: Harvard University Press).

Nee, V. (1989), 'A Theory of Market Transition: From Redistribution to Markets in State Socialism', *Administrative Science Quarterly*, 54.

—— (1991), 'Social Inequalities in Reforming State Socialism: Between Redistribution and Markets in China', *American Sociological Review*, 56.

—— (1996), 'The Emergence of Market Society: Changing Mechanisms of Stratification in China', *American Journal of Sociology*, 101.

Neuman, F. (1944), *Behemoth: The Structure and Practice of National Socialism* (revised edn., New York: Octagon Books).

Nichols, T. (1969), *Ownership, Control, and Ideology* (London: George Allen and Unwin).

Nicholson, R. J. (1967), 'The Distribution of Personal Income in the UK', in Urry and Wakeford (eds.) (1973).

Niosi, J. (1978), *The Economy of Canada* (Montreal: Black Rose Books).

—— (1981), *Canadian Capitalism* (Toronto: Jas. Lorimer).

Noble, T. (1975), *Modern Britain* (London: Batsford).

Noguchi, T. (1973), 'Japanese Monopoly Capital and the State', *Kapitalistate*, 1.

—— (1984), *Japanese Business Concentration and Multinationals* (Tokyo: Keio Tsushin).

Nove, A. (1969), *An Economic History of the Soviet Union* (Harmondsworth: Penguin, 1972).

—— (1981), 'The Soviet Industrial Enterprise', in Jeffries (ed.) (1981).

Numazaki, I. (1986), 'Networks of Taiwanese Business: A Preliminary Analysis', *China Quarterly*, 12.

—— (1991), 'The Role of Personal Networks in the Making of Taiwan's Guanxiqiye', in Hamilton (1991*b*).

—— (1992), *Networks and Partnerships: The Social Organization of The Chinese Business Elite in Taiwan* (Ph.D. diss., Michigan State University).

Nuti, D. M. (1981), 'Industrial Enterprises in Poland, 1973–80', in Jeffries (ed.) (1981).

Nyman, S., and Silberston, A. (1978), 'The Ownership and Control of Industry', *Oxford Economic Papers*, 30/1.

Oberschall, A. (1996), 'The Great Transition: China, Hungary and Sociology Exit Socialism into the Market', *American Journal of Sociology*, 101.

O'Connor, J. (1971), 'Who Rules the Corporations? The Ruling Class', *Socialist Revolution*, 7.

—— (1973), *The Fiscal Crisis of the State* (New York: St Martins Press).

Offe, C. (1970), *Industry and Inequality* (London: Edward Arnold, 1976).

—— (1972), *Strukturprobleme des kapitalistischen Staates* (Frankfurt: Suhrkamp).

Offe, C. (1981), 'The Attribution of Public Status to Interest Groups: Observations on the West German Case', in Berger (ed.) (1981).

—— (1982), 'The Future of the Labour Market', in Offe (1985).

—— (1984), 'The Political Economy of the Labor Market', in Offe (1985).

—— (1985), *Disorganised Capitalism: Contemporary Transformations of Work and Politics* (Cambridge: Polity Press).

O'Hara, M. (1981), 'Property Rights and the Financial Firm', *Journal of Law and Economics*, 24.

Ohtani, K. (1984), *Securities Market in Japan* (Tokyo: Japan Securities Research Institute).

Okumura, H. (1975), *Hojin Shinonshugi no Kozo* (Tokyo: Nihon Hyoronsha).

—— (1983), *Shin Nihon no Rokudai Kigyoshudan* (Tokyo: Diamond-sha).

—— (1984), 'Enterprise Groups in Japan', *Shoken Keizai*, 147.

—— (1991), 'Intercorporate Relations in Japan', in Hamilton (1991*b*).

Okun (1981), *Prices and Quantities: A Macroeconomic Analysis* (Oxford: Blackwell).

Oppenheim, C. (1990), *Poverty: The Facts* (London: Child Poverty Action Group).

Orenstein, M. (1994), 'The Czech Tripartite Council and its Contribution to Social Peace', *Budapest Papers on Democratic Transition*, No. 99.

Ornstein, M. D. (1982), 'Interlocking Directorates in Canada: Evidence from Replacement Patterns', *Social Networks*, 4.

—— (1989), 'The Social Organization of the Capitalist Class in Comparative Perspective', *Canadian Review of Sociology and Anthropology*, 26.

Ostrander, S. A. (1984), *Women of the Upper Class* (Philadelphia: Temple University Press).

Ottosson, J. (1993), *Stabilitet och Förändring I Personliga Näringsliv, 1903–1939* (Uppsala: Uppsala University Press).

Pahl, J. M., and Pahl, R. E. (1971), *Managers and their Wives* (Harmondsworth: Allen Lane).

Pahl, R. E. (1977*a*), 'Stratification: The Relation Between States and Urban and Regional Development', *International Journal of Urban and Regional Research*, 1.

—— (1977*b*), ' "Collective Consumption" and the State in Capitalist and State Socialist Societies', in Scase (ed.) (1977).

—— (1995), *After Success* (Cambridge: Polity Press).

—— and Winkler, J. (1974), 'The Economic Elite: Theory and Practice', in Stanworth and Giddens (eds.) (1974*b*).

Palmade, G. P. (1961), *French Capitalism in the Nineteenth Century* (Newton Abbott: David and Charles, 1972).

Palmer, D. (1983a), 'Broken Ties: Interlocking Directorates and Inter-corporate Coordination', *Administrative Science Quarterly*, 28.

—— (1983b), 'Interpreting Corporate Interlocks from Broken Ties', *Social Science History*, 7.

Palmer, J. P. (1972), 'The Separation of Ownership from Control in Large US Industrial Corporations', *Quarterly Review of Economics and Business*, 12.

—— (1973), 'The Profit-Performance Effects of the Separation of Ownership from Control in Large US Industrial Corporations', *Bell Journal of Economics and Management Science*, 4.

Pan, L. (1990), *Sons of the Yellow Emperor* (London: Martin Secker and Warburg).

Papandreou, A. G. (1973), 'Multinational Corporations and Empire', *Social Praxis*, 1.

Parkin, F. (1979), *Marxism and Class Theory* (London: Tavistock).

Parkinson, H. (1951), *Ownership of Industry* (London: Eyre and Spottis-woode).

Parkinson, J. E. (1993), *Corporate Power and Responsibility: Issues in the Theory of Company Law* (Oxford: Clarendon Press).

Parsons, T. (1940), 'The Motivation of Economic Activity', in Parsons (1954b).

—— (1954a), 'A Revised Analytical Approach to the Theory of Social Stratification', in Parsons (1954b).

—— (1954b), *Essays in Sociological Theory* (Glencoe, Ill.: Free Press).

—— (1956), 'A Sociological Approach to the Theory of Organizations', in Parsons (1960).

—— (1958), 'The Institutional Framework of Economic Development', in Parsons (1960).

—— (1960), *Structure and Process in Modern Societies* (Glencoe, Ill.: Free Press).

—— and Smelser, N. J. (1957), *Economy and Society* (London: Routledge and Kegan Paul).

Pastré, O. (1979), *La Strategie internationale des groupes financiers americains* (Paris: Economica).

Patman Report (1966), *Bank Stock Ownership and Control*, reprinted in Patman Report (1968).

—— (1967), *Control of Commercial Banks and Interlocks Among Financial Institutions*, reprinted in Patman Report (1968).

—— (1968), *Commercial Banks and Their Trust Activities*, Staff Report for the Subcommittee on Domestic Finance Committee on Banking and Currency, House of Representatives, 90th Congress, 2nd Session (Washington: Government Printing Office).

Pavitt, K., and Worboys, M. (1977), *Science, Technology and the Modern Industrial State* (London: Butterworth).

Payne, P. L. (1967), 'The Emergence of the Large-Scale Company in Great Britain', *Economic History Review*, 20.

—— (1974), *British Entrepreneurship in the Nineteenth Century* (London: Macmillan).

—— (1978), 'Industrial Entrepreneurship and Management in Great Britain', in Mathias and Postan (eds.) (1978*b*).

Pennings, J. M. (1980), *Interlocking Directorates* (San Francisco: Jossey Bass).

Perkin, H. (1978), 'The Recruitment of Elites in British Society since 1800', *Journal of Social History*, 12.

Perlo, V. (1957), *The Empire of High Finance* (New York: International Publishers).

—— (1958), ' "People's Capitalism" and stock ownership', *American Economic Review*, 48. References are to the reprint in Mankoff (1972).

Perrow, C. (1990), 'Economic Theories of Organisation', in Zukin and Di Maggio (1990).

—— (1986), *Complex Organisations: A Critical Essay* (3rd edn., New York: Random House).

Perrucci, R., and Potter, R. (eds.) (1989), *Networks of Power* (New York: Aldine De Gruyter).

Peterson, S. (1965), 'Corporate Control and Capitalism', *Quarterly Journal of Economics*, 79.

Pettigrew, A. (1992), 'On Studying Managerial Elites', *Strategic Management Journal*, 13.

—— and McNulty, T. (1995), 'Power and Influence In and Around the Boardroom', *Human Relations*, 48.

Pfeffer, J. (1972), 'Size and Composition of Corporate Boards of Directors', *Administrative Science Quarterly*, 17.

Picciotto, S., and Radice, H. (1973), 'Capital and State in the World Economy', *Kapitalistate*, 1.

Piedalue, G. (1976), 'Les Groupes financiers au Canada, 1900–1930', *Revue d'Histoire de l'Amerique Française*, 30.

Piore, M. J., and Sabel, C. F. (1984), *The Second Industrial Divide: Possibilities For Prosperity* (New York: Basic Books).

Pitelis, C. (1987), *Corporate Capital: Control, Ownership, Savings and Crisis* (Cambridge: Cambridge University Press).

Poland, E. (1939), 'Interlocking Directorates among the Largest American Corporations, 1935', Appendix 12 to *The Structure of the American Economy*, National Resources Committee of the US Senate (Washington: Government Printing Office).

Polanyi, G. and Wood, J. B. (1974), *How Much Inequality?* (London: Institute of Economic Affairs).

Pollard, S. (1962), *The Development of the British Economy* (London: Edward Arnold).

—— (1965), *The Genesis of Modern Management* (Cambridge, Mass.: Belknap Press, 1977).

Porter, J. (1965), *The Vertical Mosaic* (Toronto: University of Toronto Press).

Poulantzas, N. (1968), *Political Power and Social Classes* (London: New Left Books, 1973).

—— (1969), 'The Problem of the Capitalist State', *New Left Review*, 58.

—— (1974), *Classes in Contemporary Capitalism* (London: New Left Books, 1975).

Powell, W. W. (1990), 'Neither Market nor Hierarchy: Network Forms of Organization', *Research in Organizational Behaviour*, 12.

—— and Di Maggio, P. (eds.) (1991), *The New Institutionalism in Organizational Analysis* (Chicago: University of Chicago Press).

Prais, S. J. (1976), *The Evolution of Giant Firms in Britain* (Cambridge: Cambridge University Press).

Pratt, S. S. (1905), 'Our Financial Oligarchy', *Worlds Work*, 10.

Prentice, D. D., and Holland, P. R. J. (eds.) (1993), *Contemporary Issues in Corporate Governance* (Oxford: Clarendon Press).

Presthus, R. (1973), *Elites in the Policy Process* (Cambridge: Cambridge University Press).

Prowse, S. (1992). 'The Structure of Corporate Ownership in Japan', *Journal of Finance*, 47.

Pujo Report (1913), *Money Trust Investigation* (House Subcommittee on Banking and Currency, Washington: Government Printing Office).

Radcliffe Report (1959), *Report of the Committee on the Working of the Monetary System* (Cmnd 827, London: HMSO).

Radek, K. (1934), 'Japanese and International Fascism', Introduction to Tanin and Yohan (1934).

Radice, H. (1971), 'Control Type, Profitability and Growth in Large Firms: An Empirical Study', *Economic Journal*, 81.

—— (ed.) (1975), *International Firms and Modern Imperialism* (Harmondsworth: Penguin).

—— (1981), 'The State Enterprise in Hungary', in Jeffries (ed.) (1981).

Ramsoy, N. (ed.) (1974), *Norwegian Society* (London: Hurst).

Ratcliff, R. E. (1980), 'Banks and Corporate Lending: An Analysis of the Impact of the Interlock Structure of the Capitalist Class on the Lending Behaviour of Banks', *American Sociological Review*, 45.

Ratcliff, R. (1987), 'The Inner Circle and Bank Lending Policy', in Schwartz (ed.) (1987).

Ray, L. (1994), 'The Collapse of Soviet Socialism: Legitimation, Regulation and the New Class', in Brown and Crompton (eds.) (1994).

—— and Reed, M. (eds.) (1995), Organising Modernity (London: Routledge).

Readman, P., Davies, J., Hoare, M., and Poole, D. (1973), The European Monetary Puzzle (London: Michael Joseph).

Redding, S. G. (1990), The Spirit of Chinese Capitalism (Berlin: Walter de Gruyter).

Reder, M. (1947), 'A Reconsideration of the Marginal Productivity Theory', Journal of Political Economy, 55.

Reeder, J. A. (1975), 'Corporate Ownership and Control: A Synthesis of Recent Findings', Industrial Organisation Review, 3.

Regini, M. (1982), 'Changing Relationships Between Labour and the State in Italy', in Lehmbruch and Schmitter (eds.) (1982).

Renner, K. (1904), The Institutions of Private Law and their Social Function (London: Routledge and Kegan Paul, 1949. A translation of the 1928 revised edition).

—— (1953), Wandlungen in der modernen Gesellschaft (Vienna: Volks-buchandlung).

Rentoul, J. (1987), The Rich Get Richer (London: Unwin Hyman).

Reutter, W. (1995), 'Tripartism Without Corporatism: Trade Unions in East Central Europe', Budapest Papers on Democratic Transition, 138.

Revell, J. R. (1960), 'An Analysis of Personal Holders of Wealth', British Association for the Advancement of Science, 17.

—— (1965), 'Changes in the Social Distribution of Property in Britain during the Twentieth Century', Actes du Troisième Congrès International d'Histoire Économique, Munich.

Rex, J. A. (1974), 'Capitalism, Elites and the Ruling Class', in Stanworth and Giddens (eds.) (1974).

Richardson, R. J. (1988), ' "A Sacred Trust": The Trust Industry and Canadian Economic Structure', Canadian Review of Sociology and Anthropology, 25.

—— (1992), 'Free Trade: Why Did It Happen?', Canadian Review of Sociology and Social Anthropology, 29.

Rifkin, J., and Barber, R. (1978), The North Will Rise Again (Boston: Beacon Press).

Rigby, T. H. (1990), The Changing Soviet System (Cheltenham: Edward Elgar).

Robinson, J. (1933), The Economics of Imperfect Competition (London: Macmillan).

Rochester, A. (1936), *Rulers of America* (New York: International Publishers).

Roe, M. J. (1994), *Strong Managers and Weak Owners: The Political Roots of American Corporate Finance* (Princeton: Princeton University Press).

Rolfe, H. (1967), *The Controllers* (Melbourne: Cheshire).

Roman, Z. (1989), 'The Size of the Small Firm Sector in Hungary', *Small Business Enterprise*, 1.

Róna-Tas, Á. (1994), 'The First Shall Be Last: Entrepreneurship and Communist Cadres in the Transition from Socialism', *American Journal of Sociology*, 100.

Rose, A. (1967), *The Power Structure* (New York: Oxford University Press).

Ross, R., and Trachte, K. (1990), *Global Capitalism: The New Leviathan* (Albany, NY: SUNY Press).

Ross, S. (1978), 'The Economic Theory of Agency: The Principal's Problem', *American Economic Review*, 62.

Rostow, W. W. (1960), *The Stages of Economic Growth* (Cambridge: Cambridge University Press).

Roth, G., and Wittich, C. (eds.) (1968), *Economy and Society* (Berkeley: University of California Press).

Rowthorn, R. (1971), *International Big Business* (Cambridge: Cambridge University Press).

—— (1976), 'Late Capitalism', *New Left Review*, 98.

Roy, W. G. (1983a), 'The Unfolding of the Interlocking Directorate Structure of the United States', *American Sociological Review*, 48.

—— (1983b), 'Interlocking Directorates and the Corporate Revolution', *Social Science History*, 7.

Rubinstein, W. D. (1976), 'Wealth, Elites, and the Class Structure of Modern Britain', *Past and Present*, 70.

—— (ed.) (1980), *Wealth and the Wealthy in the Modern World* (London: Croom Helm).

—— (1981), *Men of Property* (London: Croom Helm).

—— (1986), *Wealth and Inequality in Britain* (London: Faber and Faber).

Rusterholz, P. (1985), 'The Banks in the Centre: Integration in Decentralised Switzerland', in Stokman et al. (eds.) (1985).

Rutges, A. (1984), 'Deskundigheid versus Financiële Controle: simulatiestudie van Benoemingen in het Bedrijfsleven', in Dronkers and Stokman (eds.) (1984).

Rychetnik, L. (1981), 'The Industrial Enterprise in Czechoslovakia', in Jeffries (ed.) (1981).

Ryndina, M., and Chernikov, G. (eds.) (1974), *The Political Economy of Capitalism* (Moscow: Progress Publishers).

Sabel, C. F. (1982), *Work and Politics: The Division of Labour in Industry* (Cambridge: Cambridge University Press).

Safarian, A. E. (1966), *Foreign Ownership of Canadian Industry* (Toronto: McGraw-Hill).

Sampson, A. (1973), *The Sovereign State* (London: Hodder and Stoughton).

—— (1975), *The Seven Sisters* (London: Hodder and Stoughton).

Sato, K. (ed.) (1980), *Industry and Business in Japan* (London: Croom Helm).

Saunders, P., and Harris, C. (1994), *Privatization and Popular Capitalism* (Buckingham: Open University Press).

Savage, D. (1979), *Founders, Heirs and Managers* (London: Sage).

Savage, M. (1978), 'The Ownership and Control of Large South African Companies', *South African Labour Bulletin*, 4.

—— (1984), 'An Anatomy of the South African Corporate Economy: Ownership, Control and the Interlocking Directorate' (University of Cape Town: Centre For African Studies).

—— et al. (1982), *Property, Bureaucracy and Culture: Middle-Class Formation in Contemporary Britain* (London: Routledge).

Scase, R. (ed.) (1976), *Readings in the Swedish Class Structure* (London: Pergamon).

—— (ed.) (1977), *Industrial Society: Class, Cleavage and Control* (London: George Allen and Unwin).

—— (ed.) (1980), *The State in Western Europe* (London: Croom Helm).

—— (1982), 'The Petty Bourgeoisie and Modern Capitalism', in Giddens and Mackenzie (eds.) (1982).

Schijf, H. (1979), 'Networks of Interlocking Directorates at the Turn of the Century in the Netherlands' (paper for Research Workshop, European Consortium for Political Research, Brussels).

—— (1984), 'Economische netwerkelites rond 1900', in Dronkers and Stokman (eds.) (1984).

Schmitter, P. C. (1974), 'Still the Century of Corporatism', in Schmitter and Lehmbruch (eds.) (1979).

—— (1977), 'Modes of Interest Intermediation and Models of Societal Change in Western Europe', in Schmitter and Lehmbruch (eds.) (1979).

—— (1981), 'Interest Intermediation and Regime Governability in Contemporary Western Europe and North America', in Berger (ed.) (1981).

—— (1982), 'Reflections on Where the Theory of Neo-corporatism has Gone and Where the Praxis of Neo-Corporatism may be Going', in Lehmbruch and Schmitter (eds.) (1982).

—— and Lehmbruch, G. (eds.) (1979), *Trends Towards Corporatist Intermediation* (Beverly Hills: Sage Publications).

Schonwitz, D., and Weber, H.-J. (1980), 'Personelle Verflechtungen zwischen Unternehmen', *Zeitschrift fur die gesamte Staatswissenschaft*, 136.

Schreiner, J.-P. (1984), 'Finance Capital and the Network of Interlocking Directorates among Major Corporations in Switzerland' (unpublished paper, Aix-en-Provence).

Schuller, T. (1986), *Age, Capital and Democracy: Member Participation in Pension Scheme Management* (Aldershot: Gower).

—— and Hyman, J. (1984), 'Forms of Ownership and Control: Decision-Making Within a Financial Institution', *Sociology*, 18.

Schwartz, M. (ed.) (1987), *The Structure of Power in America* (New York: Holmes and Meier).

Scott, J. P. (1978), 'Critical Social Theory: An Introduction and Critique', *British Journal of Sociology*, 29.

—— (1982a), 'Property and Control: Some Remarks on the British Propertied Class', in Giddens and Mackenzie (eds.), (1982).

—— (1982b), *The Upper Classes* (London: Macmillan).

—— (1985), 'Theoretical Framework and Research Design', in Stokman *et al.* (eds.) (1985).

—— (1986), *Capitalist Property and Financial Power* (Hassocks: Wheatsheaf).

—— (1990a), 'Corporate Capital and Corporate Rule: Britain in an International Perspective', *British Journal of Sociology*, 41.

—— (ed.) (1990b), *The Sociology of Elites* (3 vols., Aldershot: Edward Elgar).

—— (1991a), 'Networks of Corporate Power: A Comparative Assessment', *Annual Review of Sociology*, 17.

—— (1991b), *Who Rules Britain?* (Cambridge: Polity Press).

—— (1992), *Social Network Analysis* (London: Sage Publications).

—— (1993), 'Corporate Groups and Network Structure', in McCahery *et al.* (eds.) (1993).

—— (ed.) (1994a), *Power* (3 vols., London: Routledge).

—— (1994b), *Poverty and Wealth: Citizenship, Deprivation and Privilege* (Harlow: Longman).

—— (1995), *Sociological Theory: Contemporary Debates* (Cheltenham: Edward Elgar).

—— (1996a), *Stratification and Power: Structures of Class, Status and Command* (Cambridge: Polity Press).

—— (ed.) (1996b), *Class* (4 vols., London: Routledge).

—— and Griff, C. (1984), *Directors of Industry: The British Corporate Network, 1900–1976* (Cambridge: Polity Press).

—— —— (1985), 'Bank Spheres of Influence in the British Corporate Network', in Stokman *et al.* (eds.) (1985).

Scott, J. P. and Hughes, M. D. (1976), 'Ownership and Control in a Satellite Economy: A Discussion from Scottish Data', *Sociology*, 10.

—— —— (1980a), 'Capital and Communication in Scottish Business', *Sociology*, 13.

—— —— (1980b), *The Anatomy of Scottish Capital* (London: Croom Helm).

Segnana, L. (1993), 'Public–Private relations in Italy: The Experience of the 1980s', in Clarke and Pitelis (eds.) (1993).

Seierstad, S. (1968), 'The Norwegian Economy', in Ramsoy (ed.) (1974).

Servan-Schreiber, J. J. (1957), *The American Challenge* (London: Hamish Hamilton, 1968).

Shannon, T. R. (1989), *An Introduction to the World-System Perspective* (San Francisco: Westview Press).

Shaw, G. B. (ed.) (1889), *Fabian Essays in Socialism* (London: Fabian Society).

—— (1928), *The Intelligent Woman's Guide To Socialism, Capitalism, Sovietism and Fascism* (Harmondsworth: Penguin, 1937).

Sheard, P. (1994), 'Interlocking Shareholdings and Corporate Governance', in Aoki and Dore (eds.) (1994).

Sheehan, R. (1967), 'Proprietors in the World of Big Business', *Fortune*, 15 June.

Shinoda, T. (1987), 'Capitalism in Japan and the Group of Enterprises', *Ritsumeikan Sangyoshakai Ronshu*, 22.

Shleifer, A., and Vishny, R. (1986), 'Large Shareholders and Corporate Control', *Journal of Political Economy*, 94.

Shonfield, M. (1965), *Modern Capitalism* (Oxford: Oxford University Press).

Sillin, R. H. (1976). *Organization and Value: The Organisation of Large-Scale Taiwanese Enterprises* (Cambridge, Mass.: Harvard University Press).

Simon, H. A. (1945), *Administrative Behaviour* (New York: Macmillan, 1961).

Simons, A. J. (1927), *Holding Companies* (London: Pitman).

Skidelsky, R. (1979), 'The Decline of Keynesian Politics', in Crouch (ed.) (1979).

Sklair, L. (1995a), *Sociology of the Global System* (2nd edn., Hemel Hempstead: Prentice Hall/Harvester Wheatsheaf).

—— (1995b), 'Conceptualising and Researching the Transnational Capitalist Class in Australia' (unpubl. paper, London School of Economics).

Smith, D., and Tepperman, L. (1974), 'Changes in the Canadian Business and Legal Elites', *Canadian Review of Sociology and Anthropology*, 11.

Smith, E. O. (1983), *The West German Economy* (London: Croom Helm).

Smith, E. P. (1970), 'Interlocking Directorates Among the "Fortune 500"', *Antitrust, Law and Economic Review*, 3.

—— and Desfosses, L. R. (1972), 'Interlocking Directorates: A Study of Influence', *Mississippi Valley Journal of Business and Economics*, 7.

Smith, J. D., and Calvert, S. K. (1965), 'Estimating the Wealth of Top Wealth-Holders from Estate Tax Returns', *Proceedings of the American Statistical Association*.

Smith, R. J. (1983), *Japanese Society* (Cambridge: Cambridge University Press).

So, A. Y., and Chiu, S. W. K. (1995), *East Asia and the World Economy* (Thousand Oaks, Calif. Sage).

Solgow, L. (1968), 'Long Run Changes in British Income Inequality', in Atkinson (ed.) (1973*b*).

Sonquist, J. A. *et al.* (1975), 'Interlocking Directorships in the Top US Corporations', *Insurgent Sociologist*, 5.

—— *et al.* (1976), 'Examining Corporate Interconnections Through Interlocking Directorates', in Burns and Buckley (eds.) (1976).

Soref, M. (1976), 'Social Class and a Division of Labour within the Corporate Elite', *Sociological Quarterly*, 17.

—— (1980), 'The Finance Capitalists', in Zeitlin (ed.) (1980).

—— and Zeitlin, M. (1988), 'Finance Capital and the Internal Structure of the Capitalist Class in the United States', in Mizruchi and Schwartz (eds.) (1988).

Spohne, W., and Bodermann, Y. M. (1989), 'Federal Republic of Germany', in Bottomore and Brym (1989).

Spybey, T. (1992), *Social Change, Development and Dependency* (Cambridge: Polity Press).

Staniszkis, J. (1991*a*), *The Dynamics of the Breakthrough in Eastern Europe: The Polish Experience* (Berkeley: University of California Press).

—— (1991*b*), ' "Political Capitalism" in Poland', *East European Politics and Societies*, 5.

Stano, M. (1976), 'Monopoly Power, Ownership Control, and Corporate Performance', *Bell Journal of Economics*, 2.

Stanworth, P. (1974), 'Property, Class and the Corporate Elite', in Crewe (ed.) (1974).

—— and Giddens, A. (1974*a*), 'An Economic Elite: A Demographic Profile of Company Chairmen', in Stanworth and Giddens (eds.) (1974*b*).

—— —— (eds.) (1974*b*), *Elites and Power in British Society* (Cambridge: Cambridge University Press).

—— —— (1975), 'The Modern Corporate Economy', *Sociological Review*, 23.

Stark, D. (1996), 'Recombinant Property in East European Capitalism', *American Journal of Sociology*, 101.

Steer, P., and Cable, J. (1978), 'Internal Organization and Profit: An Empirical Analysis of Large UK Companies', *Journal of Industrial Economics*, 27.

Steers, R. M., Keun, S. Y., and Ungson, G. R. (1989), *The Chaebol: Korea's New Industrial Might* (Grand Rapids, Mich.: Harper and Row).

Stening, B., and Wan, W. T. (1984), 'Interlocking Directorates Among Australia's Largest 250 Corporations, 1959–1979', *Australia and New Zealand Journal of Sociology*, 20.

Steuer, M. D. *et al.* (1973), *The Impact of Foreign Direct Investment on the United Kingdom* (London: HMSO).

Steven, R. (1983), *Classes in Contemporary Japan* (Cambridge: Cambridge University Press).

Stewart, A. (ed.) (1982), *Contemporary Britain* (London: Routledge and Kegan Paul).

Stock Exchange (1977), *The Provision of Funds for Industry and Trade* (London: Stock Exchange).

—— (1983), *The Stock Exchange Survey of Share Ownership* (London: Stock Exchange).

Stokes, H. (n.d.), *The Japanese Competitors* (*London: Financial Times, c.*1977).

Stokman, F. N., and Wasseur, F. (1985), 'National Networks in 1976: A Structural Comparison', in Stokman *et al.* (eds.) (1985).

—— Wasseur, R., and Elsas, D. (1985), 'The Dutch Network: Types of Interlocks and Network Structure', in Stokman *et al.* (eds.) (1985).

—— Ziegler, R., and Scott, J. P. (eds.) (1985), *Networks of Corporate Power: A Comparative Study of Ten Countries* (Cambridge: Polity Press).

Stone, R. *et al.* (1966), *The Owners of Quoted Ordinary Shares* (London: Chapman and Hall).

Storey, J. (1980), *The Challenge to Management Control* (London: Kogan Page).

—— (1983), *Managerial Prerogative and the Question of Control* (London: Routledge and Kegan Paul).

Streeck, W. (1982), 'Organizational Consequences of Neo-Corporatist Cooperation in West German Labour Unions', in Lehmbruch and Schmitter (eds.) (1982).

Strinati, D. (1982), 'State Intervention, the Economy, and the Crisis', in Stewart (ed.) (1982).

Sugarman, D. (ed.), (1983), *Legality, Ideology and the State* (London: Academic Press).

Suleiman, E. (1986), *Elites in French Society: The Politics of Survival* (Princeton: Princeton University Press).

Swartz, D (1985), 'French Interlocking Directorships: Financial and Industrial Groups', in Stokman *et al.* (eds.) (1985).

—— (1986), 'French Corporate Leadership: A Class-Based Technocracy', *Research in Political Sociology*, 2.

Sweezy, P. M (1939), 'Interest Groups in the American Economy', in Sweezy (1953).

—— (1940), 'The Heyday of the Investment Banker', in Sweezy (1953).

—— (1941), 'The Decline of the Investment Banker', in Sweezy (1953).

—— (1942), *The Theory of Capitalist Development* (London: Dennis Dobson).

—— (1951), 'The American Ruling Class', in Sweezy (1953).

—— (1953), *The Present as History* (New York: Monthly Review Press).

—— (1971), 'The Resurgence of Financial Control: Fact or Fancy', *Monthly Review*, 23.

Szablowski, G. J., and Derlein, H.-U. (1993), 'East European Transitions, Elites, Bureaucracies and the European Community', in Derlein and Szablowski (eds.) (1993).

Szelényi, I. (1989), *Socialist Entrepreneurs* (Cambridge: Polity Press).

Tan, H. (1991), 'State Capitalism, Multi-National Corporations and Chinese Entrepreneurship in Singapore', in Hamilton (ed.) (1991b).

Tanin, O., and Yohan, E. (1934), *Militarism and Fascism in Japan* (New York: International Publishers).

Taussig, F. W., and Joslyn, C. S. (1932), *American Business Leaders* (New York: Macmillan).

Tawney, R. H. (1920), *The Acquisitive Society* (London: Bell).

—— (1931), *Equality* (4th edn. London: George Allen and Unwin, 1952).

Teichova, A. (1992), 'Rivals and Partners: Reflections on Banking and Industry in Europe, 1880–1938', in Cottrell *et al.* (eds.) (1992).

—— and Cottrell, P. L. (eds.) (1983), *International Banks and Central Europe, 1918–1939* (Leicester: Leicester University Press).

—— Gourvish, T., and Pogary, A. (eds.) (1994), *Universal Banking in Twentieth-Century Europe* (Aldershot: Edward Elgar).

Teubner, G. (1993), 'The Many-Headed Hydra: Networks as Higher-Order Collective Actors', in McCahery *et al.* (eds.) (1993).

Therborn, G. (1976), 'The Swedish Class Structure, 1930–65: A Marxist Analysis', in Scase (1976).

Thomas, A. B. (1978), 'The British Business Elite: The Case of the Retail Sector', *Sociological Review*, 26.

—— (1981), 'Managerial Careers and the Problem of Control' (paper to EGOS Conference on Capital and Control, York).

Thomas, C. (1979), 'Family and Kinship in Eaton Square', in Field (ed.) (1979).

Thomas, W. A. (1978), *The Financing of British Industry, 1918–76* (London: Methuen).

Thompson, D. N. (1978), 'Mergers and Acquisitions: Motives and Effects' (London: Canada House Lecture Series, 3).

Thompson, G. (1977), 'The Relationship Between the Financial and Industrial Sector of the United Kingdom Economy', *Economy and Society*, 6.

—— Frances, J., Levacic, R., and Mitchell, J. (eds,), (1991), *Markets, Hierarchies and Networks: The Coordination of Social Life* (London, Sage).

Thonet, P. J., and Poensgen, O. H. (1979), 'Management Control and Economic Performance in Western Germany', *Journal of Industrial Economics*, 28.

Thrift, N. (1995), 'A Phantom State? International Money, Electronic Networks and Global Cities' (paper to conference on *Sociology and the Limits of Economics*, Liverpool).

Thurley, K., and Wood, S. (eds.) (1983), *Industrial Relations and Management Strategy* (Cambridge: Cambridge University Press).

Tilly, R. H. (1974), 'The Growth of Large Scale Enterprise in Germany since the Middle of the Nineteenth Century', in Daems and van der Wee (eds.) (1974).

—— (1986), 'German Banking, 1850–1914: Development Assistance for the Strong', *Journal of European Economic History*, 15.

Titmuss, R. (1962), *Income Distribution and Social Change* (London: George Allen and Unwin).

Todd, E. (1985), *The Explanation of Ideology* (Cambridge: Cambridge University Press).

Tominomori, K. (1979), 'Big Business Groups and Finance Capital in Post-War Japan', *Hokudai Economic Papers*, 9.

Tomkins, C., and Lovering, J. (1973), *Location, Size, Ownership and Control Tables For Welsh Industry* (Cardiff: Welsh Council).

Tomlinson, J. (1982), *The Unequal Struggle: British Socialism and the Capitalist Enterprise* (London: Methuen).

Tong, C. K. (1991), 'Centripetal Authority, Differentiated Networks: The Social Organisation of Chinese Firms in Singapore', in Hamilton (ed.) (1991b).

Tonkin, D. J., and Skerratt, L. C. L. (eds.) (1984), *Financial Reporting 1984–85: A Survey of U.K. Published Accounts* (London: Institute of Chartered Accountants).

Tricker, R. I. (1984), *Corporate Governance: Practices, Procedures and Powers in British Companies and their Boards of Directors* (Aldershot: Gower).

Tsuchiya, M. (1977), 'Management Structure of Vertically Integrated Non-zaibatsu Business', in Nakagawa (ed.) (n.d.).

Turner, L. (1970), *Invisible Empires* (London: Hamish Hamilton).

Ueda, Y. (1983), 'A Quantitative Analysis of Interlocking Directorates in Japanese Firm Groups' (in Japanese), *Shoken Keizai*, 146.

—— (1989), 'Similarities and Differences of the Corporate Network Structure in Japan and the United States', *Ryutsu Kagaku Daigaku Ronshu*, 2.

—— (1990), 'The Structure of "Japan Inc." ', *Ryutsu Kagaku Daigaku Ronshu*, 2.

—— (1991), 'Types and Characteristics of Interlocking Directorates in Japan', in Hamilton (1991*b*).

Urry, J., and Wakeford, J. (eds.) (1973), *Power in Britain* (London: Heinemann).

Useem, M. (1978), 'The Inner Group of the American Capitalist Class', *Social Problems*, 25.

—— (1980), 'Corporations and the Corporate Elite', *Annual Review of Sociology*, 6.

—— (1982), 'Classwide Rationality in the Politics of Managers and Directors of Large Corporations in the United States and Great Britain', *Administrative Science Quarterly*, 27.

—— (1984), *The Inner Circle* (New York: Oxford University Press).

—— (1993), *Executive Defense: Shareholder Power and Corporate Reorganization* (Cambridge, Mass.: Harvard University Press).

—— and McCormack, A. (1981), 'The Dominant Segment of the British Business Elite', *Sociology*, 15.

Utton, M. A. (1982), *The Political Economy of Big Business* (Oxford: Martin Robertson).

van der Knoop, J., Stokman, F. N., and Wasseur, F. (1984), 'Theoretische herinterpretatie van dubbelfuncties tussen grote bedrijven: stabiliteit en carrière-opbouw in de periode 1960–1980', in Dronkers and Stokman (eds.) (1984).

van der Pijl, K. (1984), *The Making of an Atlantic Ruling Class* (London: Verso).

—— (1989), 'The International Level', in Bottomore and Brym (eds.) (1989).

van Hezewijk, J. (1986), *De Top-Elite van Nederland* (Amsterdam: Uitgeverij Balans).

Varga, E. (1928), *The Decline of Capitalism* (London: Dorrit Press).

Veblen, T. (1904), *The Theory of Business Enterprise* (New York: Scribner, 1915).

—— (1919), *The Industrial System and the Captains of Industry* (New York: Oriole Chapbooks).

—— (1924), *Absentee Ownership and Business Enterprise in Recent Times* (London: George Allen and Unwin).

Vernon, J. R. (1970), 'Ownership and Control among Large Member Banks', *Journal of Finance*, 25.

Vernon, R. (1971a), *Sovereignty at Bay* (New York: Basic Books).

—— (1971b), 'Multinational Business and National Economic Goals', *International Organization*, 25.

—— (ed.) (1976), *The Oil Crisis* (New York: W. W. Norton).

—— (1977), *Storm over the Multinationals* (London: Macmillan).

Villarejo, D. (1961a), 'Stock Ownership and the Control of Corporations', Parts I and II, *New University Thought*, 2.

—— (1961b), 'Stock Ownership and the Control of Corporations', Part III, *New University Thought*, 2.

Vogl, E. (1973), *German Business After the Economic Miracle* (London: Macmillan).

von Mehren, A. T. (ed.) (1963), *Law in Japan* (Cambridge, Mass.: Harvard University Press).

Von Otter, C. (1980), 'Swedish Welfare Capitalism: The Role of the State', in Scase (ed.) (1980).

Wallerstein, I. (1974a), *The Modern World System 1: Capitalist Agriculture and the Origins of the European World-Economy in the Sixteenth Century* (New York: Academic Press).

—— (1974b), 'The Rise and Future Demise of the World Capitalist System', *Comparative Studies in Society and History*, 16. Reprinted in Wallerstein (ed.) (1979), *The Capitalist World Economy* (Cambridge: Cambridge University Press).

—— (1980), *The Modern World System 2: Mercantilism and the Consolidation of the European World-Economy, 1600–1750* (New York: Academic Press).

—— (1989), *The Modern World System 3: The Second Era of Great Expansion of the Capitalist World-Economy, 1730–1840s* (New York: Academic Press).

Warner, W. L. (1959), 'The Corporation Man', in Mason (ed.) (1959).

—— (ed.) (1967), *The Emergent American Society*, i (New Haven: Yale University Press).

—— and Abegglen, J. C. (1955), *Big Business Leaders in America* (New York: Harper Brothers).

—— and Unwalla, D. B. (1967), 'The System of Interlocking Directorates', in Warner (ed.) (1967).

Warren, B. (1971), 'How International is Capital?', in Radice (ed.) (1975).

—— (1972), 'Capitalist Planning and the State', *New Left Review*, 72.

Wearing, R. T. (1984), 'Analyses of Shareholdings', in Tonkin and Skerratt (eds.) (1984).

—— and Seaton, J. S. (1985), 'Voluntary Shareholding Disclosures and the Assessment of Shareholding Dispersal in U.K. Quoted Companies' (University of Essex, Department of Economics Discussion Paper Series, 265).

Webb, S., and Webb, B. (1923), *The Decay of Capitalist Civilization* (London: Fabian Society and George Allen and Unwin).

Weber, M. (1914), 'The Economy and the Arena of Normative and De Facto Powers', in Roth and Wittich (eds.), *Economy and Society* (1968).

—— (1920), 'Conceptual Exposition', in Roth and Wittich (eds.), *Economy and Society* (1968).

—— (1923), *General Economic History* (Glencoe, Ill.: Free Press, 1950).

Weinstein, F. B. (1976), 'Multinational Corporations and the Third World: The Case of Japan and South East Asia', *International Organisation*, 30.

Wellman, B., and Berkowitz, S. (eds.) (1988), *Social Structures* (Cambridge: Cambridge University Press).

Westergaard, J. H. (1977), 'Class, Inequality, and "Corporatism" ', in Hunt (ed.) (1977).

—— and Resler, H. (1975), *Class in a Capitalist Society* (London: Heinemann).

Westney, D. E. (1979), 'Patterns of Organisation Development in Japan', in Dunkerley and Salaman (eds.) (1979).

Wheelwright, E. L. (1957), *Ownership and Control of Australian Companies* (Sydney: Law Book Company).

—— (1974), *Radical Political Economy* (Sydney: Australia and New Zealand Book Company).

—— and Miskelly, J. (1967), *Anatomy of Australian Manufacturing Industry* (Sydney: Law Book Company).

Whitley, R. (1973), 'Commonalities and Connections among Directors of Large Financial Institutions', *Sociological Review*, 21.

—— (1974), 'The City and Industry', in Stanworth and Giddens (eds.) (1974*b*).

—— (1992), *Business Systems in East Asia: Firms, Markets and Societies* (London: Sage).

—— Thomas, A. B., and Marceau, J. (1981), *Masters of Business?* (London: Tavistock).

Whitt, J. A. (1981), 'Is Oil Different? A Comparison of the Social Backgrounds and Organisational Affiliations of Oil and Non-Oil Directors', *Social Problems*, 29.

Wibaut, F. W. (1913), 'De nieuwste ontwikkeling van het kapitalisme', *De Nieuwe Tijd*, 18.

Williams, K., Williams, J., and Thomas, D. (1983), *Why are the British Bad at Manufacturing?* (London: Routledge and Kegan Paul).

Williams, R. et al. (1968), *May Day Manifesto* (Harmondsworth: Penguin).

Williamson, O. E. (1964), *The Economics of Discretionary Behaviour* (Englewood Cliffs, NJ: Prentice-Hall).

Williamson, O. E. (1970), *Corporate Control and Business Behaviour* (Englewood Cliffs, NJ: Prentice-Hall).

—— (1975), *Markets and Hierarchies* (New York: Free Press).

—— (1985), *The Economic Institutions of Capitalism* (New York: Free Press).

—— and Ouchi, W. (1980), 'Markets, Bureaucracies and Clans', *Administrative Science Quarterly*, 25.

Wilson, G. K. (1982), 'Why is there No Corporatism in the United States?', in Lehmbruch and Schmitter (1982).

Wilson Report (1977), *Progress Report on the Financing of Industry and Trade* (Committee to Review the Functioning of Financial Institutions, London: HMSO).

Windolf, P., and Beyer, J. (1994), 'Cooperative Capitalism: Corporate Networks in Germany and Britain' (unpublished paper, University of Trier).

Winkler, J. (1974), 'The Ghost at the Bargaining Table', *British Journal of Industrial Relations*.

—— (1976), 'Corporatism', *European Journal of Sociology*, 17.

—— (1977), 'The Corporatist Economy: Theory and Administration', in Scase (ed.) (1977).

Winter, S. (1967), 'Economic "Natural Selection" and the Theory of the Firm', *Yale Economic Essays*.

Wong, G. (1991), 'Business Groups in a Dynamic Environment: Hong Kong, 1976–86', in Hamilton (ed.) (1991b).

Wong, S. L. (1985), 'The Chinese Family Firm: A Model', *British Journal of Sociology*, 36.

—— (1988), *Emigrant Entrepreneurs* (Hong Kong: Oxford University Press).

—— (1991), 'Chinese Entrepreneurs and Business Trust', in Hamilton (ed.) (1991b).

Wood, S. (1980), 'Corporate Strategy and Organisational Studies', in Dunkerley and Salaman (eds.) (1980).

Wright, E. O. (1979), 'Class, Occupation and Organisation', in Dunkerley and Salaman (eds.) (1979).

—— (1980), 'Varieties of Marxist Conceptions of Class Structure', *Politics and Society*, 9.

—— Costello, C., Hachen, D., and Sprague, J. (1982), 'The American Class Structure', *American Sociological Review*, 47.

Wymeersch, E. (1993), 'The Corporate Governance Discussion in Some European States', in Prentice and Holland (eds.) (1993).

Yaffe, D. S. (1973), 'The Marxian Theory of Crisis, Capital, and the State', *Economy and Society*, 2.

Yamamura, K. (1978), 'Entrepreneurship, Ownership, and Management in Japan', in Mathias and Postan (eds.) (1978b).

Yamawaki, H. (1994), 'Entry Patterns of Japanese Multinationals in US and European Manuacturing', in Mason and Encarnation (eds.) (1994).

Yanaga, C. (1968), *Big Business in Japanese Politics* (New Haven: Yale University Press).

Yasuoka, S. (1977), 'The Tradition of Family Business in the Strategic Decision Process and Management Structure of *Zaibatsu* Business', in Nakagawa (ed.) (n.d.).

Yazawa, M. (1963), 'The Legal Structure for Corporate Enterprise: Shareholding–Manager Relations under Japanese Law', in von Mehren (ed.) (1963).

Young, S., and Lowe, A. V. (1974), *Intervention in the Mixed Economy* (London: Croom Helm).

Zald, M. N. (1969), 'The Power and Functions of Boards of Directors', *American Journal of Sociology*, 75.

Zamagni, V. (1980), 'The Rich in a Late Industrialiser: The Case of Italy', in Rubinstein (ed.) (1980).

Zang, X. (1995), 'Familism and Corporate Networks in Singapore' (Department of Sociology, Flinders University of South Australia).

Zaslavskaya, T. (1990), *The Second Socialist Revolution: An Alternative Soviet Strategy* (London: I. B. Tauris).

Zeile, W. (1991), 'Industrial Policy and Organizational Efficiency: The Korean *Chaebol* Examined', in Hamilton (ed.) (1991*b*).

Zeitlin, M. (ed.) (1970), *American Society Inc.* (Chicago: Markham).

—— (1974), 'Corporate Ownership and Control: The Large Corporation and the Capitalist Class', *American Journal of Sociology*, 79. Reprinted in Zeitlin (1989*b*).

—— (1976), 'On Class Theory of the Large Corporation', *American Journal of Sociology*, 81. Reprinted in Zeitlin (1989*b*).

—— (ed.) (1980), *Classes, Class Conflict, and the State* (Cambridge, Mass.: Winthrop).

—— (1980), 'On Classes, Class Conflict, and the State: An Introductory Note', in Zeitlin (ed.) (1980).

—— (1984), *The Civil Wars in Chile* (Princeton: Princeton University Press).

—— (1989*a*), 'Who Owns America? The Same Old Gang' (revised version), in Zeitlin (1989*b*).

—— (1989*b*), *The Large Corporation and the Capitalist Class* (Cambridge: Polity Press).

—— and Norich, S. (1979), 'Management Control, Exploitation, and Profit Maximisation in the Large Corporation: An Empirical Confrontation of Managerialism and Class Theory', *Research in Political Economy*, 2.

Zeitlin, M. and Ratcliff, R. (1988), *Landlords and Capitalists: The Dominant Class of Chile* (Princeton: Princeton University Press).

—— Ewen, L., and Ratcliff, R. (1975), ' "New Princes" for Old? The Large Corporation and the Capitalist Class in Chile', *American Journal of Sociology*, 80.

Ziegler, R. (1982), 'Market Structure and Cooptation' (Working Paper for Analysis of Social Networks Project, LudwigsMaximilians-Universität, Munich).

—— (1993), 'Market Structure, Ownership and Cooptation: Accounting for Interlocking Directorships', in Lindenberg and Schrender (eds.) (1993).

—— Bender, D., and Biehler, H. (1985), 'Industry and Banking in the German Corporate Network', in Stokman *et al.* (eds.) (1985).

—— Reissner, G., and Bender, D. (1985), 'Austria Incorporated', in Stokman *et al.* (eds.) (1985).

Zorzini, M. (1925), 'L'organizzazione dell'industria idro-elettrica in Italia', *Economia*.

Zukin, S., and Di Maggio, P. (eds.) (1990), *Structures of Capital: The Social Organisation of the Economy* (New York: Cambridge University Press).

Zwass, A. (1979), *Money, Banking and Credit in the Soviet Union and Eastern Europe* (New York: M. E. Sharpe).

Index

function of capital 22, 25, 278, 280
functional organization 222, 223
  see also divisional organization; holding
  company
Galbraith, J. K. 11, 12
German system of company law 5, 211
  of capital mobilization 17, 52, 141,
  142–55, 171, 211, 291
Germany 4, 5–6, 23, 28, 141, 142–50, 158,
  167, 211, 217, 224, 228, 240, 241, 243,
  247, 248, 251, 261, 263–4, 266, 270–1,
  289, 295, 307, 311
Glasberg, D. S. 135, 211
Gordon, R. A. 46, 53, 64–5
Grou, P. 247
groups of enterprises 9, 109–10
  see also financial groups and empires;
  kigyoshudan

Habermas, J. 14, 265
Hall, S. 87
Hamabata, M. 305–6
Hannah, L. 80, 259
Herman, E. S. 51, 61, 62, 63, 78, 208, 257
hierarchy and market 138, 204–6, 226
Hilferding, R. 13, 22–25, 27, 43, 103, 104,
  144, 150, 172, 274, 279
Hill, S. 209–10
Hindess, B. 174
Hobson, J. A. 79, 106
holding company 18, 51, 100, 156–7, 158,
  159–60, 168, 184–5, 222–3, 224
  see also divisional organization; functional
  organization
Hong Kong 200–1, 246, 308
Hungary 175, 176–7, 177–8, 272

ie 182
immediate control 62
  see also ultimate control
impersonal possession 15–16, 18, 41–2, 47,
  78, 142, 202, 239, 241, 278, 280, 297,
  309, 311, 312
  see also personal possession
industrial society, theory of 10–13, 16, 21,
  39, 297
inequality of income and wealth 282–91
inheritance 285
inner circle 26, 103, 114, 302, 303, 304, 305,
  306
insider dealing 9
institutions, see financial institutions
insurance companies 9, 16, 25, 47, 49, 84,
  101, 109, 144

intercorporate network 107, 109, 111–14,
  117, 118, 120, 122, 123, 126, 128, 130,
  137, 138–9, 148, 151, 163, 205–6, 217, 256
interlocking directorships 7–8, 19, 25,
  111–14, 115, 126, 128, 130, 131, 135,
  149, 193, 200, 213, 217, 248
investment trusts 25, 84, 159
invisible handshake 138, 206, 249, 256
Italy 6, 17, 28, 167–9, 211, 239, 240, 249,
  261, 263, 266, 271, 289, 295, 296

Jaher, F. 300
Japan 6, 17, 28, 141, 181–95, 199, 203, 211,
  224–5, 230, 231, 236, 239, 240, 241,
  245–6, 247, 249, 251, 261–2, 263–4, 271,
  289–90, 291, 296–7, 305–6
Japanese system of company law 6
  of capital mobilization 17, 52, 181–96
Jeidels, O. 144, 153

Kerr, C. 11
Keynesianism 268, 270
kigyoshudan 191, 192–5, 225, 261–2, 306
kinecon groups 300, 301, 307
kinship 17, 32, 64, 182–3, 197, 268, 276, 298,
  299–301, 309
  see also family control and shareholdings
Korea (South) 195–6, 246
Kotz, D. M. 72

Lampman, R. 283, 284
Larner, R. J. 59–60, 65, 66, 288
late capitalism 14
Latin America 169, 238–9, 243, 252, 271
Latin system of company law 6
  of capital mobilization 17, 52, 141,
  155–70, 291
Lawriwsky, M. 97, 216–7
Leech, D. 87
legal device 62, 109
legal relations and legal forms 3–6, 21, 22–4,
  30–1, 37, 40–1, 42–4, 277, 301, 311
Lenin, V. 13, 14, 25, 172
liberal capitalism 18, 25, 60, 78, 79, 123, 138,
  202, 221, 239, 240, 241, 297, 299, 309
liberal states 266–70
Lintner, J. 131–2
Lundberg, F. 266, 284, 286

MacEachern, W. A. 234
MACNET group of researchers 113–14, 121
McNulty, T. 211
majority control 43, 58, 82, 99, 190, 240, 278
Malaysia 200